CHARLES LANCELIN'S

Out-of-body
Method
(Méthode de Dédoublement Personnel)

Translation into English

by

CARDELLI

MMXXV

CHARLES LANCELIN'S OUT-OF-BODY METHOD

Translated by Cardelli

An English translation of original author Charles Lancelin's *"Méthode de Dédoublement Personnel"*, first published 1912.

First Paperback Edition
August 2025

ISBN 13: 978-1-7371111-4-6

Printed and bound in the United States of America

Born in 1852, Charles Lancelin was a pioneer in the research of "out-of-body" phenomena, conducting numerous paranormal experiments while researching out-of-body experiences including astral projection and lucid dreaming.

Growing up in France where a fascination with spiritualist phenomena was surging, he sought out the likes of Colonel Albert de Rochas and Hector Durville, as well as Doctors Baraduc and Papus for inspiration. He quickly became a leader in this field, delving into sleepwalking, hypnosis and regression.

As a Spiritualist, he developed a personal interest in the hidden teachings of antiquity; and worked to develop a modern system for detaching from the physical body and developing psychic abilities.

Mr. Lancelin maintained that the development and the "dynamization" of the Will to be the most vital step in successfully achieving the out-of-body experience.

Understanding that his work would only be accepted by science if it was held to the highest scientific standards, he meticulously planned his experiments in laboratory settings and achieved spectacular results, many observed by witnesses and photographed. The evidence of these are included in this book.

But even in his time Mr. Lancelin was a black sheep, investigating topics considered to be fringe theories.

Over the past century, very little has changed in the mindset of "scientific" minds when it comes to seriously discussing the subject of out-of-body experiences and the non-physical world. The few who do, do so with hushed tones in dark corners for fear of ridicule by their peers. For the most part, it is considered little more than "woo-woo" talk. The vast majority of the population, still programmed from religious dogma, fare no better, considering the practice of astral projection to be at best, harmful to the body, and at the worst, to be communing with the devil.

It is as if enlightened thinking took a pause in 1912 and has remained stagnant ever since. One might wonder what the state of human consciousness would be today if World War I, World War II and all of the other wars and conflicts that were initiated over the past century, effectively distracting the human population, had never taken place. If the curiosity and fascination with the non-physical that was evolving so passionately across the western world during that time…had not been so successfully interrupted.

Charles Lancelin left this world in 1941, but leaves behind a wealth of literary works detailing his research and experiments.

Having read the majority of books considered to be the "standard" on astral projection, I consider this work to be the premier book on the subject, at the very least an absolutely critical, if not key, piece. It is the only book available that provides not just theory and methods for success, but experiments that PROVE the existence of this phenomenon; at least to those with open minds.

And yet, this work had never been translated into English.

This is a vast and in-depth work, and the prospective reader might appreciate the long hours that went into translating this text, as well as converting each technical diagram, each photo caption, and each drawing into the English language.

During the translation process, my utmost priority was to preserve not just the accuracy of the text, but the subtle humor, mannerisms, analytical thought, and writing style that would have been Charles Lancelin.

Those who are familiar with books written in the 19th century know that people spoke and wrote much differently during that time period. In this translation the reader will find that I adhered as faithfully as possible to the writing style of that era.

As a result, the reader may find that there are a number of words and terms within the text that are not commonly used. I have thus included a glossary with these as well as other obscure terms at the end of this book that the reader may use as a ready reference.

What will not be found at the end of this book is the Annex found in the original work. I have purposely left that section out.

I will never accept this work to be perfect. It is my hope that the reader will excuse any errors that might have been made during the translation process, and instead focus on appreciating the vast wealth of knowledge and spiritual advancement that Mr. Lancelin contributed with this great work, which is now finally offered for study to the English-speaking world.

A reader may ask, what qualifications do I possess to justify taking on and producing a translation of such a high-level work?

It is certainly not my mastery of the French language.

My validation comes from my own personal experiences. At the time of this writing, I have documented nearly 600 conscious out-of-body experiences, many of which were incredibly profound.

These experiences have allowed me to gain an understanding of not only this phenomena; but also of the non-physical worlds that exist beyond this physical one, in ways very few others have.

It is with this unique perspective and awareness, and *only this awareness*, that one can truly have the correct context to accurately translate a work of this magnitude.

Mr. Lancelin was a man with whom those who question the official narrative can unequivocally identify with; he was a seeker of Truth, one who was not kept distracted by the dazzling bells and whistles of the "reality" that we know as Earth Life. He was a man whose brilliant and curious mind stirred him to think critically and seek out answers for himself.

Those who are afraid to leave the herd, intimidated by our herd masters, are rewarded with remaining in ignorance and fear.

Those such as Mr. Lancelin, and others like him, who remove themselves from the herd to go in search of answers, are rewarded with those answers. I hope the reader will find their own sought-after answers within the pages of this book.

The results of Mr. Lancelin's own personal experiences, as well as his experiments, the PROOFS of which fill this book, gave him his answers, and endowed him with the same Truths that I have known myself: that we are most assuredly NOT human beings having a spiritual experience, but rather that *we are spiritual beings having a HUMAN experience*!

It is with the greatest honor and deepest respect that I humbly present the English translation of *Charles Lancelin's Méthode de Dédoublement Personnel.*

Cardelli

Cardelli
August, 2025

Charles Lancelin (1852–1941)

Table of Contents

PART ONE

———

GENERAL INFORMATION

To Colonel A. de ROCHAS D'AIGLUN.

Dear and revered Master,

Permit me, first of all, to place your name at the head of these pages, which are merely the — very modest — continuation and consequence of your immortal works.

You were, in fact, the first to experimentally and objectively exteriorize the phantom of a living subject: — this book deals with the indication and development of a special process intended to subjectively produce the same phenomenon; it is therefore well and truly the result of the study of your works and the pursuit of your experiments; and, as such, it must bear, as a fitting tribute from the author, your name on the first page.

Allow me, therefore, to protest an assertion contained in the last letter you did me the honor of addressing: — Moreover, you wrote to me, your works, for which you know my great esteem, now surpass mine, and you are entering a world about which I have only vague notions... *What you are willing to call my works is still a hundred feet below yours, which I think I will never be able to equal; and if, later, some future reader compares — by far — the most highly regarded of my books to the least of yours, all my posthumous ambition will be satisfied.*

You are the undisputed Master, the brilliant initiator who opened a new and hitherto unknown path to the pioneers of mysterious things...

I am and have no other aspiration than to be, to remain, and to express myself.

Your very modest and very distant disciple, but also your fervent admirer,

Charles LANCELIN.

This dedication was in previous editions of this work. Today, it is addressed only to a shadow.

But my feelings of respectful gratitude and profound admiration for the man who was my master have not varied: —this dedication will not vary.

C. L.

———

TO PHYSIOLOGISTS.
TO THEOLOGIANS.

The author has only ever read a few general treatises on physiology and theology, in order to acquire an overview of these two sciences, delving more specifically and only as needed into those points that immediately relate to the subject of his current studies and his personal experiences. This certainly does not qualify him to call himself a physiologist or a theologian. He goes further: he considers himself profoundly inferior in these two sciences, he acknowledges, having the honesty to apply to himself a principle that he has always applied to others, which is this: "One loses his reason much more easily on subjects one knows only superficially than on those one has never studied."

Therefore, he repeats: he is neither a physiologist nor a theologian.

And he regrets this — deeply.

He regrets this all the more because, in certain respects, the following pages — written on a subject that he knows well from having studied it theoretically and experienced it practically, both objectively and subjectively — touch on certain very delicate aspects of physiology and theology, and his ignorance from this dual point of view, highly recognized and affirmed by himself, does not even allow him to suspect how they will be considered by a mind informed by these two sciences.

Certainly, as for the rest, the general departure of readers that this work will encounter — like any other, for that matter, on metapsychism, experimental psychology, psychophysiology, or occultism, both theoretical and practical — is, from now on, easy to establish:

On the one hand, there will be the ignorant who have never studied anything, which gives them the right, which they truly abuse, to decide everything with an unconsciousness superior to all: these will burst out laughing upon reading this volume, or will ask, with the traditional shrug, who the author intends to make believe such nonsense..., these are indifferent to him beyond all expression: they don't count, — Let's move on.

On the other hand, there will be the thinkers, and those who study because they lack the naiveté to believe that man has nothing more to learn. These people, if they are logical, *must accept* Hamlet's principle in the pillory: EVERYTHING IS POSSIBLE! — reserving the right to condemn *a posteriori* anything that a serious and in-depth study has demonstrated to them: it is for this category of readers that the author writes, it is to them that the following pages are addressed, because they will understand them, perhaps experiment with the theories developed therein, and, in any case, will only make a mature and considered judgment of them.

But what about physiologists?

But what about theologians?

Naturally, there is no question of those who belong to the first category of readers: they are, as much and in the same way as the latter, a negligible quality; and the author is thinking only of men of study and reflection, who, after reading this, will remain thoughtful and ask themselves, during their meditations: "Is all this possible?"

Once again, he asks himself with a certain curiosity: How, from what angle, in what spirit, will they consider this work?

Let us speak first of the physiologists.

They have studied and compared all the fundamental ideas that divide thinkers on the subject of life considered in itself; they have scrutinized the organic phenomena of nutrition, digestion, respiration, secretion, reproduction, lymphatic, blood and nervous circulation; they have thoroughly analyzed everything that produces movement and sensation, everything that movement and sensation produce; they have even addressed the functional modes of thought in cerebral matter; they gave the cell as the basis for life; and from all their work, all their studies, all their meditations, they drew this conclusion: being is one, and the dissociation of its constituent elements must inevitably lead to its destruction — death.

Now, the occultist movement, today of marvelous magnitude, comes to tell them: being is not one, it is multiple, and it possesses a way of life outside the cell.

Now scientists and researchers like Colonel de Rochas, Drs. Baraduc, Encausse, Moutin and others, Hector Durville, Commander

Darget, etc., add: We can dissociate the constituent elements of being, since we isolate them, since we photograph them separately!

And finally, here comes a book that tells them in turn: These are no longer laboratory experiments with specially trained subjects; you, I, the first person who comes along, anyone, we possess within ourselves the latent faculty to disintegrate ourselves, to release our neuritis from ourselves, to dissociate our own individual into its constituent parts, to send our human *double*, our living *ghost*, far away to perform this or that act, and then reintegrate ourselves.

This is, quite obviously, a phenomenon of physiology — of high physiology, of metaphysiology if you will, but ultimately of physiology — since it involves the dissociation of the elements of being and its subsequent reconstitution.

So, what do physiologists think about this?

Now it's the theologians' turn.

We know well that theology, more progressive in this respect than normal science, admits in man the existence of a plastic intermediary between the mind and the body.

"While the natural body remains paralyzed," a religious authority tells us, [1] "the soul sees itself clothed in a body in every way similar to its own, without knowing how; it sees this body ordinarily dressed in the same way, covered in the same clothes and clothes of the same color, in the same way as those that cover its true body..."

But theology admits only a cause for the phenomenon, divine or demonic, in any case external to the subject; it does not, as far as I know, recognize a subjective, voluntary, and conscious cause.

As long as we have produced mediumistic materializations from the Mystery, theology has been unanimous in proclaiming: "Beware: you are dealing with the devil! You are the devil's plaything! It is the devil who dons these deceptive appearances to make you fall into his traps!"

Yet today we produce materializations that no longer emerge from the shadows, but are emanated, in our studies, by living subjects from whom the ghost is magnetically extracted, just as gluten is mechanically extracted from wheat, just as dyes are chemically extracted from coal. Will anyone still tell us it's the devil?

But there's more. The following pages show that, in any one of us, there exists the latent faculty to dissociate ourselves, to leave the temporary corpse here or there and send the higher elements of our being elsewhere... Frankly, can we maintain that it's the devil when the *double* gives undeniable proof that it is the very personality of the subject?

Perhaps someone will reply: No, it's not the devil, but it is the devil's work!

Let's beware! One of the principal theologians of the time, a great mind moreover, one of the luminaries of Catholicism, Father Ventura of Raulica, general of the Theatine order, consultor of the sacred Congregation of Rites, examiner of bishops and the Roman clergy, covered himself, from a scientific point of view, with eternal and ineffable ridicule, the day when He wrote [2]: "Mesmerism, Magnetism, Somnambulism, Hypnotism, are nothing but Satanism!" What are we to think of this peremptory assertion today that Magnetism is one of the principal known curative agents, today when every hospital has its own hypnology laboratory?

Now, the processes used for the splitting of the being, whether auto- or hetero-dissociation, are entirely based on magnetism and hypnotism, that is to say, on absolutely natural means; and which have nothing to do with the devil, nothing to do with religious dogmas.

On the other hand, the belief in a Prince of Fire has received such blows in our time that a current has formed among the most enlightened minds of the clergy, which tends to regard Satan simply as the symbol of evil.

And the author wonders, not without some curiosity: What can a theologian in our 20th century think of this book whose sole claim is to show by what simple means the first experimenter can accomplish an operation which, in the Middle Ages, would have led its author, as a servant of the devil, straight to the stake?

This is why he offers — very curiously — these pages
TO PHYSIOLOGISTS
TO THEOLOGIANS.

---

[1] P. SÉRAPHIN, *Principles of Mystical Theology*, 1 vol. in-8, Paris, 1872.
[2] Letter. Preface to the *High Phenomena of Magic*, by Gougenot des Mousseaux, 1 vol. in.8, Paris 1864.

CHAPTER I

PRELIMINARIES

From time immemorial, it has been a very strong belief that certain individuals possess the power either to transport themselves entirely here or there, or to split themselves, leaving their physical body where it is, to send their double, their ghost, the reproduction of their person, far away.

In turn, legend and history in antiquity, then, closer to us, annalists, demonologists, hagiographers have recorded facts that, until recently, so-called sound reason considered pure fables, and that men of serious science — or those deemed so — would have considered themselves dishonored to discuss seriously.

But now, in our time, judiciously conducted scientific experiments have proved that man is not as simply constituted as had previously been thought, a theory which, moreover, has been, in all past centuries, the characteristic of the different schools of occultism that have succeeded one another in the world; and new constitutive principles of living beings in general, and of man in particular, are now studied under different names, not only by representatives of the various orders of occultism, but also by men who belong only to pure science.

Plato was the first to speak of it publicly. Ancient science was very well aware of the existence of a plastic intermediary between the physical body and the immaterial spirit; Knowledge of this element became obscured and lost during the long period of the Middle Ages, when it was transmitted only through occult doctrine, whose adherents were bound to the hart and the fagot by the then all-powerful laws of the Church, which explains why, in modern times, this notion had completely disappeared. We have to go as far back as the 17th century to see it suspected — but in what a dubious form! The work of Mesmer and the magnetizers [3] demonstrates the existence of an ignored — or rather forgotten — principle in humankind. We know with what enthusiasm magnetism was greeted in its early days, only to fall into an undeserved ridicule from which it was only to emerge in our time.

But the awakening has been given. Researchers of good faith and scientific integrity, at first few, then increasingly numerous, studied the nature of this fluid emitted by the human organism: some, whose experiments were poorly conducted, ended up with a pure and simple denial; others established still unknown possibilities of this fluid, of which every living being contains a previously unknown reservoir; it was discovered that it was of vital essence, and biologists seized upon it; one began to wonder if this semi-material principle might not be the very essence of this plastic intermediary placed by certain philosophies between the body and intelligence, by means of which the thought that conceives becomes the gesture that acts.

Meanwhile, the discovery of hypnotism, which was initially confused with magnetism, came to overturn certain parts of psychology and open a still unsuspected field to the power of will. The works of the old masters are taken up again, their assertions studied, and their conclusions, after a long and unjust disdain, are regaining the place they should never have left, in high science, which today is only the science of the pioneers of mystery; but which tomorrow will be official science.

Finally, the emergence of Spiritism gave unprecedented impetus to all these investigations into the unknown. The existence of ghosts was proclaimed; denied by some who refused to study them, ridiculed by others who found it simpler not to concern themselves with them, it soon asserted itself to the point that a medical doctor could write, "The phenomena of Spiritism, for whatever reason they are reported, can no longer be denied except by ignorance and bad faith!"

---

[3] See Hector Durville: *Magnetic Physics; Theories and Processes of Magnetism; Personal or Psychic Magnetism*; etc.

Now, if ghosts exist, what are they made of, if not those semi-material fluids that have been debated for so long and which do not follow the physical body in its *process* of posthumous disintegration?

And Spiritists study this fluidic body that they call the *périsprit*, that is, the envelope of the spirit.

But the birth of Spiritism — or rather its renaissance, for its phenomena were known from all antiquity — gave a new impetus to the renewal of occult science, which is none other than the High Science of the ancient temples and the Mysteries of antiquity, hidden when political upheavals devastated the ancient sanctuaries of Egypt, Greece, Latium, and Gaul and put an end to the sacred Mysteries, whose teachings were henceforth preserved — and jealously hidden — only by a small number of the faithful who transmitted them, from age to age, to carefully chosen and tested disciples. And the occult theories, slightly differentiated among themselves by several parallel schools, showed us that there is not just one, but two kinds of fluids in man: those that die with his physical body and those that survive with his immaterial spirit; They told us that the ghost of the dead is composed only of the latter, but that the former are also found in the apparitions of the living. And, with occultism, the composition of the *double* and the astral body (*périsprit* of the spiritualists, which itself is made up of several types of fluids) was studied.

In turn, theosophy was born, bringing us the teachings — somewhat distorted, in truth — of the old Hindu philosophies, themselves born in the sacred crypts of the Himalayas, and according to which the living body is composed of seven different material or fluidic elements, differentiated from each other, and whose reactions with each other produce the diverse and multifaceted states in which the ghost appears to us — sometimes visible, audible and tangible, sometimes assuming only one of these aspects, and sometimes revealing itself in the appearance of a more or less dark, more or less luminous nebula...

But all this was only theories, if I may put it that way, to explain the various ways in which ghosts exist. There remained to be done what this ancient philosopher who walked did to prove movement: — it remained to uncover the great unknown of the problem — to uncover the ghost itself from the living body, in order to experimentally prove the existence of this ghost.

Colonel de Rochas's greatest claim to fame was to have been the first, albeit fortuitously, to resolve this problem.

By repeating the experiments of the Chevalier de Reichenbach, he wanted to see what results he would achieve by placing a gifted magnetic subject into increasingly profound states of hypnosis: the result was the splitting of the subject into a physical body and a ghost. But the experiment, by this method, was extremely dangerous, and the initiator preferred not to pursue further an experimental study in which a human life was at stake.

Very recently, barely four years ago, Hector Durville [4] repeated Mr. de Rochas's experiments using simpler and less dangerous procedures. Very quickly, he managed to disengage the human ghost from a subject, by the dissociation of this same subject whose *sarcosôme* (material body) remained in an armchair, while his freed *aérosôme* (ghost) was isolated, photographed and prepared for any subsequent experiment, the main ones of which were the successive dissociations of this same *aérosôme* into its main constituent parts, or of the less in those parts that were most immediately accessible, that is, the double, holder of the subject's physical life, and, consequently, mortal itself — the astral body properly speaking, holder of the subject's sensitivity — and finally, the mental body, holder of its intelligence.

I have just said that Colonel de Rochas was *the first* to isolate the living ghost: this must be understood from the point of view of normal science, for occult science has always known the phenomenon itself while carefully concealing its processes of production; the works of Paracelsus, in particular, in modern times, prove that this occultist knew, for certain experiments, how to isolate the living *aérosôme*.

On the other hand, nowadays, there is no one who does not know or has not heard of individuals who, endowed with a particular sensitivity, permanent or occasional, make themselves seen or heard, in such and such circumstances, far from the place where they are in reality; Dr. Gurney, Dr. Myers, and Dr. Podmore

---

[4] See his work: *The Ghost of the Living, Anatomy and Physiology of the Soul.*

conducted a vast investigation on this subject, the results of which, recorded in a book, *Phantasms of the Living* (partly translated into French by L. Marillier and prefaced by Professor Ch. Richet under the title *Telepathic Hallucinations*), note more than four hundred absolutely proven cases of apparitions of this kind. In France, Dr. Dariex, the astronomer C. Flammarion, and others have collected several hundred such cases, the reality of which is well established.

Finally, who has not heard of, or experienced in their circle, apparitions, visions, or "intersigns" [5] of the dying, that is, individuals who, at the moment when their being is disintegrating, send their thoughts, their will, and, consequently, their *aérosôme* toward a friend or relative whose memory particularly strikes them at this final moment?

It is therefore surprising at first glance that a phenomenon reported by legend, recorded by history, cited by the most serious annalists, and scientifically observed in our time, should have always seen its means of production remain in a state of secrecy that no one has ever revealed. And yet, upon closer inspection, it could hardly be otherwise for anyone who historically follows the state of mind of the ages that successively preceded our own.

In the earliest times, when the Sacred Mysteries summarized the high science of antiquity, the initiate who divulged such a secret could have inevitably expected to fall under the anonymous dagger of another initiate whom the temple, where his oath of secrecy had been received, would have sent to him with orders to kill him.

Later, we come to the late Empire, where the people were concerned only with circus rivalries, while the quarrels between the *blues* and the *greens* set Constantinople ablaze; where all minds were absorbed by the Byzantinism of religious disputes, where people killed each other over an *iota*, over the question of whether the Son was *homoiousios* (of similar substance) or

---

[5] On the Breton coast, when a sailor perishes at sea, and his wife, his mother, his children, on the cliff, anxiously await the return of the boat and try to penetrate with their eyes the curtain of storm covering the ocean, a patch of sky is torn away, revealing the vaguely luminous image of a gigantic cross toward which a soul ascends, bearing the appearance of the deceased... this is the intersign.

homoousios (of the same substance) with the Father. One need only consider the religious ferocity that dominated this period to understand that the author bold enough to reveal a new way of being in the constitution of man could only be regarded as a dangerous innovator from a doctrinal point of view, a heretic of the first order, and, consequently, must arouse deadly hatred on all sides.

At the same time, in the West, all knowledge, following the Barbarian invasions, had taken refuge in cloisters. Only one monk could hold this secret, but he could not speak of it to anyone. The proof? The persecutions to which, a few centuries later, Roger Bacon was subjected by his peers for having written the *opus majus*: his invention of the water-drawing pump was, in all monasteries, regarded as a demonic work.

In the Middle Ages, this revelation would have led to its author being stoned as a sorcerer.

Later, the Inquisition would have had him dragged to its bar, and the stake or the hemp tie would have been the ransom for his excessive knowledge.

In times closer to our own, the Bastille did not extend its hospitality only to political writers, but to anyone who held secrets that were embarrassing to some; and it must be recognized that such a notion could very easily be disguised as a state secret, as harmful to the great, or be regarded from a doctrinal point of view as more dangerous than the propositions of Jansenius or the quarrel of the Quietists.

Finally, in the century preceding ours, one important reason certainly curbed any desire for disclosure: this secret can be fatal for anyone who wants to put it thoughtlessly into practice. Now, it was only held in our days by high occultists, because to extract its essence, one must have studied a lot and for a long time; these high occultists were, consequently, imbued with the dogma of human fraternity, which made it their duty of conscience not to throw into the public, within the reach of the first comer, the elements of a formidable experiment in which the experimenter, dissociating his physical organism to make an "astral projection"[6], finds himself exposed, through lack of composure or for any other reason, to being unable to reintegrate his material body: then, for him, it's either death or madness. This serious reason is enough to explain, in contemporary times, the silence of those who know.

But today, the situation is no longer the same. Since the experiments of Colonel de Rochas, and especially since the very recent ones of Hector Durville, which showed that the human personality can be dissociated with relative ease, a certain number of researchers have tried to apply to themselves the conditions required by personal out-of-body experience. On the other hand, there are curious individuals who, having discovered by chance that they themselves fulfilled the required conditions, and dissociating themselves without too much difficulty, wanted to continue, out of curiosity or for other motives, these experiments, which are not without danger. Personally, I know several of them in my circle.

It therefore seemed to me that at the present time, the best course of action was to provide the necessary guidance for the pursuit of this higher-order experiment, but on the condition of drawing particular attention to the undeniable dangers inherent in such experiments, and consequently providing them with all the information relating to the precautions to be taken to avoid the abyss into which the imprudent, the thoughtless, and the audacious can fall.

This is what I will attempt to do in the following pages.

But, as can be seen from what has just been said, I have no predecessors in this field; I am, in a way, opening a path that has yet to be explored. Moreover, the elements of the question are scattered throughout works of all kinds, some of which are quite difficult to obtain. I therefore do not claim to indicate here a *ne varietur* line of conduct; this work will undoubtedly be improved subsequently; doubtless, other researchers and experimenters, taking advantage of the path opened up, will do better in the future... My sole intention here is to bring together in a single work the conditions of the experiment scattered until now in other books, to coordinate them, to make them as complete as possible, by verifying them with all the information gathered from personal

---

[6] This term, which technically designates the operation in question, shows that it is well known in occultism.

experimenters, and, why not say so? By my own attempts in this direction. It seems to me that the task will be quite large, if I manage to fulfill it, by limiting myself to saying what exists, what our predecessors have given us, what we are doing at present, and above all by pointing out — I insist — the inherent dangers of experimenting with a phenomenon as transcendental as personal out-of-body experience.

————

CHAPTER II

DEFINITIONS — LEGEND — HISTORY — SCIENCE

This phenomenon of high physiology, which consists of leaving the physical body — let us say the quasi-corpse, to be clear — in the place where it is, while the ghost is sent far away to perform a certain defined act, has had in the past and still has many names.

Fig. 2. — The double among the Egyptians.
Bas-relief relating to the birth of Amenhotep III, the child and his double — who carries on his head the banner surmounted by the hawk — are presented to Ammon-Ra.

The ancients saw it as *théophanies* when it was the earthly vision of a divine personage, *idolophanies* when the subject was a human being.

People today call it an *apparition* or *revenant* when it applies to the dead, and an *apparition* or *vision* when it applies to the living.

Religious annals use the term *bilocation*, which clearly expresses what it means: the simultaneous presence of the same person in two different places.

Hagiographers use the words *bicorporeality* more specifically when they want to convey that the subject actually possesses two bodies, each of which is seen in one of the two places; or *representation* when they believe that one of the two bodies belongs to the subject while the other is merely a representation modeled and animated by an angel. When it comes to the apparitions of Jesus, the special term *christophany* is used.

For sorcerers who, rightly or wrongly, are believed to manifest in animal guises, particularly in the form of a wolf, the terms that characterize their vision are *zoanthropy* and *lycanthropy*.

Spiritists, who usually deal with the spirits of the dead, call this phenomenon *materialization*.

Occultists who have experienced and practiced it throughout history rightly call it *astral projection*; indeed, the mechanism of the phenomenon consists in the intelligent and semi-material part of the being *leaving* the physical body and projecting itself onto the astral plane — an intermediary between the divine and the material planes — to manifest itself from there onto the physical plane according to the proposed purpose.

Modern science, which deals with it, initially began by classifying it, so as not to compromise itself, among *telepathic hallucinations*; at present, it applies to it the names of *dissociation* of the being, *splitting*, *exteriorization*, etc., and in cases of visual impression, that of *phantasmatophany*.

Legends abound, both in antiquity and modern times, of living or deceased figures who appear bodily.

One of the earliest known idolophanies is found in the *Iliad* (XXIII): Patroclus, killed by Hector, appears as if he were still alive.

Everyone knows the stories told of the splitting of Apollonius of Tyana, and Simon Magus seems to have had at least equal renown.

The *Lives of the Saints* teems with legendary tales of a similar nature, and this belief in the dissociation of human beings was well established, since we see the Apostle Paul cite (II Cor. 2-4) a man who was caught up — bodily or not — to heaven to hear ineffable words.

Rightly or wrongly, the same power has been attributed to all miracle workers, to all the mysterious figures of the Middle Ages and Modern Times, Cagliostro, the Count of Saint-Germain, etc., and the *blue tales* of our ancestors are filled with stories of the same nature.

Today, all cities and country sides have their own special traditions relating to a particular character renowned for his virtues, the Curé of Ars, for example — a skilled sorcerer like Thorel — or simply having played a prominent role, in one way or another, in local chronicles, particularly in regions like Brittany, where belief in the marvelous is, in a way, an article of faith.

Finally, there is perhaps no family in which a story of this nature does not circulate — the apparition of a living or deceased person — more or less well established, more or less fabricated, perhaps born of a real event and perhaps of an imaginary one, which, passing from mouth to mouth, from grandfather to grandchildren, has not, over time, acquired the right to exist.

All this is only the legendary side of the question, but it shows, by its very tenacity, that there must be some serious basis for such a long succession of beliefs and narratives, one after the other.

We will now turn to history, that is, to the enumeration of facts collected by serious authors, subject to criticism, and appearing clearly established enough to be trusted.

Ancient science was well aware of this phenomenon, which we find figuratively described on the monuments of ancient Egypt. We provide five reproductions of Egyptian sculptures depicting a *double*, showing that in this remote period the phenomenon was widespread enough among the public to be part of religious exotericism (*figs.* 2, 3, 4, 5, 6).

Fig. 3. — The double among the Egyptians.
Bas-relief relating to the birth of Amenhotep III, the queen gives birth;
the double of the royal child (carrying on his head the banner of Hathor-
Sat) descends to earth.

Fig. 4. — Double among the Egyptians.
The child (Amenhotep III) and his double, suckled by the goddess
Hathor-Sat.

The Child and His Double

Fig. 5. — Double among the Egyptians.

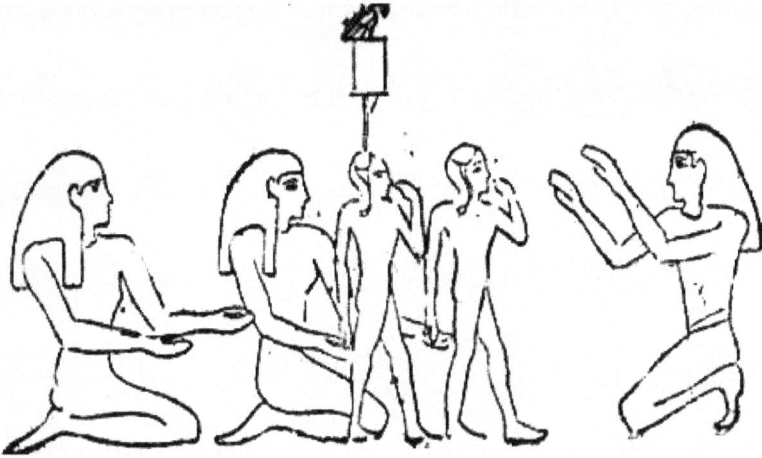

Fig. 6. — The double among the Egyptians.
The double of Amenhotep III carries on his head the banner of Horus,
surmounted by the hawk.

Furthermore, Fig. 1 shows that this phenomenon of personal out-of-body experience was taught by Chinese Buddhism in ancient times. Finally, Fig. 7 depicts the myth of the exteriorization of the ghost as symbolized in Greek mystery teachings.

It is not my intention to write in detail the history of the question. This work, completed and very well established, with all the necessary citations, can be found in chapter III, of *The Ghost of the Living,* to which I refer the reader curious for details.

In Saint Augustine (*Civ.*) we encounter the much-studied case of exteriorization of a certain Prestantius. [13]

Tacitus (*Hist.*) and Suetonius (*XII Caes.*) both cite the bilocation of Basilides.

Görres and Abbot Ribet, in their *Mystics*, report numerous cases, some still legendary, but others supported by serious evidence, of the bilocation of Saint Clement, pope; seen simultaneously in Rome and Pisa — that of Saint Alphonsus Liguori who was both in Arienzo and in Rome — that of Saint Francis Xavier who made an act of Presence simultaneously on his ship and on a longboat in distress far away, the ecstasies of Mary of Agreda during which she was both in Spain and in America.

Glanvil, an English philosopher, cites the now somewhat classic cases of exteriorization of Jeanne Brooks and Juliane Cox, both witches.

Fig. 1. — The solitary Ma-Wing-Tsun escapes persecution by freeing himself from his physical body.

Based on a Buddhist painting, borrowed from *Memoirs of China* by Count D'ESCAYRAC de LAUTURE.
(We see the fluidic link which, starting from the top of the head, connects the physical body to the astral body.)

Fig. 7. — Minerva emerging armed from the brain of Jupiter.
(Copy by M. A. Teyssandier, after a Greek vase.)
Myth of the teaching of the Mysteries symbolizing the splitting: —
Armed Minerva represents intelligence and strength; emerging from
Jupiter, she constitutes the exteriorization, by one who is master of
himself, of the phantom composed of the astral body (neuric force)
directed by the mental body (intelligence).

In 1851, the Justice of the Peace of Yerville brought up in his court a well-known case of splitting now known as the Cideville affair. [7] Besides the authors of *Mystics* already cited, serious discussions of the facts will be found in Fr. Seraphim's *Principles of Mystical Theology*, in Bishop E. Méric's *Imagination and its Prodigies* (one of the religious writers who have best studied the various aspects of the Mystery), in Dom Maréchaux's *The Divine Marvel and the Demonic Marvel*, etc.

The works of Madame Blavatsky, Sinnett, Col. Olcott, Dr. Pascal, and other theosophical writers will provide numerous documents for researchers. The same is true, from a spiritualist point of view, of the works of Gabby Delanne, notably his *Materialized Apparitions of the Living and the Dead*.

The innumerable contemporary facts are set out, without discussion but with supporting evidence, in *Phantasms of the Living*, by Drs. Gurney, Myers, and Podrnore, translated, partially into French, under the title *Telepathic Hallucinations*, by Marillier and with a preface by Prof. Ch. Richet. Many others can be found in the works of Flammarion, notably *The Unknown and Mental Problems*, by Dr. Dariex, Papus, Colonel de Rochas, d'Assier (*Essay on Posthumous Humanity*), Gougenot des Mousseaux, in the aforementioned book (*The Ghost of the Living*), Hector Durville, etc.

On the other hand, there are absolutely proven cases, such as, among many others, that of Emilie Sagée, whose ghost all her students constantly see in the garden while she herself occupies her chair.

Finally, there is undeniable proof that the living can split into two: it is photography that provides this. Among the most well-known photographs of this type, I will cite that of the priest, that of the Pinard girls (obtained by Commander Darget), those of a young girl, reproduced in the *Annals of Psychic Sciences* (October 1905) by Colonel de Rochas, that of Captain Volpi's fiancée, etc.[8]

---

[7] The details and the text of the judgment can be found in *Sorcery of the Countryside*, by the same author, (1 vol. in-8, Paris 1910).

(2 vol. in-8, Paris, 1849; 1 vol. Paris, 1905; 1 vol. in-8, Paris s.d.; 2 vol. in-8, Paris, 1909; 1 vol. in-8, Paris 1892; 1 vol. in-12, Paris s.d.; 1 vol. in-12, Paris, 1883.)

But here we have entered the scientific side of the question: I will return to it from a little further up.

It had long been noted that, under certain conditions, man — like all things — emits rays of light that are perceived by certain subjects endowed with special sensitivity. The Chevalier de Reichenbach, who had the opportunity to study these radiations, called them odic from the term *od*, which occultism applies, after the Hebrew Kabbalah, to a kind of mysterious light.

Magnetism, by developing the sensitivity of special subjects, had provided greater facilities for observing the radiations in question; nevertheless, this study had remained stationary when Colonel de Rochas resumed Reichenbach's experiments; using magnetic subjects immersed in increasingly deep states of sleep, in order to enable them to better distinguish the radiation they themselves emitted, which was both more abundant and more perceptible as their magnetic state became deeper.

First, they noticed that these effluvia formed concentric curves around them, a sort of *aura* more or less distant from the subject, in which the experiment demonstrated that the subject's sensitivity was externalized (*fig. 8*).

This sensitive layer, invisible to normal individuals, was very visible to the subject and to the adjunct sensitives, on whose instructions the subject's sensitivity could be damaged — by a prick or a pinch — in this *aura*, while the subject physically perceived the sensation of the lesion. [9]

The magnetization continued; the subjects saw luminous clouds escaping from them, to the right and left, reddish on one side, bluish on the other, which gradually took on their resemblance, each forming a half-ghost of the subject, to the right and left of him. As the subject continued to deepen his sleep, he saw the two half-ghosts reunite into a single phantom uniting within itself the colorations of its two constituent fragments.

From then on, the living human phantom was exteriorized.[10]

---

[8] All these photographs and several others, among the most interesting in existence, are found in the body of this book.

[9] I urge the reader to note this particularity, which will later provide us with the key to the phenomenon of repercussion.

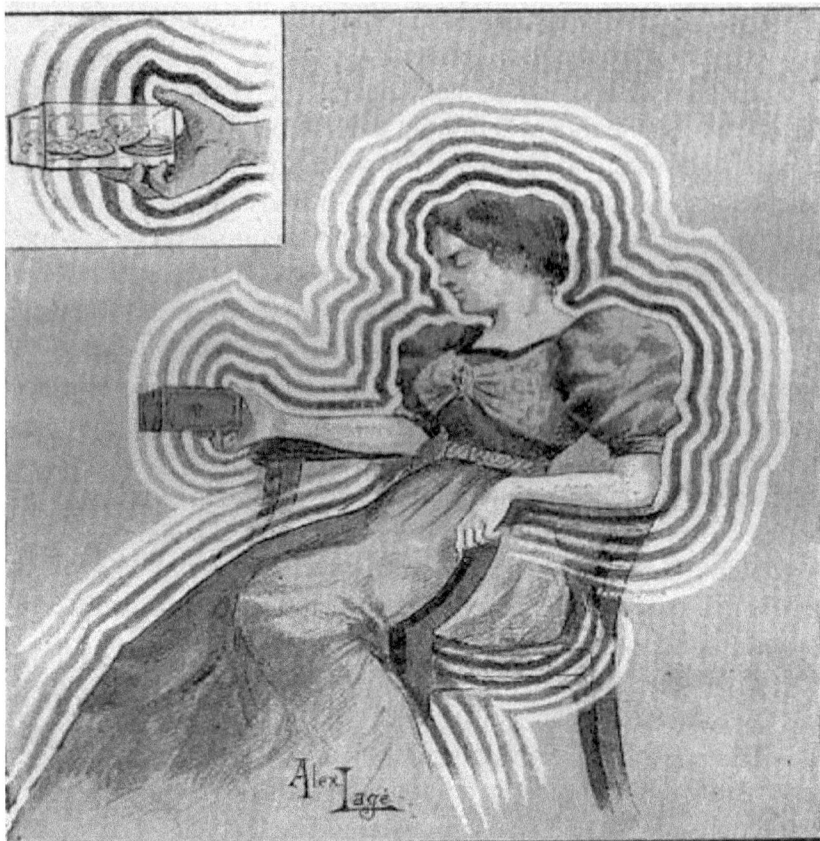

Fig. 8. — Externalization of sensitivity.
Diagram showing the successive zones of the subject's externalized
sensitivity — Above, the detail of the hand holding a box shows how the
subject can become aware of the objects enclosed in this box.

Here are the terms in which Colonel de Rochas describes his
admirable discovery. [11]

"After a variable amount of time, generally after the seventh
or eighth phase of lethargy, the layers whose intensity developed
mainly on the sides of the subject coagulate so to speak into a sort
of bluish phantom placed to the subject's right, at a distance of
about one meter.

This phantom quickly takes on *the form and position* of the
right half of the subject's body, which now only feels the actions
exerted on the portion of space occupied by this phantom, or (but
to a much lesser degree) on *the links that unite* the corresponding

parts of the material body and the fluidic body. The latter, moreover, repeats, like a shadow, all the movements performed by the former.

Further passes determine the formation, to the left of the subject, and at approximately the same distance, of a second half-phantom enjoying the same properties as the first, but which is red instead of blue.

Let us continue the magnetization, and, after one or two further phases of lethargy, the two seeing-subjects will agree that B.'s two half-ghosts gradually stretched out on the operator's side, emitting moving flames, and eventually fused together, forming, between the operator and the subject, a complete phantom, blue on the right, red on the left.

---

[10] Magnetism plays such a role in cases of objective out-of-body experience that it sometimes happens that this phenomenon occurs without even realizing it. — One of the most curious cases, and the only subjective case I know of under these conditions, is that of Mr. Bouvier, a well-known magnetizer in Lyon, who recounts it in these terms:

"A few years ago, in the first days of September, I was taking the 6:20 p.m. light train from Vienna to Lyon. I found myself completely alone in the front carriage and right in the middle of the first compartment, with my back to the engine. As soon as I was seated, and finding myself undisturbed by anyone, the idea came to me to magnetize my hat to see if I could make it move under my own power, with no effort other than that of my will.

"After a few minutes of magnetization, thinking of something else after the whistle of the engine announcing arrival at Estressin, I mechanically put my hat back on my head, while following the train of thought. What happened? Suddenly I saw myself sitting opposite me! The first thought that came to me was this: 'Is it over? The train has derailed, an accident has occurred, and I have passed into the other world.' To realize reality and know which of the two selves was the real *me*, I pressed my hands against my sides, and, oh! Amazement! I felt no resistance; then, I approached the one in front of me, who wasn't moving, and grabbed him by the middle of the body: my arms also passed through! This time, I was seized by real anguish; I thought of my family, my friends; In a few moments that seemed like centuries, I retraced the course of my life whose actions unfolded in an apotheosis, which ended with me seeing myself again, still small, in my mother's arms; then I felt myself, so to speak, melting into myself, while thickening instead of diluting myself, and finally I regained full possession of my individuality." (Quoted by A. de Rochas, *Successive Lives*, 1 vol. Paris, 1911).

[11] *Exteriorization of Sensibility*, 1 vol. in-8, Paris, 1899.

This phantom becomes more and more tangible, and also less and less sensitive, as the magnetizer's fluid replaces (at least this is a hypothesis that can be accepted) in the subject's body the fluid of the one who externalizes himself in the double. His clothes, which at first presented only an indeterminate shape and recalled the white shrouds that tradition attributes to ghosts, become more precise, taking on clear shapes, while remaining transparent, like the rest of the astral body through which seers perceive objects placed behind them."

Here, moreover, is a very clear summary of the operation, published in the *Psychic Annals* of 1895:

2 January 1894.

"I placed myself in front of Laurent and magnetized him with passes in semi-darkness. After a while, he saw a blue column of light form on his right, then move away as the states of hypnosis succeeded one another, separated by their phases of lethargy. At the same time, a red column of light developed on the left, which had appeared after the blue column, and which also moved away. These columns became more and more luminous, but without distinct shapes; these are clouds of his size and height, roughly representing the profile of his body: when he raised one of his arms, a bulge appeared in the cloud on the corresponding side, I then briskly pressed his epigastrium, so as to draw out fluid. Laurent declared that he *felt himself empty*; after a few moments, he saw the columns come together between him and me and form a column half red and half blue, still representing the shape of his body.

"I brought a burning ember close to it; he felt a strong burning sensation. When I touched his phantom with my hand, he felt the pinch, but he no longer felt it as soon as my hand lost contact with the phantom. I placed my hand between the phantom and his leg for thirty seconds; after waking up, the leg was completely inert, and I had to rub it vigorously to return it to its normal state..."

For years, the question remained static, Colonel de Rochas seeming to have neglected it on the one hand, and, on the other, the danger of the experiment distracting researchers. It therefore seemed that one could not go further; it was known that the living phantom could be, had been exteriorized: that was all.

It was then that, very recently, Hector Durville had the idea of repeating Colonel de Rochas's experiments using methods that simplified the operations.

First of all, he noted certain differences in the mode of formation of the phantoms; they did indeed condense to the right and left of the subject, but in the form of fluidic masses bearing no resemblance to him. They showed no more resemblance when the two fluidic masses united on his left; it was then "an indecisive mass, a vaporous column, noticeably taller and wider than the subject; still under the action of the magnetization directed at the latter, this mass diminishes in volume, condenses, becomes more luminous, and gradually takes on a human form; soon, this form, which condenses further, takes on exactly that of the subject; it is his *double*, his *ghost*, who is always standing to his left, and sometimes a little in front... the contours are more or less clear and precise, especially in the upper part which is much more active than the lower. Under the action of the magnetization which continues, the ghost condenses and becomes more luminous, especially towards the head; having reached a certain point of condensation, it takes on the attitude of the subject; the latter being comfortably seated in an armchair, the former sits in another arranged for him in the place he must occupy, and there, like a shadow, it repeats all the movements and gestures of the subject; it is the image of the subject, an objective, real image, because it is reflected by the mirrors, refracted as it passes from one medium into another, like light: it can be photographed." [12]

Thus, we have arrived at proof of the splitting of the living subject, whose physical body can be photographed separately, and whose ghost can be photographed separately; we are no longer reduced to the assertions of sensitive subjects, loyal certainly, but ultimately fallible.

But Mr. Hector Durville goes further. [13] Through a series of well-conceived and well-conducted experiments, he studies the phantom thus produced, from all sorts of points of view; he notes that its senses are identical to those of the physical body, but

---

[12] H. DURVILLE. (loc. cit.).
[13] A detailed account of all these experiences can be found in the work of Mr. H. DURVILLE: *The Ghost of the Living*, already cited.

infinitely more developed; he examines separately and successively, in the living phantom, sight, hearing, smell, taste, and touch, and notes the acuity of these senses; he experiments with its action on other living phantoms, on non-split subjects, on random assistants, on matter; and the inverse reactions that follow; from magnetized subjects, witnesses, matter, on the phantom.

In this regard, I must quote in full a passage relating to the action of the living ghost on calcium sulfide, a process which, in conjunction with photography, will later allow for the control of personal out-of-body experiences:

"The ghost releases N rays in great abundance, which illuminate phosphorescent screens in a very remarkable way.

"I will give some information about these rays for those who are not familiar with the latest discoveries in physics.

"At the beginning of 1903, Mr. Blondlot, professor of physics at the University of Nancy, while studying X-rays, which do not refract, observed rays that do refract.

"He soon discovered that these rays are independent of X-rays, and that their main characteristic is to increase the brightness of a small flame.

"These rays are found in abundance in sunlight and in the light from an Auer burner when the sleeve is new; in the human body, as Charpentier, another professor from Nancy, demonstrated, and in certain agents of nature, as other observers have noted.

"The professors from Nancy named these new rays, which increase the brightness of a small flame, *N-rays*, as having been discovered in Nancy.

"Practice has shown that the small flame can be advantageously replaced by a black screen on which small areas of calcium sulfide have been previously placed here and there, provided that this screen has been exposed for a few moments to a source of N-rays, or, preferably, to sunlight. The screen thus isolated is kept in the shade, in a dry place, and when one wishes to use it, one places oneself in relative darkness, if complete darkness cannot be achieved, and the screen becomes luminous as soon as one brings any secondary source of N rays close to it.

"It was with these screens that I conducted my experiments on the phantom. Here is the account of a study session:

"I have two large screens and a certain number of small ones. For the experiments I am going to present, I took the two large screens and one small one that I had exposed to sunlight. Here is the result of an experiment conducted in complete darkness. The subject is Mrs.

François; the witnesses are Mr. François and Mr. Sigogne, a professor at the University of Brussels.

"The subject being split into two, I take the three screens in question and present them to the witnesses, who observe that they are *completely* dark. Momentarily setting the small one aside, I place one of the large ones on the subject's abdomen, and I hold the other in the phantom, which is sitting on an armchair, to the subject's left.

"The screen placed in the phantom *quickly lights up*, and the one on the subject remains completely dark. After a few minutes, I take them both and present them to the witnesses, who are very surprised by this phenomenon. I then take the last screen that remained dark on the subject and place it in the phantom. It lights up immediately, like the first; I present it again to the witnesses, who see them sufficiently illuminated for them to be able very easily to count all the calcium sulfide spots from a distance of one meter.

"I then take the small screen that has not yet been used and place it on the subject's abdomen for two to three minutes without it giving off the slightest trace of luminosity. I then place it in the phantom, and it illuminates to a very high degree. The witnesses note that it illuminates enough to allow one of them to *see the time on a watch*.

"These experiments, repeated about ten times with seven or eight different subjects, have always given me similar results, very intense results when the screens were well exposed, less significant when the exposure was insufficient.

"It is worth adding here that I had previously observed their effect on the same screens with almost all the non-doubled subjects. When, in the dark, they bring their hand close to the screen, especially if they make a firm fist, the screen lights up more or less, as it does with any person. But it should be noted that the luminosity is always considerably less than that observed when the screen is placed inside the phantom.

"This series of experiments with phosphorescent screens demonstrates once again that the physical body of the split subject is no longer the site of any activity; in any case, it produces no N-ray, while the phantom becomes an extraordinarily intense source of these rays."[14]

Continuing his studies on the living ghost, H. Durville noted various noises, knocks, nearby or at a distance, weighing on a scale, movements without contact of objects, even quite heavy ones such as an armchair, a table, etc., the lifting of objects and even individuals, luminous phenomena, in a word, all the

---

[14] Hector DURVILLE, loc. cit.

phenomena one usually encounters in a session of psychic materialization; he also noted the action of the ghost on Dr. P. Joire's sthenometer, an instrument used to measure psychic strength. He even goes so far as to study the ghost's clothing, which leads him to this conclusion, which he presents as a hypothesis: *The ghost is draped in a fluidic gauze or vaporous veil (fig. 11) when, having no serious reason to reveal itself, it floats undecidedly in an early state of materialization; on the contrary, it is dressed like the subject when, for whatever reason, it is heavier and more material* – and also, I might add based on my studies and personal observations, when it has an interest in being recognized by the people to whom it reveals itself.

But Hector Durville went even further.

He divided the living ghost into:

a) Double, etheric or odic body, semi-material, but colored blue on the right, pale red on the left, holder of the life of the subject from whom it departs only very slightly. This double still has human form and seems to die a few days after the physical body.

b) Astral body, luminous, possessing the subject's sensitivity, from which it can move great distances.

It has, in principle, a human form; [15] but it can, under certain circumstances, change this form into any other. [16]

c) Mental body consisting mainly of a luminous ball occupying its apex. [17]

It possesses the subject's intelligence and always follows the astral body, which is, in a way, its support. It seems to have no form of its own but rather an ellipsoidal appearance, with the mental ball occupying the upper end. In a normal, complete individual, it would be like an aura overflowing from the physical body, which it envelops. [18]

It was then, at the beginning of 1910, that H. Durville kindly admitted me, for which I thank him most cordially, to his experiments to study a detail: the nature of the cold breath that is felt at the beginning of each session, a phenomenon about the nature of which he could give me no information, but which seemed to me similar to that experienced at the beginning of any spiritualist materialization séance, and which is due to the mixing of the fluids of the participants. Subsequently, I was given the

Fig. 9. — Dr. Baraduc (photograph of his mental ball).

Fig. 10. — Dr. Ixon's Mind Ball of London.

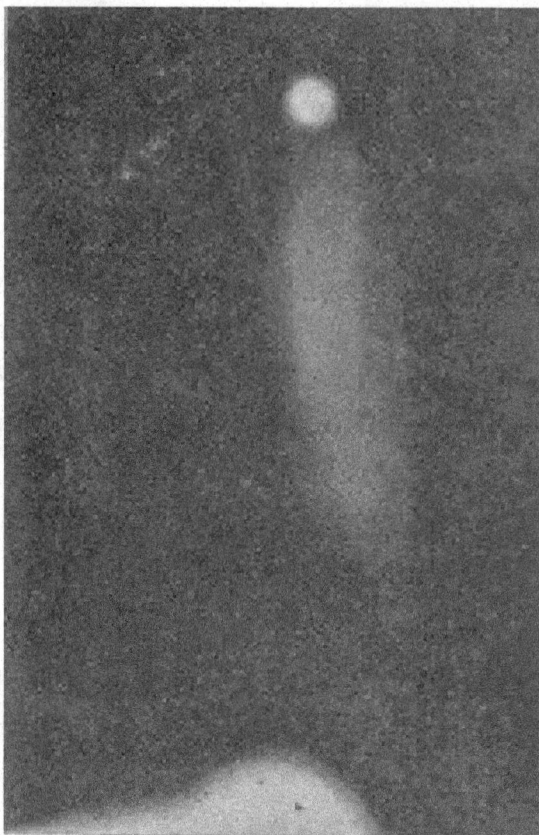

Fig. 11. — Mental ball in the split.

Fig. 12, 13, 14. — Ghost with Mind Ball.

opportunity to feel the living ghost (with caution since it is not solid and carries within itself the subject's sensitivity), which produced a sensation similar to that experienced by plunging one's fingers into an icy medium.

Therefore, the ghost thus obtained is neither solid nor visible to the participants whose sensitivity has not been developed in this way.

It was then that, while Hector Durville sought to further condense it through magnetic processes in order to give it these two qualities, I, for my part, was led to pursue the same goal by entirely different means: the use of hyperphysical operations and aids.

This is not the place to develop the account of these experiments, the details of which will be found in another work [19] and which will be repeated and completed in due course.

Furthermore, I will provide later [20] the material proof of the objective reality of the phantom thus produced.

Figures 12, 13, and 14 show photographs of living ghosts with the mental ball.

It remains to draw the general conclusion of this chapter, which is this:

---

[15] From very recent experiments, it would seem that it only assumes human form through its habituation to this form in the physical body, but that in reality it has no form of its own. In any case, when it has human form, it is always smaller than the physical body to which it belongs.

[16] This would explain the phenomenon of zoanthropy (werewolves).

[17] The late Dr. H. Baraduc, in his psychic photographs, often obtained this luminous ball which, by intuition, he called the mental ball because it seemed to him, in a normally constituted personality, to always envelop the brain. We provide here several photographs of the mental ball (*figs.* 9, 10, 11, 12, 13, 14).

[18] We seem to have gone even further down this path, and the causal body, characterized by a flame whose apex is circumscribed by a halo, holder of higher intellectual principles, memory, will, etc., appears to have been isolated recently by Mr. L. Lefranc, a student and collaborator of H. Durville; but the discovery is too recent, and moreover not mine, for me to discuss it at greater length.

[19] *Sorcery of the Countryside*, 1 volume octavo, Paris, 1910; Messrs. H. and H. DURVILLE, publishers, 23, rue Saint-Merri, Paris. — See the final note added, relating to the conditions of occult collaboration, cases of repercussions of injuries, etc.

[20] See chap. VI.

Currently, through magnetic processes, we have succeeded in separating the phantom of a subject from his physical body. [21]

This living phantom moves and acts like a normal individual, whose intelligence, will, and sensitivity it carries within itself; it is endowed with the same senses as the living, but, it seems, to a higher degree than the latter. It has an effect on matter and on living beings. But it is not normally tangible, and is only completely visible to special sensitives and to the photographic plate.[22] However, this lack of tangibility and normal visibility is only partial and temporary since, on the one hand, the ghost moves objects and, on the other hand, there are moments when we perceive in the place it occupies vague luminosities that are its fluids in the process of condensation: these two shortcomings will therefore disappear one day or another, this can be considered certain.

Now, this being admitted, since it is absolutely, undoubtedly acquired through experience, is it possible for a normal, normally constituted human being to exteriorize their own ghost?

------

[21] It has even been possible to exteriorize, from a physical body and in isolation, the *aérosomatic* part of the sensory organs. This discovery, at first a little bizarre, was the result of chance; here is how it happened: During the winter of 1910-1911, Commander Darget was led to photograph, during a mediumship session, a young boy who was an auditory medium. The plate, upon development, showed a sort of ball connected to the subject's right ear by a fluidic cord. Commander Darget initially saw in this strange device only the image of a sort of telephone or ear trumpet for the use of "Spirits" and used by them in their auditory communications with human beings. He brought this curious photograph, which we present opposite (*fig.* 15), to the *French Institute for Psychical Research*, where Mr. Lefranc suspected that it could well represent the actual capture of the phantom exteriorization of the auditory system; subsequent experiments demonstrated the validity of this hypothesis; after magnetically exteriorizing the subjects' sense of hearing, pinching the air at the location that this part of their astral body should occupy, produced the image of a small sphere connected to the physical ear by an extremely sensitive fluidic cord. From then on, they were on the right track, and other senses were exteriorized in the same way. It is certain that from this point of view, there is still much to be done in experimental research, but it is nonetheless established that, at present, we can exteriorize the fluidic body of a subject not only as a whole but also in each of its parts.
[22] We still do not fully understand the conditions under which it impacts the sensitive plate.

Fig. 15. — Young boy whose hearing apparatus is externalized.
(From a photo by Commander Darget.)

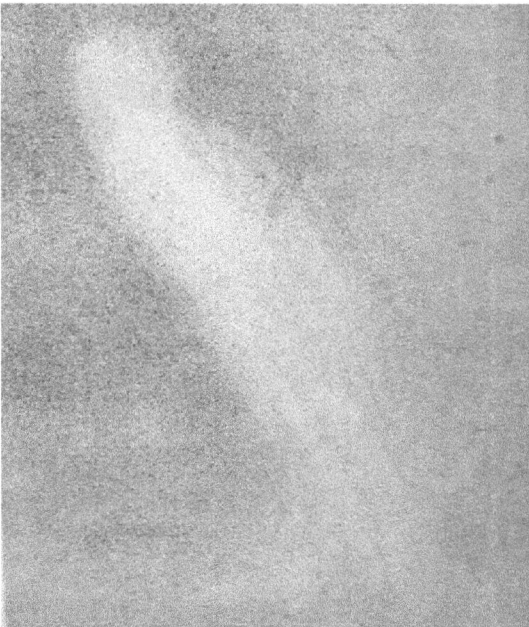

Fig. 16. — Mrs. Lambert's ghost swinging in front of the lens.

Yes, since the experimental exteriorization of the ghost is caused by the use of hypnotic or magnetic processes, since there are well-known processes of self-magnetization and auto-suggestion — suggestion, I remind you, being the mainspring of all hypnotization — based on will, and since will is a psychological faculty, entirely personal.

Is it possible, on the other hand, to direct this exteriorized phantom so as to make it perform a deliberately desired act?

Yes, since it carries with it, upon leaving the physical body, the same will that exteriorized it and that directs it.

Finally, is it possible for this exteriorized phantom to make itself absolutely visible, audible, and tangible?

Yes again, I would reply, despite the deficiency that exists in this regard in the laboratory exteriorizations carried out to date, but based on two convincing reasons in themselves:

1. The releases carried out until now in the laboratory are only the effect of an external will: The resulting phantoms therefore represent only a reflection of the will and would be infinitely better condensed if the will that animates them were within themselves instead of being external to them.

It is therefore possible, beyond doubt, to give the consciously exteriorized phantom qualities of visibility, audibility, and tangibility that are, if not complete, at least sufficient.

At each instant, moreover, the photographic plate records images of the partial exteriorization of the *aérosôme*, obtained voluntarily or involuntarily. These images are so frequent that they have received a special name: they are called *effluviographies*; Dr. Baraduc of Paris and Narkiewicz-Iodko [23] have provided, in their works, indications of techniques suitable for obtaining them. I will limit myself to reproducing two specimens here, one produced voluntarily (*fig.* 17) and the other fortuitously (*fig.* 18).

2. The hundreds of cases, observed and studied to date, of fortuitous or voluntary releases prove to us that the exteriorized ghost that manifests itself always enjoys one of these faculties (without which its presence would be imperceptible), very often two of them, and quite frequently all three combined.

---

[23] See also the study by D. G. De Régare: *The Exteriorization of Nervous Force* (magnetic force) and the work of M. De Jodko with 5 fig. *Review of Experimental Psychism*, July 2014. MM. H. and H. Durville, editors.

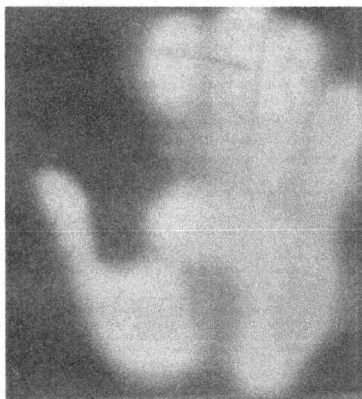

Fig. 17. — Photograph of the voluntary effluvia of the hand.

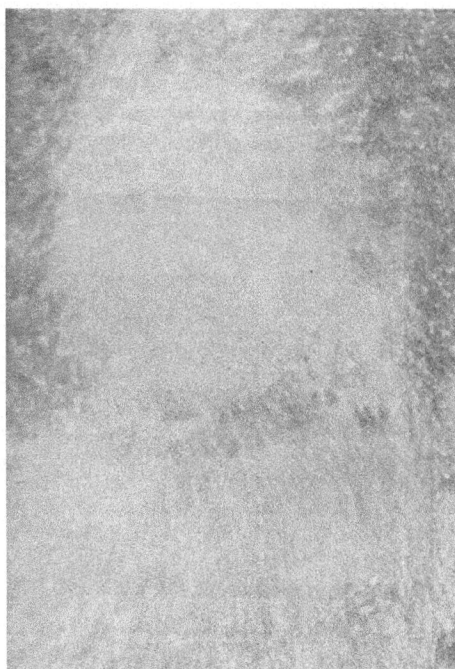

Fig. 18. — Photograph of involuntary effluvia.

A mother takes her young daughter to a photographer to have her portrait taken. There is a discussion between the daughter and the mother about the pose to strike. The mother, irritated, slaps her daughter, who submits. Immediately, without a word, the photographer hurries to take the picture; when developed, he obtains this image: he has photographed the young girl at the moment when the slap, given by the mother, provokes in the girl a movement of violent indignation and suppressed anger, causing a partial exteriorization of the ghost.

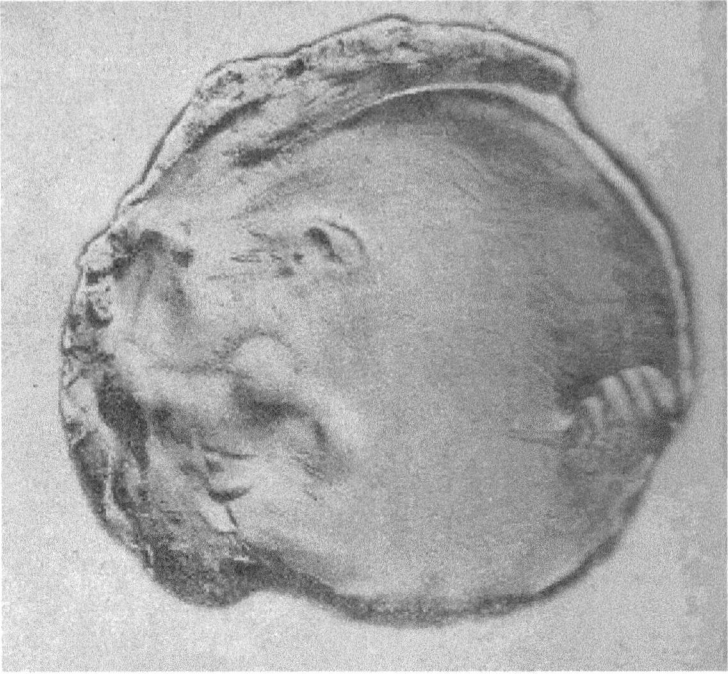

Fig. 19. — Sketch of face and hand obtained remotely, in clay, with EUSAPIA, by Lt VISANI SCOZZI.

Fig. 20. — Handprints obtained in clay, from a distance, with EUSAPIA, by M. GELLONA.

The material action of the exteriorized ghost is not only exerted on the photographic plate but also on any substance, leaving traces of its passage when this substance is plastic. In this regard, I provide the photographic reproduction of various prints obtained on clay with Eusapia Paladino (*figs*. 19 and 20). We will see later how to use this property of the living ghost to establish its identity by applying the ordinary procedures of anthropometry.

———

CHAPTER III

STATEMENT OF FACTS

Before tackling the study of the process to be implemented to achieve self-dissociation, it seems appropriate to say a few words about how I managed to establish it, by outlining the sequence of conditions in which I found myself and the deductions I was led to make, which will certainly destroy the aura of wonder that at first glance seems to surround this phenomenon, reducing it to the level of a simple psychophysiological experiment.

Let me first state that the time had come, today, when we so easily dissociate a magnetic subject to externalize its phantom, when any researcher, placed in the same circumstances as me, pursuing the same experiments, engaging in the same reasoning, and making the same series of deductions, would inevitably end up at the same point as me. So I take no pride in having been, rather than someone else — perhaps more competent than me — favored by a fortunate combination of circumstances.

But I am not a lover of the marvelous, far from it! I am only a modest experimenter, and I believe it useful to show, by simply stating the facts as they occurred, and the series of conclusions I successively drew from them, how sometimes chance, or at least what is wrongly called by that name, can, when one knows how to reflect on it, make those it favors find what they themselves do not seek… For a long time, personal out-of-body experience has been a well-known phenomenon in occultism; but the processes indicated by occult theories, and which it is unnecessary to detail here, have always seemed to me very absorbing and, in summary, quite dangerous. In short, upon reflection, they arrive at the same method that I will develop later, and which, I am convinced, students of Higher Science, in the sacred crypts of Thebes or the subterranean temples of the Himalayas, have known and put into practice; it is, at least I think so, only the *popularizers* of times more recent than our own, who, to ward off the imprudent, have surrounded the operation with difficulties of all kinds, difficulties foremost among which must be placed the long retreat which, technical works affirm, must precede the operation in order to prepare for it.

Now, I will say quite frankly that, some time ago, I wanted to ascertain, through personal experience, the possibility of this operation. There were certainly results — at least enough to prove the possibility of the event to me, but, I repeat, considering the experiment dangerous in itself and too absorbing in its preparations, I had long since abandoned any attempt — and years passed.

In 1910, as explained above, I was admitted to follow H. Durville's experiments, and I observed with what ease, in about a minute, a magnetizer could split a subject in two to exteriorize the ghost.

The operator was, it is true, one of the masters of magnetism, and the subjects highly trained, but that doesn't matter! The ease and speed of the operation made a profound impression on me from the very first experiment. And each of H. Durville's sessions that I attended subsequently confirmed my idea that splitting a human being is, for those who know, an operation of extreme simplicity.

Then a question imposed itself on my mind, logically, inevitably, arising from the circumstances themselves: Why couldn't one do to oneself what one does so easily to a subject? And I didn't need to think long to give this question an affirmative answer — at least theoretically — because self-magnetization, that is, the union in a single individual of both the magnetizer and the subject, is not new.

Such was the answer in *principle*; but then it was necessary to explore the idea in depth, down to the smallest details.

First, what elements were involved in such an operation? On the part of the magnetizer, an active will and magnetic passes; on the part of the subject, a passive will and a phantom. Now, can these elements be found united in a single individual? Obviously yes. Is it possible, moreover, to make them react upon each other by operating on oneself? Theoretically, the fact presents no impossibility. It remained to be seen whether, in practice, this would be the case.

To do this, it was important to know how the subject's phantom behaves in the event of splitting, because the will of this same subject, which must be purely passive, that is to say, annihilated, presented no obstacle to experimentation and, therefore, required no prior study.

The living phantom, as I explain elsewhere, is composed of:

1. Etheric double, holder of vital energy;
2. Astral body, holder of neurological force;
3. Mental body, holder of intelligence;
4. Higher elements of the being not yet addressed by experimentation. [24]

When the living phantom is exteriorized, it contains within itself the etheric double, which is its apparent basis as long as it evolves in the immediate vicinity of the subject; but this etheric double, holding physical life, is rather a constituent part of the material body. Indeed, while it follows the astral body in its exteriorization, it *never* strays far from the *sarcosôme*, where it returns as soon as the astral body — and with it, the higher elements of the being — is sent far away. The true basis of the phantom is therefore the astral body, and, since the latter is the repository of sensitivity, that is, of the subject's neurological force, it is consequently on the side of neurologicality that the starting point of the operation must be sought.

So much for what concerns the experimenter understood as a subject; this aspect of the question is very simple, since, in this case, passivity must be complete, to the point that there is no need to even consider the question of will.

Things are quite different when, in the experimenter, we no longer study the subject, but the operator. The latter, referring to the mode of production of objective splitting, must act on itself by means of magnetic passes and by the implementation of its own will.

_____

[24] However, as I said above, we have reached, but without being able to isolate it yet, nor, consequently, study it, one of these higher elements which appears to be the causal body.

So, for a while, I studied all the processes of self-magnetization in order to see which one would best suit the proposed goal: the dissociation of the experimenter himself.

I admittedly found none of these processes that satisfied me, since the simplest of them require a certain amount of reflection on the part of the operator, that is, sustained attention, whereas, understood as a subject, this same operator must passively abandon himself. There was, in short, within the same individual a radical and necessary opposition of dispositions that presented a seemingly insurmountable obstacle to the realization of the phenomenon, the two factors of this phenomenon seeming irreconcilable with each other.

For some time, I pondered the problem without even seeing a satisfactory solution, when, upon reflection, I had the intuition that I was coming up against an obstacle that was, in short, very easy to eliminate purely and simply.

What, in fact, is the purpose of the passes made by the magnetizer? To render the subject to his own will by making said will, conveyed by the magnetic fluid, pass through the subject.

Now, in the case where the operator and the subject form only one and the same individual, the former, as operator, *wanting* to dissociate himself, is by that very fact, as subject, subject to this will: as a logical consequence, the passes are superfluous.

We can see how the problem was simplified, reducing it to the study of two terms: neuropathy and will.

To study the development of the first factor, I only needed to open a few books on special physiology; but it was far from the same with regard to willpower. Indeed, in our time, when this faculty tends more and more to be regarded as a force of the human being, analogous if not superior to muscular or nervous forces, [25] works abound in which it is considered from the multiple aspects of the services it can provide and the different developments to which it is capable. However, only a few of them can be considered serious; the vast majority are the result of simple compilations and are, in short, nothing more than banal bookselling undertakings. The most appreciable provided me with a basis for establishing a method of development; but there is one special point that I could only reach through my own research and personal experience:

All the books in question deal solely with the will as it is in the waking state; none of them considers it from the point of view of sleep.

Now, my first attempts to realize the phenomenon showed me, beyond any possible doubt, that, on pain of failure, one must place oneself in a special hypnoid state, less profound certainly than magnetic sleep, but similar to it. There is even more: for the beginning, a deep sleep — ordinary, non-magnetic sleep — is, or at least seems to me so far, absolutely indispensable. I therefore had to experiment on myself to know exactly what happens to the will during the period of sleep, and, after having observed its almost total annihilation during this period, to study sleep itself in practice to understand the forces and faculties of man that subsist in this state, and can be called upon not to supplement the will, which must be at its strongest at the beginning of the experience, but to prolong it, in a way, in this phase despite its almost total annihilation. And this is how I was led to combine it, in order to achieve the desired result, with memory, which will store the order given by the will in the waking state, to present it to the astral body at the moment when sleep, numbing the will, will at the same time loosen the bonds that unite the astral body to the physical body. There are therefore only two elements of the phenomenon left: a will developed enough to know how to give an order, at first terrifying, which must be preserved by memory; and a neurological ability trained enough to be able to execute this order transmitted by memory, after having received it from the will.

In summary, at the point I have reached, the production of the phenomenon can be understood with the help of a very simple comparison.

---

[25] It seems to be a law of nature that the power of a force is inversely proportional to its materiality. To understand this, it is enough to compare the various types of forces: — solid (muscular and mechanical) — liquid (hydraulic press and ram, etc.) — gaseous (water vapor, deflagration of explosives, etc.) — imponderables (light, heat, electricity, etc.). Will is therefore a force (magnetism, hypnotism, etc.) that is not entirely immaterial, since its production leads to the destruction of brain cells, and which, as such, can act on other forces that themselves act on matter: it is enough to direct it properly... — but how many people know how to will?

A test tube, a simple drinking glass, will represent a human organism; the liquid it contains at normal height will represent the neurosity of the same organism in its normal state.

What means do I have at my disposal to force the water out of the test tube, that is, to externalize the organism's neurosity? Only two, at first glance: — either tip the test tube over (making the organism sick) — or break it (killing the organism).

But upon reflection, a third means will present itself by which I can make the liquid pass outside the test tube without even needing to touch it: it will suffice to fill the test tube with liquid, to the point of creating a meniscus above its edges, so that the liquid is ready to spread outward (develop the neuritis sufficiently so that the slightest cause determines its exteriorization); then place on the edges of the test tube a cotton wick, acting as a siphon, which will quickly soak the excess liquid, forming the meniscus and which will then cause the liquid to flow by capillarity: this wick represents the action of the will aided by memory for the production of the phenomenon of personal out-of-body experience.

From then on, I possessed a sufficiently well-founded theory of the phenomenon to guide me in this terrain, which was still completely unexplored by investigation. For two years, I closely followed experiments in objective splitting, which only confirmed the theory I had ultimately extracted from the facts!

So, all that remained was for me to experiment and have this theory tested in practice: this is what I did, and the results obtained proved to me that I had not been mistaken overall, and that only a few details needed to be modified in practice.

This is where and how I ended up.

Certainly, the phenomenon itself seems unacceptable; this is not the case when one considers the simplicity of the methods employed and the logic of the deductions that led me to the goal I was pursuing. Perhaps another researcher could have solved the problem better than I; this is possible, and will almost certainly happen in the future.

In short, the first observer to come along, placed in the circumstances in which I found myself, could have, should have arrived at the same point as me; it was therefore a matter of simple chance that it was I, rather than someone else, who found myself in favorable conditions; I therefore, I beg you to believe, and I repeat, derive no vanity from this. Only one point, in this series of studies and deductions, is strictly personal to me: the alliance that I was able to establish between will and memory, the latter substituting itself for the former to bring about the realization of the experiment.

But, someone told me to whom I presented these results, this is truly magic!

This person didn't believe he was speaking so true, but then again, one must understand one another. Magic, the kind that emanated from ancient sanctuaries and came down to us under the mysterious aegis of the initiates; this haughty and formidable science that, to break with a disparaged term, is today called hyperphysics; is in no way, as the common people think, the grotesque art of pronouncing a barbaric formula as misunderstood by the makers of grimoires as it is incomprehensible to those who repeat it, by virtue of which the sun, for example, must transform itself into the moon, or man into an animal... no! This magic is purely imaginary, that of the naïve and the swindlers; it has no reality, and its phenomena are pure sleight of hand.

On the contrary, real magic, the kind that was once part of the mystery teachings of India, Egypt, Greece, and the Druids, which was transmitted to us by devoted converts, and which holds incredibly dangerous secrets, this magic exists today as it has always existed, as it always will, increasingly unmasked by the research and experimentation of normal science [26]; the formulas it uses are either Sanskrit *memtrams*, Hebrew-Chaldaic invocations, or Greek and Latin prayers; it can be defined as: the domination of human or natural forces known or still unknown to normal science, by the hyper-dynamized will of man.

In this respect, hypnotism is nothing other than a detached fragment of the initiatory magic of sacred antiquity, and the illustrious German scholar Carl du Prel was able to publish, under the title *Magic, Natural Science* [27], a work in which he studies magical physics and magical psychology.

I have just said that this magic, the true kind, whose adepts once bore the sacred name of "Magi" and today bear that of "Magists", results from the action of human will on the *known* or *still unknown* forces of being and nature... It can, in fact, operate only on a *real* element and not on a *fictitious* one.

This is how a Hindu Yogi [28] will be able, in a few minutes, to make a plant germinate, grow, and bear fruit; because he finds in nature the necessary force; he simply has to activate it by the energy of his will. But it will not be able to produce the seemingly much simpler phenomenon of making a pineapple grow on a mango tree, because it has no natural force at its disposal capable of bringing about this result.

Now, to what terms does the phenomenon we are studying in these pages boil down? To the action of the will on the astral body, unknown to normal science, but whose existence is undeniable since we isolate it daily in our laboratories.

This is therefore undeniably magic, as the person I just spoke of was astonished; but scientific magic, hyper-physics, and not the low, non-existent witchcraft magic of charlatans and their dupes. On the other hand, let me say here, I have extensively studied this high science of ancient initiations, which can be summed up in two terms: hyper-dynamization of the will and knowledge of the subtle forces of nature, not yet cataloged by official science, upon which the will can act. Now, the study I have been given to conduct of the human will and of certain particular dynamics, specific to man although still unknown to the public, will allow me to give this work all the breadth and precision that the reader may require.

That said, I close the parenthesis and return to my subject.

To summarize the above, there are three elements to consider in the study of this phenomenon:

a) The agent, that is, the will producing the release of the phantom.

---

[26] The circulation of life was unmasked by Harvey; the unity of matter is now a given; microbiology leads us to understand the theory of elementals, etc., etc. Yesterday's occultism is today's high science, which will become tomorrow's commonplace science.

[27] Translated into French by Nissa. 2 vols. octavo, Paris, 1908.

[28] The fakirs, who are merely high-level conjurers, produce only the imitation of the phenomena that Yogis give reality to; they know only one aspect of the high hidden science, but this aspect they know and practice with a mastery unsuspected in the West: it is the art of arousing collective hallucinations; as such, they produce, or at least seem to produce, phenomena that a Yogin could not realize, precisely because they are simple illusionists.

b) The object, that is, the living organism that must be brought to dissociate.

c) The external conditions that aid or hinder the splitting of the body.

In other words, to achieve the accomplishment of the phenomenon, three objects must first be studied and understood:

a) The will, its essence, and its means of energization.

b) The constitution of man and the means of training that can be applied to his organization, threefold, to achieve the proposed goal.

c) All the external conditions of the operation, and the study of the means to neutralize those that are harmful, and, on the contrary, to utilize those that are favorable.

This is what the following pages will address.

———

PART TWO

———————

THEORY

CHAPTER IV

WILL AND ITS PROCESSES OF ENERGIZATION

A) *Outline of the normal will.*

There is perhaps no philosophical term that has so aroused the enthusiasm of definition seekers as the word Will; this is due, I think, to the fact that there is no faculty that presents so many degrees within itself, nor whose degrees are so different from one another, from simple whim to *volitodynamia*, passing through impulse, inclination, intention, desire, envy, volition, resolution, obstinacy, stubbornness, etc., etc.

If, therefore, we do not want to get lost in the depths of metaphysics or end up with definitions that are false in their breadth, like those of lexicons [29], or in their restriction, like those of theology [30], we must remain within the simple domain of fact, and draw our definition from the fact itself.

---

[29] Faculty of command, of desire, of consent...

[30] The extent to which man escapes the domination of external forces, and governs the impulses of life that arise within. Understood in this way, wills are rare; almost all men fall into two categories: the apathetic and the excessive. In the former, impulse is lacking. Vital resources remain buried in inaction, activity does not rise to the level of duty. This languor of soul is the most dangerous disease of the will. In the excessive, impulse is, on the contrary, violent, and disordered, like the untamed ardor of those teams that the bit does not govern. Neither of them has willpower nor can they have it, we add, if they do not submit to the methodical training that will allow them to activate or moderate this state of mind that is particular to them, because willpower must be, above all, measured and persistent action. (*The Development of Willpower through the Training of Thought*, by G.-A. Mann, 1 vol. octavo, Paris, 1910).

Under these conditions, we can say of Will that *it is one of the two forms of activity.* Activity is force in action; but action involves two modes of production: it occurs spontaneously or voluntarily; spontaneity and will are therefore the two forms of activity.

I will leave aside spontaneity here, which is of no interest to us, and focus only on will.

Will is therefore a force, as a form of activity, which is, as just said, force itself in action.

But, as a force, will possesses material organs: What are these organs?

Here is what Dr. Lavrand [31] says about it:

A volition is composed of a concept, a deliberation, a decision, and an execution. [32] Consequently, one cannot claim that volition is a purely psychic phenomenon; it therefore includes both psychic and physiological or somatic elements. There is, in fact, such an intimate union between the soul and the body that they always remain associated and participate to varying degrees in all human acts, moral and physical, in a healthy or pathological state. In the act of will, we also find conscious phenomena and phenomena that are not currently perceived by consciousness; among these are some of the physiological elements taking part in the act of will. We believe it is useful to say a word about the physiological elements, for they exert, as we shall see, a not insignificant influence on the will.

Will is generally considered to be linked to reflex acts, but to one of the most complicated forms of reflexes. It certainly seems that volition only results in determining the appearance of ideas; how then can reflexes be involved? Now, we are inclined to admit that every idea tends toward its realization, that it is always accompanied by more or less apparent movements; we therefore arrive at reflex acts both when the will results in ideas and when it generates motor phenomena. The simplest reflex arc is constituted by a centripetal or sensory nerve, a cellular center, and a centrifugal or motor nerve.

---

[31] *Treatment of Willpower and Psychotherapy*, 12vo, Paris, 1909.
[32] These elements will be studied further.

At the very bottom of the scale, we have the centers of the spinal cord and the medulla oblongata; higher up, we encounter the higher reflex centers; they are located in the basal ganglia of the brain (quadrigeminal tubercles, optic layers, striated bodies, etc.), and also in the cerebral cortex. Grasset distinguishes between lower automatism and higher automatism, or lower psychic reflexes: consciousness and intelligence are involved to varying degrees, and finally, at the highest level, higher psychic acts, that is, conscious, voluntary, and free. The hypothetical center O groups the centers of the higher psyche; the other centers would constitute what this author calls the polygonal centers. [33]

For all these reflexes, there are groups of neurons higher and higher in the nervous axis; only the acts of the higher psyche are controversial. Indeed, Grasset believes in the existence of a special group of neurons [34] for conscious, voluntary, and free acts. However, he does not want to establish the seat of the soul there, he says, and he admits that this hypothesis "does not have a precise basis in topographical anatomy." However, since there are higher and lower functions, one must assume corresponding neurons, or attribute diverse functions to the same neurons.

Consider a trivial example: in a large city, I am crossing a busy street; I suddenly hear a loud horn. Looking, recognizing an electric tram or a car and the direction they are traveling, parking accordingly — this whole complicated ensemble reproduces the various phases of the act of will, with an auditory impression as the starting point.

How many nervous acts are performed by a large number of nervous elements in this banal event we are analyzing, and how many muscular acts: the cerebral cortex, the ganglia, the spinal cord, the nerves, and finally the muscles take part. All these organs function for the slightest act of will, but they still need to understand each other, their functions need to coordinate, and finally, they all need to act synergistically.

"We see," writes Paulhan, "to what broad physiological reality the psychic fact of the will corresponds, and what a number

---

[33] GRASSET, *Hypnotism and Suggestion.*
[34] BALTUS, *The Nervous System. The Brain.*

of somatic facts it implies, which are specific to it or which also characterize other forms of activity. Whenever we speak of volition, we are not talking about a psychic act supposedly independent of the organism, but a psychic act which, like all psychological facts, realizes a complexus of physiological facts." »
Let us rather say that it constitutes, like all psychological facts, both a complexus of psychic and somatic phenomena, for we have seen that there is an intimate dependence, a close concordance, between the soul and the body. Psychology is not a chapter of physiology: it has its own laws and special phenomena that are irreducible.

It has been said, with a large degree of truth, that genius is a long patience. Not only does the man who knows how to will considerably increase the productive value of his intelligence through the concentration of his efforts and perseverance in his studies, but he also masters his passions, directs them, and uses them; even more, he imposes himself on his fellow men and tames nature itself, as demonstrated by the magnificent artistic works of engineers.

How do you recognize that a person has willpower?

By knowing how to make up their minds, by carrying out what they have resolved to do, and above all by persevering in their resolutions and undertakings. The essential condition for this is that the soul be in normal health and the psyche be healthy.

The decision remains entirely internal; however, it requires a process of comparing options and demands a genuine effort to make a choice, to decide to act. The effort is so real that some people cannot make it and remain indecisive for a long time. Then, volition reaches the execution phase. This requires greater effort, sometimes very painful; many make up their minds, a great many begin to realize their will, but ordinarily few people possess enough persevering energy to see it through, because they become discouraged along the way: asthenia of the will, *abulia*, are morbid, purely psychic phenomena (such as neurasthenics).

All these notions about the organs of the will were necessary to give here; but they will be applied especially in the following chapter, which will deal with auto-suggestion. We will now study the elements of the will taken in itself, which have just been touched upon.

The will is a complex faculty, which can be broken down into four interdependent elements: possession, deliberation, determination, and finally, action. These four constituent facts of the will are indissolubly linked together and absolutely dependent on one another; deliberation stems from possession; determination is the logical consequence of deliberation; and action is the natural conclusion of determination. Indeed, if the soul is not free, there is no possession; if it does not possess itself, there is no possible deliberation; if, on the other hand, deliberation is false or incomplete, there can be no healthy determination; and finally, action is always in proportion to determination, energetic or weak depending on whether the determination has been strong or indecisive. Everything therefore rests, in short, on the first term, the absence of which vitiates all the rest. From which we can conclude that the will cannot exist unless one is absolutely master of oneself.

But, as everything is linked together, the will can, in turn and by its very essence, react on self-control, strengthen it, and increase it significantly; and this self-control, thus developed, will contribute to increasing the strength of will. From this we can conclude that, when both are developed in parallel and simultaneously, the will shall acquire, as a final result, a dynamization that will be in direct proportion to the efforts made in each direction, which amounts to saying that it is capable of strengthening, development, and dynamization. There are various methods for achieving this goal, which will be examined later; for the moment, I will continue with the analytical study of the will itself.

I will pass over in silence the two objections raised against human freedom, and consequently against self-control, from divine foresight and the power of motives; these two objections — the principal ones, if not the only ones that exist — can be taken seriously by a weak and fickle character; they do not exist for anyone who is truly aware of their moral strength and self-possession.

We have just analyzed the four factors that together constitute the will; we must now see what the elements of its mode of action are.

These elements are three in number: knowledge of the goal pursued, the felt power to achieve it, and the internal judgment that the action of the organs must immediately follow the wish of thought.

I. — Knowledge of the goal pursued is incompatible with instinct or any other organic determination. If, therefore, we *want* to perform an act, we must free ourselves from everything in us that instinctively tends to demonstrate the impossibility of performing this act.

An impulsive idea arises in us, stemming from the previous general belief: "The dissociation of the physical and living human personality is, can only be, a dream"... we must react against this idea, otherwise your will shall vanish; we must tell you that laboratory experiments, that the observation, in all countries of the world, of hundreds and hundreds of studied and proven cases, collected by people who are not visionaries but men of science, are there to demonstrate to us the possibility, the reality of the phenomenon.

The instinct of self-preservation tells us that this experiment must be excessively dangerous... far be it from me to absolutely deny the existence of these dangers to which, on the contrary, I reserve the right to draw attention later; but they must still be analyzed in order to examine them, and consequently to find a palliative for them; a vague fear, without a precise object, is the most deplorable factor in any experience, because its imprecision inevitably leads us to collide head-on with the real danger that we have not previously been able to define, and consequently, to be shattered. No one will dispute that the use of dynamite in mining is extremely perilous, and yet we have managed to handle this formidable explosive with almost absolute safety, lacking only as a result of imprudence. Why? Because certain absolute rules have been established, to the observation of which all those called upon to handle this agent conform.

This is the case when it comes to the splitting of the human being. We must know the dangers that accompany it, we must know the precautions with which we can ward off these dangers and which, taken by a man sure of himself, sure of his intellectual and moral strength, sure of his will, will be enough to neutralize them. [35]

II. — I now turn to the second element of the question.

The felt power to achieve the desired goal is incompatible with desire. Desire, in fact, is only a vague aspiration toward an object, whereas will presupposes a firm and certain proposition of success.

The man who says, "I want to achieve such and such a goal, but I don't know if I will succeed," is putting forward two contradictory, if not irreconcilable, propositions; since he is not sure of achieving the proposed goal, it is because he lacks willpower, for the very nature of willpower is precisely to remove or annihilate every obstacle. The man who has willpower, on the other hand, will say, "I want to achieve such and such a goal; for another it might be impossible; for me, it is not because I *want* to!" Why can he express himself with such assurance, with such firmness? Simply because he feels within himself the power to realize his will.

He must therefore, before beginning any attempt, analyze himself, examine himself seriously: if he feels only the desire, without more, to succeed, he will inevitably end in failure. After rigorous self-examination, he must feel he has the power to act. And how will he acquire this power to act? Through study and reasoning on the one hand, and on the other, through the awareness he possesses of the dynamization of his will and the training of his triple organism.

We will say a word about each of these three factors.

a) Study — acquired from his previous studies — will affirm to him: You now know all sides of the question; you have delineated the strong and the weak; you know what the risks of failure are and the chances of success; you have weighed both; you are in full possession of the means; both physical, and intellectual and moral, to use to neutralize the former and to increase the latter; you have identified and secured your starting point; you have foreseen all the obstacles that may arise on your path and hinder your progress, but you also know how to remove them and how to

―――――――
[35] The reader will note that everything said here about the will relates exclusively to the subject at hand. There would be too much to say if I were to go into other generalities, and it would be pointless to give insights which, however interesting they might be, would have no use with regard to the experimental phenomenon studied in these pages.

break them; you have finally clearly defined your point of arrival; now leave the books that have taught you only theory, and get up: take with you your Viaticum of science, and walk; your previous knowledge gives you the assurance of reaching the goal: *you must reach it because you have the power and the will to reach it!*

b) Reasoning, on the other hand, will assert to him: Are you then the first to attempt such an experiment?

Far from it. Laboratory successes have shown you how possible it is and even, to a certain extent, easily achievable; observations made everywhere by serious men, by yourself, prove to you that it has been carried out many times, that it is commonly done, sometimes unconsciously, but other times with the operator fully aware of it. What others have done, can't you do? And were your predecessors better equipped than you? Did they have more knowledge than you? More willpower? More energy? No, you are their equal in every way; why then should you fail where they have succeeded?

Is it, on the contrary, their contempt for danger that was greater than it is in you? But contempt for danger is only a word, a word of madness. In this, no more than in anything else, one must not despise danger; one must recognize it, appreciate it at its true value, and guard against its hazards by the means taught to you by the experience of your predecessors combined with theoretical knowledge of the subject. Are you then less informed than they? Is your knowledge inferior to theirs? No! You are in full possession of all your faculties, all your means, all your technical training: through all this, you have the sense of your power, and everything depends on your will, since *to will is to be able!*

c) Finally, the awareness one possesses of having judiciously applied special training procedures to the will and the psycho-physical organism and of having achieved certain results is perhaps the best agent that can give a man the sense of his special power.

Your will was, if not weak, at least indecisive and soft; through a constantly repeated auto-suggestion, the mechanism and details of which will be studied later, you have come to have proof, in the thousand incidents of daily life, that you know how to will, that is to say, when an obstacle arises in your path, you judge it quickly, you clearly see the means to overcome it, you make a precise decision, and you put it into action immediately; unlike what would have happened before your training, where you would have hesitated, procrastinated... you have the experimental and personal proof that now you know how to will: in a word, you feel undeniably that you have the power to act because you have the will — I repeat, *to will is to be able.* [36]

An identical moral assurance will arise in you from the fact that, having clearly understood that the occult constitution of the human being is essentially different from what the public commonly believes, having clearly grasped the mechanism of its various cogs as well as the procedures that must be used to activate this or that, and having implemented them to achieve the desired goal, you have understood that in you, self-control not only directs your external actions, does not only dominate your physical body and your moral being, but also extends, as a result of special training, to the entire psychic organism and the hyperphysical energies found there.

During this training, a number of small events, the cause of which you will be able to discover, will clearly show you the progress you have made in this direction, the acquired knowledge you will have acquired, and you will thus acquire the awareness of your power to act.

III. — I will finally analyze the third element of the will's mode of action.

The internal judgment that the action of the organs must immediately follow the will of thought excludes any idea of mechanism. It would therefore be a mistake to believe that the will is only an initial instrument of action; it must act by itself not only throughout the duration of the action but also in all the particular modes of that same action.

A worker wants to start a machine: he presses a button, and immediately, as a result of accumulated energies, a spring activates cogs that react on each other, communicating the force that each of them transforms and uses according to the data that presided over its construction. In this case, the worker may have wanted to start

---

[36] It is obvious that the application of this aphorism must be guided by reason; only a madman can want what is materially or logically impossible.

the machine, and he acted in this direction to the end, that is, from the knowledge of the goal pursued to the final act of pressing the button; but he did not have, he could not have had, the will to make this machine work, which moves only through the use of external mechanical forces to which his will was limited to restoring their freedom of action. This is a matter of mechanism and not of will, which ceased to act at the precise moment the machine began to move.

Consider, on the contrary, a battle. It has been rightly said that in every combat, victory belongs to the one of the two adversaries who desires it with the most energy, with the most tenacity. The leader does not limit his will to simply engaging in the struggle, to giving the order to march forward, mechanically anticipating final success, no; he extends his will to all phases of the action, monitoring what is happening to his right, to his left, to his center, ready to give new orders according to the twists and turns of the day, ready to ward off any event; in a word, maintaining his will in full activity, and, if he knows how to will longer, more firmly than his adversary, he ends up imposing his will on him. Woe to the general who believes, at any moment in the struggle, that final success is merely a matter of technical mechanism and that his will can rest!

On June 14, 1800, French and Austrian troops clashed at Marengo. Mélas, after repelling all attacks and forcing Bonaparte to retreat, judged that it was now a matter of pure military mechanics and left the day to his chief of staff to finish: in a word, he ceased to want. Desaix arrived, and Bonaparte, continuing to want, judged that, if the battle was lost, he still had time, before nightfall, to engage in another and win it. Bonaparte wanted more tenaciously than Mélas, and Mélas was defeated.

To want! The whole secret of the military successes of the First Empire lies there. All the generals of allied Europe saw only a battle, all the military academies advocated only geometric order, which only results in tactical mechanics. Napoleon would arrive, having set himself a goal, wanting to achieve it — and his will would shatter his adversaries' mechanisms.

To return to the point at hand, we must not believe that will is only the initial instrument of personal splitting; it must be its constant driving force. It is not enough to have willed for a moment for the constituent parts of the human being to mechanically dissociate and for the ghost to be freed from the physical body; one must will for the entire duration of the operation, each phase of which must be monitored and activated by will.

In summary, the will is the principal agent of any hyperphysical or other operation, by the very fact that it dominates the whole of the being: — its intellectual system through attention and reflection — its moral system through intention and premeditation — its psychophysical system, through the training it has subjected it to and as a result of which it knows how to energetically impose itself; in a word, the human will is man himself.

From all of the above, I will draw the following four propositions, which I ask the reader to kindly remember, in view of what follows:

I. — Will is a force.

II. — Will depends on self-control, upon which it in turn reacts.

III. — Like any force, will is susceptible to diminution and augmentation.

IV. — Energy variations in the will can be obtained either by acting on the will itself directly, or indirectly, on self-control. [37]

B) *Will in sleep.*

Everything that has just been said applies to the will considered in its normal activity, that is, in the waking state; but splits are exceedingly rare in the normal state; the phenomenon most generally occurs when the subject is either in a state of complete sleep—which constitutes the majority of cases—or in a state of drowsiness, numbness, or torpor that is very close to sleep.

We must therefore examine what becomes of the will in such

---

[37] One will read with interest the work of M. H. DURVILLE: *Personal or Psychic Magnetism, Education of Thought, Development of Will. To be happy, strong, healthy, and successful in everything*. This very practical method allows one to quickly develop one's will and personal magnetism through a natural process.

an occurrence, without disguising the fact that the question is extremely obscure and, consequently, highly controversial.

First, what is sleep [38] from a physiological point of view, the only one that interests us here? We can define it from this perspective: a period characterized by the rest of the organs that serve the life of relationships, and by a redoubled activity in the functions of inner life. On the one hand, indeed, one of the principal causes of sleep is the prolonged exercise of the functions that connect us with the objects that surround us, from which follows the weariness of the organs that pertain to these functions. On the other hand, while the organs of relational life are struck by a sort of paralysis during the period of sleep, those of inner life not only continue to act but also generally enjoy greater energy than in the waking state; thus, for example, all fractures, dislocations, etc., heal more quickly under the influence of sleep.

In summary, despite the suspension of activity of certain organs, sleep is an essentially active state. [39]

On the other hand, there appears to exist a certain analogy between the laws that govern our physical faculties and those to which our intellectual faculties are subject, worthy of attention. Just as during sleep there is a redoubling of the activity of the vital, internal, and passive forces of the human body, favored by the suspension of the expansive forces of action, so there is an increase in power and intensity in what we can call passive intellectual forces — for example, memory and imagination when left to their own devices, while attention and will, these expansive forces of the soul, are noticeably weakened and can no longer be exercised without effort.

Therefore, the will is weakened during sleep; it is even completely abolished, according to certain authors, [40] Darwin, Boerhave, and Formey among others; Darwin is even resolutely

---

[38] I am naturally speaking here only of normal sleep, leaving aside abnormal sleep, coma, lethargy, hypnosis, etc.

[39] *Dictionary of Medical Sciences*, art. *Sleep* by Montfalcon.

[40] I reject the opinion of physiologists who believe that the exercise of attention and will is totally suspended in our dreams, but I do not go so far as to say that these faculties usually retain all their energy during sleep. (*Dreams and the Means of Directing Them*, without author's name (D'Hervey de Saint-Denis), 1 vol. in-8, Paris, 1867).

affirmative in this regard: "The power of volition," he says, "is totally suspended during sleep." [41]

For my part, I do not share this opinion, and I rather agree, at least partially, with that of Dugald-Stewart when he asks: [42] "In sleep, is the faculty of willing suspended?" and replies: "The efforts we make in sleep and of which we are aware clearly show that the faculty of willing is not suspended. Thus, in a dream, we believe ourselves to be in danger and we want to call for help. This desire, it is true, is usually ineffective and the cries we utter are weak and indistinct, but this is precisely what confirms the opinion that, during sleep, the connection between the will and voluntary movements is broken. *The will continues to act, but its action remains insufficient.*

"Likewise, during a frightening dream, we feel that we are making efforts to escape by flight from the danger that threatens us; but despite our efforts, we remain lying in bed. Most often, in this case, we dream that some obstacle stops us. The fact is that then, probably, the body is not subject to the action of the will.

"We can therefore conclude by saying: *during regular, natural sleep, the faculty of volition subsists, but it has lost all authority over the organs of the body.*"

Here, the Scottish philosopher is too absolute in his conclusions: one cannot say that the connection between the will and voluntary movements is abolished: it is simply relaxed. Nor can one say that the faculty of volition, while subsisting, has lost all authority over the organs; only that this authority is more difficult to exercise. Many people have proof of what I am saying, which consists in this: while willpower alone is powerless to emerge from a nightmare by awakening, it can nevertheless produce a violent movement; for example, by causing a sudden relaxation of the extensor muscles of the leg (making one kick), the result of which will be to awaken. And this is so simple, so within the reach of most people, that we will later see how to use this method for the purpose that interests us. I continue the quote:

"Let us go further: when we seek to fall asleep, which happens often, our mind naturally assumes a state close to that in

---

[41] DARWIN, *Zoonomy of Sleep.*
[42] *Elements of the Philosophy of the Human Mind* (3 vol. in-4, Edinburgh 1792-1814-1827).

which it will be when sleep is fully established. Now, it is clear that the means dictated by nature to induce sleep do not consist in suspending the faculty of volition, but rather in the exercise of the faculties that depend on the will. If the faculty of will were to be suspended before falling asleep, it would be impossible for us, by any kind of effort, to hasten the moment of sleep. The very supposition of such an effort is absurd, for it is to say that the will would be in a sustained activity to suspend the very acts of will.

"From which one is led to conclude that the effect of sleep on mental operations has the most perfect resemblance to that which it has on the body. The faculty of will subsists, but it has no influence over the faculties of the mind..."

Here again the conclusion is too absolute. Yes, the faculty of will remains, but, as we saw above, if its action seems abolished on the expansive forces of the soul, on the contrary this action seems more powerful on the passive intellectual forces (memory which gives birth to dreams, imagination which nourishes them, etc.)

We cannot therefore truly say that, despite the subsistence of the will, its action is totally abolished, for who among us has not experienced more than once, upon falling asleep, the desire to wake up the next day at a certain time, and in fact, wake up at the appointed time? Therefore, the will remains active... and yet daily practice shows us it is dozing itself, virtually ceasing to act as sleep approaches. How can we reconcile these two seemingly irreconcilable phenomena? In a very simple way.

Everyone is familiar with this particular hypnotic phenomenon called suggestion. An operator says to his subject in a state of hypnosis: "Tomorrow, two weeks from now, at such and such a time you will perform such and such an act." Then he wakes the subject, who remembers nothing. But the next day, two weeks later, at the appointed hour, the thought arose in him: "I must perform such and such an act." And he did so. This is ordinary suggestion reduced to its simplest mechanism. But there are others that are infinitely more complicated: there is suggestion in the waking state, there is auto-suggestion. This last word gives us the key to the enigma.

The sleeper, before falling asleep, autosuggests to himself:

"Tomorrow, I must wake up at such and such a time." The suggestion slumbers with him, but it has been stored by the astral body, [43] by the astral part of the brain, if you prefer, where it remains in potential existence while the physical body sleeps, and which gives it at the appointed hour all the force of which it is capable, a force whose measure is in direct proportion to that of the will that produced it.

In other words, the will, before falling asleep, has created a monoidism that watches and acts at its own time. We will see later [44] that although physically asleep, the will retains its own action on certain cerebral faculties, but for the moment, we need only concern ourselves with this other mode of action which constitutes the creation of a monoidism by the will. The transition from wakefulness to sleep is always characterized by a more or less lengthy period of daydreaming during which ideas and reminiscences flow together and unfold spontaneously, following their laws of association. As a result, for this daydreaming to occur, attention must be suspended; now, the suspension of attention is the suspension of the action of the will, which then only exerts itself on certain cerebral faculties outside of our consciousness. It is therefore before this moment of daydreaming, when our will is still in consciousness, that it must be made to act to create with all its energy the monoideism, the fixed idea, if you will, which will remain awake despite physical sleep, which will normally replace the will, then manifested under other conditions and with greater difficulty, which will preside, in a word, over the entire series of operations. We now understand how the will can act during sleep by first creating an order that will be executed passively if given firmly. The situation is identically similar to that of a ship's captain who, before falling asleep, has given a special order to the officer of the watch; he can fall asleep, he can lull his will with him; the order emanating from his will shall be executed in a sort of mechanical way.

C) *Dynamization processes.*

In his *Education of the Will*, [45] J. Payot demonstrates that

---

[43] See Chap. VI, Occult Constitution of the Human Being.
[44] Chapter XI, § E.
[45] 1 vol. in 8, Paris, 1900.

the internal means whose infallible effectiveness is in creating, strengthening, or destroying certain affective states, and which must necessarily precede external means, include *meditative reflection* and *action*. To which it must be added that this action, to be effective, must be essentially continuous, because it is precisely continuity that gives action its omnipotence.

We will find the application of these two principles in the following pages.

First, with regard to preliminary meditation, it is appropriate to thoroughly understand what has just been said about the will in general and its mechanism, both in the waking and sleeping states; this is elementary. It is the application of the principle by virtue of which one can only drive a horse well if one knows it thoroughly; that one can only draw well if one is familiar with all the practical processes of drawing, etc. It is therefore necessary not only to understand the above well, but also to study within oneself, in the ordinary acts of daily existence, all the psychic phenomena to which the normal exercise of the will gives rise; to analyze them, to dissect them, in order to fully understand their mode of production, and consequently, to be aware of the theory and practice of the will.

Only after this study can we fruitfully implement the means to energize the will.

These means are quite numerous but are generally only variations of a single principle: the application of auto-suggestion. I will therefore give only the two simplest ones that everyone can modify and adapt to their personal development.

But first, I must say it once and for all: what I call *will* — for we saw at the beginning of this chapter that the word itself has many meanings because will itself has many degrees and takes multiple forms — what I call *will* is neither the capricious will of the child who *wants* to eat a cake, nor the disordered will of the madman who sees red and *wants* to kill, no! *Willpower*, if I may give such an example, seems to me to be that which a passenger who has fallen from a moving ocean liner, unable to swim but having retained all his composure, has and seems to display; he sees the boat that has been put out to sea to rescue him; he calculates that it will take five minutes before anyone reaches him, and says to himself with full self-knowledge: "I *want* to keep myself afloat during this time!" Willpower, therefore, to be truly such, must have a threefold character; it must be calm without respite, energetic without violence, and continuous without variation in intensity.

I now turn to the processes of dynamization.

The reader is asked to recall here two of the propositions stated above: "Willpower depends on self-control..." and "Variations of energy in the will can be obtained either by acting directly on the will itself or indirectly on self-control." This distinction will give rise to the examination of two processes that I will study successively.

1. — Direct action.

Will is a force; it is perhaps the greatest of all those at the service of man, and in any case, it is the one with which he can master all others.

Now, what other force can act on this force, which is the most powerful of all? None, except will itself when it possesses a superior degree of energy. This is the principle of hypnotism, whose phenomena are brought about by the influence of a strong will on another will.

But hypnotism is based on suggestion, and while hetero-suggestion acts on the subject, auto-suggestion acts on the operator himself. We can see the full extent to which, in the present question, auto-suggestion can be used. [46]

It is therefore a matter of formulating an idea whose simple, clear, and precise enunciation is easily engraved in the brain and makes an impression on the imagination.

This one is recommended because it says what it means: "I HAVE WILL AND I AM ENERGY".

Keep it always in mind, repeat it mentally when you find yourself in the presence of other people in a low voice, and even out loud when you are alone.

But this is not a purely mechanical task; mechanically repeating this formula like the good women who believe they are

---

[46] I am only examining auto-suggestion here as applied to this particular case; I will later (Chapter V) deal more fully with auto-suggestion in general.

praying because they are always muttering to their rosary beads the same words from memory, no! First of all, immerse yourself in the meaning of these words, so that when you repeat them, it is not only the image or the sound of the word that attracts your attention, but also the intimate meaning of these two little phrases.

To this end, begin by making a commentary, a paraphrase to yourself, so that their meaning is clearly defined in your mind. Think, for example: "*I have will*, that is, I am my own master and I must do not what I *can* but what I *want*, whatever the work or action I undertake. When I speak of will, I mean a serious will, but not one that is fickle or proceeds in fits and starts; therefore, before each act, before each task, I must clearly see what I want and stick to it no matter what. My will should only waver in two cases: 1. if an unforeseen event occurs that completely changes the aspect of the question and gives it a completely new appearance; 2. if judicious advice reveals to me a side of the same question that had escaped my reflection. But in either case, my will should only be suspended until after further meditation on the new conditions; in order to then, according to my decision, taken in complete freedom, in all self-power, either strive more strongly toward the same goal to regain lost time, or turn toward another goal; but also stronger to neutralize its previous effects toward a goal that is no longer mine. *I am energetic*, that is to say, I can only be dominated by a will more powerful than my own. Now, I do not want this other will to exist; I must therefore develop the energy of my own in such a way that it can *never* encounter an external will capable of dominating it. But my energy must not only manifest itself externally, for in that case it would only result in transforming my will into stubbornness, a quality into a vice; I must be the absolute master of myself. It is therefore on my inner strengths that my energy must, before all and above all, be directed, which will increase accordingly. My body and my intelligence must be nothing but the slaves of my will, the corpses that it alone animates and vivifies: if, in a word, I am master of myself, I am master of all, and no opposing will shall succeed, not only in bending mine, but even in reacting against it."

As you can see: the theme is inexhaustible, and new commentaries will constantly be found to establish along these lines; and the further we advance along this path, the better we will understand what a perfect will must be, one that is sure of itself and unassailable by anyone. These two little phrases, "*I have willpower, I am energetic*," or any other of the same kind that you have adopted, must be the companions of your existence every day, every hour, every minute, whether you are at work or at play, at table or traveling, at rest or in activity. These are the ones you must keep in mind in the morning as soon as you wake up, and it is by meditating on them that you must fall asleep at night; in this way, that very night, their meaning will penetrate you, for before giving yourself over to sleep, you have created within yourself a monoideism that will not be affected by the momentary slumber of your will, and which will act on your sleep itself; that is to say, during this period of rest, on your subconscious, on your dreams, in a word, on all your latent activity of the night.

But there are especially moments when these little phrases must be present to you with their meaning as complete as you have been able to establish it until then; this is when it will be a question of moving from theory to practice, in other words, when the opportunity arises to translate these two little phrases into action.

Now, whether for a trivial determination or an important decision, these moments occur one after another for each of us, throughout the day, and it is only then, through experience, that we realize whether we have repeated the words in question like a parrot repeats its lesson, or whether we have said them with the awareness of an intelligent being; that is, by delving into their innermost meaning and becoming immersed in their significance.

You must therefore translate into action the theory that you constantly have in mind, make a firm decision, and then pursue its implementation. To this end, you must bring great precision to the mental operations that follow: gain an exact understanding of the entire question; clearly define what is to be desired; take in at a glance the starting point, the path to be taken — and, along this path, the possible obstacles as well as the means to neutralize them — and finally, the clearly defined goal to be achieved. This preliminary meditation must be quick and complete; quick to develop the spirit of decision, which is a precursor to complete willpower, so as not to have to subsequently undertake a new examination, which would only weaken the will. [47]

From this meditation must emerge, for the operator, the certainty that there is nothing impossible in achieving the proposed goal; and from the determination that follows must be born an unshakeable will to achieve this goal. Let us recall in this regard Nietzsche's great saying: "There is only one thing that can demonstrate whether someone has value or not: to stand firm!"

Thus, there are two parts to this training: theoretical reflection, which must be constant, without interruption, and create in you the certainty that you have willpower and energy; and practical application to each of life's acts, from the smallest to the most important, but a clear, decisive, and rapid application, followed immediately after the decision by an implementation of the will as you have created or developed it.

I will also indicate in Chapter V, and more explicitly, how one can practice developing auto-suggestion and how it can be used to educate the will; I have only wanted here to outline the simplest application to the subject at hand.

2. — Indirect Action.

We have just seen what kind of influence man has directly over his own will; it remains for us to see how he can energize it indirectly by developing self-control, which is the principal factor of willpower.

Self-control, the meaning of which is understood without further definition, is the characteristic of the informed man, and especially of the strong soul. It exists in each of us; to an infinitesimal degree in some, to a very high degree in others; no one is devoid of it, but no one possesses it absolutely. Just as in the weakest of character, in individuals who might be considered the most devoid of it, it reveals itself under the influence of certain circumstances; so too certain circumstances can take the most self-controlled man unawares, and rob him of all composure; in this regard, there is no one who does not have a flaw in his armor and his own Achilles' heel.

---

[47] From this point of view, the practice of fencing is an excellent will-builder because it accustoms one to judging at a glance the strength and weakness of the opponent's attack, to instantly deciding on the appropriate response, and to carrying it out with lightning speed.

Self-control, existing in all of us, more or less pronounced, has an infinite number of degrees; it is, therefore, capable of development.

This development is achieved in different ways, some purely mechanical, others based on auto-suggestion. I have just spoken of auto-suggestion and briefly explained its mechanism, and I will have to return to this later to go into greater detail; for the moment, I will simply leave to each person the choice of the suggestion that best suits their abilities. I will cite only one mechanical training process that has the advantage of being able to be used concurrently with the auto-suggestion process discussed above to act directly on the will. And I cite it because its use has always seemed to me to produce excellent results.

This mechanical process consists of the following:

Every morning, wait in your bed until you are fully awake, recalling to yourself the memory of everything you have to do during the day. When these memories are clear, when you are fully awake, sit up on your bed, with your back unsupported by pillows or any other means. This slightly awkward position will prevent you from falling asleep again. Then cover your head with the bed sheet to avoid any external distraction of your senses. Then, meditate. Review all your actions for the coming day, from the moment you jump out of bed until the moment you get back into it.

Establish your schedule hour by hour. Carefully review all the tasks awaiting you. For your letters to write, consider the direction in which you will write them. For your actions to take, develop a preliminary plan of what you will need to say in view of the goal you have set for yourself. Even establish a schedule for the additional time you will have left if the people you have to see must be absent. [48]

Do you intend to take some diversion, some relaxation? Set the program in advance, as well as the amount of time you wish to devote to it. In a word, plan all your actions for the day. In this

---

[48] Above all, we must be careful not to imitate those weak beings who, having a tiresome process to do, present themselves preferably at the time when they are most likely not to meet anyone, and this for the vain satisfaction of telling themselves that it is not their fault if their process was useless: this way of acting is childish and only serves to waste time and weaken the will.

mental work, let your thoughts be neither vague nor floating, but clear and precise, fully encompassing the object of the moment. Just as you have covered your head with your sheet to avoid any external distraction, so keep your attention firmly fixed on the project that must then occupy it, so that it is not distracted by any side issue; in a word, avoid all daydreaming, the mother of a dull drowsiness that quickly brings the lazy back to sleep. When your day's program is carefully and minutely established, only then do you get up and carry it out in all the details you have previously determined. Follow it point by point without letting yourself be sidetracked by all those trivial daily incidents that are so easy to distract from your attention. However, you must not live your day mechanically and hypnotized by the sole execution of the prepared program. Events may arise whose importance compels your attention; there are others that will impose themselves on you (such as the arrival of a visitor, the receipt of a letter forcing you to leave immediately, etc.). It is obvious that you must comply with all these unforeseen circumstances. It would be childish, moreover, to regard them as null and void; not to receive the visitor, to neglect the instructions in the letter; for the sole satisfaction of blindly following your program for the day. But as soon as these circumstances have ceased or as soon as you are freed from their consequences, return immediately to your program. Quickly review those items you are forced to postpone, and those you still have time to complete, and resume their course as strictly as possible.

In the evening, mentally summarize your day; consider which of your details you have completed, those you have inevitably neglected, and those you have shied away from through apathy, and thus gather the elements of your program for the next day.

It is certain that this regime will initially cause you boredom; it is no less certain that, at first, you will notice many shortcomings in the way you spend your day; but apply all your tenacity to carrying out the decisions made in the morning every day, and you will notice, after a short time, how easily you will succeed.

Why? Because once this practice was well established and firmly observed, your self-control increased daily, without your knowledge, and you quickly became master of your actions and thoughts. Your will has certainly helped you in this, since it found in this way of proceeding its constant application; and it has, by this very fact, benefited directly from this training. But it has also given you great self-possession, and this self-possession is the source from which your will shall draw both its own energy and the awareness of this energy.

Gradually, the reactions between self-control and will, shall become increasingly important, and the latter will eventually acquire a superior dynamism that will truly make it the most considerable force that man has at his disposal.

As we can see, these two methods of training, direct and indirect, can be followed simultaneously without interfering with each other; the results produced by each of them, taken in isolation, have always been among the best, and I have no doubt that their combination produces a first-rate boost to the will.

CHAPTER V

AUTO-SUGGESTION

A) *General Principles*.

In the previous chapter, I explained the mechanism of willpower. It remains for me to discuss one of the most curious effects of exercising this faculty: suggestion, and, especially in what concerns us in these pages, auto-suggestion, of which it is essential to have some understanding in order to achieve the phenomenon of personal out-of-body experience.

Already, in the study of the development of willpower by means of direct action, I have indicated the simplest process of auto-suggestion; there are others to examine from this point of view.

Later, we will have to consider the development of neuritis: here again, certain processes of auto-suggestion will come to our aid.

Finally, when I approach the practical part of this work, we will see the production of the phenomenon based on monoideism. Now, what is monoideism if not the result of a suggestion, whether objective or subjective? We can therefore see that from all points of view, it is necessary, before going any further, to understand the principles of auto-suggestion, which will be useful to us later.

But, before discussing auto-suggestion, it is necessary to proceed in order and to ask ourselves: What is suggestion?

Suggestion is the result of the influence exerted by the word, action, or simple will of one person on another person of a certain sensitivity. This is what is properly called *hetero-suggestion*, to distinguish it from *auto-suggestion*, which is the result of a concentration, voluntary or not, of personal thought on an object either existing objectively or imagined subjectively.

"We know that to will is to be able... We therefore want only what is possible, what is reasonable. There is thus no exhausting tension in the will, but only the exercise of a power of the soul, of a faculty, where ideas awaken inclinations and feelings; these come to set in motion motor activity with a view to the execution of the will. Now, the starting point, the guiding idea, is an idea suggested to the patient: it can come from outside, for example, from the doctor; in this case, there is *hetero-suggestion*. On the other hand, *auto-suggestion* is realized when the idea has presented itself to the patient; when it has been cultivated and made fertile, when it has impressed the affective centers, when it has given rise to a will, with realization in action of the volition thus elaborated."[49]

We can already see, from the beginning, suggestion being divided into two orders, depending on whether it comes from outside or from ourselves.

In the state of hypnosis [50], hetero-suggestion can act alone; in the normal state, hetero-suggestion cannot act alone unless it subsequently provokes auto-suggestion, for, as Bernheim put it, hetero-suggestion provides the seed, auto-suggestion fertilizes it. This explains why in the normal state, auto-suggestion is preponderant, can act alone, and can bring about a result alone, since, as Levy [51] so aptly put it: Every idea is an act in its nascent state.

In the most general sense, auto-suggestion is any influence exerted on cerebral functions and perceived by the brain, when this influence comes from an internal impulse. The primary cause of this impulse may, moreover, have its origin in an excitation coming from outside and which provokes an internal reaction.

In a narrower sense, auto-suggestion is a mental operation by which our thoughts are focused, concentrated, and maintained on a fixed and exclusive idea; the result of this operation is the transformation of the idea into action, or the tendency toward this transformation.

The name auto-suggestion is also given to the idea that is the object of the mental operation, and also sometimes, to the effect that results or should result from it. [52]

Thus, this word has four different meanings: 1. the initial impulse; 2. the mental operation; 3. the resulting idea; 4. and finally the actual realization of this idea. But there can be no confusion since, in short, these four objects of definition represent the four different phases of the total operation.

Who are the people capable of auto-suggestion? To this question, we can answer in principle: Any individual, whoever they may be. The state of auto-suggestibility [53] can be considered general. Indeed, the state of hetero-suggestibility is considered very common, even normal; Liébault and Bernheim claim to achieve successful suggestion in at least 90% of subjects, and Forel and O. Vogt in 97%. However, auto-suggestion is infinitely more common than hetero-suggestion, since the latter needs the assistance of the former to produce its full effect, while, on the contrary, the specific characteristic of auto-suggestion is spontaneity.

Auto-suggestion is, in short, so common in each of us that it can be said to be the driving force behind each of our actions.

It is usually only imagined in well-defined and very specific cases: a person who, having a cold without his brain knowing it, cannot perceive a scent, imagines himself to be the victim of a loss of smell, and can no longer distinguish any odor; someone who, having read a medical book, imagines that he feels all the symptoms of the illnesses he believes he knows; a man condemned to death who is led to believe that he is to perish in a scientific experiment as a result of the flow of his blood, and who, after a

---

[49] Dr LAVRAND, *Treatment of the will and psychotherapy*, 1br. in-12, Paris, 1909.

[50] Bernheim professes that: *there is no hypnosis, there is only suggestion.* I agree with him; therefore, I only considered hypnosis as a result of suggestion.

[51] *Rational Education of the Will.* 1 vol. in-12, Paris, 1910.

[52] Dr. GÉRAUD-BONNET, *Summary of voluntary autosuggestion*, 1 vol. in-12, Paris, 1910. An excellent work from which I will borrow more than once, and on which this chapter will be specifically based.

[53] I will be excused for speaking French. The term commonly used is *suggestibility*: this word can only be applied to things and not to people. The day official science was forced to deal with these matters, it did so reluctantly that it lost all sense of the correct expression; and its error from then still persists today.

harmless injection to each of his limbs, dies upon hearing water running from a faucet, which he believes to be his blood; the imaginary patient to whom his doctor assures that he should be cured if he simply has the patience to take every quarter of an hour, for two days, a pill of *mica panis* in a spoonful of hydrogen protoxide, etc. These are only special cases, but which, usually presented, seem to limit auto-suggestion to certain categories of more or less well-defined facts.

In practice, it is quite different, and we can say of it, I repeat, that it is the driving force behind each of our seemingly instinctive and thoughtless daily actions.

Let's take an example: we are walking along a road; a noise catches our attention: auto-suggestion; we recognize the horn of a tram, a vehicle we know to be dangerous for pedestrians; an auto-suggestion then makes us look where we are, and realize that we are actually traveling on its track; we move away from this track as a result of another auto-suggestion; then, instead of continuing to walk on the road where cars are moving, we reach the nearest sidewalk: another auto-suggestion... We see the permanent role of auto-suggestion in our actions at every moment. We can therefore say that auto-suggestion is, by far, the main motive for our actions, and that no one can escape it.

This is, it is true, only spontaneous auto-suggestion, whereas we will have to implement voluntary auto-suggestion, but who does not understand that the environment naturally accustomed to the former is even more naturally conducive to the development of the latter? When, in a previously uncultivated field, a farmer observes that wild grasses thrive wonderfully, he concludes that those he sows there will grow with the same ease.

This brings us to the subject of voluntary auto-suggestion, that is, not that which arises spontaneously and produces its normal result on its own, but that which we can arouse within ourselves for a specific purpose. Here is what Dr. Géraud-Bonnet says about it:

"Voluntary auto-suggestion aims to give oneself a useful suggestion.

"It can also be referred to as personal auto-suggestion to differentiate it from foreign suggestion made by another person.

"The practice of personal auto-suggestion can never be harmful or cause any inconvenience. It may not be successful if one does not put enough energy or persistence into it. But when it is regularly and properly applied, and focuses on a feasible idea, it can lead to inestimable results.

"It is based on the following principles, which govern the practice of suggestion in general:

"1. Any suggested idea that enters the brain produces a mental impression.

"2. Any idea, repeated sufficiently, eventually causes the corresponding action to be performed.

"To implement its principles, three essential elements are absolutely indispensable and must be used to their maximum power to obtain rapid and certain effects.

"These elements are: the will to succeed, confidence in success, and concentration of thought on the idea that constitutes the auto-suggestion. There is also no doubt that the operation must be carried out under conditions that facilitate the use of ordinary suggestion, that is, the brain must be placed, beforehand, in a more or less passive state, and even, when possible, in a certain degree of self-hypnotization that will make it more suggestible. [54] During the session, brain activity must not be stimulated by any idea unrelated to that relating to the desired auto-suggestion.

"These latter conditions entail, as accessories, other adjuvant conditions which it will be good and even necessary to satisfy in order to avoid distractions and maintain fixity of attention on the suggestive idea: isolation, silence, the absence of any noise coming from outside, occlusion of the eyes, inertia of the body, and the suppression of all voluntary movement."

We have already indicated above, in the explanation of the process of direct dynamization of the will, how one can go about it, in the ordinary course of life, to fully imbue oneself with an idea; here I will explain how to proceed, according to the preceding principles, when one wishes to devote a few moments specifically and solely to the genesis and development of an auto-suggestion.

Lock yourself in a secluded room, where outside noises do not penetrate, where you are sure not to be disturbed, and where you have closed the curtains; then, facing the darkest part of the room, lie down on an armchair, a chaise longue, or a sofa where your body will remain inert and without any discomfort.

To apply a principle of hypnotism here, place a watch or a monotonously ticking clock within earshot; if it is evening, have no other light than the flickering and trembling light of a small alcohol lamp, after having macerated in alcohol for twenty-four hours a large pinch of hemp flowers per liter [55]. Sight and hearing, the two senses that put us most in touch with external things, will thus be numbed and place your brain in a good state of suggestibility. First avoid thinking about anything; in a word, make your brain as inert and passive as the rest of your organism; when you feel yourself gradually overcome by a sort of torpor, then fix your thoughts on the idea you wanted to suggest, thoroughly understanding the meaning of the words. Rest while breathing slowly and fairly deeply (without, however, this act being uncomfortable or holding your attention); then repeat as many times as you can within the time you have decided to devote to this exercise, which you can repeat several times during the day, especially before going to bed. If you act in this way with assurance and conviction of success, it will only take a short time for the desired auto-suggestion to take effect.

Sometimes, in the beginning of this practice, excessive or poorly balanced restraint of the mind leads to insomnia; if it is brief and accidental, it is best not to worry about it; but if it becomes prolonged and becomes chronic, one could use the following formula indicated by Curtin. [56]

Potassium bromide .... 10 grams
Ammonia valerianate, Pierlot form 30   "
Orange blossom water 30   "
Simple syrup 60   "
Distilled water 150   "
To be taken by the spoonful, morning and evening, twenty minutes before the meal.

---

[54] The simplest process used is detailed below.
[55] The light obtained by this process is both flickering and fascinating, and emits very gentle narcotic emanations, capable of drowsing the brain.
[56] *Youth and Beauty*, 1 in-16, Paris.

However, it should be noted that bromide and valerianate are powerful anti-nervous systems; this formula can therefore only be used if the development of neuritis, which will be discussed later, has not yet begun, as this treatment would hinder it.

Otherwise, it would be necessary to consult a doctor who, knowing the subject's temperament, would prescribe a medication that has the least possible effect on the nervous system, since all soporifics, bromides, chloral, countless opium derivatives, and other sulfonamides produce a more or less intense effect on neuritis.

In the event that no product is found that can act without harming the development of neuritis, the operator who truly wishes to experiment would have the choice of either self-suggestion in this direction or enduring a few sleepless nights, which would soon be overcome by fatigue.

B. *Application to the will*

We will see later, when we consider the development of neuritis, that will is an emanation of nervous force and that the increase in one is in direct proportion to the increase in the other, since will is a function of the brain and it is the brain mass above all that emits nervous force.

If, therefore, one *wants* to acquire or increase willpower, that is, if one has self-suggested in this sense, one will quickly realize that if willpower depends on the increase in nervous forces, these — for everything is connected, everything is linked in man as in nature — in turn depend on general bodily forces. The ancients said: *Mens sana in corpore sano*, which we will translate as: A strong will is created by a vigorous organism.

It is therefore necessary, first of all, to develop muscular forces and organic energies: these, in turn, will produce neuritis from which emanates the will. This is achieved, as is universally known, by adopting a lifestyle based on hygiene and exercise. Building muscles first, that is all! Therefore, a life in the open air, or at least daily walks, a moderate but substantial diet, only seven or eight hours in bed, but all of it spent sleeping and not daydreaming so dear to the lazy, a well-organized daily routine, to combine intellectual and physical exercise, so as to seek in one relief from the fatigue produced by the other: such should be the ideal way of life for anyone who wants to develop a will.

Compare, in this regard, two children, two brothers born in the countryside and of equal strength. One remained in the fields, cultivating the estate; the other wanted to seek his fortune in the city and entered a trading post or an office where he gradually weakened from lack of exercise, from the confinement of life, from all sorts of causes imaginable. Let some time pass, and then say which of the two has the stronger willpower? You hesitate to answer because, even if you admit that the bodily strength of one has declined, his willpower may nevertheless have remained intact; and you hesitate to pronounce on a general and abstract case. But place these two brothers in a concrete situation, this one for example: — In time of war, two corps of troops march against each other, each as well trained, as maneuverable, as well commanded as the other; but the former is composed mainly of office or commercial employees; the latter's contingent is formed mainly of agricultural workers, accustomed to marching and resistant to fatigue. Let us not forget that all military writers agree on the principle that the outcome of a battle depends on whichever of the two adversaries *wants* it with the most tenacity. Each of the two troop units is, in principle, animated by a will equal to that of the other. But the former arrives at the scene of the engagement tired by a long march, partially demoralized by lack of rest, and brings to the fight only a superficial will, a purely nervous will, that is to say, artificial, since it does not rely on muscular strength, and it can only maintain it with artificial stimulants, such as alcohol, which will turn out to be the opposite of what it expects once the moment of overexcitement has passed. [57] Compare this body of troops to its adversary, dominated by rugged country folk, they have cheerfully endured the fatigue of the march and the weight of the pack; they arrive in combat unfazed, in possession of all their composure, well in the hands of their leaders... The question no longer even arises as to who will be the victor, that is to say, in the end of the analysis, who will have, at the end of the day, displayed the most will.

It is the same at any level of the social hierarchy. Compare, for example, in the higher ranks, an administrative office manager and an army captain, and say whether, at first glance and without knowing either better than the other, you would not instinctively attribute a stronger dose of willpower to the soldier accustomed to the elements, muscled by physical exercise, than to the office manager accustomed to a secluded life, and valetudinarian by the very nature of his occupations? [58]

So muscle is the essential basis of willpower; but there are several kinds of willpower: one that emerges only after long meditation and procrastinates, and one that asserts itself immediately and goes straight to the point. Which is preferable?

Certainly, a decision made without reflection is generally unfortunate; however, reflection must be swift, because a half-satisfying decision, but one toward which one marches against a storm, is always preferable to another excellent decision, but in the accomplishment of which one hesitates.

To return to the military example cited above — for war has always been the best school of willpower — let us suppose that two enemy troop corps encounter each other unexpectedly. Both leaders make their combat dispositions with equal speed, but both have different tactical ideas, aided by unequal decisiveness. The leader of party A, less maneuverable than his adversary, sees only one solution: withdraw his troops and charge at the enemy center so as to cut the enemy in two: this is a somewhat simplistic conception; the leader of party B, on the contrary, conceives the plan of taking advantage of a terrain accident to outflank his adversary, to force him to retreat; it is certain that this decision is far superior to the first, but on one condition: that it be executed quickly, otherwise the troops of party A will break through the center of party B, momentarily weakened by a movement on the wings, before being themselves forced to withdraw by a turning movement that did not have time to succeed. Of the two decisions, it is the more inferior one that prevails due to its speed of execution.

---

[57] See in this regard the charge of Ponsomby's cavalry at Waterloo, where men and horses had been saturated with alcohol, and where riders sabered their own mounts.

[58] There are obviously exceptions to this; but these exceptions are based on intelligence, and one can admit in principle that, of two men taken at random, the weaker must possess infinitely more intelligence than the stronger to be endowed with a superior will.

As we can see, in many circumstances, promptness of decision is preferable to excellence of the decision itself.

Now, to acquire this spirit of decision, what in many cases is called a *quick glance*, what is the best method to employ? The practice of sports. I mentioned above fencing, which requires great speed of decision and lightning-fast execution; but there is no sporting game — tennis, football, swimming, hunting, etc. — that is not capable of developing to a high degree these qualities by means of which the exercise of the will gives it a value it did not previously possess.

But speed of conception and decision is not enough to create an absolutely superior will; to be perfect, it must possess three qualities that are rarely found together in the same individual: strength, persistence, and continuity.

The need for strength is understandable, since a will without strength ceases to be a will, and, moreover, the present pages are devoted to the development of this quality.

Persistence and continuity also contribute to forming a will sure of itself; indeed, it is difficult to imagine a will truly worthy of the name when it is intermittent, that is, when it ceases at times to tend toward the proposed goal, or when it proves versatile and diverse, changing its goal at every moment.

These last two qualities are also acquired by auto-suggestion, not, like strength, by directing the suggested monoideism toward the will itself, but toward the object it sets out to achieve.

For example, we have seen that will develops if one autosuggests: "I have willpower! I am energetic!" On the contrary, to acquire or develop persistence and continuity, the monoideism created will not be: "I want *to want* constantly!" but it will consist in not losing sight of the goal to be achieved.

A general and very simple means — because its use is, in a sense, constant — of acquiring these qualities consists in completely changing one's habits. This process also has the advantage of showing the degree of development the will has reached. [59]

Indeed, everyone has their own small practices to which they are all the more attached because, most of the time, they cannot understand the *reason* for this or that habit; it is therefore a matter of changing one's habits, not as a whole, which would disrupt one's existence, but by taking them one by one, so as to gradually change one's way of life.

For example, you are accustomed to reading your newspaper every morning before breakfast; make the decision, which you will maintain, to read it from now on only before going to bed. — As soon as a letter arrives, you unseal it immediately, overcome your curiosity and each day leave your mail *in front of you* for an hour before touching it. — When you go out, you experience a certain pleasure in strolling, lingering in storefronts; from now on go straight to your business without stopping.

This reversal of your habits will exercise your willpower, and the tenacity you bring to maintaining these small changes in your lifestyle will produce persistence and continuity.

Here, moreover, is the advice given by Dr. Géraud-Bonnet in his aforementioned work for directing auto-suggestion toward increasing willpower:

Choose a physical or muscular exercise that you know, in advance, you can accomplish easily, and complete it to the end, in one go, without repeating it several times if possible.

Ensure that your willpower is active throughout the entire exercise; do not abandon yourself to any foreign ideas, distractions, or daydreams; take care that your attention is firmly focused on what you are doing; that your mental effort is real and persistent from beginning to end.

If, while performing the exercise, you recognize that your will has ceased to act, that a different thought, no longer related to the desired activity, arises and disturbs you, hasten to resume the interrupted thread of your initial idea, or stop and start again.

If the same thing happens again, it is because the chosen exercise is too difficult or too long. Simplify it, or choose another easier or shorter one.

For example, you have decided that you are going to clap your hands together for two consecutive minutes. At a certain

_____

[59] In America, I've been told, there exists an instrument for mechanically measuring the intensity of willpower. I mention its existence here, but I can't say anything more about it, because I've never held it in my hands, and I don't know on what principles it's based; I don't even know if it's not purely and simply a bluff, like so many others that arise on the other side of the Atlantic.

point, you realize that your thoughts are wandering to some unrelated idea; stop, it is too long.

Start again, setting a duration of only one minute. To be successful, your attention must be unwavering throughout this minute, firmly focused on the clapping of your hands, and the movement must be constantly conscious and not become automatic.

Here are some examples of easy exercises to perform.

With your upper limbs extended horizontally, bend your right forearm over your upper arm and extend it again, then repeat the same movement with your left limb. Start again on the right and continue until the end point set from the beginning. To ensure the rhythm of the movements is regular and your attention more sustained, you can count each partial movement: 1-2-3-4.

You can also perform the two flexion movements simultaneously with both forearms, then the two extension movements.

You can make it more complicated by adding flexion and extension movements of the forearms while the arms are moved vertically downward, then upward, or vice versa.

The lower limbs can also be used for flexion and extension movements, or for forward or backward movements.

A good exercise consists of walking every day, at the same time, a certain distance along a road, and returning to the starting point. [60] During this walk, which should take place regardless of the weather, the season, and any opposing motives, one should not allow oneself to be diverted by any fortuitous incident, nor by acquaintances one might encounter on the way. Only under these conditions shall the will be subjected to a serious test of real value.

One can also force oneself to count, once or several times in a row and at a fixed time, the beads of a necklace or the beads of a rosary.

This exercise does not require significant muscular effort, but rather sustained attention; it requires little more than willpower, without any physical fatigue. As such, it is particularly

---

[60] A man who would engage in this exercise with the sole aim of touching the same pebble placed there on purpose each time would, in the long run, turn this pebble into a marvelous talisman of will.

suitable for weakened or ill people whose physical debility prevents them from exercising their muscles.

A more difficult exercise will be to get up, for a certain predetermined time, for a specific number of days, at an earlier hour than usual. If you are afraid of not being able to wake up at the desired time, you should bring an alarm clock or ask someone to warn you.

If you are a smoker, or if you are in the habit of going to a club or a café, decide that you will no longer smoke or that you will stay at home, without going out, for eight days.

These last exercises are difficult. Any exercise that goes against an acquired or inveterate habit should be considered as such. They should be reserved for perfecting the education of the will when it has already acquired a certain development and has been strengthened by other easy exercises. Their success testifies that the will possesses, at that moment, a vigorous firmness. If you fail in an exercise, or if you are truly tired before its completion, you must modify it and take another. Failure or a painful effort will indicate that you have overestimated your strength; that your training is not advanced enough.

Focus long and hard on simple and easy procedures; vary them, change them often, but get used to doing them well and succeeding. Only add complications or new difficulties slowly and cautiously.

And above all, remember that to achieve your goal, you need time and perseverance...

Willpower increases through training, that is, through the repetition of simple exercises, continued for a long time, and of increasing difficulty; it is maintained by the continuation of these same exercises or similar exercises.

This training must be practiced intermittently, separated by intervals of inaction, since we have seen that after any work, a sufficient period of rest is necessary for the nervous system to recover the energy expended and perfect the results acquired during the action.

It will be advisable to carry it out at fixed, well-chosen and well-defined times, always the same, because there is a law of the nervous system that leads it to reproduce, at a similar time, the act to which it was previously subjected in a similar circumstance.

The execution of the new act is thus made easier; so that, with the same expenditure of energy as before, the nervous system can be called upon for a more energetic act, involving greater length, greater fatigue, or greater difficulty.

This latter result corresponds to an increase in general strength. Training strengthens the entire organism, develops the energy of the will, and allows us to constantly increase this energy.

Through this will, constantly supported and strengthened, we can influence all our functions and achieve self-control, both intellectually and psychologically, as well as physically...

The training of the will can be undertaken at any stage of human life. However, whenever possible, it is better to begin at a young age in order to develop good habits that will later eliminate the need for painful efforts, physical labor, and intellectual application.

If this training is begun late, we may encounter bad habits, already ingrained, which increase the difficulty and delay success. Nevertheless, despite these obstacles, it is possible, even in old age, to achieve appreciable and beneficial results.

All the results obtained through exercises aimed at training the will, and all the benefits acquired through this training, can be maintained and increased by using voluntary auto-suggestion.

Indeed, if willpower is essential for achieving good auto-suggestion, conversely, auto-suggestion can be used to train and increase willpower. It will allow one to concentrate all available nervous force, all the power and activity of the brain, on this faculty.

The auto-suggestive process consists of mentally repeating to oneself that one has a strong will, an energetic will. This is a lesson that the brain must learn; by dint of repetition, one will end up deeply imprinting it; the idea will be accepted, will persist, will develop increasingly, and, on occasion, will translate into action.

Moreover, auto-suggestion intervenes unconsciously in all physical, muscular, and intellectual exercises used for the development of the will and applied especially to the idea of willpower.

It can be consciously added to willpower whenever one wishes to use it to improve another particular cerebral faculty, to perform an act considered difficult, to correct a defect, or to eliminate a vicious habit.

For example, if one is naturally hot-tempered, violent, and irascible, one should, during voluntary physical exercise, suggest to oneself that one is calm and patient. If one realizes that one has a weak character and is easily influenced, one should suggest to oneself that one has a firm character and is not subject to anyone's influence.

If, for a few days, one wishes to get up early in the morning, earlier than usual, one should, during this same physical exercise, focus one's attention on the idea of getting up without fatigue and without boredom, at the desired time.

Similarly, if one is a smoker, an alcoholic, or in any way vicious, one should, while working physically, perform the curative auto-suggestion appropriate to that particular case.

One should engage in the practice of auto-suggestion combined with voluntary exercise in the most favorable external and incidental conditions, that is, in silence, recollection, isolation, sheltered from unexpected distractions, and, as much as possible, always at the same time.

The calm and tranquility of the night, the moments of rest that precede sleep, are eminently propitious for this operation. Every night, before falling asleep, one can take a retrospective look back at the events that occurred during the day, at the deeds that have been accomplished, and use auto-suggestion combined with voluntary physical exercise to increase willpower, combat actions, ideas, and feelings recognized as bad, to strengthen all that is good and useful, and maintain confidence in success and faith in a prosperous future.

It is not necessary to devote a lot of time to this; the important thing is to think about it; a few minutes may be enough.

Finally, to conclude this chapter, I will indicate two exercises recommended by d'Alba [61] and all the better, in my opinion, because they can be applied to all possible types of auto-suggestion.

---

[61] *Elementary Treatise on Scientific Magic*, 1br. in-8, Paris, s.d.

— Retire to a very quiet room, and, having made it dark, lie down on a bed and put yourself in a state of muscular relaxation; that is, the suspension of muscle tension, which alone can bring about perfect rest for the body.

Then concentrate your thoughts as forcefully and for as long as possible on any undertaking whose success you ardently desire: try to clearly present the object of your desires, and, during the exercise, which can last half an hour, your thoughts should be focused exclusively on it. Repeat to yourself mentally or aloud affirmative words of success.

The difficulty of this exercise lies in the absolute and sustained concentration, as well as in the suggestion one must give oneself. If one cannot convince oneself deeply enough of success, the result will not manifest, since the astral matter will not have been activated. This exercise must be repeated several times, while always pursuing the same achievement until it is successful. This very powerful process can be applied to happiness, love, and health; in any case, it will provide astonishing results. Anyone who wishes to undertake it successfully should not pursue the achievement of things that are too difficult.

— The following exercise will facilitate the previous one: try to form a mental image of objects, monuments, people, faces, etc., that you have seen depicted or that you know. The more this exercise is repeated, the clearer the image will become. This representation is very strong during dreams, when scenes that we believe to be real unfold before our mental eyes.

All the practical precepts of preparation and auto-suggestion contained in this chapter have yielded excellent results to students who have applied them consistently and tenaciously. Their reasoned and correctly pursued use is a prime will-forming factor, and anyone who applies themselves to them patiently, even if they are endowed with the weakest and most indecisive character, must succeed in creating a will that will no longer be desire, wishful thinking, nor, on the contrary, stubbornness, obstinacy, or obstinacy; but a will truly worthy of the name and containing within itself the future will-power that will in turn be developed and affirmed by appropriate, increasingly difficult physical and mental exercises, and above all the diligent application of auto-suggestion.

CHAPTER VI

OCCULT CONSTITUTION OF THE HUMAN BEING

Each school of occultism teaches a particular theory regarding the general constitution of man, in nine, seven, five, or three elements to which each of them attributes special names that differ for each school, such that the beginner who begins this study finds himself singularly troubled, not to say confused, by this multiplicity of terms. But he who would see such differences of doctrine between each school, and consequently, believe that in each everything is false, or almost, would be seriously mistaken. Let us examine the whole question, and we will see that all these differences are limited, I will not even say to quarrels over words, but to a lesser or greater degree of analysis of principles, combined with this reason for particular obscurity that, among occultists, some, those who adhere to the ancient teachings of India, use Sanskrit terms; the others, following the data of Kabbalah, use Hebrew names; and finally, the last, those who can be called the modernists of the question, seek to make the use of French words prevail — in France, at least — so as to be better understood by all.

Add, as a further cause of confusion, that contemporary scholars who have studied one of these principles in its material manifestations, wishing to avoid being classified in a particular school of occultism whose terminology they might have used, have given the principles they studied names either taken from antiquity by analogy (Reichenbach's *od*), or composed in harmony with current scientific data so as not to frighten the academies (Barthez's *vital principle*, Pététin's *animal electricity*, Richnowski's *universal fluid*, Barety's *radiant neurotic force*, the *nervous fluid* of some, the *dynamic force* of others, etc., etc.).

It is understandable that, in such conditions, the student no longer finds himself faced with a complicated nomenclature, but with a veritable *imbroglio*, in which it is very difficult for him to find his way without the advice and guidance of a competent guide.

But the subject I have undertaken to address presents sufficient explanatory difficulties, by its very audacity, that I wish to avoid complicating it further with more or less justified considerations on the fundamental analysis of the constituent elements of the human being. First of all, I want to be clear, I believe I have been so far, and it is not by bringing to light the processes of a phenomenon which is already inexplicable, incomprehensible and paradoxical for many, that it is appropriate to add to the mystery due to the obscurities of language.

I used above, in analyzing H. Durville's experiments, the terminology of the theosophical school because H. Durville himself had employed them as responding better than any other to his successive dissociations from the living ghost; but in these pages, where I study only personal out-of-body experience, I have no use for this nomenclature: I will therefore refer simply to the theory of the spiritists because it is the least complicated, the simplest, and, consequently, the most immediately understandable of all.

What then are the constituent elements of the living human being?

A single principle, reply the materialists, mechanists, monists, etc.: *matter*, that is, the *physical body*. But then, without addressing the element of *will*, about which there would be much to say, they deny phenomena that are now absolutely proven: out-of-body experience, clairaudience, clairvoyance, etc. and even foreboding.

— Two principles, respond the Western religions forgetful of their origins: [62] the *soul* and the *body*. But then, one seeks, in vain, the explanation of a host of phenomena; one wonders what link unites the immaterial element of being to its material element, how the thought that meditates becomes the gesture that executes. "We arrive, by applying this theory, at saying that a man is consumptive because he has a consumptive soul, which is a bit far-fetched" (Papus). Some thinkers have therefore long wondered whether, between the soul and the body, there was not an intermediary, a mediator, a middle ground, participating in the nature of both.

Occultism has, from the outset, answered this question in the affirmative: "Man," says Eliphas Levi, "is an intelligent and corporeal being, made in the image of God and the world, ONE in essence, TRIPLE in substance, immortal and mortal; within him is a spiritual soul, a material body, and a plastic mediator."

The existence of this *plastic mediator* was once taught in the sacred crypts of India and Egypt; it was part of the Great Mysteries and constituted one of the principal revelations communicated to initiates. It is therefore known by the most varied names, under the most disparate appellations. In our time, it is commonly called the *astral body* [63], *périsprit* [64], *aérosôme* [65], etc.

It should not be believed that these three constituent principles of man form three clearly separate parts, as is wrongly thought with regard to the body and the soul, because their natures seem at first glance to be totally different and opposed. On the contrary, they interpenetrate in the most intimate way. The composition of the human being can be aptly compared to the following example:

Into a metal box, throw pebbles until it is full, and you will have a box full of pebbles. If, on top of these pebbles, you throw powdered cement, it will penetrate all the spaces left between them by the stones; your box will always be the same, and yet it will

---

[62] Early Christianity recognized three principles: the *body*, the *soul* (plastic intermediary), and the *spirit*; today, religious exotericism confuses the soul and the spirit, and the plastic intermediary is found only in esoteric teaching. See *Sorcery of the Countryside* by the same author (1 large octavo volume, Paris, 1910), where this question is thoroughly addressed.

[63] This term, at first glance bizarre, used by occultists, comes from the fact that the universe is divided into three principal interpenetrating planes, each of which, in principle, lives one of the three constituent elements of man:

Divine plane	Spirit
Astral plane	Astral body
Physical plane	Material body

[64] Lit. *Envelope of the spirit*, a term used by spiritualists.

[65] Fluidic body, as opposed to the *sarcosôme* or carnal body.

then contain two different bodies. On top of these two bodies, you throw water; this water penetrates the interstices of the cement and, with its help, binds all the pebbles together. So, in this box, there are three disparate elements, completely united. Can you say that this forms three distinct blocks? That's right. You now have only one block, which is called concrete.

So it is with the human being. The creator emanated his breath, and the spirit, [66] moving away from its primordial source, assumed a body borrowed from the atmosphere; that is, formed of astral fluids; [67] when it enters our physical plane, this fluidic body envelops itself in flesh. [68] Can we say that there are three different entities here? There is only one: man.

So, man is triune; through his spirit, he lives on the divine plane and enters into communion with the soul of the universe, of which he becomes aware in certain states (prayer, ecstasy, etc.); through his astral body, he lives on the intermediate plane, and is aware of it through certain phenomena (clairvoyance, presentiment, etc.); finally, through his physical body, he lives on the material plane, and when it disintegrates, everything returns to its natural plane: the physical body to matter, and the astral body to the higher plane, carrying with it the spirit, which rises and will one day return, after countless incarnations and avatars, to the source from which it emanates: — To merge there, according to the great Eastern beliefs? — To retain its individuality there, according to the religions of the West? — This is the secret of the Mystery, and we do not need to examine it here. It suffices for us, for the moment, to know that the astral body of the living being exists only accidentally in matter and lives primarily on the astral plane from which it emanates and to which it has a constant tendency to return as soon as the opportunity arises, that is, when the material body no longer has a temporary need for it (sleep, somnambulism, catalepsy, etc.). This is a fact worth remembering, because we will find its application later when studying how to disengage the astral body from the physical organism.

The three constituent elements of the living being can be considered as having their seat (I speak theoretically, because practically, I repeat, they interpenetrate each other), namely: the physical part in the belly; the astral part in the chest; and the spiritual part in the head.

Indeed, the stomach produces material life (which is the basis of the living being) through digestion, the principal result of which is the production of blood. [69] This blood, the vehicle of physical life, carries it to all the systems and organs, where it is modified, becoming here *cerebral physical life, cardiac physical life,* elsewhere *nervous, muscular physical life,* etc.

Physical life is sufficient for some of these organs; but there are others that refine it, in a way, like the nervous system, to create life of a higher essence, that is, astral life. [70] This astral life is maintained in the chest by the action of the lungs, which draw from space a higher life intended both to maintain the already formed astral life, [71] and to recreate new life by purifying the blood. But the work of life itself tends to sublimate the higher energy thus produced; if the motor nerves have to perform only almost purely mechanical work, this is no longer the case for the sensory nerves, and if we go back to the brain substance, we find there a very refined energy appropriate for mental work: [72] this is why we consider the brain to be the physical seat of the mind. [73]

---

[66] In our time, there is great confusion between the spirit and the soul. According to theologians, the soul is the incarnate spirit, just as the spirit is the soul freed from the physical body. As a result, for them, the ghost is a soul since it has a visible body (which, in reality, is either the double or the astral body), while the spiritualists, taking the higher part for the whole, call this same ghost a spirit. In the long run, when the terms are well defined and the definitions better known, this regrettable confusion will dissipate.

[67] In reality, the mechanism of the operation seems to be more complicated than I am saying, for the astral plane appears to be subdivided into a certain number of sub-planes on each of which the spirit, in its involution, assumes an envelope that is all the denser the closer it is to the physical plane. But in these pages, I am only concerned with the astral body, and to be clearer and better understood, I prefer simplicity of exposition to meticulous precision that would risk confusing the issue.

[68] Here again, the reality is much more complicated: before taking on a human organism, the involvating spirit must practice physical life by going through its most rudimentary manifestations.

[69] I warn the reader that I do not claim to write a treatise on physiology here; just as above I summarized in one sentence the phenomena of the involution of the spirit, its contact with physical life, etc., so here I do not go into the details of physiological phenomena; I am content to explain these phenomena in their general process, as well as the way in which they relate to one another, as in a simplified diagram to better grasp the overall picture.

Thus, the basis of the astral body in the physical body is the nervous system.

"We have seen," says Papus, [74] "that the matter produced by the stomach served solely as a support for that force that the chest draws from the external atmosphere and which constitutes life. [75]

"Likewise, this astral body, the ultimate product of the chest, serves as a support for something that comes directly from the outside, but on a plane different from the material plane; this something is what makes us have presentiments, what makes love or hate dilate or contract our heart [76], in a word, what makes us passionate.

"This new element, located not in the ganglion but in the plexuses (groups of ganglia) near the heart, is the fourth principle, the animal soul, *Kama Rupa*; it is there that instinct resides. This principle is more developed in animals than in humans, more in the uneducated than in the educated. Comparative anatomy further shows us the reality of this through the number of abdominal and thoracic ganglia that form the true brains of lower animals, especially insects.

"The astral body is therefore the intermediary between two different worlds; it is indeed the highest element of the physical body, the soul of the physical body, but at the same time it is the lowest element of life itself; [77] it is the body of life, the matter of the vital body. This third principle is common to both worlds, that of matter and that of life.

---

[70] In reality, the astral body possesses its own life; but it would have no effect on the physical body if nervous life were suspended, just as the physical body, deprived of neurogenicity, could not react on the astral body. The nervous system can therefore be considered the material basis of the astral body.

[71] See further, chap. VIII, § A.

[72] Physiologically, the work of thought results in the destruction of brain cells.

[73] The mind also has another secondary seat, the heart: we need not concern ourselves with it here.

[74] *Methodical treatise on occult science*, 1 vol. in-8, Paris, 1891.

[75] The poverty of our language and my desire to be clear above all can lead to confusion here. There are several kinds of life, each with its own particular technical name in Hindu and Hebrew philosophies. What I called life above is purely material and physical life, understood in a general sense, vitality; the life Papus speaks of here is animal life, which does not exist in lower beings, plants, minerals, etc. (*Author's note*).

"The animal soul constitutes the central element of being, the origin of its egoism and its passions...

"The study of the evolution of the nervous system throughout the animal species reveals a very curious fact. The nervous system is first represented by a simple filament in the lower ages (e.g., the tapeworm). At this point, three of the principles are developed, the others are in embryo. The developed principles are the PHYSICAL BODY (*Rupa*), VITALITY (*Jiva*), and the rudiments of the *astral body* (*Linga Sharira*). These beings therefore belong almost exclusively to the physical world. If we move up in the animal series, we see this nerve filament presenting a few ganglia along its course. The astral body is then more developed. These ganglia can be theoretically considered to be produced by the folding of the nerve filament on itself. In insects, the ganglia together form two crowns, a thoracic crown and an abdominal crown. There is therefore a union of ganglia, that is, plexuses, and consequently the development of the fourth principle, the origin of instinct, the ANIMAL SOUL (*Kama Rupa*).

"These beings therefore belong almost exclusively to the astral world.

"However, we see a small ganglionic mass pointing at the upper part of the animal: in the head. This indicates that the fifth principle is there in embryo.

"What then is the fifth principle?

"It is the one that develops at the same time as the brain, the characteristic principle of the human being, the one that allows one to learn the sciences when it is developed, the principle of intellectuality in all its orders; the HUMAN SOUL (*Manas*).

---

[76] The reality of this moral influence on the physical was proven by Claude Bernard, *Experimental Science* (Papus).

[77] This theoretical duality comes from the division of man into nine principles reduced to seven by the union of two of them, as the following table shows:

	9	Soul of the spiritual body	. . .	7	Atma.	
Spirit . .	8	Life of the spiritual body	. . .	6	Buddhi.	
	7	Matter of the spiritual body	. .	5 Manas.	upper
	6	Soul of the astral body	. . . .		lower
Aérosome .	5	Life of the astral body	. . .	4	Kama rupa.	
	4	Matter of the astral body	. .	3 Linga sharira.	
	3	Soul of the physical body	. . .		
Sarcosôme	2	Matter of the physical body	. .	2 Jiva.	
	1	Life of the physical body	. .	1 Rupa.	

"The nervous fluid constituting the astral body and enclosed in the sympathetic ganglia has condensed on itself in the plexuses to receive the principle of instinct; it spiritualizes itself in the brain to receive the principle of intelligence."

Despite my desire not to indulge in scientific considerations and not to use technical terms, in order to remain clear and understandable, I must nevertheless, precisely to be well understood, summarize the constitution of man in a table where each element will be briefly described and differentiated from the others by its particular name.

<table>
<tr><td rowspan="3">Sarcosôme (physical body)</td><td>1. RUPA:

Matter of the physical body. — Material part of the body, renewing itself by the various functions performed by the stomach, carried by the liquor of the blood.</td></tr>
<tr><td>2. JIVA:

Life of the physical body. — Mediating part of the physical body. Combination of the material body with the immediately upper principle. Life of organic cells. This element may be external but never leaves the body, or it returns as soon as the upper elements are sent away (1).</td></tr>
<tr><td>3. LINGA SHARIRA:

Soul of the physical body. — Animating part of the body. Spiritualization of the blood under the influence of vegetative life. Element located in the ganglia of the great sympathetic and which can exit the physical body. It is materially renewed by the functions of the chest.

This higher element of the body combines with the next one which is the lowest of the astral body.</td></tr>
</table>

---

(1) Experiences of H. Durville. See his work: *The Ghost of the Living.*

Aerosome (astral body)

Material of the astral body. — Material part of the astral body located in the ganglia of the great sympathetic nerve. — Support of the following principles.

4. KAMA RUPA:

Life of the astral body. — Mediating part of the astral body. Combination of the astral body with the next higher principle. Life of the astral body. Element located in the plexuses of the great sympathetic nerve. Origin of instinct and passions.

5. LOWER MANAS

Soul of the astral body. — Animating part of the astral body. Spiritualization of the conscious nervous fluid. Element located in the cerebral convolutions. Seat of intelligence and memory. Renewed materially by the functions of the head.

This higher element of the astral body combines with the next, lower element of the spiritual body.

Spirit (spiritual body)

HIGHER MANAS:

Material of the spiritual body. — Lower part of the spiritual body. Element located in the brain. Seat of intellect. Intermediary between the astral body and the spirit. Support of higher principles.

6. BUDDHI:

Life of the spiritual body. — Mediating part of the mind. Combination of the human soul with the higher soul (atma). Partial influence of Atma on Manas. Element located in a few higher nerve cells. In embryo only in current races. Seat of inspiration, conscious double vision (prophecy), and morality.

7. ATMA:

Soul of the spiritual body. — Animating part of the
spiritual body. Spiritualization of human
faculties under the influence of the
divine Word. Non-localized element in
man. Principle of immortality (1).

Until now, it was believed that the life of the physical body
(*Jiva*) never exteriorized; Durville's recent experiments have
shown that this element can momentarily leave the *sarcosôme*, but
without ever moving away from it. From this observation, it
follows that the exteriorized phantom can have several
compositions. If seen near the physical body, it can contain the
Jiva element; in this case, it is slightly blue and orange; if seen far
from the physical body, its base is the *Linga Sharira*, [78] an astral
immaterial of a bluish white.

In the following pages, we will not have to concern ourselves
with the split between the *Jiva*, which always remains near the
sarcosôme, and the other higher principles, which can move away
from it, since this split occurs automatically without any need to
take any special precautions in this regard.

----

(1) These nine constituent elements of the human being represent the Eastern
theory, which was used when the first editions of this work appeared, and which,
moreover, still is.

But since then, Western experimentation has studied the soul — the plastic
intermediary between the organism and the spirit — and constitutes man as
follows:

1. Physical body or *sarcosôme*.
2. Etheric double or *odic* body or vital Soul (*material life*).
3. Astral body, desire body or sensitive soul (*sensibility*).
4. Mental body or intelligent soul (*Intelligence*).
5. Causal body or causal soul (*memory, volition*).
6. Moral soul (*Distinction between good and evil*).
7. Intuitive Soul (*Relationships with the spirit*).
8. Conscious soul (*seat of the Self*).
9. Mind (*Pure ideation*).

This experimental division, where each element presents itself in a particular
and distinct form, differs a little from that given by the oriental theory, but there
is no doubt, in my opinion, that further, more in-depth studies will bring about a
perfect concordance between the two systems.

But that's not all: the ghost itself is not always identical, and its composition can vary due to different circumstances.

Jiva (Vitality) and the lower part of the *Linga Sharira* (the soul of the physical body) are two elements that die only after *Rupa* (the matter of the physical body) — a short time (a few days), after him, it is true, but ultimately survive him. Moreover, during life itself, the human body, like any physical object, possesses its image, its reflection on the astral plane.

It follows from this, as we have just seen, that *Jiva* (Vitality) may or may not be part of the ghost; this ghost itself may be either the ghost itself (elements of the astral body and the spirit) or simply the reflection, the image of the material body emerging for a moment from the astral plane to manifest on the physical plane; this manifestation very generally occurs within a few days following death. But it can also occur, in certain cases that are still poorly understood and insufficiently defined, while the subject is still alive. This is what is called the *astral form*, which is like a reflection of the physical body and which, after death, remains for a certain time near the corpse. When this apparition occurs under these conditions, it presents exactly the appearance of the dead person but is, in a way, only a pseudo-ghost.

According to the teachings of the Mysteries of antiquity that had spread among the people, the ancients were much better informed than we are about this particularity; the Egyptians called the physical body *Khat*, the reflection of the physical body *Ka*, the astral body *Khu*, and the luminous intelligence *Ba-baï*; the Persians called the reflection of the physical body *Djan*, and the astral body *Ferouer*; the Kabbalah called the reflection *Nephesch*, and the astral body *Ruach*; the Latins gave the material body a *shadow* (reflection) and an *image* (astral body), of which *Manas* was the life soul and *spiritus* the higher intelligence.

It is therefore necessary to distinguish between these two kinds of apparitions: astral images and true ghosts.

The former behaves exactly like a reflection in a mirror; it is visible, photographable, and animated.

---

[78] I have said it elsewhere and I repeat it here: immaterial is not zero.

The latter will generally be much more visible, more easily photographed, will speak, and, if sufficiently condensed, will be palpable.

But all this is primarily intended for receptive subjects so that they can distinguish the type of apparition they are dealing with; as for the experimenters of out-of-body experience themselves, this is of little interest to them, since we do not yet know what laws govern the manifestation of the astral image on the physical plane; it can therefore only be, for them, purely accidental, and what they will exteriorize, above all and very generally, is their astral body. What concerns the astral image should have been said to warn the percipient subject, but I will only deal with the exteriorization of the astral body — intermediary between the spirit and the physical body — for which I will now examine the training conditions for its exit from the material body.

However, before closing this chapter and going further, since, on the one hand, studies of the exteriorization of the living ghost are currently very actively pursued, and on the other hand, they use theosophical nomenclature without basing themselves on the theosophists' theories, and since, consequently, the student may find himself confused amidst this multiplicity of different appellations, I will quickly establish the relationships that exist between the terminology commonly used since its use by Dr. Baraduc and Durville, and that of occultist theory. And, to be clearer, I will proceed based on experimentation.

A subject is magnetized by ordering them to dissociate; after a certain time, it is observed that the subject is dissociated; their physical body (*Rupa*) is still in its seat; but to their left, [79] and external to them, a fluidic substance has condensed, invisible to the normal eye, but visible to a certain category of individuals (sensitives, magnetic subjects placed in a state of clairvoyance, etc.) and whose reality is easily ascertained by purely material processes: [80] this is what Colonel de Rochas called — and all experimenters after him — the PHANTOM.

---

[79] At least very generally; but exceptions are known.
[80] Air pinch, photography in certain cases, etc.

This word — now also called *AÉROSÔME* — is therefore a general term designating all the exteriorized fluidic elements forming a whole, as opposed to the physical body, the *sarcosôme*. This phantom contains within itself the various properties specific to each of the elements of which it is composed.

This experiment, which I have already discussed, may seem absolutely incredible to people who are not familiar with this aspect of science: I will therefore be excused for digressing here to provide objective, material proof of the fact.

At the beginning of 1911, Mr. Lefranc wanted to attempt to photographically capture the various phases of the operation at the *French Institute of Psychical Research*, and for this purpose used Mrs. Lambert, a former subject of Colonel de Rochas (Miss Lux) and our devoted subject at the time.

The subject was asleep, and when the formation of sensitive areas around her was observed, photographed (*fig.* 21), this was the period of formation of the phantom: the physical body is obsessed by moving fluids.

The magnetization continued, and about half a minute later, when the subject announced that her double was completely exteriorized, another photograph of the subject was taken, in the same pose, in the same place, with the same lighting and the same exposure time (*fig.* 22).

The subject is completely obsessed with the fluids, and to her left appears a vague human form that appears to be the ghost still in the process of condensation. Note that the print does not allow us to see certain details that appear on the photographic plate.

The experiment was not pushed any further that day; but previously, during a series of experiments at Hector Durville's, the same Mr. Lefranc was able to take three successive photographs of Mme Lambert's ghost, in which the double is more or less well condensed (*figs.* 23, 24 and 18).

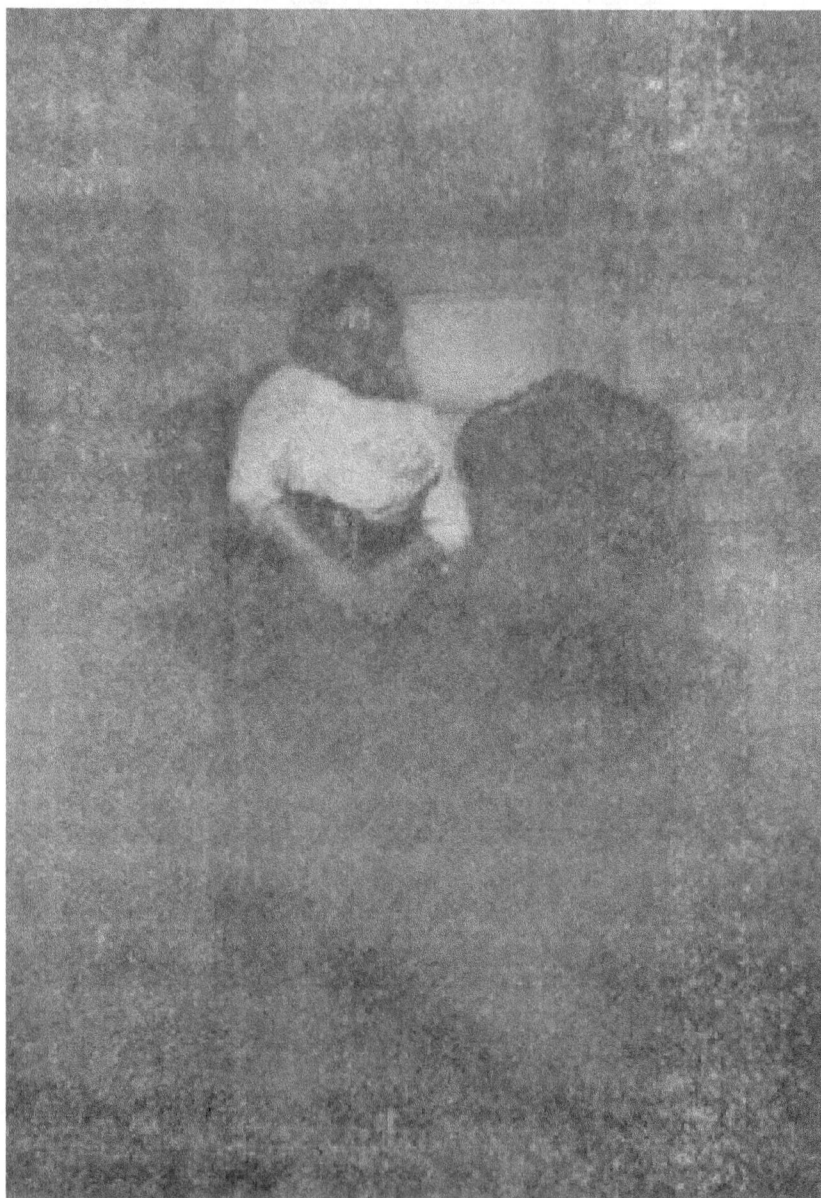

Fig. 21. — State of exteriorization of sensitivity.

Fig. 22. — State of splitting.
The subject is invisible, and to her left is, in a light cloud, her ghost
during a period of condensation.

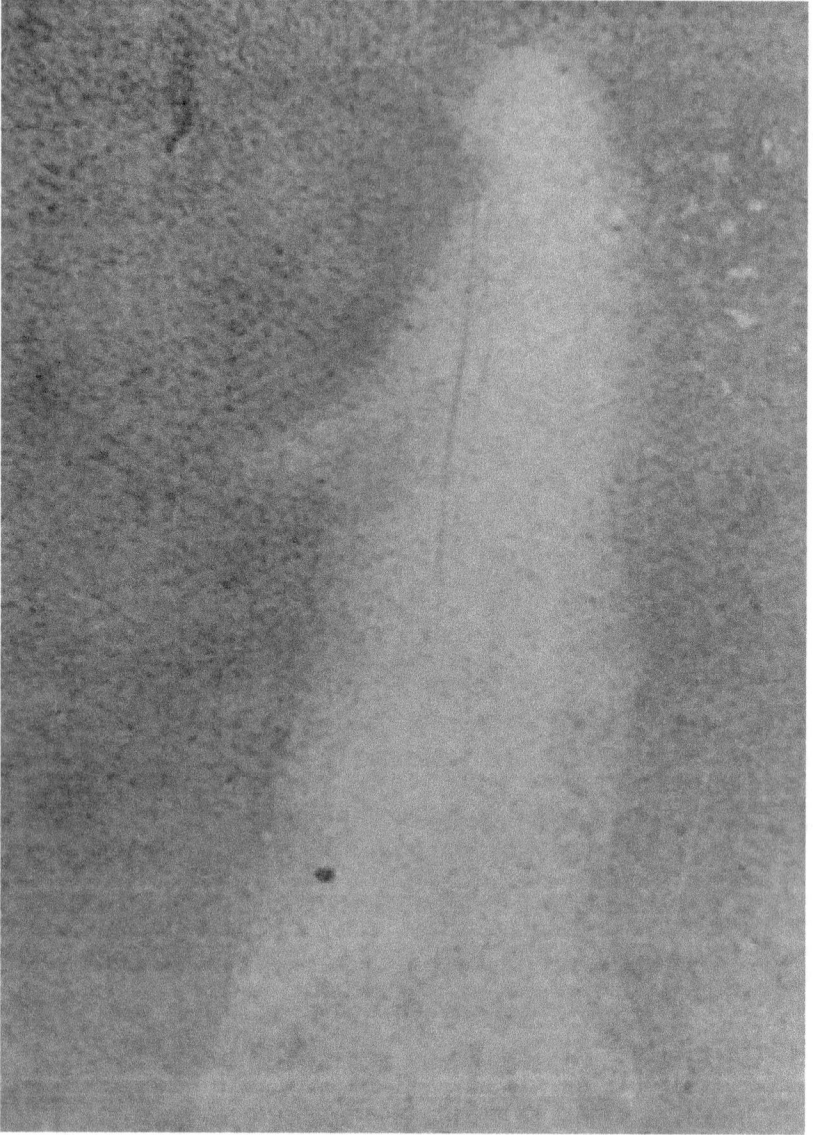

Fig. 23. — First photograph of Mrs. Lambert's ghost.

Fig. 24. — Last photograph of Mrs. Lambert's ghost [81]

[81] Figure 18 shows another photograph of Mrs. Lambert's ghost, swaying before the camera. For full details, refer to Mr. Durville's book, *The Ghost of the Living*, already cited.

Madame Lambert is not, moreover, the only subject with whom experiments have been carried out in this way. Around the same time, Madame Léontine, asleep in Villejuif, about ten kilometers from Paris, but following an earlier suggestion from Hector Durville, exteriorized her ghost, which she sent to pose in his study in Paris, in front of a sensitive plate. The result, a little blurred, is shown in figure 26 [82].

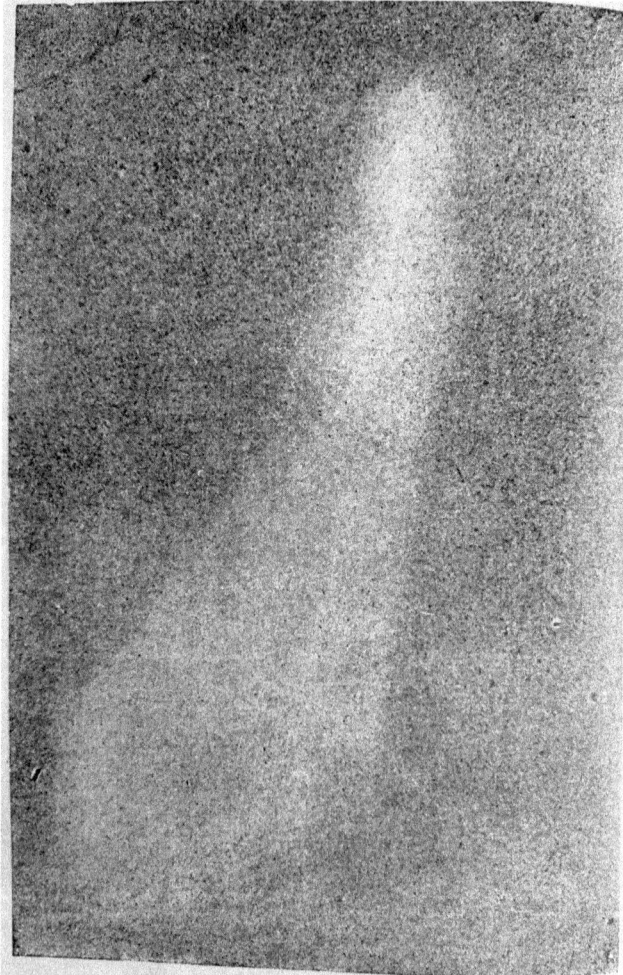

Fig. 26. — Ghost of Mrs. Léontine.

[82] Figures 12, 13, and 14 provide other photographs of living, exteriorized ghosts.

So, if the exteriorized ghost is not normally visible, except to people who possess a certain degree of natural or acquired clairvoyance, it can be captured by the photographic plate under certain conditions that are still poorly understood, because, it must be said, this kind of transcendental photography is not always successful, and a study must be done to define the conditions necessary for its realization.

Finally, the ghost's reentry into the physical body has been photographed several times by H. Durville.

In this regard, I provide two photographs, the first (*fig.* 27) representing the normal reentry of the ghost — where the ball is mainly visible — and the second (*fig.* 28) representing the sudden reentry following a fright.

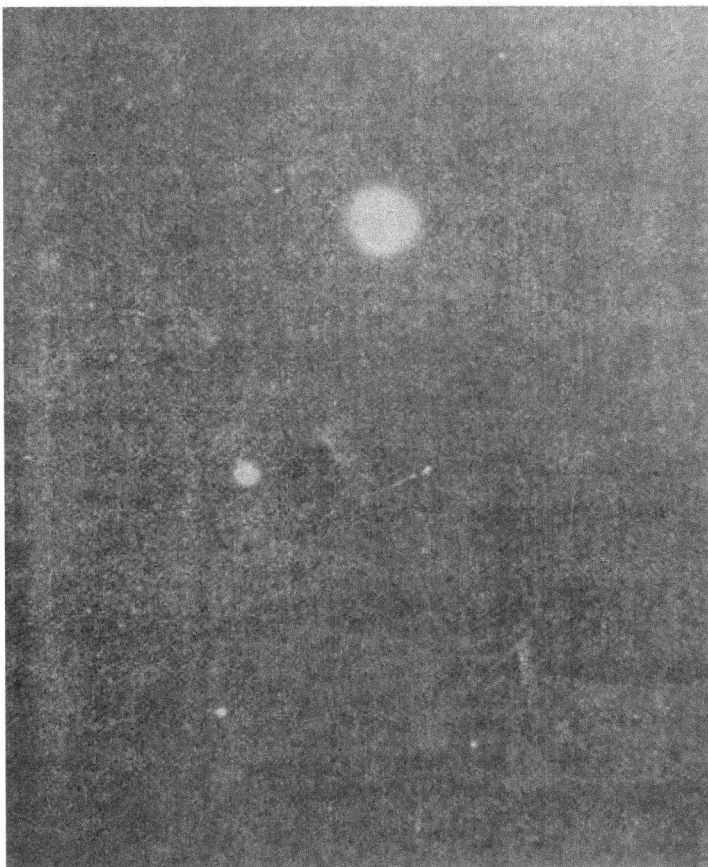

Fig. 27. — Normal return of Mrs. Léontine's ghost.

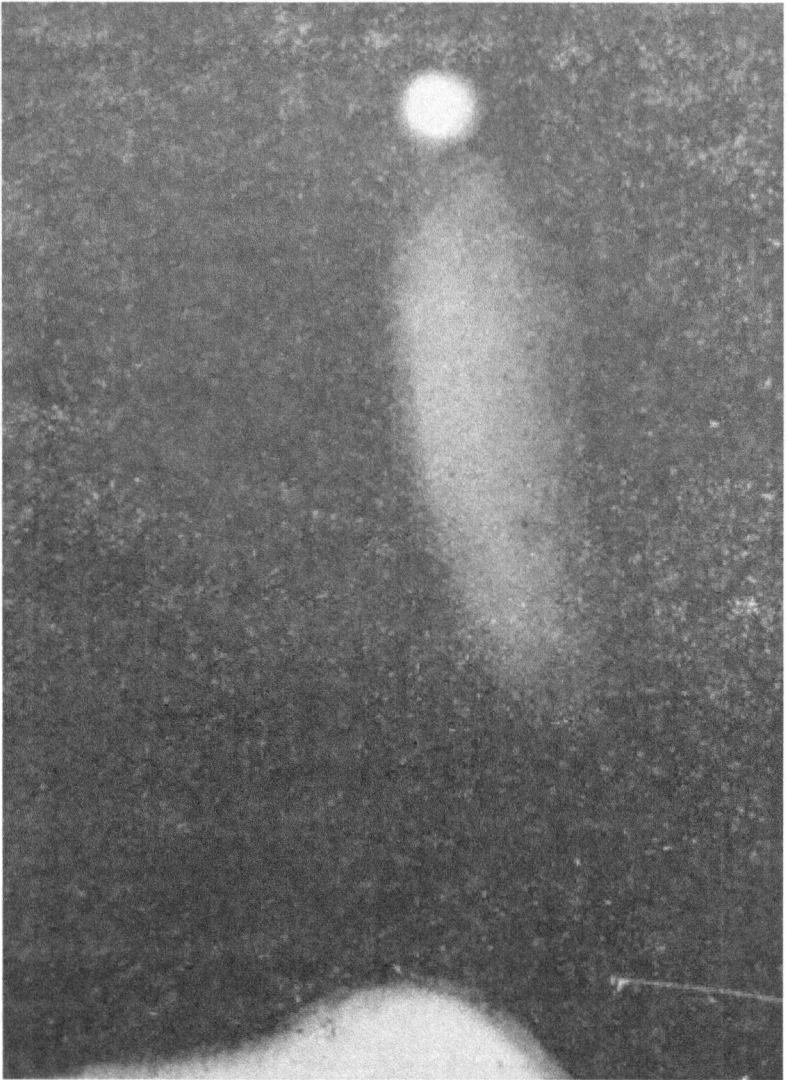

Fig. 28. — Sudden return (following a fright) of the ghost of Mrs. Léontine.

But the exteriorized living ghost is not only visible in certain cases: it also exerts a mechanical, physical, chemical, etc. action on matter, which reveals its objective reality, for example: when it weighs on a scale, conducts an electric current, etc.

To achieve these phenomena, it must be very condensed; but in this case, we do not know what the limit of its strength might be.

To give an example, I reproduce the plan (*fig.* 29) of an experiment carried out by chance, at H. Durville's with the exteriorized phantom of Mrs. Lambert: —

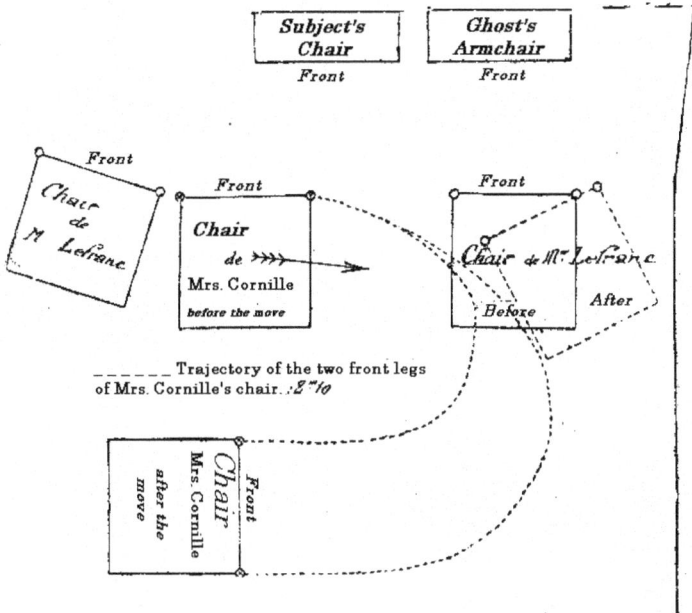

Fig. 29. — Moving of (occupied) seats by an exteriorized living ghost.

while the subject was inert in her armchair, her phantom left her own, advanced towards Mrs. C.'s chair, made it describe the trajectory indicated by the dotted line, and, in this movement, struck the chair occupied by Mrs. L., so violently that these two ladies were thrown onto the parquet floor; the phantom also dragged Mrs. C. across the parquet floor for about two meters. However, Mrs. Lambert does not normally have the strength necessary to act in this way. [83]

---

[83] We will see later that the force of the exteriorized ghost is of a composite order, constituted both by the odic force that the double contains within itself, and by that which it borrows from those of the assistants whose organism lends itself to this communication; now, in this case, the assistants were two magnetizers and two magnetic subjects; that is to say that all four belonged to the category of people who can, better than all others, exteriorize their odic forces.

I think that after all this successive proof, the objective reality of the exteriorized living ghost is sufficiently established to allow me to close this long but necessary parenthesis.

So, as I just indicated, the subject's phantom is exteriorized by magnetic means.

When this phantom is magnetized under certain conditions, it divides itself into two, and the second phantom thus obtained is placed to the left of the first, where the reality of its presence is easily observed by the same processes as above.

If we study each of these two phantoms separately, we see that the first (which is reddish and bluish) contains the subject's material life, to which it is connected by a fluidic link made of its own substance. It has been called the *double*, the *etheric body* and the *odic body*; it corresponds absolutely to *Jiva*, which is material vitality, and to *Linga Sharira*, which is the animating part of the living organism. [84] Enclosing the subject's physical life within itself, this *double* never moves more than a few meters away from it, and it returns as soon as the second phantom is sent away.

This one, slightly azure white, is joined to the first by an indefinitely extensible bond, of the same material as its own. It is called the *astral body*, and by pinching it, pricking it, or placing substances of various flavors on the tongue, it can be seen to possess the subject's sensitivity, for the latter immediately registers the sensations produced in its physical body, while, on the contrary, this material body is completely insensitive.

The astral body and the etheric double have human form. [85]

---

[84] If the occultist theory is true, we will one day be able to decompose the etheric double into its two constituent elements, which is all the more likely since it is seen in two different and very distinct colors, polarized one to the right and the other to the left.

[85] The etheric double *always* has a human form; the astral body *ordinarily* possesses it, but it can modify it under the influence of will. — Certain very recent experiments would suggest that the astral body *may not* have a form of its own, and that if it generally assumes a human form, it is simply out of habit.

In all cases, when the astral body assumes a human form, it is smaller than life: the astral body of a man assumes the form of a child of about eleven years old.

The astral body corresponds perfectly to the *Kama-Rupa* of occultism, accompanied by its own matter — or rather, substance, for the matter of which it is composed is so fluidic that, by itself, it cannot act on matter itself; in this case, he is obliged to use the semi-material forces he encounters in the etheric double, either his own or that of another person in his environment, as we will see later.

If the magnetization of the astral body is continued, sensitives and clairvoyants see a luminous *aura* emanating from it, ovoid in shape, which completely surrounds it and is especially bright around the head, where it constitutes a sort of particularly luminous sphere; it is this sphere that Dr. Baraduc has photographed many times under the name of *mental ball*. [86] Hence the name *mental body*, which is given to this special aura. The mental body corresponds very exactly to the *lower Manas*. It holds intelligence: convincing proof of this was obtained in 1911 at the *Institute of Psychical Research*, where the secretary, Mr. Lefranc, had attempted to isolate it; of the exteriorized ghost of the subject, Mrs. Lambert, he successively brought into the physical body the etheric double and then the astral body; but then the subject, having at her disposal her neuritis (astral body) and her muscular strength (etheric double), but deprived of intelligence (mental body), had a fit of furious madness which almost caused accidents and from which it was very difficult to bring her out by restoring her *mental body*.

Finally, when the magnetization of the exteriorized mental body enveloping the astral body continued, sensitives and seers described the formation, above the mental ball, of a sort of flame whose summit was surrounded by a brilliant halo: it was believed to be the *causal body*, but since it has never yet been possible to isolate and photograph it, we are reduced to hypotheses about it; it appears to hold the highest faculties of the soul, such as memory, and seems to correspond to the *higher Manas*; but we will only be able to be certain in this regard after being able to subject it to experimental study.

As for the other higher elements of the being — Buddhi and Atma — we have not yet been able, in the current state of these studies, to approach them.

Theosophists do indeed affirm that beyond the causal body there still exists a body called *nirvanic*, another they call *paranirvanic*, and finally a third called *mahaparanirvanic*: this is only a theory — certainly respectable like any theory not yet disproven by the facts, but one that a prudent man will only truly believe when it is verified by experimental study.

But, since these lines were written, as we saw in a note a few pages above, experimentation has brought to light the higher elements of the soul (plastic intermediary between the organism and the spirit), which allows us to summarize here in the simplest way, to be well understood, the occult composition of the human being.

Spiritualist theory.	Occultist theory		Experimental theory
	Atma		Spirit
Higher principle, Spirit.	Buddhi		Conscious soul
			Intuitive soul
		higher	Moral soul
	Manas		Causal soul
		lower	Intelligent soul
Intermediate principle, Perispirit, Aerosome, Life	Kama-Rupa		Sensitive soul
	Linga-sharira		Vital soul
Lower principle, Physical body	Jiva		
	Rupa		Sarcosôme (1)

---

[86] Photographs of *mental balls* have been provided, *figs.* 9, 10, 11, 12, 13, 14.
(1) These correspondences should only be regarded as provisional, while waiting for an experiment which is currently continuing to have its definitive basis.

CHAPTER VII

TRAINING

All training requires three elements:
A. — An object to which this training applies.
B. — A mode of action.
C. — A goal pursued.

In this study, the object is the astral body, which we must consider in a special way; we will then study the process by which we can act upon it; finally, the goal pursued, that is, the exteriorization of this astral body or, in other words, the personal unfolding of the human being, the theory of which is presented in the preceding pages, will be examined practically.

Therefore, this chapter is divided into two parts: — the astral body considered as based on neuro-psychic force, and the training process.

A) *Neuro-psychic force* [87]

Everything that lives exists with a life of its own: the star and the plant, the animal and the stone. This universal life, constantly

---

[87] This force has received many other names that can confuse the student; it has been called — and is still called — dynamic, vital, biotic, neurotic, radiant, magnetic, physiological, odic, etc., etc. It is, in short, the astral light of occultists specialized in an organism; if I use the term *neuro-psychic*, it is because this name corresponds exactly to the study pursued in these pages, since, emanating into an organism by the nervous system, it sublimates there to become an energy, a hyperphysical force-substance that constitutes the *substratum* of the astral body.

emanating from its primordial center, the knowledge of which is closed to us, spread throughout the entire universe, reaches the Earth via the sun; on our globe, it changes, making all modalities possible: animal, vegetable, mineral, and, in the animal, it penetrates every organ and becomes cerebral, cardiac, nervous, etc. life. Life is therefore a secondary force, but it is not energy of its own. As Mr. Lodge, president of the mathematics section at the *Congress of the British Association for the Advancement of Science*, pointed out, "the death of an animal does not affect, in the least, the sum of energy; however, a living animal exerts an action on energy that it no longer exerts after its death; life is therefore a *governing principle...*"

On the other hand, H. Spencer says somewhere: "The existing universal forces of attraction and repulsion, which set a rhythm for all the minor changes in the universe, also set a rhythm for the totality of these changes, producing sometimes an immense period during which the attractive forces predominate and cause a universal concentration, and sometimes an immense period during which the repulsive forces predominate and cause a universal diffusion, alternating eras of evolution and dissolution..."

Thus: attraction and repulsion are the two manifestations of Life. Attraction produces the centripetal force, universal gravitation, and repulsion gives rise to the centrifugal force which tends to project moving bodies out of their orbit: the parallel functioning and, consequently, the balance of these two forces constitute the life of the universe.

Now, man, the microcosm, must be constituted like the universe, the macrocosm. Let us therefore see what man is in this respect.

In man, we find three currents of vivification: the lymphatic system, which forms life; the blood system, which maintains it; and the nervous system, which governs it. [88]

These three systems each produce a double current, one of which flows toward the periphery and the other toward the center;

---

[88] Hence the symbol of the three ancient Fates: Clotho who weaves the thread, Lachesis who spins it, and Atropos who cuts it (or respects it); I developed this theory in *Sorcery of the Countryside*, to which I prefer to refer the reader (MM. H. and H. DURVILLE, editors).

for example, blood flows through the artery toward the skin's surface, where it ends in the capillaries, which, through the veins, return it to the heart, etc.

But, for the specific study we are pursuing in these pages, it is primarily nervous force that interests us, and it is this that we will study above all.

Let us first see how it is formed.

The nervous system, as a whole, is made up of two kinds of substances, each with a different structure and color.

One, the gray matter, is composed of cells (or neurons) placed side by side; the other, the white matter, is composed of long filaments.

The gray cells produce a force that is probably analogous, if not identical, to electrical force, and which constitutes nervous force. The white filaments serve as conductors for this force (just as electric wires serve as conductors for electricity) and distribute it to the various organs so that they can perform the work assigned to each of them. It increases and renews itself through continuous *inputs from outside* in the form of light, heat, electricity, etc., and also through the forces released within the body and the innermost tissues during the physical and chemical phenomena of assimilation and dis-assimilation, during the transformation of compound foods into simpler foods.

Nervous force is distributed throughout the smallest branches of the nervous system; but it is mainly produced and stored in the ganglia of the greater sympathetic nerve, in the spinal cord, and in the masses contained within the skull. And, since the brain is by far the largest and most important part of the entire system, it must be considered the principal seat of nervous force. Thus, unless otherwise stated, we can assume that nervous force emanates entirely or almost entirely from the brain.

But cerebral activity not only produces nervous force; it also produces will: that is, will can be considered an emanation of nervous force, which, in turn, it governs and can put to use for useful work.

A consequence of cerebral activity, it reacts inversely on this activity and can apply it to a specific operation.

In the case of the functioning of the will, the available nervous force is divided into two parts, two secondary forces: one feeds the cerebral center that presides over the will; the other is directed to the cerebral location that governs and activates the organ called upon to perform the work.

These two forces are expended simultaneously and separately while the will is active; their intensity therefore tends to diminish and would soon be exhausted if new and continual inputs did not compensate for the loss they experience.

But while the will is in action, the brain continues to receive and produce, or, better said, to elaborate, to transform nervous force whose primordial origin is external to the organism, as we will see later; the elaboration of this nervous force can never stop; a complete halt or too great a decrease in this production would lead to a rapid slowdown and, soon, the cessation of all vital phenomena.

The expenditure of force that maintains the will, and the expenditure of force used for the desired work are therefore compensated by the continuous supply of new nervous force.

If this supply is considerable and sufficient, the activity of the will and the work being performed can be sustained for a long time.

If the intake is low and insufficient, willpower will weaken, work will stop; the body will show its helplessness through a sensation or feeling of fatigue.

The final result is therefore dependent on this influx of new force, that is, on the brain; it will be all the greater the stronger and faster the brain's capacity to produce nervous force.

Consequently, if we wish to accomplish considerable and sustained work — whether this work be physical or cerebral — it is essential that the willpower on the one hand, and the brain's capacity to produce it on the other, be as intense as possible.

All this shows us how closely united on the one hand, the will — which we have already studied in its essence and mode of use — and on the other, the neuro-psychic vital force are.

We are only examining here its elaboration by the brain and how to use it for the proposed goal.

It was stated above that this force increases and renews itself through continuous inputs from outside: how to use these external influxes will be studied later [89], with a view to finding ways to increase and accelerate the work of developing the organism's neuro-psychic force. For now, we will only see how it exists in the normal organism, and how it can be used to achieve personal out-of-body experience.

Let us not forget that the basis of the exteriorized phantom is the astral body, that is, the part of the being where sensitivity resides. Now, since sensitivity is a function of neuro-logicality, it is neurological force in general, and it is its development that must be addressed above all, since the more developed the neuro-vital force is, the more it will tend to exteriorize itself.

Just as our globe — or our universe, as you will, since, according to the teaching of the Emerald Tablet, "as above, so below, and as below, so above" — absorbs the life emanating from its source to return it, modified, purified, *evolved*, to the common center, so man must be subject to this law. In other words, the vital currents within him must not stop at his skin, but have their origin and their outpouring outside him: this is indeed what exists. Magnetism has long taught that man, any living being, is traversed by a current of external force, taken by him from his environment and returned to it after a sort of evolution. To be more precise, man is in some way a compound of three magnets (see *fig.* 30), each of which corresponds to one of the three dimensions, and whose poles are arranged as follows:

	POSITIVE (Emissive)	NEGATIVE (Receptive)
LENGTH	Head	Feet
WIDTH	Right side	Left side
DEPTH	Chest	Back

Since man is much more extended lengthwise than in the other two dimensions, it follows that the left-right current is more powerful than the other two. It is therefore on this current that Dr. Baraduc relied to establish the theory of the reception and emission of vital force, and, consequently, of temperaments and various states of health.

A few words on Dr. Baraduc's conception are necessary here.

According to his theory, [90] which may undergo modifications in detail, but whose general idea remains, a man in perfect health, a well-balanced man, is one who returns to the environment as much force as he has received. [91] To measure both the force received and the force returned, this biologist used the Fortin magnetometer, of which he simply modified a few details.

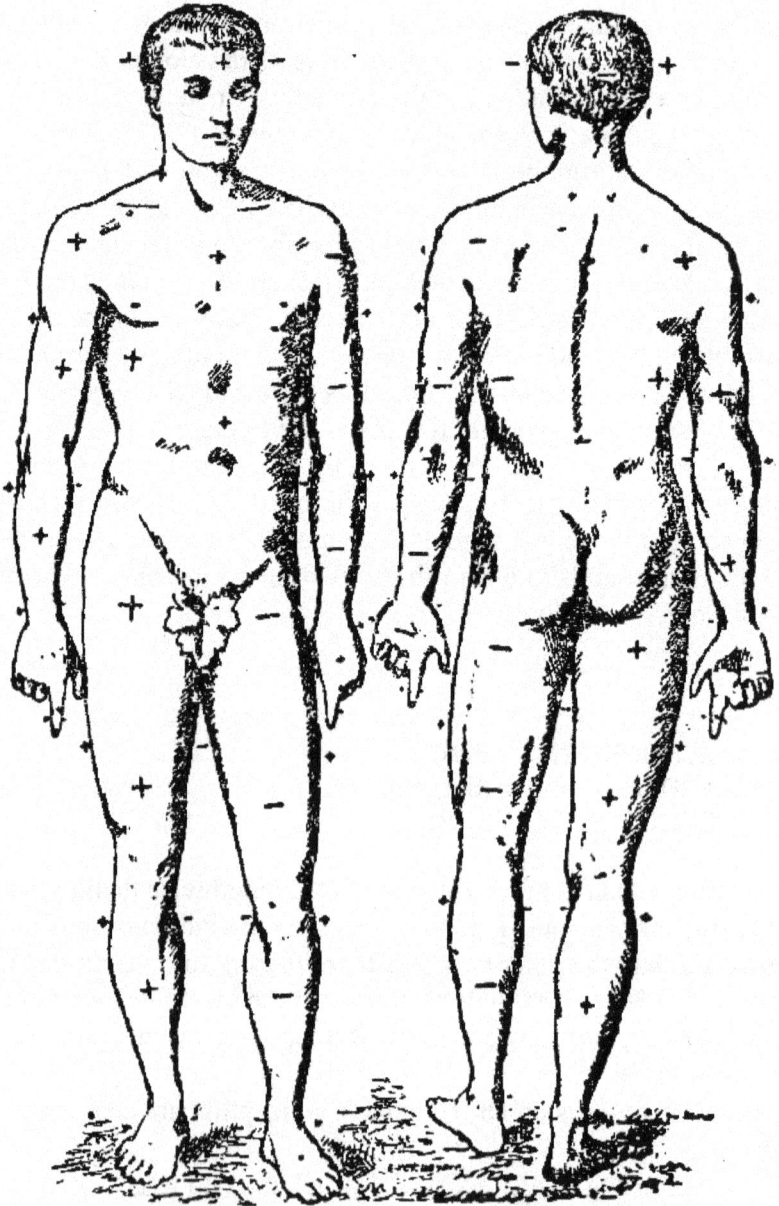

Fig. 30. — Overall polarity of the human body.

This instrument consists essentially (see *fig.* 31) of a very fine, untwisted cocoon thread, fixed at the top to a support and terminated at the bottom by a needle of annealed copper wire, around which the cocoon thread is wound in the middle, without any binding or loop at this point. The copper needle is movable on a dial divided into 360 degrees, below which is a coil of fine wire surrounding a horizontal glass cylinder. The whole thing can be contained in a glass cylinder of sufficient diameter, designed to insulate the apparatus from any draft and heat, in which case the upper part of the cocoon thread is fixed to the center of the plate — also made of glass — which closes the top of the apparatus. The subject places their fingers (right or left hand) about five centimeters from the apparatus, and the phenomena of attraction or repulsion take place.

There are also some precautionary measures to take: for example, fix the apparatus in the corner of two thick walls to avoid external vibrations, — and in relative darkness to neutralize the influence of light. Furthermore, the apparatus must be oriented along the S-N line so that this line passes through the subject's vertical median plane. Finally, the digital tip of the hand (right or left) must be presented to one end of the needle, in such a way that, through the convexity of the glass, the plane of the hand is perpendicular to the plane of the end of the needle; and the duration of observation must be two minutes or one hundred and twenty seconds, until the moment when — attraction or repulsion — the needle has settled at a point different from the one where it was observed before the experiment.

---

[89] See chap. VIII, § A.

[90] *Vital Force, Our Fluidic Body, Its Biometric Formula*, 1 vol. octavo, Paris, 1893. See also: Dr. BONNAYMÉ: *Psychic Force and the Instruments Used to Measure It* (1 vol. H. and H. Durville, Editors).

[91] Strictly speaking, there is no such thing as an absolutely balanced individual: each person, depending on the time of day, the season, their moral state, etc., gives back more than they receive, or *vice versa*. — On the other hand, the principle of equality of reception and restitution of force, although in itself very accurate from a theoretical point of view, cannot be understood, in practice, in an absolute manner, in the sense that only one-third of the force taken from the environment is returned to it as is; the other two-thirds form, as it were, the life capital and are returned to the environment only after undergoing certain modifications in the organism.

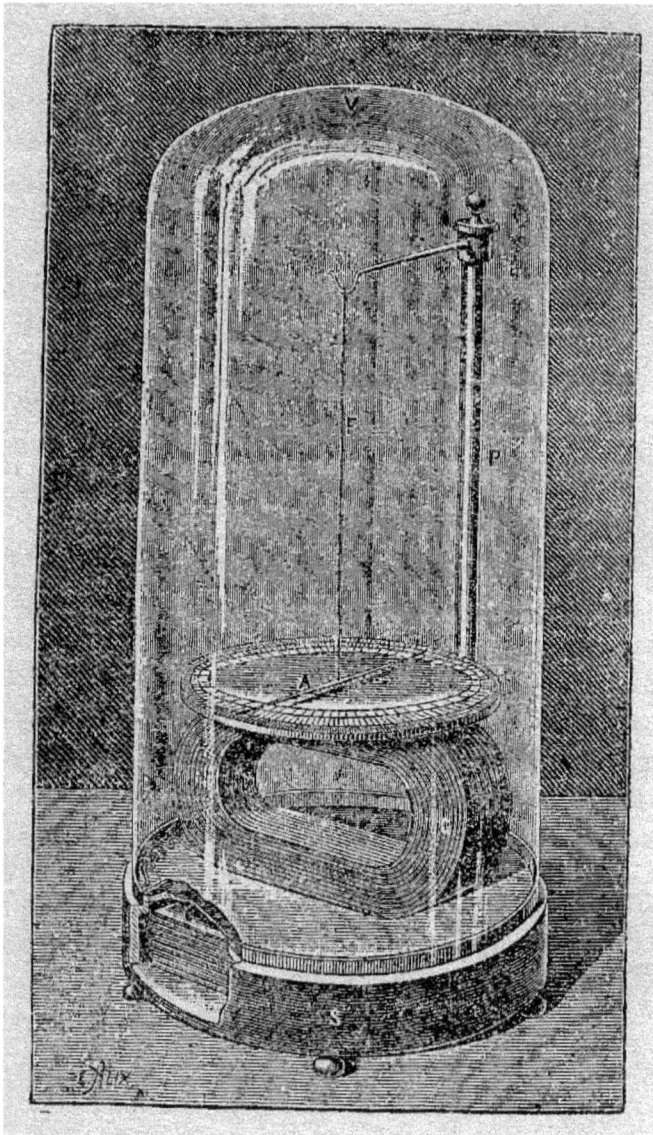

Fig. 31. — The BARADUC biometer

The force that the being takes from the environment is any astral force, which we do not need to concern ourselves with here; that which it emits is, before all and above all, neurologically modulated vital force, as results from the work of Dr. Barety [92]: this is to be remembered in view of what will be said later.

Having explained that the living being, depending on the circumstances, and depending on the side of itself that it observes, can give rise to three formulas: attraction, neutrality, repulsion; Dr. Baraduc has deduced nine different types, which are:

		Right. Left.
Main types (very rare)	⎱⎰	O/O A/A R/R
Secondary types	⎰⎱	A/O O/A R/O O/R R/A A/R — the most frequent.

(+ 5° — 5° marks the perfect balance).

Now, if we recall, on the one hand, that, as has just been said, the human force that is externalized is neurotic force, and, on the other hand, that neuroticity largely constitutes the astral body, it will be logical for us to deduce that the individual who will have the greatest ease in externalizing their astral body will be the one whose biometric formula is R/R.

But it is obvious that such a formula can only occur exceptionally and very momentarily, since, in order to externalize force, it is first necessary to hold some in reserve, which must be taken from somewhere, that is, ultimately, from the common reservoir; consequently, the individual who presents the R/R formula is, at least in principle, subject to enormous variations in both the positive and negative directions, since he or she must have previously presented, if not the A/A formula, at least a formula close to it.

There is therefore only one piece of advice to give to the experimenter who, from the outset, presents the R/R formula: — his or her neural equilibrium being extremely unstable — to abstain from such experiments: it is dangerous for him or her to engage in them. [93]

The conclusion to be drawn from the above is that the training to be followed must lead the experimenter to present a formula as close as possible to R/R, and, to this end, he or she must monitor his or her own progress daily using the biometer whose mechanism was indicated above.

B) *Measuring devices*

Dr. Baraduc's biometer is one of the most accurate instruments available for measuring neuro-psychic vital force; but it has the disadvantage of being quite expensive. Furthermore, despite the simplicity of its construction, we do not recommend anyone setting it up themselves, because, with any precision instrument, it only takes one poorly understood or defectively executed detail for the instrument to render no service, or even — what is worse — to give results that are falsified in advance.

However, since it is important for each operator to assiduously monitor the development of their own neurological activity, as will be established in the following paragraph of this chapter, and since, for this purpose, everyone needs to possess a special monitoring instrument, we believe we are doing experimenters a service by indicating here the method of construction and use of other instruments, including some that anyone can set up without difficulty, but which, it goes without saying, should not be considered precision instruments and can only be used to make rough observations.

It is also useful to know the main features of these various devices, since some work well with some people and poorly with others, or vice versa. Could humans emit several types of forces? Rather, I believe that these are the various modalities of the same force, differently developed by each organism, and that these instruments are applied, depending on their method of construction and the materials they are made of, to different modalities of the same neuro-psychic force.

---

[92] *Animal magnetism, studied under the name Radiant Neural Force*, 1 vol. in-8. Paris, 1887.
[93] When the phenomenon of personal out-of-body experience occurs unconsciously, it is generally in individuals exhibiting this R/R formula.

I will pass over Dr. Baraduc's biometer, which I have just studied, and Dr. Collongues's dynamoscope, which was sometimes used to take observations of psychic force, but in a completely accidental manner, to first say a few words about:

— *Dr. Collongues Bioscope.*

This device, intended in principle to indicate the weakest side of the body and to accurately assess the degree of health through perspiration, is based on the principle that nervous force is the cause of the vitality of the hands through its directing and predominant action on skin secretion. It can be seen that by relating the indications of this instrument to the nervous polarity of the human body, this bioscope can, in a pinch, be used to replace Baraduc's biometer. Here is a brief description. [94]

Fig. 32. — Bioscope of Dr. Collongues

[94] This description, as well as several of the following ones and some passages in this section, are borrowed from a work by Dr. Bonnaymé of Lyon, *Psychic Force, the magnetic agent and the instruments for measuring them*, 1 vol. in-12, Paris. This work, which should be referred to if necessary, contains numerous details relating to the construction and use of certain devices, details that could not find their place here, where I simply and quickly review the most well-known, simplest, and most recent devices for measurement or simply for psychic observation.

It is a sort of large lantern (*fig.* 32) with two equal appendages on each of the two sides to allow either hand to be inserted into the bioscope. The metal-supported cage, fitted with four glass windows, is roughly cubic in shape and topped with a truncated pyramid roof. From the center of the ceiling, inside, hangs a cotton Alsace thread twisted from left to right, which carries, suspended from its lower end, a long aluminum needle. Below this, to measure its travel, there is a clock face glued to the floor of the bioscope. These are the essential parts.

To take an observation, one first waits until the needle is still, then carefully inserts one's right hand, up to the wrist, into the right appendage of the device, the ulnar edge resting on the floor of the bioscope, and the palmar surface turned toward the thread. Once these arrangements have been made, after two or three minutes at most, the hand of the bioscope will begin to rotate due to the swelling of the thread under the influence of the humidity produced by perspiration, and will travel a certain number of degrees on the dial. This movement is usually continuous and always in the same direction, from right to left.

It is more or less rapid, depending on the amount of perspiration produced. When the hand is moving, after any oscillation due to an external cause has ceased, the distance traveled, in one minute, by this hand, on the enameled dial divided into hours and minutes, is noted. Then, one removes one's hand from the device, opens the windows of the bioscope widely, and wipes them with a dry cloth to remove the condensation that has settled on their internal walls. The device is left open long enough for this humidity to disappear completely, then the windows are closed.

The same series of operations are then repeated, but with the left hand, and the degrees traveled by the needle are noted during one minute.

The bioscope, as can be seen, indicates the proportional intensity of perspiration, whether sensible or insensible, in the hands, and, following the application of the principle on which it is based, the greater or lesser psychic activity of the right or left side of the body. It therefore provides only elements of comparison, not absolute figures; but as such, it can provide certain services.

— Lafontaine apparatus.

To verify Mesmer's hypothesis on the existence of magnetic fluid, the magnetizer Lafontaine constructed a small apparatus, a description of which we will provide, given the simplicity of its construction, which anyone can accomplish.

One must take a copper, platinum, gold, or silver needle, pierced in the center, suspend it horizontally by an unspun silk thread in a hermetically sealed glass vessel twenty to twenty-five centimeters high; then attempt to act on this needle by presenting one of its points with one's fingertips, through the glass, at a distance of five to ten centimeters. Under the magnetic influence, one will see the needle turn to the right or left, according to the experimenter's wishes. [95]

As can be seen, this apparatus is extremely simple, but the results it produces are, from the point of view of precision, in direct proportion to its simplicity.

— Mr. Boirac's device.

The device of Mr. Boirac, Rector of the Academy of Dijon, Vice-President of the *Society of Hypnology and Psychology*, is described as follows in the *Annals of Psychic Sciences*:

A straw, similar to the one used to suck up iced drinks, is cut to a length of about ten centimeters. The two sections are oblique, so that the two ends are pointed. Each end is lightly colored a different color to ensure they are always distinguishable from each other in their various positions when the apparatus is completed. Using a little modeling wax, a cocoon thread is attached to the precisely determined middle of the straw. The other end of the thread is similarly attached to the inner top of a glass bell jar, whose diameter is slightly greater than the length of the straw, so that the straw can move freely within it. Then the glass bell jar is placed on a circular glass plate, carefully tightening the lid to close the apparatus.

---

[95] LAFONTAINE: *Art of magnetizing* and BONNAYMÉ: *Psychic Force.*

This apparatus is based on the same principle and is used in the same way as Dr. P. Joire's sthenometer, which we will study later. If it has been mentioned here, it is because it is much easier to construct than the other.

— *Galvanometer of Mr. de Puyfontaine.*

Fig. 33. — The Puyfontaine galvanometer.

It is, in principle, an ordinary galvanometer, with the difference that instead of 30 or 40 meters of copper wire, it is composed of 30,000 and 80,000 meters of silver wire, which gives it extraordinary sensitivity and allows it to record very minimal currents of vital electricity, in other words, neuro-psychic force. This galvanometer, of which we provide a reproduction (*fig. 33*), is mentioned here only because of its extreme sensitivity, which allows it to be of great service; but its construction, rather complicated, is only possible for a specialist, and its price is quite high. It should therefore be mentioned here, but it will not detain us further.

— *First device by W. Crookes.*

This device is, in summary, a recording scale intended to measure the increase in gravity by contact; consequently, it is only called upon to be used in fairly rare cases from the point of view that concerns us here; we will therefore be content with the figure of the overall view, and that of the detail of the recorder (*figs*. 34 and 35); these figures will suffice to demonstrate the mechanism of the device; as for the complete description, it will be found in the new research on spirit phenomena and psychic force and in the work of Mr. Bonnaymé: *Psychic Force.*

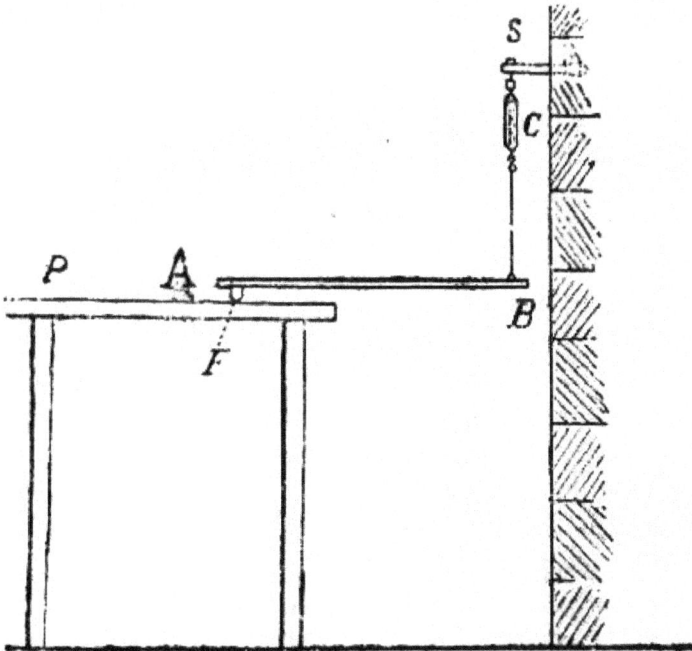

Fig. 34. — First CROOKES device (general figure)

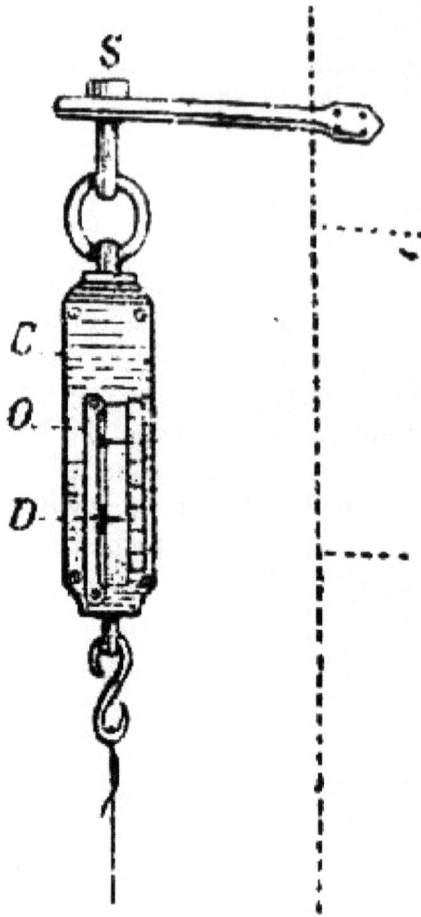

Fig. 35. — Detail of the C recorder.

— *W. Crookes's second apparatus* will not interest us, for the same reasons. It is in total only a modification of the first by the addition, at the precise point of support, of a glass tank full of water, on the surface of which a copper vessel, pierced below, therefore, communicating with the water in the vessel, and intended to receive the subject's hand, eliminates by this very fact all mechanical force and records absolutely only psychic force.

The two attached Figures (36 and 37) will suffice to demonstrate the main features of the apparatus. As for a detailed description, it can be found, if necessary, in the work of Crookes and that of Dr. Bonnaymé, both mentioned above.

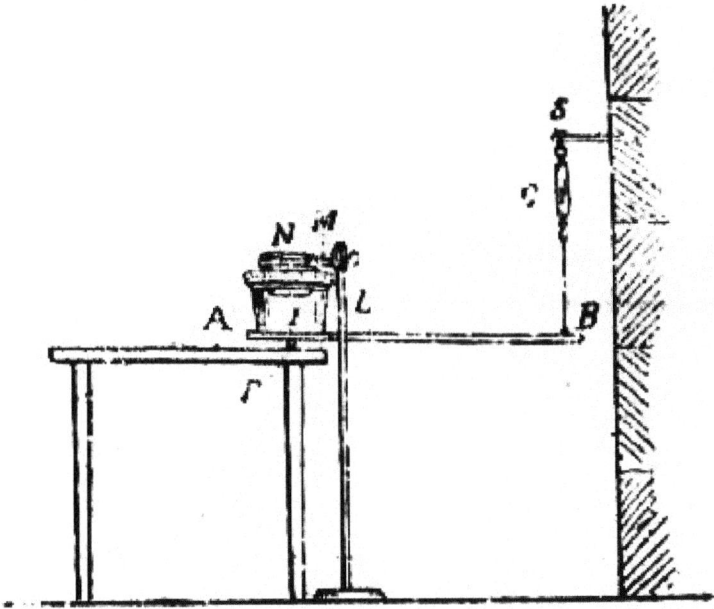

Fig. 36. — CROOKES' second device

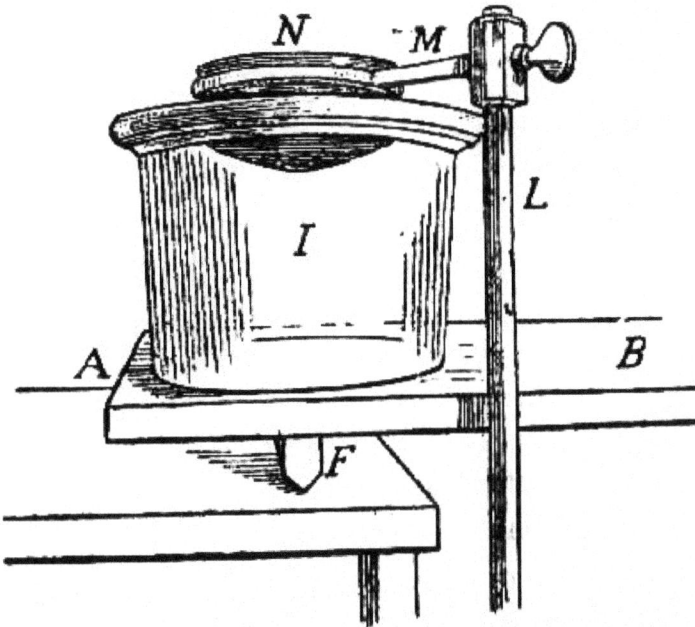

Fig. 37. — Detail of CROOKES' second device

— The third device of W. Crookes will detain us more, because the occasion can arise quite frequently to use it, and, in short, it is quite simple to construct.

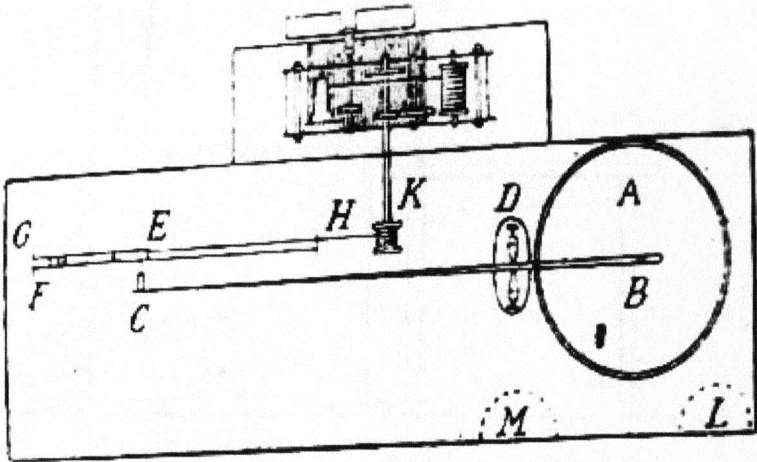

Fig. 38. — CROOKES' third device

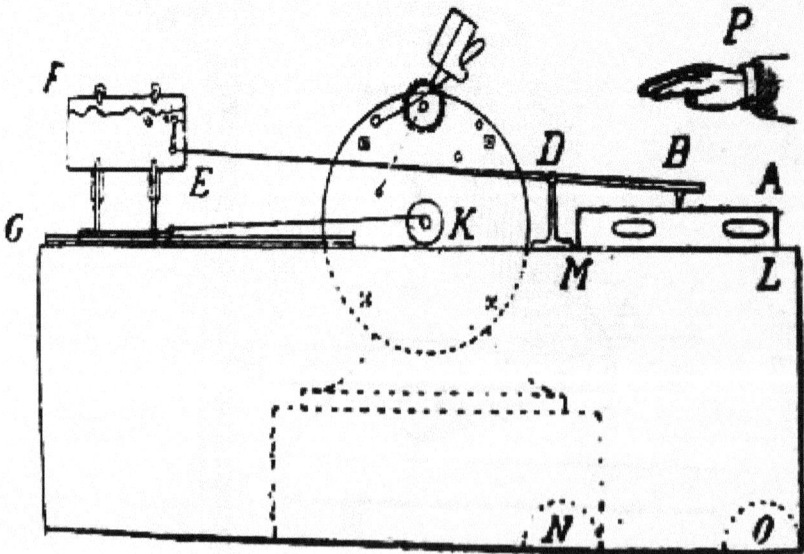

Fig. 39. — Section of CROOKES' third device

A sheet of parchment A (*figs.* 38 and 39) is tightly stretched over a circular wooden hoop. BC is a light lever rotating at point D. At end B is a vertical needle whose point touches membrane A. At the other end C is a second needle whose point projects horizontally and touches a blackened glass plate EF. This glass plate is driven in the direction GH by a clockwork movement K. End B of the lever is arranged to quickly follow the movements of the center of disk A. These movements are transmitted and recorded on glass plate EF by means of the lever and needle point C. Holes are made around the rim of the hoop to allow air to pass freely under the lower part of the membrane.

In this state, W. Crookes' third apparatus indicates only the existence of neuro-psychic force in the subject; it would be simple to improve it by tracing graduated divisions on the EF glass plate, relative to a standard weight, to make it indicate the quantity of force emitted.

With the following devices, we truly enter into the quantitative assessment of vital force.

— *The sthenometer of Dr. P. Joire*, president of the Universal Society for Psychical Studies, is a relatively recent device.

Fig. 40. — Dr. JOIRE'S Sthenometer

It consists (*fig.* 40) of a base on which is placed a dial divided 360 degrees; at the center of the dial is fixed a pivot on which is placed a long straw needle fitted with a cap resting on the tip of the pivot. The dial, raised two centimeters above the base, is covered with a glass globe that protects the needle from air movement.

To use the instrument, place your hand at the level of the needle, as shown in the figure, with your fingers close to the surface of the globe without touching it, and perpendicular to the tip of the needle.

After a few minutes, in most cases, a very pronounced attraction movement of the needle is observed. This movement is sufficient to move the needle 15, 20, and sometimes up to 50 degrees.

As can be seen, the Joire sthenometer, which has been compared, in experimental terms, to Dr. Baraduc's biometer, gives much less precise readings from a quantitative point of view. However, it is more sensitive in detecting the existence of a very minimal odic force.

— *Thore's apparatus* consists quite simply (*fig.* 41), says the author [96], of an ivory cylinder 24 millimeters long and about 5 millimeters in diameter, suspended by a single-strand silk thread, so that its axis is in line with the suspension thread; the latter is attached to a folding support, which allows the cylinder to be lowered or raised without giving it sudden jolts that would inevitably cause the thread to break: in a word, it is a small pendulum that is placed in the open air in the center of a well-supported table, itself placed in the middle of an apartment with all openings closed, to avoid atmospheric movements as much as possible.

When the cylinder is completely still, if one gently approaches, to within a millimeter of this cylinder, either a second ivory cylinder, a thin wooden ruler, a card, or even a simple sheet of paper held vertically in the hand, one sees an accelerated rotational movement occurring in the first cylinder, which seems to have no limit other than the opposing force developed by the twisting of the wire.

---

[96] *First, second and third communication on a new force*, by J. THORE, Dax, 1887.

This rotation always occurs in a clockwise direction when the second cylinder is placed to the left of the first in relation to the observer (I assume the latter is facing the apparatus), and in the opposite direction when this second cylinder is placed to the right.

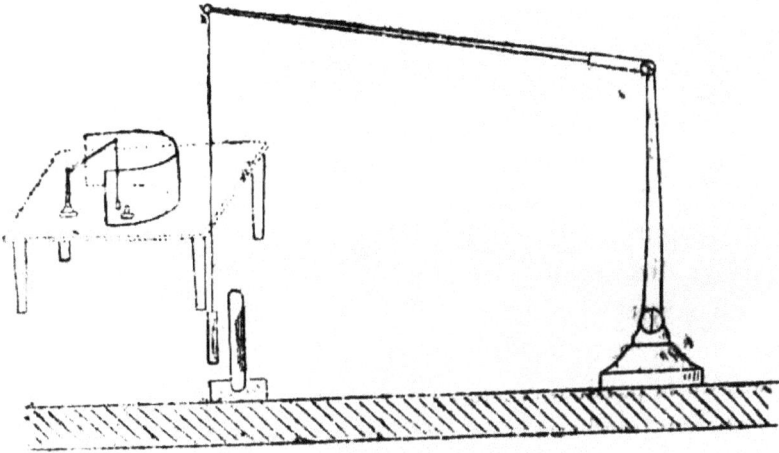

Fig. 41. — THORE'S apparatus

This double movement always occurs, regardless of the observer's position around the table when approaching the second cylinder. The nature of the substance of the two cylinders has no effect on the production of the movement; the same is true of their mass. Liquid or solid, full or empty, the rotation always remains the same. The second cylinder can even be replaced by a taut hair, or a single-strand silk thread, which is even thinner, without there being any noticeable change.

Flat screens placed between the experimenter and the apparatus, or beyond it, when they are less than 20 centimeters from the cylinders, disrupt the movement.

On the other hand, when placed laterally to the right or left, or above or below, they remain without influence. A semi-cylindrical screen (at least 0.25 in height by 0.35 in diameter), set up as indicated by the small plate on the left of the figure, has the singular property of reversing the direction of rotation (the observer must face the open part).

We know that the direction of this rotation is closely linked to the observer's position, which would seem to indicate that the origin of this force lies within the observer himself. But then what is its nature?

At the time Mr. Thore was writing, nothing was yet known about radioactivity; it is therefore understandable that he hesitates to pronounce on the nature of the force to which his apparatus obeys. It is now undeniable that this is the neuro-psychic force emanated by the observer, and that the fixed object, held in the observer's hand near the moving cylinder, plays only a role of presence, or, at most, of accumulator, unless its role consists simply of maintaining the absolute immobility of the hand from which the vital radiations escape.

Mr. Thore concludes by making the following recommendations:

1. Keep the hand in permanent contact with the fixed cylinder or its support for the duration of the observation.

2. The observer must position themselves in front of the apparatus, at a distance of approximately 40 centimeters.

3. Operate alone, or avoid the presence of people too close to the apparatus.

— *Mr. de Tromelin's fluid engines* [97]. We now turn to Mr. Le Goarant de Tromelin's devices, which are certainly among the easiest to construct.

Here is the description of Mr. de Tromelin's first device, as given in 1908, in the *Antwerp Spiritist Bulletin*, by Mr. Le Clément de Saint-Marq.

"It essentially consists of a vertical cylinder that can rotate around its axis (see *fig. 42*).

---

[97] Mr. de Tromelin presented his work in two books entitled *The Human Fluid* and *New Research on the Human Fluid*. MM, H. and II. Durville, publishers, 23, rue St-Merri, Paris.

ROTATING CYLINDER

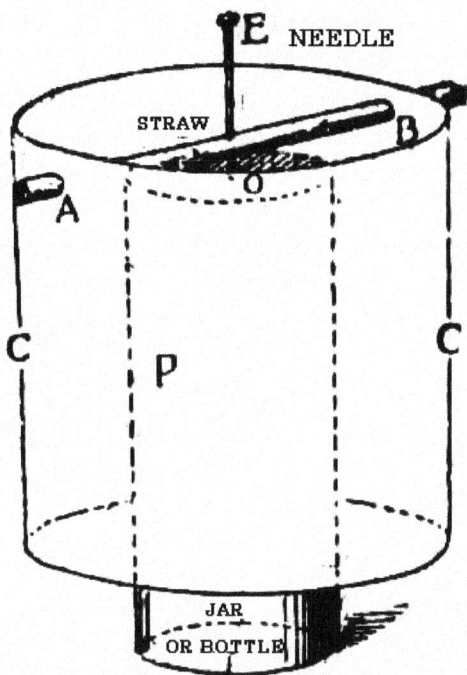

Height and width 55 to 60 millimeters.

🔥 Latency pot on glass bottle.

Fig. 42. — First device of Mr. de TROMELIN

"The cylinder consists of a 50-millimeter-wide strip of paper glued to itself in a circle. The diameter is approximately 55 millimeters. To mount the pivot formed from the tip of a pin, a straw is placed as a horizontal crosspiece at the top of the cylinder. Carefully balance the straw, then glue the two ends of the straw to the paper at the pierced points. The pivot's support point will be provided by the bottom of a small porcelain or glass vase, narrower and taller than the paper cylinder.

"The apparatus, thus arranged, rotates on itself with great ease. If left to its own devices, the agitation of the air is sufficient to produce small movements of varying amplitude and duration, but which are generally characterized by a complete lack of systematic appearance. According to Mr. de Tromelin, by bringing the right hand, placed a few centimeters away from the cylinder, to the camera, one imparts a continuous counterclockwise rotational movement, and the left hand produces a movement in the opposite direction in the same way.

"In the experiments we conducted, we were able to obtain:

"1. Irregular movements with the right hand, however, including fairly prolonged periods of rotation in the indicated direction.

"2. Even less regular movements with the left hand. The continuous rotations seemed to occur in the same direction as with the right hand, contrary to the indications given by Mr. de Tromelin.

"3. With both hands interlaced, I was able to obtain much more regular movements. I was able to count, during a single series, twenty-five complete rotations of the camera, without stopping or reversing the movement.

"4. In the experiments conducted with the right hand, it seemed to me that I could cause the movement or stop it at will. The influence of a concentration of thought directed toward this intention seemed noticeable, without being immediately and absolutely effective. [98]

"These initial observations are sufficient to prove that the device invented by Count de Tromelin is indeed capable of being remotely activated by the human body. It merits in-depth study."

I have quoted this report in full, firstly because it indicates in general terms the method of construction and the principle on which Mr. de Tromelin's other devices are based, but also because it shows how this type of device generally behaves when a person uses it for the first time; they only produce their full effect — at least that seemed to me to be the case — after a certain period of testing, and it seems that a bond of habituation must be established beforehand, like a bond of habituation between them and the organism they are intended to control. Here, moreover, are the indications given by the inventor:

---

[98] I managed to externalize the will, wrote Mr. de Tromelin later, that is to say, having placed a large pastry mold arranged like the cardboard box on a pivot, Miss Pauline Bernard could turn it at will to the right or to the left, with Miss Pauline Bernard's mental acceptance.

"I recognized," he said, "in the externalized nervous fluid certain analogies with static electricity and the magnetic field of magnets.

"I was led by these analogies to admit and then observe that the human fluid potential should theoretically be zero inside closed vessels and practically almost zero.

"This explains why, in jars or under glass bell jars, all devices malfunction, since the energy that should move them becomes almost zero.

"As a result, I had to completely abandon placing any of these devices under a glass dome, because they would be in conditions contrary to the theory.

"Always guided by my theoretical research, I found that the best hand position to rotate any of my devices was to place it directly behind the device, in front of which one is seated, with the hand touching the table or not. If the hand does not touch the table, the rotation is much slower.

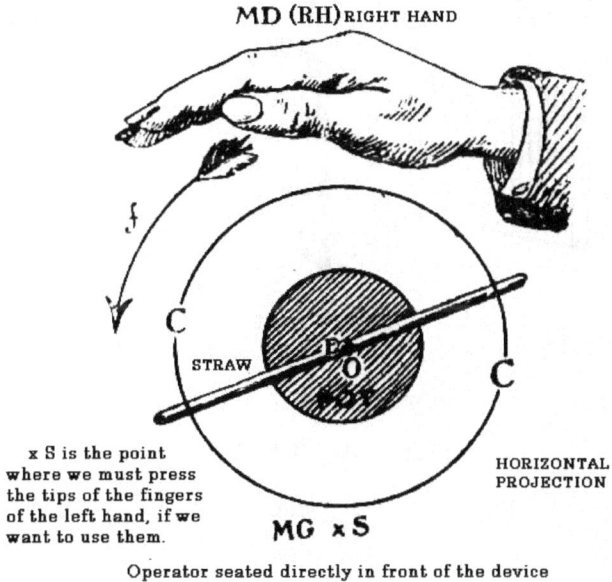

MD (RH) RIGHT HAND

STRAW

x S is the point where we must press the tips of the fingers of the left hand, if we want to use them.

HORIZONTAL PROJECTION

MG x S

Operator seated directly in front of the device

Fig. 43. — Hand position.

"If, having thus placed the right hand behind a cardboard box that one wishes to rotate, one wants to achieve the same effect with the left hand, one must touch, with the fingertips of this left hand, the point placed in front of the apparatus and corresponding diametrically to the hollow of the right hand which is behind the apparatus (*fig.* 43).

"This hand must not be placed flat, but rather inclined towards the table."

Since Mr. de Tromelin's other apparatuses are based on the same principle and inspired by the same theory, I will limit myself to describing them briefly; a quick exposition attached to the corresponding figure should suffice to assist the potential constructor.

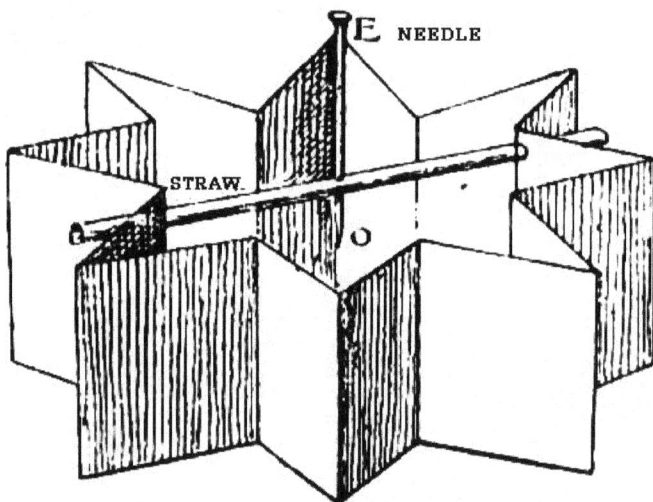

Life-size for fast turning
PLEATED PINION OR CYLINDER

80 m/m to 150 m/m diameter

VERY GOOD DEVICE

Fig. 44. — The pleated cylinder.

— *The pleated cylinder,* called the *pinion* cylinder (*fig.* 44), is the same as the rotating cylinder, with the difference that the paper is equally pleated around its entire circumference.

This device appears to rotate more easily than the previous one, but the rotations are less precise and generally seem to be in an abnormal direction. Furthermore, it is quite difficult to balance, and it is a good idea to use two straws in the shape of a cross to support it.

— *The Tromelin tube* (*fig.* 45) made of metallic paper, pivots on a needle fixed with its point in the air on a piece of cork itself placed on a metal box which seems to play a role of condensation.

It offers the advantage that, moving horizontally, it can replace needle devices.

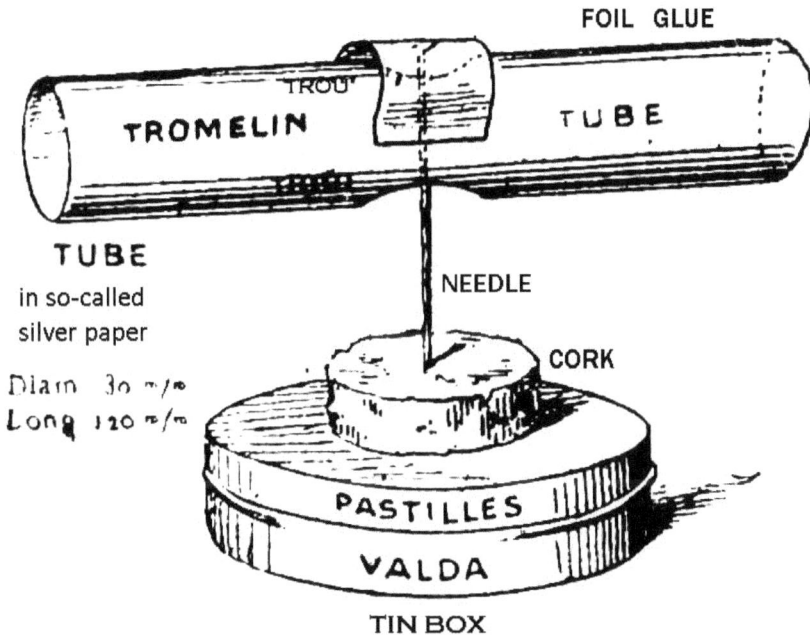

Fig. 45. — Tromelin Tube

— *The commercial box* (*fig.* 46) made of cardboard has a thin metal cap glued to the center of the bottom. As with the previous device, the pivot rests on a metal box serving as a capacitor.

This instrument is heavy and therefore difficult to rotate, but is useful when the previous ones are no longer sufficient for highly developed neuron activity.

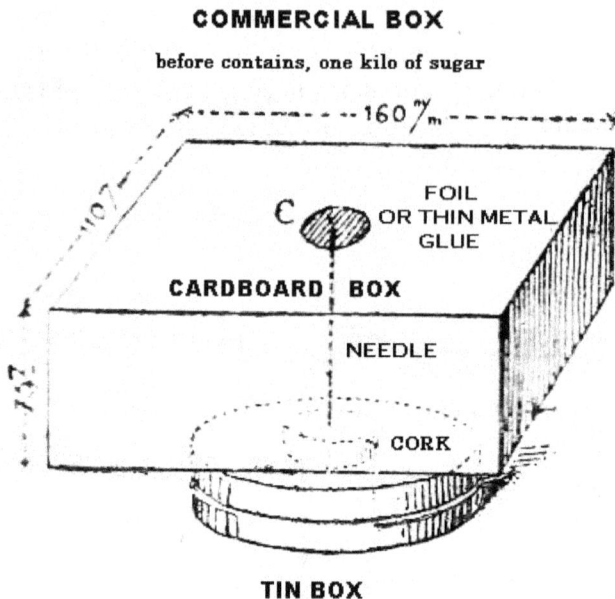

COMMERCIAL BOX

before contains, one kilo of sugar

Fig. 46. — The commercial box

— Finally, *the baking pan (fig.* 47) is used to increase the capacitor's power. It replaces metal boxes. At the bottom of this mold is placed any of these preceding devices.

These instruments, operating in the open air, can be suspected of moving under the influence of air currents, heat radiation, or simply light rays. They have therefore been carefully studied for the purpose of testing, from this point of view, by Mr. Le Clément de Saint-Marcq [99], Mr. de Backère [100], Mr. Fayol [101], etc. All these experimenters were led to conclude that the driving force of these devices is indeed the external human fluid, that is, the neuro-psychic vital force.

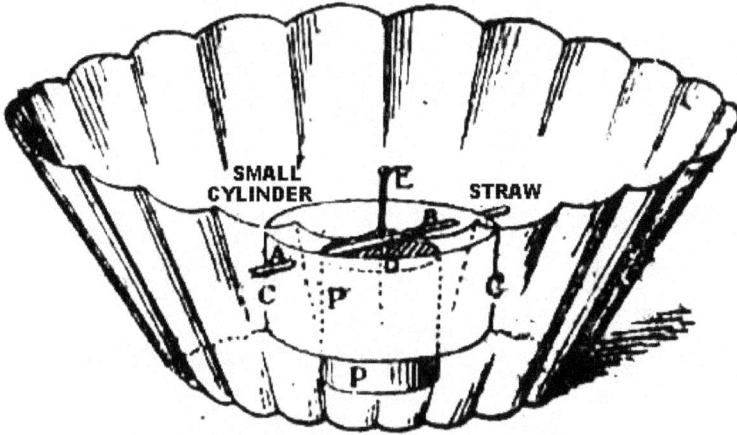

TIN PASTRY MOLD

To rotate a device placed on the bottom
of an upside down cake tin

Fig. 47. — The baking pan.

But this testing work — and this is what primarily interests us — has led to the construction of genuine scientific instruments, the most important of which is the one described by Mr. Fayol in the June 1912 issue of the *Journal of Magnetism and Experimental Psychism*. Here is the description:

— *The Fayol Apparatus* irrefutably eliminates the intervention of heat in its movements and rotations.

It is made of drawn and tempered steel foil, and is composed (*fig. 48*):

A — A cylindrical body with a diameter of 50 millimeters; height 50 millimeters; uniform thickness: five hundredths of a millimeter.

B — A steel yoke, also attached to its upper part, diametrically to the outer walls, serving as a fulcrum and allowing it to rotate on its axis, supported by a pivot. Length: 80 millimeters; width: 5 millimeters.

[99] *Spiritist Bulletin of Antwerp*, 1908.
[100] *Psychic World*, 1912.
[101] *Journal of Magnetism and Experimental Psychism*, June 1912. Messrs. H, and H. Durville, Editors.

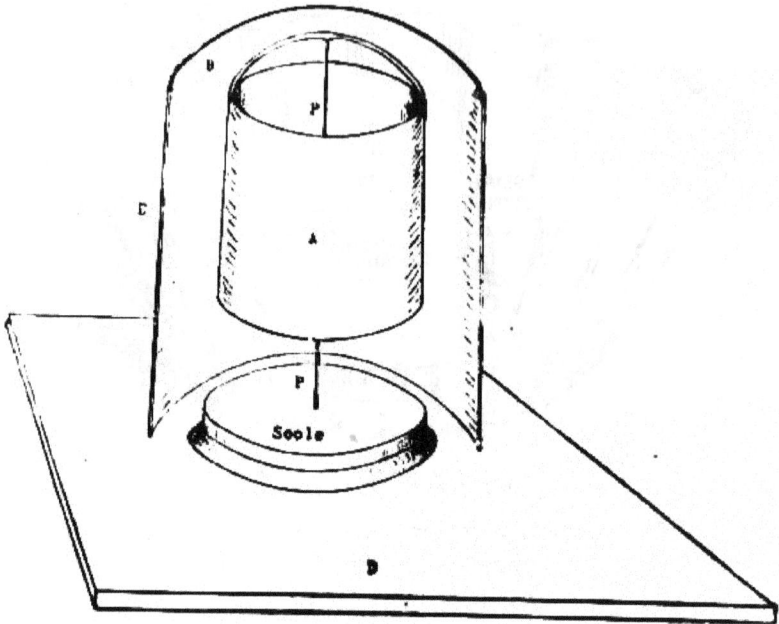

Fig. 48. — Fayol device.

P — A cast steel pivot, with a hardened, needle-shaped tip. Length: 90 millimeters; diameter: 3 millimeters.

G — A wooden base, pierced with a hole, holding the pivot vertical: for tightening, a rubber washer.

D — A wooden board (length: 25 centimeters; width: 15 centimeters; thickness: 1 centimeter) serving to support the assembly and secure the screens.

E — Several screens accessory to the apparatus and of various molecular compositions. They have a semi-cylindrical shape and serve to insulate the hand from contact with the device, to determine the accumulation of projected force and the approximate conductivity of the materials used (Materials used to make the screens: 1. tinned iron, 2. copper, 3. zinc, 4. flannel, 5. straw, 6. cotton wool, 7. cardboard).

R — Finally, an accessory essential to eliminate the heat action. It is made of tinned iron (*fig.* 49) and constructed in such a way that liquids and solid materials can be used indiscriminately. It exactly matches the shape of the screens in its smallest diameter. It has an essential feature in its shape and dimensions: the proportions of an ordinary human hand are observed as meticulously as possible. Its dimensions are as follows: height 90 millimeters; small diameter 95 millimeters; thickness at the fingertips: 10 millimeters; thickness at the wrist (shown): 40 millimeters; arrow: 60 millimeters. Diameter of the screens: 75 millimeters; height: 85 millimeters; thickness varies depending on the material used.

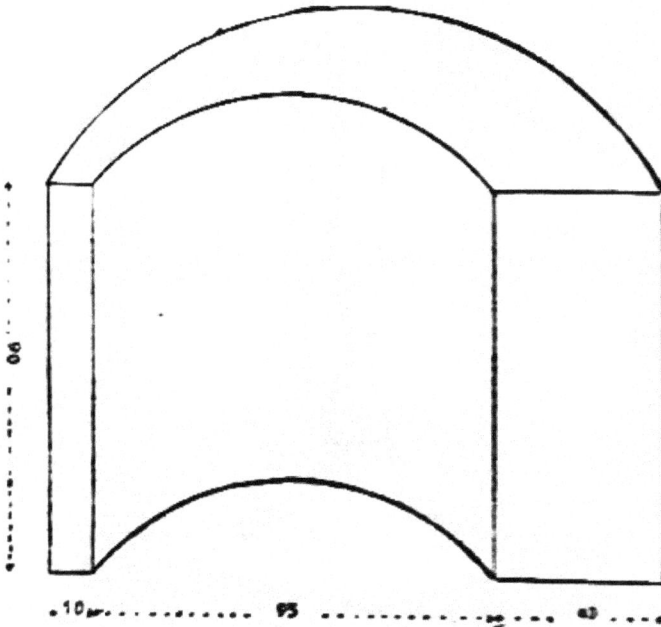

Fig. 49. — Accessory R

This device is used like Mr. de Tromelin's fluid engines; the various experiments carried out with this instrument can be found in the aforementioned publication, under the signature of Mr. Fayol. [102]

— Furthermore, through the hands of various experimenters, Mr. de Tromelin's devices have undergone various modifications and improvements, the most interesting of which are shown in Figures 50 and 51.

These modified instruments do not require any special description; their appearance alone should provide an understanding of their construction system if one refers to the description of the devices from which they are derived.

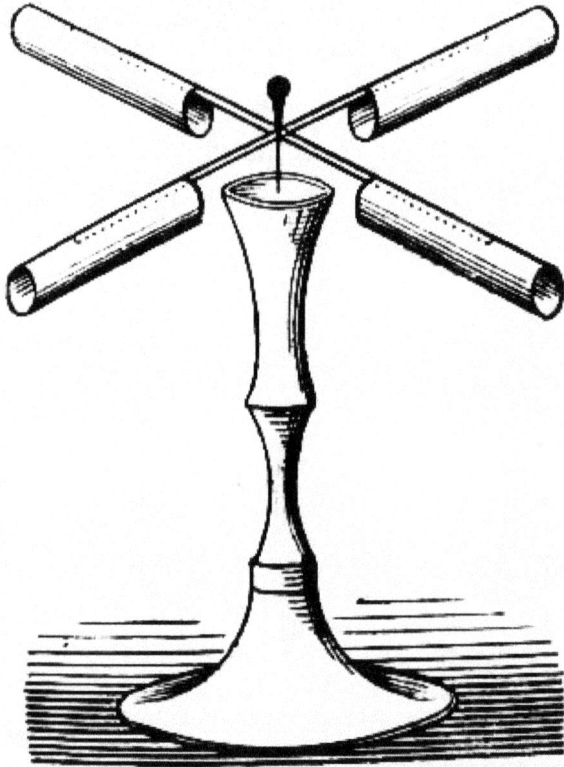

Fig. 50. — Modifications to Tromelin's devices

[102] Since then, Mr. Fayol has constructed a new, highly precise, all-metal apparatus. Mounted on two pivots, it rotates rapidly under the influence of human fluid and seems to meet all the requirements of experimental science. A description of this new apparatus and the results to be expected can be found in the *Journal of Magnetism*, December 1912 issue and subsequent issues. Publishers.

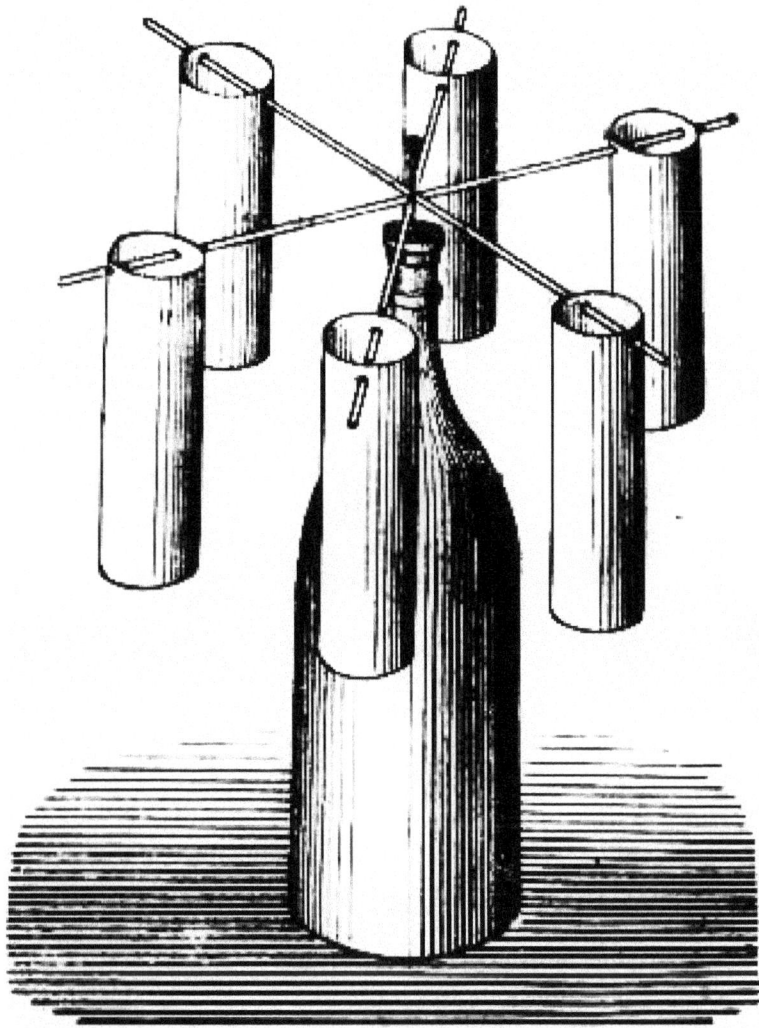

Fig. 51. — Modifications to Tromelin's devices

— Finally, the devices recently devised by a Russian experimenter, Mr. Vladimir Pravdin, eliminate air currents considered a possible cause of rotation.

We simply provide a reproduction (*figs.* 52, 53, 54), the clarity of which will easily supplement any description. These biolic motors, like all others of the same type, are of the simplest and easiest construction.

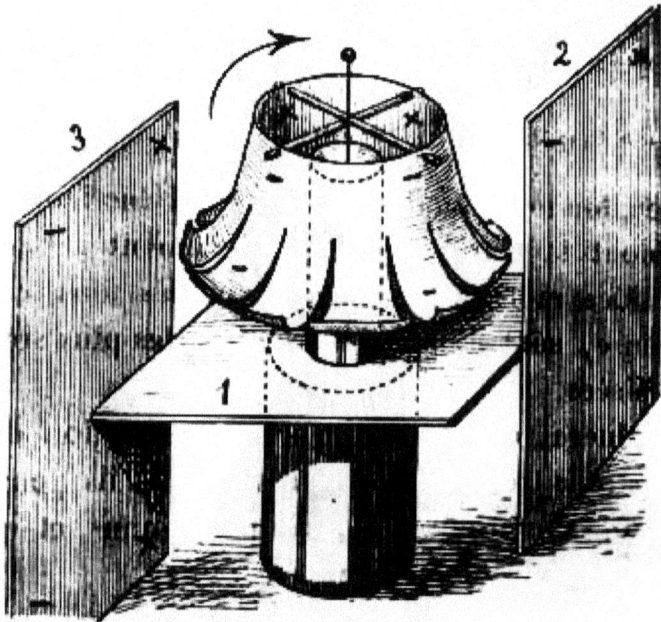

Fig. 52. — Mr. Pravdin's Biolic Engine

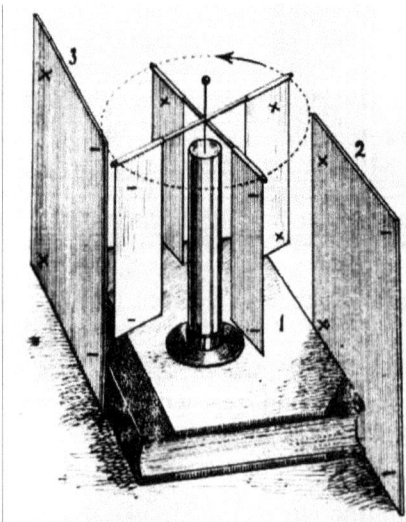

Fig. 53. — Mr. Pravdin's 4-blade
Biolic Engine

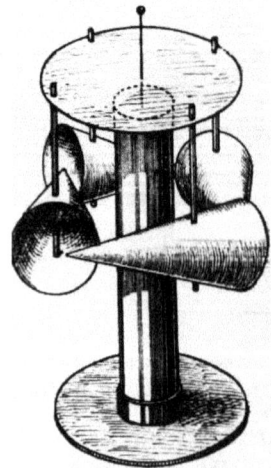

Fig. 54. — Mr. Pravdin's
Anemometer

I will conclude this chapter with the description of two devices that are easy to construct — they can, in a way, be improvised — very little known, but which can provide real services.

— *Float apparatus*. It essentially consists of a fishing float from which the feather has been removed, leaving only the varnished cork; on this float, either a straw tube about 20 centimeters long or an aluminum wire of equal length is fixed in the middle, the ends of which are fitted with a paper fin [103]; to balance the system, an iron nail of sufficient weight is placed below the float, with a quadrangular head and the corners of which have been carefully sharpened to a point to provide the least possible friction.

At the bottom and center of a circular glass vase, such as a jam jar, a small liqueur goblet, also made of smooth glass, is placed. The container is then filled with water to a suitable height, and the cork float just mentioned is placed on the surface of the water, so that the head of the nail is held in the small goblet, against the walls of which its corners will slide, preventing the surface float from obeying the attractive force of the container's edges.

Since this object is circular and moves in water, the work of friction can be considered zero, and it will respond with the utmost sensitivity to the propulsion of the external fluid (*fig. 55*).

A person who had the opportunity to use this little device told me that they could even eliminate the friction of the nail head against the inside of the small glass goblet by removing the small goblet itself. In this case, it annihilates the force of attraction exerted on the float by the edges of the container by raising the water level inside the container above its edges, creating a meniscus whose edge pushes the float back and forces it to remain in the center of the instrument. I was unable to achieve this requirement, and it is likely that there is a question of diameter that I was unable to study. In any case, I leave this detail for the reader's experimentation.

---

[103] Two straws or two aluminum wires can be used, which, in this case, are placed crosswise.

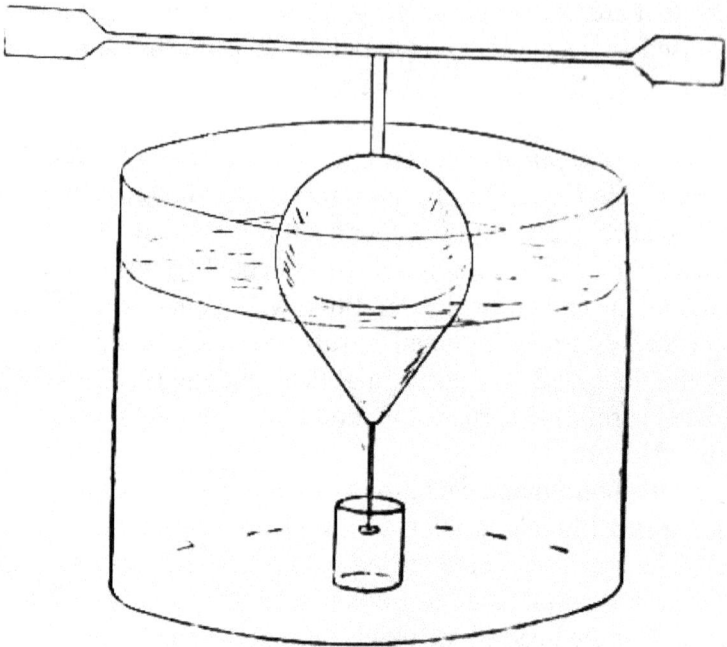

Fig. 55. — Float device.

I now turn to the simplest and perhaps most unknown device in existence.

— *The Paper Tourniquet.* A cork, a needle, and a sheet of cigarette paper are sufficient to set it up, and it can be improvised at anytime, anywhere, and in any circumstance.

An ordinary sewing needle is fixed vertically on a cork by the side of the eye. A sheet of cigarette paper is then folded twice on the same side, from opposite corner to opposite corner; the folds are then evened out so as to give the object as regular a shape as possible; finally, it is placed in perfect balance on the needle, in such a way that the intersection of the two folds rests on the point of the needle. This produces an object that is extremely light and mobile, therefore capable of feeling all the currents that may influence it, and, naturally, the currents of attraction or repulsion emitted by the fingers. It is used under the same conditions as similar instruments; but it goes without saying that, from the point of view of precision, such an instrument is most defective, since the slightest breath, the simple agitation of the air caused by the operator's breathing, is enough to move it and consequently to distort the results it is designed to present. We are not even sure, unless the external temperature is exactly 37° C, that is, that of the human body, that its movements are not influenced by heat radiation; but ultimately, from this point of view, it presents the same drawbacks as the vast majority of other devices.

As it is, nevertheless, it can be useful, provided that it is supplemented, from time to time, by the use of another, more precise instrument. Such are, at present, the devices used for the measurement of psychic force. As each of them applies better to one individual than another, and is more appropriate for certain organisms, it is up to each experimenter to conduct the necessary tests to acquire the device that will give them a daily approximate measurement of the exteriorization of their neurological strength; because it is necessary to keep abreast of the progress made in the neurodevelopment of the body, as will be explained in the following chapter; it is, in fact, very imprudent to undergo any training without carefully monitoring its progress, so as to guard against any possible accident.

In any case, and whatever device is adopted, it will be good, from time to time, to keep abreast of one's own biometric figures by using, at least incidentally, the Baraduc biometer, for it is the only instrument scientifically established on precise bases for measuring the repulsion of the right hand and the attraction of the left hand. All the other devices examined above are fairly conclusive with regard to the right hand (which is, in short, the main side to follow, since it is this side that primarily exteriorizes neural force), but very imprecise with regard to the left hand, for which some of them alternately show, and without any well-defined cause, attraction or repulsion for the same organism: there must be a particular law here whose details we do not yet know.

We will now consider the method of training appropriate for bringing about the exteriorization of the astral body.

C) *Mode of action*

The astral body being primarily composed of neurological force, and neurological force being the force that man primarily exteriorizes, this amounts to saying that increasing neurological force is both energizing the astral body and facilitating its exteriorization.

Therefore, we must say a few words about temperaments, which are too often confused with character [104] and which I will define as: Physiological states determined by the predominance of an element, organ, or system.

To avoid any misunderstanding, I will explain later what physiology understands today by temperament; but for now, and in order to be better understood by the reader, I will retain the meaning of this term in everyday language, because the old notion of temperament has survived the advances in biology, physiology, and psychology.

So, in common parlance, temperaments are divided into four main classes: lymphatic, sanguine, bilious, nervous — although some physiologists deny the existence of the bilious temperament, which they regard simply as the beginning of a pathological condition of the liver.

1. LYMPHATIC TEMPERAMENT. — Lymph, which dominates in this temperament, is the transparent, salty, highly coagulable liquid, containing leukocytes whose role is to expel, as it were, or neutralize, all hostile elements that can enter the body. The lymphatic system, therefore, lives primarily, if one can express it that way, within its own interior. It exhibits a remarkable ability to resist harmful external influences, but, consequently, is not capable of exteriorizing itself.

---

[104] Temperament constitutes the dynamic value of an organism, and character is its psychological translation; character is, in a way, a function of temperament.

2. SANGUINE TEMPERAMENT. — Blood, which is the characteristic of this temperament, is the basis of physical strength; this means that, in individuals endowed with this temperament, material forces predominate over astral or psychic forces, and that, for them too, exteriorization is not easy.

3. BILIOUS TEMPERAMENT. — Bile serves the assimilation of nutrients by completing the transformation of fatty substances and liquefying nitrogenous bodies: it is therefore a general factor of a force that can take both the sanguine and nervous forms; as such, it aids in out-of-body experience, and individuals endowed with this temperament can exteriorize themselves more easily than the preceding ones, but they are more apt, in principle, to passively experience psychic phenomena than to actively produce them. From the special point of view that concerns us, a bilious person will be a good receptive subject rather than a good experimenter.

4. NERVOUS TEMPERAMENT. — Since nervous force is the principal element of the *aérosôme*, it follows that the nervous temperament is truly that which suits the operator: it is therefore the organism's neurosity that must be developed above all.

One observation should be made: since the exteriorization of the astral body is the result of a deliberate imbalance, it follows that, to achieve this goal, it is better to emit a lesser quantity of neuric force that is not replaced in the organism by the recovery of external force, rather than to exteriorize a torrent of nervous fluid that would immediately be counterbalanced by the entry into the astral organism of an equal quantity of external forces. It follows that the subject presenting the very balanced biometric formula A 60° / R 60° will be much less able to split himself than one whose formula is, for example, A 10° / R 50°.

From all of the above, it follows that, from the point of view of psychic experimentation, the pure lymphatic is susceptible to almost no phenomena, but, on the other hand, is completely immune to hallucinations; the sanguine will be exposed above all to subjective and objective hallucinations; the bilious will be more able to observe objective phenomena, and the nervous will be able to produce them while being subject to objective hallucinations.

[105] Hence, in our case, two classes of temperaments: the negative or passive (lymphatic and bilious) and the positive or active (sanguine and nervous). But it is quite rare to encounter the absolute temperament, that is, purely nervous, purely bilious, etc. Very generally, a temperament is of a composite order: sanguine-lymphatic, nervous-sanguine, etc., with often a marked predominance of one element over the other.

Under these conditions, these temperaments can be classified in the following order:

Nervous.
Nervous-bilious.
Bilious-nervous.
Nervous-sanguineous.
Sanguine-nervous.
Nervous-lymphatic.
Lymphatic-nervous.

Since the others are only susceptible to exceptional psychic manifestations, we do not note them.

The training effort must therefore be directed primarily toward modifying temperament in the nervous sense, following the processes we will examine later.

But first, we must precisely indicate the characteristics of each temperament, so that they can be recognized and distinguished from one another at first glance.

LYMPHATIC TEMPERAMENT. — Becquerel indicates the characteristics specific to lymphatic individuals as follows: fine red or blond hair; blue eyes; fine, white skin; underdeveloped hair; soft flesh; poorly colored mucous orifices; exaggerated volume of the nose, lips, and ears; altered teeth; reddish-brown cheeks; large hands and feet. Furthermore, according to Dr. L. Thomas, their muscular system is underdeveloped, their gait is nonchalant; they have poor resistance to fatigue, and sweat easily. A slight swelling of the ankles is frequently observed in the evening, especially in women. Finally, in these individuals, illnesses are persistent and tend to become chronic.

On the other hand, Dr. Leniez [106] says that subjects of this temperament are distinguished by their fine, white skin, blond hair, blue eyes, rounded, somewhat feminine shapes, soft tissue, slow movement, and general apathy. They appear to feel less keenly than others, and are usually very slow to make a decision. This temperament, which was believed to be based on the predominance of lymphatic tissue, is simply a function of slowed nutrition.

SANGUINE TEMPERAMENT. — The sanguine temperament is characterized by circulatory activity, the development of the capillary system, and the lively coloration of the skin and mucous membranes. It is the most hygienic and most conducive to health. Individuals with a sanguine temperament are generally endowed with developed muscular strength, broad intelligence and imagination; in them, illnesses give rise to a violent febrile reaction; they generally have a frank onset, well-defined symptoms, a regular gait, and frequently end in recovery. It is generally accepted that the sanguine temperament predisposes to hemorrhages and apoplexy, but this tendency is far from being proven (Dr. L. Thomas).

According to Dechambre, the sanguine temperament is characterized by an increase in blood mass and the proportional number of blood cells, by a more considerable development of the vascular system, and by the functional hyperactivity of the general and parenchymal capillaries. It almost inevitably leads to the predominance of nutritional functions over those of relationship. Sanguine people generally have rosy skin, a ruddy face, supple brown hair, a lively and cheerful countenance, and rounded and graceful figures. Their muscular strength is developed, their imagination ardent, their passions violent but fleeting, their character amiable and generous. Finally, it is noted that they are very inclined to the pleasures of love. Henri IV and Mirabeau are said to be types of the sanguine temperament.

---

[105] M. Decrespe, *Research on the Conditions of Personal Experimentation in Physio-Psychology* (1 br. in-12, Paris, 1896), an excellent study from which I will subsequently borrow more than once.
[106] *Temperaments*, by Dr. Leniez, 2nd Class Medical Officer at Saint-Cyr, in the *Bulletin of the French Military Medical Society*. Issue of April 1, 1909.

BILIOUS TEMPERAMENT. — As mentioned above, a number of physiologists deny the existence of bilious temperament, which they consider a pathological condition denoting the onset of a liver disorder. Nevertheless, here are the main characteristics attributed to this temperament: dark, slightly yellowish skin tone; black hair; abundant body hair; vigorous muscles; rugged, not overweight features; strong bone structure; easy digestion; developed intelligence; firm, decisive, persevering character; ambition and stubbornness (Dr. L. Thomas). The skin is more or less dark brown, the body hair is abundant and strongly colored black, and the eyes, also black, complement the strong facial features, giving the face a character that is both intelligent and firm.

Individuals of this temperament, writes Adelon, generally have great capacity, their feelings and passions are intense and lasting; their determinations are strong, bold, and pursued with unfailing perseverance; they are distinguished by great ambition and by an equally great stubbornness in satisfying it. It is above all the characteristics of this temperament that are exhibited by the greatest men who have honored humanity by the elevation of their character and those who have devastated it by their unbridled ambition. And he gives as examples of this temperament Alexander the Great, Julius Caesar, Tsar Peter, and Napoleon.

NERVOUS TEMPERAMENT. — It is difficult to give precise characteristics to the nervous temperament; it is characterized, says Fleury, by irregular functions, exaggerated mobility and excitability of the nervous system. In nervous people, the muscles are generally slender, movements abrupt and jerky; the imagination is ardent, the passions violent, but they arise suddenly and fade away in the same way; the intelligence is lively, but incapable of long-held attention; sensitivity is exaggerated; they fear pain and exaggerate it when they feel it. The nervous temperament exerts a remarkable influence on most illnesses; it causes innervation disorders that are more apparent than real. Nervous people are subject to a large number of conditions such as neuralgia, gastralgia, hysteria, hypochondria, mania, etc.

Adelon — but in this he introduces a new confusion between temperament and character — finds that with an intelligence that can rise to the highest point, these nervous temperaments exhibit all the grandeur and misery of human moral character, sometimes combining nobility, dignity, love of humanity with susceptibility, fear of ridicule, envy, hatred, cruelty, and the deepest misanthropy. Here then, says Dr. Leniez, is a so-called nervous temperament, based, moreover, on thinness and muscular weakness. It is obviously the cause of this thinness and weakness that constitutes this temperament, and it is difficult to understand why it was called a nervous temperament, for it is nothing other than a psychic meaning that served as the basis for the classification. For him, in summary, the characteristic that has been attempted to be established amounts to a temperament of chronic intoxication, which is the part of organisms that are poor at eliminating waste products.

Before going any further, it is appropriate to explain here what temperaments actually are, according to the conception of current physiology.

The terms — bilious — nervous — lymphatic — sanguine — are only a relic of old humorist theories that are no longer current in our time, where they have been replaced by biological and, above all, physio-psychological theories.

Currently, there is a tendency to consider temperament only from the point of view of nutrition and elimination, which gives rise to the classification of three temperaments which are:
1. The temperament of balance of exchanges;
2. The temperament of incomplete elimination;
3. The temperament of insufficient nutrition.

This is the classification of temperament understood scientifically, and it has, as one can see, no connection with the one that has remained in common understanding.

I could, of course, have based myself on this classification, but there is some evidence that I would have been much more difficult for the reader to understand.

So, I return to the old-style temperaments, the data for which are more readily available to everyone, with the certainty that the reader will be grateful to me for it.

From a sexual point of view, the nervous-sanguine temperament is found mainly in men, and the nervous-lymphatic temperament most often in women.

From a professional point of view, we can classify in principle and with some exceptions:

Among the nervous: people of the world;

Among the lymphatic: clergymen and small income earners;

Among the sanguine: butchers and sportsmen.

And finally, among the bilious: small shopkeepers, small employees, failures, the unknown, the jealous, the coquettes, all those dominated by money or tortured by passion.

From the foregoing, it follows that, in order to provoke the exteriorization of nervous fluid at will, one must, when one is bilious, sanguine, and especially lymphatic, seek to become neurotic at least temporarily, and within a certain limit that the most elementary prudence urges one not to exceed, a limit that varies, moreover, with the resistance of one's organism.

Thus, a lymphatic patient suffering from congenital debility, a tubercular rickets, for example, should not rise above the biometric formula A 30°/R 30° to A 40°/R 40°, or another similar one; a nervous, unbalanced person should, on the contrary, aim to become calmer, more insensitive, so as not to risk losing their balance completely and seeing their nervousness become pathological neurosis, the slightest drawback of which, from the point of view that concerns us, would be to cloud their judgment and consequently distort the indications they believe they find in their physio-psychological experiments. It would therefore be *very imprudent* to undertake psychic training without a competent guide, unless one is perfectly familiar with one's own temperament and the rules of this training. In all cases, *it is essential to always remain absolute master of one's will* and to know exactly what one is doing: this is why the lymphatic temperament is infinitely valuable, because it protects, better than any other, from suggestion, hetero or auto-suggestion.

Before committing to developing one's own neuritis, one should bring one's temperament back to normal by eliminating any incidental causes of disorder it may contain. To this end, a vegetarian diet and the following rule of life are recommended, which should be adhered to for about a week.

PREPARATORY REGIME

DIET: Light vegetables, green vegetables, barley, oatmeal, rice, semolina, tapioca, salad.

SEASONINGS: Oil, butter, and fat.

BEVERAGE: Red wine with plenty of water.

FORMAL ABSTENTION: Alcohol, beer, liqueurs, meats.

RECOMMENDED ABSTENTION: Sugar, milk, eggs, cheese, fish (those eaten should preferably be grilled and very lightly salted).

DIET: A sober, quiet, regular, animal-based life, as much as possible in the countryside, in solitude: seven hours of sleep at most on a hard, lightly covered bed. Upon rising, a cold shower or cold bath in running water. Light purgation at the beginning, middle, and end of this preparatory phase. Moderate exercise in the open air (without going outside if possible), walks in the garden. No worries or emotions. No futile pursuits.

This regimen should preferably be followed during the most favorable seasons, that is, in spring and autumn, especially in spring.

After about eight days of this regimen, rest for a few days, then follow the regimen designed to increase the body's neuritis.

Now, is it possible to modify temperament? Yes, under certain conditions and to a relative extent.

Temperament is the result of two causes, one that seems specific, innate, characterized from the birth of the individual, and which depends on their anatomical and physiological constitution; this cause, constitutional and organic, is beyond our control, and we can do nothing about it. [107] The other, perhaps dependent on the first, lies in the variety or species of performance and functioning of the human machine: it is the activity coefficient of organic exchanges; on this other cause, we have a real influence and can modify it to a certain extent through an appropriate regimen which, in this case, must naturally be directed towards the neurification of the organism.

---

[107] At least, this was the general opinion held until recently. Currently, psychophysiology teaches that certain processes can influence all parts of the body, even the most resistant. See on this subject the *Outlines of Voluntary Auto-suggestion* by Dr. Géraud-Bonnet, already cited.

This regimen should, in the most ordinary cases, be established as follows:

NERVOUS EXCITEMENT REGIME

DIET: Very restrained, light vegetables as above: milk, eggs.
BEVERAGE: Watered white wine.
FORMAL ABSTENTION: Fish and cheese.
DIET: Little sleep (five to six hours). Absolute chastity. Cold shower upon rising. Absorbing and gentle occupations; intellectual work; little manual work and, in this case, only patient work. Development of physical and moral sensitivity: meditations, reflections.
MORAL EXCITING AGENTS: Multiplied emotions, deep but not violent.
PHYSICAL EXCITING AGENTS: Rather static electrification. Dark colors (live in semi-darkness, go out at dusk and in the evening).
CHEMICAL EXCITING AGENTS: Coffee, incense, cola.
Stimulants should only be used at the end of the diet, as simple adjuvants, and their abuse is strongly discouraged. On the other hand, mild narcotics (tobacco, chloral, etc.) have no effect on the actual training, but their effect on the brain can only be detrimental in experiments where the primary goal is to maintain the fullness of one's intellectual faculties.

This definitive diet should last at least six weeks to two months to produce results. [108] If possible, it is a good idea to combine it with a high-altitude treatment (500 to 1,000 meters), but in a quiet environment, that is far from any casinos or social gatherings.

The above regimen is applicable in the majority of cases; but if the temperament to be modified has too strong a predominance of lymphatism, going as far as weakness, or, to return to the question at hand, is too devoid of neuritis, it is advisable to first use the intensive and very detailed regimen that follows.

---

[108] During this time, an electric belt with a moderate current can be worn, so as to excite the nerves without causing irritation.

This treatment includes:

1. DIET: Bread, eggs, fish, meat, fats (butter, grease).
Flavorful foods rich in legumes, potatoes, beans, peas, and lentils, and a fair amount of salt. From a *medicinal* point of view, the main bases to consider are bromine, iodine, and especially arsenic.

2. VENTILATION AND CLIMATE: Outdoor living. Plenty of sunlight. Marine climate (superior in effectiveness to mountain climates).
Sea air is excellent, firstly for its purity, and secondly for the respiratory stimulation it causes, increasing tissue oxidation and, consequently, enhancing the activity of nutrient exchanges. It is also a nervous system stimulant.

3. HYDROMINERAL TREATMENT: Sodium chloride waters are mainly used in baths, lotions, and showers (for example, Balaruc/Hérault) and especially Bourbon-l'Archambault/Allier, Bourbonne-les-Bains/Haute-Marne, which stimulate the nervous system.
Equally valuable from this point of view is the water from La Bourboule/Puy-de-Dôme, which contains, in roughly equal proportions, sodium chloride, sodium bicarbonate, and, above all, a certain amount of arsenic (28 milligrams per liter), and which is drunk, used in baths, and showers.
Similarly, strong sodium chloride waters, such as those from Dax and Salies-de-Béarn. Finally, a final variety of mineral waters used to combat lymphatism is represented by chlorinated-sulfur waters, such as: Amélie-les-Bains, Barèges, Cauterets, Challes, Luchon, Uriage.

4. NERVOUS STIMULATION: Nerve stimulation can hardly be achieved through medications; it must be sought primarily through psychological or physical means (see above): static electricity, aero and climatotherapy, and especially balneotherapy and hydrotherapy.
In these latter methods, it is the nervous action that, along with the cold, activates nutrition. Cold baths increase urea,

carbonic acid, and uric acid, i.e., activate organic combustion. This hydrotherapy will be used in the form of cold showers, cold baths, and Scottish showers.

5. MORAL, PHYSICAL, AND CHEMICAL EXCITING AGENTS, OCCUPATIONS, etc.: As above.

In all cases, whether using the ordinary regimen mentioned above or this intensive regimen, use Dr. Baraduc's biometer twice a day, upon rising and going to bed (if a third attempt can be added in the middle of the day, this will be even better), or at least one of the psychic measurement instruments mentioned above, each reading of which will be recorded in a diary.

Carefully take into account the information recorded in the *laboratory log*, which will also include: the number of meals, the quantity and nature of solid and liquid foods ingested at each meal; the number of hours of sleep, and the daily activities, with an indication of their duration; meteorological elements (temperature, electricity, humidity, barometric pressure, wind, etc., are natural physical stimulants of the body), the nature, method, and duration of application of artificial stimulants, as well as the effect they produce, etc. Physiological observations should also not be forgotten: pulse rate and regularity, respiratory rate, body weight, skin color and temperature, appearance of the tongue, face, mucous membranes, suppleness and dryness of hair and beard, dynamometric tests, etc. — Above all, carefully note any pathological symptoms: migraines, torpor, insomnia, gastric disturbances, constipation or diarrhea, etc., and, if these indications diagnose excessive fatigue, *do not hesitate to immediately stop the diet*. It is better to postpone the experiment or even abandon it completely than to risk damaging your body.

It should be noted that this regimen is primarily intended for adults in the prime of life; it is therefore not suitable for incompletely formed young people (up to 22 or 24 years old), nor for men who are beginning to decline (45 to 50 years old), nor especially for women whose organic delicacy could be seriously affected.

When all the observations just discussed agree to demonstrate that neurological development is occurring, then, and only then, can stimulants be used, but, I repeat, only as adjuvants and not as a basis for training. In all cases, none of the stimulants used should have any effect on the brain. Then, the final push will occur, and you can proceed with the exteriorization of your astral body.

Does this mean that you will then be master of your astral outings? It would be a grave error to believe this; you will have in hand only the necessary tool, the instrument of your exteriorization; you can dissociate yourself, but you still do not know how to direct your exteriorized phantom, nor make it perform a particular act, nor retain the memory of those it has performed, etc. You are, in a word, in the situation of a child who, wanting to take a boat ride, has managed to jump into a boat moored at the quayside, but lacks the key to the lock to sail away, the oars and sails to navigate, and the rudder to steer. All this — direction, action, memory — is a matter of will, but it is also, above all, a matter of practice; and only when this study addresses practice will I be able to say how one can achieve these *desires*. What should be made clear from the outset is that the attempts, before achieving complete self-mastery, will last — apart from extremely rare exceptions — months, and perhaps years.

There are certainly other methods for achieving a kind of personal splitting, but I absolutely advise against them, some because they are too violent and attack the brain (opium, morphine, etc.)[109] , others because they take away your free will and your will (hypnotism, etc.), and both because, while they quickly lead you to splitting, they destroy all self-control once this splitting takes place, and therefore run counter to the ultimate goal.

It can be said with certainty that anyone who resorts to such means can only achieve an incomplete exteriorization — either because they cannot manifest themselves objectively, or because consciousness is abolished within them, or finally because their will, their very personality, are no longer theirs. By using these methods, they will either mark time in place, destroying their material organism (opium smokers), or they will become nothing more than a *thing* in the hands of their guide (hypnotic subjects); in any case, they prevent themselves from going further, higher, by taking their consciousness with them.

Moreover, there are still other means that facilitate the exit of the astral body, but which I also advise against, although for entirely different reasons: they have not yet been studied, or have not been studied sufficiently to allow us to know what to do with them. Among these, I would point out to researchers — but only to researchers endowed with knowledge of the subject and not to the first amateur who comes along — the use of electricity. There is, I believe, a fruitful path to follow in this direction by developing and applying to the complete out-of-body experience of the human being the principle by which Dr. Baraduc facilitated his psychographic experiments using electric current: for these experiments, in short, constituted nothing other than a partial

---

[109] Among the psychic agents that undeniably produce out-of-body experiences and whose use I strongly advise against, firstly because they have a harmful influence on the body, and secondly because they very rarely leave the memory intact, is, first and foremost, chloroform.

Individuals, says Dr. Simonin, who are under the influence of anesthesia, when they retain the intelligence to realize it, believe they have a body of impalpable subtlety.

One of Dr. Isidore Bourdon's clients told him that, during the operation he had just undergone under the influence of chloroform, "it seemed as if a delicious breeze was pushing him through the spaces like a soul gently carried away by its guardian angel."

According to Dr. Sédillot, "The flesh may be crumpled, bruised, split, but the client doesn't feel it; his mind soars through unknown regions, crosses endless spaces, accomplishes in a few minutes the events of several years; or he is plunged into ecstasies and dreams often accompanied by a vivid feeling of well-being and happiness."

Fletwood Cromwell Warley, the inventor of transatlantic cables, recounts that, having used chloroform one evening to soothe a sore throat that was causing him insomnia, he fell into a deep sleep, and saw himself, shortly afterward, with his fluidic body, outside his material body, which was deeply asleep.

Captain Volpi made a similar observation. "Six years ago," he wrote in 1889, "I inhaled some to deaden the spasms that would be caused by the extraction of a stone; I then realized with astonishment that my *Ego*, that is, my soul and my thinking reason, clothed in corporeal form, were two meters from my body; consequently, my *Ego* was outside my organs. It saw, stretched out and motionless on the bed, my body, to which it imbued movement and life."

Captain Volpi spoke of this sensation to several doctors who told him they had heard similar things expressed, though with less clarity, by patients they had chloroformed. "My patients have often told me," said one of them, "that during my operations they had not suffered, but that they had watched everything I did like spectators watching operations performed on other individuals" (*Successive Lives*, by A. de ROCHAS, 1 vol. in-8, Paris, 1911).

exteriorization of psychoneuric force; and, by properly applying their principle, it seems to me that one should succeed in greatly facilitating the total exteriorization of the *aérosôme*.

Whatever technique is used, the *sarcosôme* must *always* be placed in relation to the negative pole of the current, and the point toward which the *aérosôme* is to be released in relation to the positive pole. Numerous experiments have indeed proven that electricity repels exteriorized fluidic bodies, while positive electricity attracts them.

Moreover, it seems established that high-frequency currents are powerful generators of neuro-psychic force; consequently, it appears that the prior application of electricity in this form could only aid the success of the subsequent experiment.

A few lines above, I advised against the use of hypnotism; the same is not true of magnetism. Certainly, and for the same reasons I explained when discussing hypnotism, I am opposed to the complete magnetization of the operator, who must *never* expose himself to losing consciousness; but it seems to me that certain procedures (for example, insufflation into the pit of the stomach, mouth-to-mouth vital breath, etc.) performed by a strong and powerful magnetizer could only be good adjuvants for subsequent splitting. Finally, I would like to point out — but still only to researchers — the possible use of the Jansé *multiplier*.

This device has until now only been applied to land prospectors and baguetters, for the search for underground water tables and metal deposits. Without going so far as to specify and say, like its inventor, that this instrument increases fluidic forces in the proportion of 1 to 26, it does seem that it helps their production and accumulation in the individual to whom it is applied: there would therefore be some interest in knowing whether it could not be used in the case in question.

CHAPTER VIII

CAPTURING HYPERPHYSICAL FORCES

(Exclusively for
those who know)

Up to the point this study has reached, we have only been concerned with the development of two forces that everyone recognizes as existing within themselves: will and neuritis. In this, I have kept within the limits of normal science; and, in practice, it is appropriate to consider that the use of these two forces combined must lead to the realization of the phenomenon of personal out-of-body experience. Several practitioners whose experiments I have followed have gone no further in theory, and, in practice, have achieved certain results.

But it is nonetheless true that, on the one hand, these methods may not be sufficient for everyone, and on the other hand, those experimenters for whom they were sufficient could have, by adding other training procedures, either acquired this supernormal faculty more quickly or achieved superior results in its exercise and applications. In any case, this foray into the realm of occult science had to be made, and this chapter had to be written. I will be left to ask the proponents of official science who would leaf through this volume — probably with a disdainful and distracted finger — to skip these few pages, which are intended only for the initiated, and which the nature — and I would say almost the absolute — of their previous studies will prevent them from understanding much, for here we are about to enter into this science which is almost unknown to the West, and which Eastern initiation calls YOGA.

Although I intend to write here on a somewhat abstract subject, I will make every effort to be as clear and comprehensible as I have tried to be so far.

I will first take the reader back a little by reminding them that the physical body is a triple support comprising the material organism, the astral body, and the mental body (to which the higher principles of being are joined) or, to refer to the simpler and better-known spiritist theory, the *sarcosôme*, the *périsprit*, and the spirit. The physical body therefore possesses three centers of activity, each of which has its own specific domain:

1. The principle of instincts, a completely physical principle, which has its domain in the abdomen.

2. The principle of feelings and astral forces, which has its domain in the chest, [110] with the cardiac plexus as its center.

3. The principle of the mind and spiritual forces, which has its domain in the head. [111]

To separate the second principle — and consequently the third that usually follows it — from the first, that is, to produce the unfolding of oneself, we have seen that it is necessary to act above all on the astral body by training its principal constitutive force, neuricity, and on the mental body by training its primordial faculty, will; but the neuric force alone does not constitute the astral body: it is only its basis, if one may express it thus, the most accessible to us since it derives from the *sarcosôme* over which we have complete power; but the will does not constitute, on its own, the mental body of which it is, so to speak, only a property; There are therefore, in these two higher principles, the *aérosôme* and the spirit, other forces that, by certain processes, we can energize, and whose increase, it goes without saying, will facilitate the dissociation of the individual.

Hence, this chapter is divided into two parts: the absorption of astral forces and the assimilation of mental forces, the operations of which will ultimately greatly increase the energy of the higher part of the organism, which must be separated from the grossly material part.

---

[110] And particularly in the lungs.
[111] Dr. ENCAUSSE, *Reincarnation*, 1 vol. in-12, Paris, S. D. (1912).

A) *Absorption of astral forces*

Like the material organism, the astral body possesses its own Energies and particular weaknesses. While the physical body suffers in an apparatus or system, for example, when an individual is subject to heart problems or suffers from arteriosclerosis, the *aérosôme* is also subject to certain weaknesses, for while its quasi-material basis is constituted by neurological force, it is actually composed of different types of fluids, that is, force-substances whose lowering below a certain average can create in it states comparable to the pathological states of the *sarcosôme*. These are, in fact, true illnesses whose repercussions on the physical body create certain morbid conditions that are the despair of medicine; for while current materialistic science can, to a certain extent, protect the organism against this kind of contamination, it is powerless against the disease once it has manifested. I will cite as examples cancer and gangrene, [112] whose physical manifestations, that is, their effects, it merely treats — unnecessarily, moreover — without knowing how to trace the cause, which is an imbalance in the *aérosôme*.

Thus, this *aérosôme* is not composed solely of neurological force but also of force-substances, of fluids, some of which it draws — the most immaterial — directly from its astral environment and others of which arrive transformed by the organic work of the physical body. Indeed, the astral plane obviously includes, like the physical plane, a certain number of sub-planes (without us yet knowing how to distinguish them), each of which possesses its own particular fluids and energies. In the astral plane, the astral body must, obviously, behave like the material body on the physical plane; but, for the latter, what do we see? It is a composite of elements borrowed from each of the seven sub-planes of the physical plane, which correspond to different states of matter and which are:

---

[112] Cancer is a disease originating in the astral body, which is transmitted to the physical body, where it undergoes a material evolution in conjunction with its astral evolution. — Gangrene is a disease of physical origin, but whose vehicle is the astral body, which transmits it from the contaminated parts, after their detachment, to the healthy parts.

1. under the solid plane;
2. under the liquid plane;
3. under the gaseous plane;
4. under the radiant plane;
5. under the molecular plane;
6. under the etheric plane;
7. under the atomic plane.

Just as, in the *sarcosôme*, one can increase or decrease the proportion of this or that element, so too, the *aérosôme* is capable of receiving a greater or lesser influx of either quintessential fluidic forces or fluids approaching more or less the material essence. To aid in capturing the former, we must have some power, but we still do not know how to exercise this power, and we are forced, in this regard, to let the *aérosôme* act on its own. But as for the latter, I mean the astral forces which, drawn from the astral plane by the *sarcosôme*, reach the astral body through the intermediary of this same *sarcosôme*, we have an influence on the process of their assimilation, and we can, at our discretion, increase or decrease their quantity, I would even say raise or lower their quality.
Since the *aérosôme*, I repeat, is not composed solely of neurotic force, it is utterly obvious that if we succeed in giving it an increase in astral forces superior to neurotic force, its own energy, that is, its faculty of dissociation, will increase accordingly.
I will therefore study here how we can capture, in some way, these astral forces to transmit them to the astral body.

We have just seen that the center of astral forces in the human organism is located in the thorax and especially in the lungs. This shows us that it is breathing that connects us with the astral plane; and, indeed, it is with the newborn's first breath that the astral body takes possession of its newly hatched organism, while, from conception, the etheric double emanating from the father with the spermatozoon directs the evolution of the embryo.

We must therefore here concern ourselves with respiration, with the way in which it is used, and with the manner in which, through respiration, man can absorb and assimilate as much as possible of the astral energies. As this will be the main subject of this chapter, I will say a few preliminary and general words about it here; later, I will study it from the specific point of view that concerns us.

To proceed in order, we must first give some rather unknown notions about the lungs.

Mathias Duval tells us, [113] according to Kuss, that the total surface area of the pulmonary alveoli is equivalent to 200 square meters; it follows that the capillary vessels form a layer of 150 square meters. [114] This layer is very thin and is barely the thickness of a blood cell. It nevertheless results in a volume of blood roughly equal to one or two liters. It has also been calculated that in 24 hours, 15,000 to 20,000 liters of blood pass through it: [115] this layer of blood is therefore constantly renewed. These figures are important because they already allow us to predict the magnitude of the gaseous exchanges that take place between the blood and the air masses placed in contact with it, since they are separated only by the thin wall of the capillaries and a very thin epithelium. We must therefore study the mechanism by which the outside air is brought into contact with the respiratory surface, and how it is renewed after gaseous diffusion has taken place between it and the blood. These phenomena are comparable in every way to digestion; but while the elements introduced into the digestive tract must, before being assimilated, undergo a large number of metamorphoses, the respiratory elements of the air are directly assimilated. The alveoli of the lung are very numerous; it has been calculated approximately that their number is 1,700 or 1,800 million.

In summary, respiration is an exchange between the organism and the atmosphere, but, from a purely mechanical point of view, it is far from being as simple a phenomenon as is believed. Here is what Dr. Smester [116] says on this subject:

"When respiration exceeds half a liter, which is *normal*, it is always voluntary or pathological.

"In either case, it is constantly done through the mouth and the nose, never through these two passages at the same time.

"When breathing is normal, that is, equal to half a liter, it obeys the same rule as deep breaths, whether voluntary or not.

---

[113] *Physiology Course.*
[114] These figures have been slightly modified by Marc Sée.
[115] This enormous figure helps us understand the crucial role of respiration in physiological phenomena.
[116] *On Respiration through the Mouth and Nose*, octavo, Paris, 1884.

"Through various experiments and observations, I have found that small breaths below normal are no exception to this rule. If one breathes through the nose while keeping the mouth open, during small breaths, the tongue presses against the pharyngeal opening, which it tightly closes. During the smallest breaths through the mouth, with the nostrils free, certain movements of the soft palate are observed; which remain exactly the same when the nostrils are tightly closed."

It now remains beyond doubt whether breathing occurs through the mouth alone or through the nose alone. Everything proves that it is impossible to breathe through both passages at the same time.

Until now, we have remained within the realm of normal physiology; we will, with E. Bose, enter the domain of Hindu Yoga.

We will go even further, says this author [117], by adding to Smester's conclusions that, "even in nasal breathing, very often, if not always, one never breathes through only one nostril at a time, either the right, solar respiration, or the left, lunar respiration." The fact is easy to observe: by pressing the index finger on one or the other nostril, one will see that one breathes completely freely through one, while inspiration must be forced through the other; therefore, by breathing through both nostrils, one can conclude that inspiration is only through the one that is completely free. These two modes of breathing take place in turn, and each have different influences.

It would take too long to present here the theories of solar and lunar respiration, which alternate with each other under certain external influences, such as oral and nasal breathing.

We see, in short, that there is not just one way of breathing, as the public thinks, for whom the entire operation is summed up as: inhalation of air, ingestion into the lungs, and exhalation. There is also daytime respiration and nighttime respiration, for it must not be believed that during sleep we breathe in the same way as when awake; masculine and feminine respiration, for men and women do not breathe in the same way; clavicular, costal, abdominal, and diaphragmatic respiration, depending on whether it is caused by a movement of the shoulders, ribs, abdomen, or diaphragm; long (active) breathing and short (passive) breathing, jerky breathing, panting, coughing, etc. [118], each of which has its own particular properties and influences. Finally, each of these breathing modes can be infinitely varied by the greater or lesser duration of the breathing pause.

The number of respiratory movements is 14 to 16 per minute for adults, and, since it is the need for oxygen that motivates inhalation, it can be said that the longer the breathing, the less frequent it is: per hour, a human absorbs an average of 2 liters of oxygen and expels 16 liters of carbonic acid. The Egyptians, in the antiquity of the sanctuaries [119], and the Hindus still today [120], have attributed the highest importance to the science of respiration, because it is through it that the material organism, while drawing the oxygen necessary for the lungs from the air, captures from the etheric sub-plane and the astral plane the forces necessary for the life of the double and the astral body.

Physiologically, respiration can be divided into five main types, which are:

1. Normal breathing in a state of rest.
2. Forced breathing (when shouting, coughing, yawning, sneezing, etc.)
3. Breathing during muscular exercises.
4. Breathing under the control of will or attention.
5. Breathing under the influence of yoga exercises.

It is mainly these last two types of breathing that we will have to deal with. Naturally, I will not go into all the details that the subject may entail: I will leave aside, for example, the study of the processes of retaining the breath for a few seconds, then a few minutes, then hours, and finally entire days, which ultimately produces anabiosis and allows yogis to allow themselves to be buried for months. [121]

I will only concern myself with what is the subject of this study, that is, the capture and assimilation of hyperphysical forces to combat the possible asthenia of the living ghost; I will even pass over in silence the various systems of bodily mortifications relating to food [122], clothing, temperature, etc., which the true Yogi forces himself to undergo in order to establish a more intimate relationship with the higher planes, by reducing matter and its influences within himself to the bare minimum: I will, in a word, stick to the common standard of a normal Westerner, as he commonly lives in our circles, and I will only consider what he can accomplish without any hindrance to the multiple occupations of existence in society.

High Hindu philosophy calls Yoga the set of sciences that apply to the *self*, as opposed to *Gupta-Vidya* or esoteric sciences that apply to the *Non-Self*; this means that there are several kinds of Yogas [123] which are, going back: *Hatha-Yoga* or physical yoga; *Yoga-Bhakti*, or psychic yoga; *Râja-Yoga* or spiritual yoga; and finally *Laya-Yoga* which identifies the mind with physical sounds in such a way as to give the perception of the primordial, ineffable, and sacred sound AUM of the eternal *Logos*. I will deal initially only with Hatha-Yoga, speaking of the others only as necessary; in the last division of this chapter, *Râja-Yoga* will be dealt with more specifically.

Hatha-Yoga, says E. Bosc de Vèze [124], is a Hindu method that consists of subjugating one's personality and physical body in order to increase, to a certain extent, one's powers over the body itself and its environment; *Hatha-Yoga*, in a word, is a realization of the union between the physical and the astral, as its name indicates. This method deals exclusively with the will without

---

[117] *The Book of Breathing*, 1v. in-12, Paris, 1905.

[118] To these various modes of breathing, we can add cutaneous breathing, which we do not need to address here.

[119] *The Book of Breathing*, translated by J. de Harrock, Papyrus du Louvre, no. 3284.

[120] Currently, *Prânayama* (the practice of deep breathing) is the basis of all yoga.

[121] The Hindus are not alone in achieving these results, so prodigious that it is hard to believe them. I will cite, in particular, Colonel Thownsend in England, who, after a long stay in India where he had become accustomed to the meticulous practices of Yoga, succeeded in stopping, at will, the movement of the heart and arteries, in dying and reviving at will, in a word, in practicing all the phenomena of the Samadhi of the Yogis.

[122] However, I will draw attention to one important point: it is generally advisable to avoid heavy foods and prolonged meals; in short, anything that causes fatigue to the stomach would cause the nervous forces to converge on this organ instead of leaving them free.

Furthermore, a diet, not strictly vegetarian but based on plant matter, will significantly facilitate the practice of the exercises discussed later.

[123] Literally *union*.

[124] *Treatise on Yoga*, 1 vol., octavo. Paris, S. D. (191.0).

concern for the moral. [125] The principles on which it is based, which serve as its foundation, we might say, are those very ones that govern the elements of the lower planes of nature, and whose specifications can be found in all theosophical treatises; this is why we do not believe it useful to enumerate them here. The processes used in *Hatha Yoga* consist of extensive internal and external ablutions, and frequent and gradual application of the will to the various organs of the body, principally to the respiratory organs, in order to achieve, over time, the most perfect control of the physical organism. When the desired result is achieved, the *Yogi* can at will *abstract himself* from the surrounding environment, *free himself from his physical body*, and, just as his astral has been organized and transformed following the trials and long efforts of his will, the Yogi has the faculty and power to act on the astral plane, even to link the two neighboring consciousness's, and to operate as on the astral plane, within his physical body itself.

To study Yoga practically, two types of processes must be practiced simultaneously: mental processes and material processes; the first are summed up in meditation, and the others in the way of sleeping and breathing: we will say a few words about these processes.

1. *Meditation.*

At first glance, nothing seems simpler than meditation: in practice, it is very difficult to keep one's mind fixed on a single object for long enough to study all its details.

Many people replace meditation with reading: the two things have no connection, in the sense that one reads with more or less attention, but one can only meditate with sustained attention. And yet, says E. Bosc de Vèze, one cannot train oneself too much in this exercise of thought by which one manages to fix one's thoughts on an idea, to analyze it, to study it, to consider it from all its aspects, and then to compare it with other ideas of the same kind or of a different order, according to the case that presents itself to the mind. It is in meditation that lies the secret of noble

---

[125] Also, developed in a certain sense, it leads to black magic.

and powerful ideas, of those that know no defeat; it is finally through meditation that one can support the soul in its trials, in its aspirations, in its impulses toward the ideal, toward infinity, toward the Absolute, or God... Through meditation alone, the mind learns to free itself from the disturbing atmosphere that surrounds it; it is through meditation that the human soul rises above the petty concerns of daily life, and that it can, under these conditions, remain entirely devoted to its reflections and devote itself completely to the object of its reflections without being distracted by any passing thought, foreign to the idea of its meditation.

It is only then, when it has acquired control over its ideas, that man is truly the master of its thoughts and can practice perfect meditation.

Now, in this as in everything, there is a path that must be followed if one does not want to go astray. It is obvious that, in the case at hand, the object of meditation must be the study of the conditions for personal out-of-body experience; but it would be a mistake to approach such a subject without any preparation. Let us therefore follow the path indicated by Eastern instructions.

We must first train ourselves by using external objects. This is understandable. It is, in fact, much easier to reflect for a certain time on an object, an objective image that we have before our eyes, than on any abstract idea. We can consider the external object as a magnet, which attracts our thoughts, retains them, and fixes them, just as iron is attracted, retained, and fixed by this magnet. Although the effort required is still considerable, it is less painful when considering this external object, visible, graspable, palpable.

Let us therefore try meditation before practicing yoga, and make every effort to think and meditate; Let us compare one external object to another; let us study what differentiates them; let us analyze, dissect these objects from each other; and when we have practiced this exercise for a long time, we will begin to know how to think, how to meditate, for, as we like to repeat, meditation is a profound teaching that prepares us for the practice of Yoga, and which leads us to know how to pray, a teaching that nothing can replace.

Meditation shows us, among other things, how little control we have over ourselves in the pursuit of a thought; how difficult it is for us to delve into a single subject. We have no sooner fixed our mind on one idea than another, arriving, drives out the first, and successively, other new ones take possession of our minds.

We must not allow ourselves to be led by these vagabond travelers, who leave, arrive, appear in turn with disconcerting nonchalance, who impose themselves and disappear in spite of us, whether we want it or not, and of whom, in fact, we who should be their master, are only the submissive slave.

In summary, the practice of meditation, as it concerns us, must begin by focusing on material objects, at first simply any kind, then on others related to the goal pursued, for example, the images contained in this work, objects intended to measure neuro-psychic strength, or the plates representing out-of-body experiences; after which, when the strength of meditation is sufficient, thought must focus on the study of all the processes that we detail here, with a view to training any of the forces that contribute to producing the phenomenon, and finally on the whole experience.

It might be thought that what is said here about meditation would be better placed later, when we will be dealing with mental forces. Certainly, we will then have to return to this; but it was necessary to say a few words about it here, for, just as the moral and physical aspects of man have hidden but undeniable relationships, and the health of one influences that of the other, so the mental body and the astral body, in man, are united by bonds that are easier to observe than to describe, and the forces of one consequently react on those of the other. The subjects of meditation that have just been proposed to the reader are intended for the production of forces reacting on the astral organism: later, we will have to indicate others more specifically suited to strengthening the mind.

2. *Sleep.*

I will say little here about sleep, which has already been studied in the chapter devoted to the will, and I will only speak of it enough to draw attention to a few details that are useful to know.

Sleep, as I have said elsewhere, is a period of rest for the organs of relation, and on the contrary of redoubled activity for the internal and passive forces of the organism.

The duration of sleep varies according to the age, sex, and strength of each individual; it can be said, in general, that women need less sleep than men, and that this need diminishes with age. It can be established that the average for a healthy adult male is about seven or eight hours a day. The person who wishes to practice the experience of personal out-of-body experience must strive to obtain sleep that is always equal in depth and duration. The best way to achieve this is to lead a life perfectly regulated from a material point of view (meals, work, etc.), and as free as possible from worries, so that the individual's neurological system is in a perfect state of balance and can easily submit to the training discussed elsewhere. One can even gradually reduce the amount of food a man must ordinarily consume per day; but this reduction should especially affect the evening meal, even if one feels the need, to proportionally increase the food consumed at the morning meal.

It is also advisable, for this purpose, to sleep in a well-ventilated room, as an impure atmosphere tends to disturb and, consequently, prolong sleep.

Finally, let us remember, in view of what follows, that breathing is not the same during sleep as during waking; during this period, it operates more slowly and lasts about ten seconds.

In a word, one must strive to achieve that eminently restful, deep, and perfect degree of sleep, which the Hindus call *Sushupti*, where all thought, all sensation, all mental emotion ceases — where, consequently, the soul is freed from its earthly bonds, where even, according to Eastern doctrine, man is freed from all his faults.

3. Breathing.

I have already said a few words about the respiratory system and breathing in general: I will now deal with it from a special point of view; that is by considering it as the principal means of attaining, if not yoga as a whole, at least the degree of yogism necessary for what concerns us. I will therefore have to deal in detail of the main processes applicable to what we have been able to call the *Art of breathing*.

It seems *a priori*, says Dr. Lavrand [126], that the respiratory act is instinctive and that one can do without a master in such matters. The newborn, however, sometimes does not breathe; it needs an abnormal excitement to trigger the first inspiration [127]. Not all children and adults know how to breathe normally, that is, usefully and efficiently.

Education, even here, often proves necessary, and respiratory gymnastics imperatively requires the attention of the doctor and is increasingly entering into medical practice; but, says Colonel Amoros: "Gymnastics is the reasoned science of our movements, of their relationship with our senses, our intelligence, our feelings, our morals and the development of all our faculties" [128].

When we talk about respiratory gymnastics, we hear the reasoned, methodical exercise of a function, and its adaptation to a perfectly determined goal. According to Maurice Faure [129], "Many of us who have never learned to distinguish one movement from another, whose eye has not undergone that special education which only instructors of men and those whose own taste have driven them to the study of sports, will not see what multiple nuances separate the movement executed by the competent gymnast, of an identical movement performed by someone whose culture and training have not meticulously prepared them to understand and execute the healing gesture."

The act of breathing is of prime importance because it provides oxygen, the fuel that allows us to use ingested food by releasing the energy it contains [130]. This is the role of inspiration: this time must therefore be accomplished widely, fully, in order to provide as much air as possible. Its role also consists of ventilating all the pulmonary alveoli several times a day, leaving no dead or stagnant points. We thus have several meals of air during the day, practicing slow and deep inspirations methodically at set times.

---

[126] *Physical and mental rehabilitation*, 1 vol. In-12, Paris, 1909.
[127] The one by which the astral body takes up the new organism which, until then, was made up only by the material body and the etheric double.
[128] *Medical press*, 1908, n ° 29.
[129] quoted by GUERMONPREZ, *Respiratory gymnastics*.
[130] The physiologist sees in breathing only the absorption of oxygen considered to be fuel; The occultist sees it as the absorption of oxygen considered as the basis of astral, lower energies and as a vehicle of higher energies.

The second phase is represented by exhalation, which aims to rid the lungs of used air, laden with useless or even dangerous substances. The perfection with which it is performed precedes the next inhalation by preparing it and making room for it. It is therefore necessary to occasionally take deep, ample, and long breaths in and out if we want to ensure sufficient air supply to the body.

Even more: a full, ample, and regular breathing rhythm exerts a most favorable influence on the movements of the upper limbs, and also on the intensity of any effort: a well-developed thorax, possessing a large capacity and breathing amply, regularly, and deeply, allows the patient to make much more considerable efforts, and therefore much more effective ones, not to mention physical vigor, which reaches a higher degree in the subject who knows how to breathe.

In short, there must be no nasal insufficiency, no thoracic insufficiency, and no diaphragmatic insufficiency if one wants to achieve full breathing, because insufficiency can be due to anatomical causes, pathological causes, or even purely functional causes.

Rehabilitation aims to teach the patient that they can, and must, breathe better and more fully. Through repetition, the patient, once instructed in the proper way to perform their breathing movements, will become accustomed to them: what was initially conscious and willed will become automatic and unconscious, that is, habitual.

Technique. — To achieve this goal, slowly perform deep inhalations, followed by equally deep exhalations, on command, while counting aloud. Active, then passive movements of the arms, then the lower limbs, will be added, rhythmically and in time. The subject will stand upright, or lie on their back, or on their stomach; they will imitate swimming movements. The diaphragm will be exercised by pushing as if moving a heavy weight, maintaining each effort for a few seconds. Breathing must be nasal during these exercises, as this is what allows the thorax to expand to its maximum: it is, moreover, the only truly normal and physiological one. Elementary singing exercises, declamation, and well-directed reading aloud are excellent exercises. The wise clinician will elaborate endlessly on this pattern.

This is the process for achieving ideally normal breathing, that is, the breathing that must first be acquired because it is the indispensable basis for all other types of breathing; it is purely physiological, but when properly mastered and practiced commonly, normally, and effortlessly, it will allow one to try out the various types of yoga breathing with the help of which one can achieve more intimate communication with the higher planes, and especially with the astral.

Before discussing the higher processes of respiration, I must say a few words about its influence on the physical organism.

The movements of the heart, first of all, are directly dependent on the nervous system; now, the quantity of nerve impulses varies according to the composition of the blood: the physical and chemical actions that occur during the act of breathing therefore indirectly, by purifying the blood and modifying its condition, have a beneficial effect on the innervation of the heart. Furthermore, the increase in volume and the alternating collapse of the lungs, causing changes in the rib cage, act mechanically on the heart since it is contained within the thorax and is, so to speak, in immediate contact with the lungs. Consequently, regular and methodical breathing, performed under the control of the will, has the undeniable result of promoting the natural and normal functioning of the heart.

And let us not forget that the heart is the great regulator of blood circulation. Thus, the blood, purified on the one hand by a greater flow of oxygen to the lungs, will see its circulation increase under the movements of a more vigorous heart; and blood is the factor of the nervous force on which the astral body is based. We can therefore see how certain breathing processes can, through their judicious use, increase the energies specific to the astral body.

But there is more.

Rhythmic breathing, especially when deep, also beneficially influences the functions of the stomach and intestines. These organs, through the diaphragm and through variations in the extent of the base of the thorax, are subjected to a veritable massage and forced movements that facilitate their blood circulation, their movements, and the mixing and progression of the food materials they contain.

We thus see that everything depends on the mode of breathing, for what ultimately results from the work of the stomach and intestines? To the creation, through a series of physiological operations and reactions too long to describe here, to the creation of a new quantity of blood — this blood, the primary factor of neural strength.

Finally, we can add that when respiratory movements are performed with the intervention of a firm and energetic will, when they are executed methodically, consciously, regularly, and with amplitude, they have a reactive effect on the will and brain power, activated for their execution, and contribute to their growth.

After the above, it is easy to see the capital importance of breathing from the point of view that concerns us here.

Here is what Dr. Géraud-Bonnet of Oran has to say about it, who studied the use of breathing in voluntary auto-suggestion [131], that is, in a subject with which we ourselves have had to deal in these pages; he first analyzes the mechanism of slow and deep breathing.

It is necessary, he says, for the access of air, bringing the essential oxygen, to take place right up to the last bronchial branches, for the air to penetrate to the most distant alveoli. This result will be achieved all the better if the inspiration, which constitutes the first stage of breathing, is fuller, more powerful, and deeper: it must be long enough for the inspired air to have the opportunity to penetrate everywhere, as far as possible, and in sufficient quantity.

The second stage of breathing is formed by exhalation. Regardless of its intensity and duration, the bronchial cavities never empty completely, and they always retain a gaseous residue that is absolutely unsuitable for hematosis, or the transformation of venous blood into arterial blood.

This gaseous residue will be less the longer the exhalation; it will form a mixture with the atmospheric air introduced by the next inspiration, and it is this mixture that will come into contact with the venous blood for the exchanges intended to transform this venous blood into arterial blood.

It is obvious that this mixture will be all the more active the more new gas it contains, and in particular the more oxygen, which will depend on the greater quantity of air inhaled.

Now, an ordinary, natural, and effortless inhalation introduces on average half a liter of air.

A deep and forceful inhalation, taken under the influence of will, can reach three and a half liters. If a man takes eighteen breaths per minute (and many authors accept the figure as sixteen), he brings into his lungs a total volume of nine liters.

By taking slow, deep breaths, one can achieve only four per minute; even with this reduced number, but at a rate of three liters at a time, one obtains twelve liters. Consequently, deep and prolonged inspiration, sustained for a certain time, promotes the purification of the blood and contributes to increasing the vitality of the organism.

It is also good that the air and venous blood brought together have all the time necessary to carry out their exchanges; consequently, the exhalation movement should be delayed as long as possible; one should only exhale the stale air when the need to expel becomes imperative and almost irresistible.

Since this stale air must be expelled almost entirely, it must have time to escape, which requires that expiration be complete, until there is a general collapse of the pulmonary organs and total relaxation of the thorax.

All these physiological considerations lead us to the following conclusion: for the entire act of breathing to be performed in full and under the best conditions, for it to be truly beneficial, it is essential that the two stages of breathing and the intervals of apparent inaction that separate them each be as long as possible.

It follows from this that slow, deep breathing, pushed to its extreme limit, in its two alternating movements, is the ideal breathing, the one that should, theoretically, be performed constantly and out of habit.

But, as the cited author notes, this is not possible, given the maximum effort of the lungs, diaphragm, and thoracic muscles, and, moreover, the powerful intervention of conscious will, all causes that lead to a considerable expenditure of nervous energy, and consequently, fatigue. However, if the efforts required by this type of breathing can only be sustained for a limited period of time, one can at least increase the duration of this period through frequent and regular training.

The breathing pattern indicated above by Dr. Lavrand must become normal; it will always remain exceptional; but at least it is advisable to approximate it as closely as possible in everyday use; this can be achieved by the following procedures indicated by Dr. Géraud-Bonnet.

Make yourself comfortable, sitting or lying down, in a room where you are certain not to be disturbed, where outside noises are difficult to reach, and cannot distract you.

Relax your entire body and close your eyes as if you were going to sleep. Concentrate your thoughts on the action you are about to undertake, and use all the energy of your will to direct, govern, and execute it consistently and completely.

To maintain attention and avoid acting automatically and unconsciously, you can force yourself to count the number of complete breaths as you complete them; after the first, count *one*; after the second, *two*; and so on.

Breathe through your nose; do not breathe through your mouth. The nose is the first organ of the respiratory system: it is through it that air should always pass before reaching the lungs.
[132]

Inhale slowly, very slowly, and pull it all the way out, until your chest can no longer expand or inflate; make an effort to support this distension and swelling; then, expel the air little by little, imperceptibly, taking as long as possible. Force yourself again to resist the urge to inhale, and only begin a new inhalation when absolutely necessary.

This complete exercise must be repeated several times in a row.

At first, you will only be capable of a very limited number of breaths; but, with practice, you will be able to successfully complete it ten, fifty, sixty, or even more times.

---

[131] Summary of voluntary auto-suggestion, already cited.
[132] This corresponds perfectly to the theories of Hindu occultism which we will deal with later, and according to which each of the two nostrils controls a particular current of force, to the right and left of the spinal column.

You may also find yourself unable to complete it entirely from the beginning: a few medium breaths, of progressive intensity and duration, will be necessary first to allow air to penetrate the terminal alveoli and restore the permeability of certain small bronchi. However, these difficulties are only temporary and are easily overcome after a few attempts.

It is best to perform this exercise in a spacious, well-ventilated room with the window open. When it is possible to go outside in the fresh air, it is even preferable.

During the day, the most favorable times are those before lunch and dinner, when digestion is complete and the stomach and intestines are sparsely filled or empty. If your activities do not leave you enough leisure and if you cannot do better, do it in bed, in the morning before getting up, and in the evening before going to sleep.

When you have done the same exercise for several days in a row, you will soon recognize that it becomes easier, that it requires less and less effort, and, finally, you will perform it out of habit, without any apparent intervention of conscious will.

At this point, you can stop and suspend it, even if you start again later, if the result you are pursuing relates exclusively to the concentration of thought and the training of the will. For this special purpose, your exercise becomes useless from the moment that thought and will no longer play any part in it. For any exercise to be truly beneficial in this sense, it must be performed consciously and require a real effort of thought and will, however slight that effort may be. But you can continue it indefinitely if your intention is to exercise and strengthen your lungs.

You can combine slow, deep breathing with muscular movements such as lateral movements and elevations of the upper limbs.

Stand in front of an open window, or in the open air, with your arms hanging down, neck straight, and head held high.

As soon as you begin to inhale, slowly raise your arms, keeping them extended and straight; spread them away from your torso and position them so that they are horizontal or slightly above the horizontal at the moment you finish inhaling; keep them in this position while you stop breathing, then, lower them very slowly to the vertical position at the start, during the exhalation movement and the final rest.

This exercise strengthens certain muscles while strengthening the development of the rib cage. It can and should be repeated several times in a row. It has the slight disadvantage of dividing one's thoughts between two different objects: respiratory movements and limb movements, but it contributes powerfully to establishing the habit of deep and regular breathing.

The exercises can be varied by changing the posture and movements of the limbs, trunk, and head. It is easy to imagine a large number of different combinations; the simplest are sufficient in most cases.

Sometimes, especially for people who are accustomed to a sedentary and withdrawn life, and consequently to short and shallow breathing, they have some difficulty taking a very deep breath; they then experience, when their inspiration has reached its usual maximum, a feeling of discomfort and anxiety in the rib cage; it seems to them that they can no longer lift their chest and that their lungs are going to run out of air: this is only a minor inconvenience that can easily be eliminated by applying — which one can do oneself — a dry cupping glass to the side of the chest, at the height, or better, towards the base of the lungs.

Dr. Géraud-Bonnet, who, according to his aforementioned work, deals with breathing only from the perspective of voluntary auto-suggestion, also offers the following advice, which may, from this special perspective, be of great benefit to our readers.

"Physical and muscular exercises intended to train the will and develop self-confidence can also be used to make auto-suggestions. The same is true of those used for the concentration of thought.

"All these methods are good and applicable to the various eventualities for which they have been indicated; but I consider regular breathing movements, whether medium or deep, to be the best of all; they are always available to us; they lend themselves to all circumstances, and can be implemented at any time, in any place, and whatever the goal one sets for oneself.

"They produce multiple and general results because they simultaneously promote self-confidence, concentration of thought, and energy of the will. They can therefore be used advantageously for the practice of voluntary and personal auto-suggestion.

"Depending on the nature of the auto-suggestion, whether the idea to be instilled into the brain is simple or complicated, whether it is expressed by a single word or several, whether one is working on a single idea or a group of ideas, one can choose breathing movements of medium duration and intensity, or slower and deeper movements. This is a matter of intuition, convenience, or individual appreciation.

"The method of operation includes two main varieties.

"First, the auto-suggestion will be performed while the inhalation and exhalation movements are being performed; it will begin at the beginning of the inhalation, continue with it, continue during the exhalation, and end at the same time.

"Secondly, we will make an effort not to think of anything during the respiratory movements, and we will perform auto-suggestion at the end of the exhalation and during the rest that precedes it.

"We use both movements (inhalation and exhalation) when the idea can be subdivided: we only use the second phase (exhalation) which is the main one, when the idea is condensed into a single word."

Everything we have seen so far gives us the means to develop, through a well-understood mode of breathing, the neural energy that constitutes the force of the astral body closest to matter; but there are breathing processes that allow us, in a way, to capture and assimilate higher energies. The study of the theories would take us much too far; I will limit myself to giving practical indications, referring the reader curious about these theories to specialized works.

The method of Western magic is summarized by d'Alba [133] in four main exercises which must be practiced above all every day, in the morning before taking any food, that is to say, on a completely empty stomach.

A. — This breathing exercise — like the following ones, should be practiced by breathing through the nostrils, with the mouth completely closed; it should be performed slowly and outdoors, twice a day, on an empty stomach. It is divided into four steps:

    1. Inhale the air while mentally counting to five.

    2. Retain the air in the lungs while mentally counting to five.

    3. Exhale the air while mentally counting to five.

    4. Remain without air in the lungs while counting to five.

    This complete breath should last twenty seconds. As the pulmonary alveoli develop, and consequently, the organ of respiration, the rib cage will tend to expand.

    B. — 1. Stand upright with your arms hanging naturally; raise them sideways, while inhaling very slowly and counting to five.

    2. Keep your arms raised for the same amount of time, with your palms pressed together.

    3. Exhale in the same way, while returning your arms to their original position.

    4. Remain without air in your lungs.

    You can perform the same exercise with your arms outstretched.

    C. — 1. Stand in the correct position, then, gradually bending your knees, let yourself sit back on your heels while raising your arms laterally, bringing your palms together, and breathing deeply.

    2. Stay in this position, holding your breath.

    3. Stand up slowly while exhaling.

    D. — 1. Keep your right nostril closed by pressing your thumb on its side, then inhale air through the left while mentally counting to seven.

    2. Keep the air in your lungs while mentally counting to seven.

    3. Exhale air through your right nostril while keeping your left nostril closed and mentally counting to seven.

    4. Remain without breathing while mentally counting to seven.

This exercise can, after several months of practice, be increased to: 1. = 12; 2. = 20; 3. = 12; 4. = 20; but this result should not be rushed in any way.

This last exercise is obviously borrowed from the preliminary exercises of Yoga; we find it in Bosc de Vèze with the original numbers and the progression it includes; we give it here so that one can refer to it after having practiced it successfully as indicated by d'Alba.

One must inhale the air slowly, very slowly, through the left nostril, after having kept the right nostril closed with the finger, long enough to be able to mentally count up to 60... 1, 2, 3, 4, 5, etc. — After this exercise (when the inspired air is enclosed in the lungs), one must close both nostrils and keep them closed for a long enough time to be able to mentally count up to 1, 2, 3, 4, 5, etc., about two numbers per second. Then, one must slowly exhale the air through the right nostril, for a long enough time to be able to count 34 or 35. — This is the initial process in Prânayama (control of the breath). — Gradually, each day, the breathing exercise can be increased by 10 as a number thought, and one soon arrives at counting up to 50 and beyond. [134]

For this last teaching, there is, in my opinion, a distinction to be made.

The practice is very simple for Hindus who, from an early age, have been accustomed to mastering their breathing; it would be very difficult for a Westerner who has no notion of the science of breathing. We therefore believe that the best is to begin with the number, as d'Alba indicates; when one has mastered this breathing method, one can increase to 10, and, when this progression is acquired, successively increase to 15, 20, 25... without ever exceeding 60.

---

[133] *Elementary Treatise on Scientific Magic*, 1 br, in-8, Paris, S. D.

[134] The practice of this exercise must last at least six months; it will give, say the Yoga treatises, a great number of qualities, increase digestive power, greatly calm cerebral fatigue, and make the body luminous, but for seers first of all, which is not excessive, since seers perceive the colorations of the human aura; later, they affirm, after long practice, everyone will be able to see the luminosity of the student's body (?)

4. *The surrounding environment.*

To conclude the absorption of astral forces, it remains for us to expound on a particular theory, that of cosmic currents, which can be used for the subject at hand.

Normal science recognizes that our globe is not isolated in space. It is part of the Cosmos, to which it is connected by cosmic currents that carry undulations of forces known to us, in part, as electricity, light, heat, etc. Thus, there exist, circulating around and through the Earth, considerable currents going from north to south, penetrating all things. These magnetic currents are, for the most part, invisible; they manifest themselves materially in the form of the aurora borealis, zodiacal light, etc. Others become perceptible to our sight, under certain conditions, in laboratory experiments conducted using special tubes in which a vacuum has been created. The electrical corpuscles move with great speed, imparting considerable luminosity to the tube, as well as beautiful, velvety colors; this is what occurs in the Crookes tube. X-rays, radium, and all luminous materials are a manifestation, a proof of cosmic forces and currents of etheric force.

The ether currents flow from the north pole to the south pole in great bands of light, above and through the Earth. This unique force of space is attracted to the magnetic center of the Earth; it manifests itself in layers, in the form of vibrations, and these are related to the various densities of matter, which they pass through and set in motion.

The Earth is surrounded by several layers of a very pure and invisible, yet luminous, substance, forming the lower layers. Now, when the different regions of this matter are set in motion by a single force, they act as several forces.

The lower layers, being of different densities, consequently their atoms vibrate at different degrees, which means that the currents, composed of unequally vibrating matter, not only have a uniform forward movement, but they also have an *internal vibration that produces colors* as numerous and varied as the different degrees of vibration.

On the surface of the earth, all the ether currents are found together and intermingle so well that man, who is a universe in miniature, attracts to himself these forces which enter through his right side and carry his aura: when they have passed through his body, these forces exit partly through the left side, after having magnetized each atom of the body and brain by their vibrations.[135]

This theory of colored cosmic currents, an integral part of the teachings of ancient occultism, has been verified in our time by a number of independent researchers, notably by C. W. Leadbeater [136]. It can therefore be taken for granted, although normal science has not yet addressed it. [137]

I will not go into detail about the various colorations and their specific meanings; these details can be found in the aforementioned authors. I will simply say that animal forces are found in orange-colored currents, psychic forces in blue currents, [138] and mental forces in yellow currents.

Furthermore, we know that visualization is a means of inducing these currents. It is therefore sufficient, to induce any current to pass through our organism, to live in a similarly colored environment. As a result, one will acquire astral powers by living in the color of the astral substance, that is, in an apartment dominated by the light blue hue. [139]

I will say right away, so as not to have to return to this theory further, that mental powers will develop if one lives in a light yellow environment.

Finally, to avoid constantly changing the coloration of the environment, one can resort to a general combination of desired colors. In the case at hand, and to assimilate both astral and mental energies by bringing into oneself the appropriate cosmic currents, the most favorable general tonality of the environment should be white, light blue, and gold, with white bringing in all the neutral currents and the other colors specializing them.

In this environmental coloring, it is important to avoid all shades of orange, which only develop bodily forces, and especially green shades, which generate selfishness, [140] and red, which stir up passions. This is elementary, since anyone who wishes to acquire supernormal faculties must, before all else, kill selfishness within themselves and control their passions.

Moreover, one must not believe that this environmental coloring acts by itself: it only acts by induction. Indeed, the only true means of drawing a particular cosmic current into oneself is mental appeal; but, by itself, mental appeal is very fragile, and if the will is not carefully trained, it can become distracted by this appeal, while, on the other hand, it is very tiring to keep one's thoughts constantly fixed on the same object. The coloring of the atmosphere, by acting continuously on the sensory organ of sight, arouses mental visualization, and, consequently, the unconscious call of the special cosmic current.

This paragraph may seem superfluous to some readers; personally, I believe the breathing processes indicated above to be much more effective in achieving the desired goal; but, since the influence of colors on the organism now appears to be established, a few words had to be said here, if not as a purely theoretical indication of useful colorations, to at least allow experimenters to avoid harmful colorations.

B) *Assimilation of mental forces.*

Just as — as was said above — the moral reacts on the physical of man (and vice versa), so the mental body, which, in the exteriorizations of the living ghost, always accompanies the astral

---

[135] G. MANN, *Thought force*, 1 vol. in-8, Paris, 1910. – See also *The human soul, its movements, lights*, by Dr. H. BARADUC, 1 vol. in-8, Paris, 1897. – See finally *The Formation of Worlds*, by M. TURPIN (the inventor of melinite). For this author, it is solar energy which, projected onto the Earth in the form of a wave (light, heat, electricity), makes the Earth rotate and produces the Earth's magnetic current. This solar current induces a constant electric current around the Earth, from west to east, which makes the Earth a true solenoid rotating under the influence of the energy received, and not by its own force.
[136] *Thought-Forms*, 1 vol. in-8, Paris, 1905, etc.
[137] Note, however, that there are medical systems based on chromotherapy or healing by means of colors.
[138] See in this regard what is said above about the coloring of the etheric double reddish on one side and bluish on the other.
[139] One can give the desired color to the entire atmosphere by wearing glasses of the appropriate shade, but this artificial process is no match for natural coloring.
[140] Throughout the universe, green is the color of individualization. On our globe, where green dominates, altruism is still only in its primary manifestations.

body, reacting on the latter by communicating its own energies to it; it is in this that it is good to strengthen the mind by making it assimilate certain higher forces: this will be the subject of this last division of the chapter.

It is always through the mastery of breath, directed in one way or another, that we are able to capture the energies of the higher planes, because it is breathing that brings their various emanations into us: on this point, Western occultists and mystics are in perfect agreement with Eastern magicians and yogis.

We will therefore first present the Western methods, which are very well summarized by A. Caillet. [141] We will not follow this author in all his considerations on the various types of breathing: we will simply reproduce what is said in his work about the most powerful mode, which he calls *Rhythmic breathing*, surrounding it with all the explanations necessary to enable everyone to practice it.

Rhythmic breathing. — The laws of vibration and rhythm have shown us that everything in the Universe is nothing but rhythmic vibrations. Now, man's breath is precisely the manifestation of the rhythm by which he indefinitely draws his own life from the *Prâna* [142] of the world.

When he voluntarily, consciously, follows by thought, clearly manifested in his consciousness, this *vital rhythm* in a regular and continuous measure, he succeeds in absorbing an ever-increasing quantity of *Prâna*, which he can then use as he pleases. The entire human being begins to vibrate, to harmonize completely with this desired rhythm, and in this state, the entire unconscious [143] becomes perfectly and directly docile to the commands of the will.

---

[141] *Mental Treatment*, 1st vol. duodecimo, Paris, 1912. *General Overview of Mental Treatment* and *the Science of Life* — Messrs. H. and H. Durville, publishers, 23 rue Saint-Merri, Paris.
[142] Sanskrit word. I will explain exactly what *Prâna* is a few pages later; for now, it will suffice to say that it is the vital principle outside the physical universe and its localized manifestations, the principle of human life and that of other living creatures. From a purely material point of view, it is the breath itself. It corresponds to the *nephesh* of the Hebrew Kabbalah.
[143] Perhaps it would be better to say the *subconscious*. In short, it is the *Self* opposed to the *Ego*.

This *rhythmic breath* is therefore the basis of all energetic mental treatment, whether magnetic or suggestive, or purely mental and metaphysical: all operate through the effect of *Prâna*, of life, whose only driving cause differs.

According to the tradition of the yogis, [144] the *rhythmic breath* is based on the operator's *pulsation of the heart*.

It is practiced by mentally counting an equal number of pulses during inhalation and exhalation, and only half that number of the same pulses following each of these two periods. We recommend paying the utmost attention to its constant practice, for its use is, so to speak, contained in all branches of both physical culture and mental treatment...

Practice. — Here is the exercise that must be practiced until absolute familiarity is achieved:

1. Sit upright, but not stiffly, and pay particular attention to keeping your spine as straight as possible... with your chin tucked in, your shoulders slightly back, and your hands resting naturally on your thighs. This is what yogis call *sitting on your sides*. It is impossible to practice rhythmic breathing with your chest tucked in and your stomach protruding.

2. Slowly inhale a *full breath* [145], counting *six heartbeats*: 1, 2, 3, 4, 5, 6.

3. Hold the air in your lungs while counting *three* heartbeats: 1, 2, 3.

4. Slowly exhale the air through your nose, counting, as before, *six* heartbeats: 1, 2, 3, 4, 5, 6.

5. Count *three* heartbeats with empty lungs: 1, 2, 3.

6. Repeat the same cycle indefinitely, but above all, do not overexert yourself at the beginning.

---

[144] Throughout this chapter, we have repeatedly used this term, which should not be confused with the Fakir; the Fakir is a simple trickster, an illusionist who masters only the art — still unknown in Europe — of creating collective hallucinations; the Yogi, a follower of Yoga or transcendent science, possesses the means to produce in reality the supernormal phenomena of which the Fakir only gives the illusion. There is as much difference between them as between a professor of advanced physics and a conjurer.

7. When you are about to stop this exercise for good, practice the *purifying breath* [146] to clear and rest your lungs.

With practice, you will quickly be able to gradually increase the number of beats in the cycle, gradually counting *eight* beats during inhalation, *four* while holding the air, and *eight*, then *four* again in the last two beats of the cycle.

---

[145] This is the first stage of *full breathing*, which is as follows:

Step 1. — Inhale air through the nose in a continuous movement, first expanding the *lower* part of the lungs, by lowering the diaphragm, which gently presses the abdominal organs, then by advancing the anterior wall of the abdomen itself. Next, fill the middle part of the lungs by expanding the ribs, the sternum, and the entire thorax to their full extent. Finally, finish by filling the upper part of the lungs, by moving the upper part of the chest forward and up as much as possible, which draws the six or seven pairs of upper ribs into the same movement. During this last stage, the abdomen will draw in a little of its own accord, which will provide firmer support for the lungs and help fill their upper part.

At first glance, one might think these are three distinct movements; but this is not the case; inhalation must be continuous; the entire thoracic cavity, from the diaphragm at its most depressed point to the clavicles at their maximum elevation, must expand in a uniform movement. It is absolutely essential to avoid a jerky inhalation and to acquire a regular and continuous movement. Practice will bring perfection and ease.

Step 2: — Hold the breath for a few seconds, with the lungs completely filled.

Step 3: — Exhale slowly, keeping the chest firm and pulling in the abdomen slightly, then raising it slightly and slowly, as the air leaves the lungs. When the exhalation is complete (which is also important to ensure), relax the chest and abdomen.

As can be seen, this method encompasses all known modes of breathing and consists simply of methodically and deliberately filling the lungs with all the air they can contain, acting in a single, continuous movement.

[146] The *purifying* or *resting breath* is a form of breathing practiced by Yogis to purify and ventilate the lungs thoroughly. They generally end all their breathing exercises with this form, which aims to rest tired organs and is performed as follows:

1. — Inhale a *full breath* (see the previous note).

2. — Hold the air for a few seconds.

3. — Contract the lips, as if you were about to whistle (but without puffing out your cheeks), then forcefully expel a little air through the opening of the lips. Pause for a moment, holding the rest of the air, and so on, until all the inhaled air is used up. In short, it's a bit like blowing out a candle from afar, in several bursts.

This exercise should be practiced frequently: it rests and restores strength when fatigue sets in.

This will give you an initial beat of *fourteen* or *fifteen* beats, a number that should not be exceeded because the regularity of the rhythm is more important than the duration of the periods.

You must practice until you can feel the rhythmic swaying and the vibrations of your entire body. This obviously requires a great deal of perseverance, but this quality is inseparable from any mental cultivation; and, moreover, the initial results are such that it quickly becomes *impossible not to persevere*, you feel so good about the efforts you have made.

As we can see, Western processes are purely mechanical; more logical in this respect, since it involves the development of mental forces, Eastern processes are also based on meditation. It would seem that from this special point of view, meditation should be sufficient: this is not the case.

In a powerful machine, it is the flywheel that starts moving first; its movement is transmitted to less and less crude cogs, until the most delicate ones work in harmony with the whole. Now, breathing is this flywheel which, from a material point of view, provides and regulates the motive force that each part needs; and, moreover, from a psychic point of view, it imbues us with the higher energies that we must assimilate.

We will therefore return to Yoga and enter into *Râja Yoga*, [147] which, unlike *Hatha Yoga*, presents no drawbacks. But before going any further, we must clearly understand the distinction that exists between the two kinds of Yoga with which we are concerned here.

As we saw in the previous section of this chapter, *Hatha Yoga* deals primarily with the lower forces: on the one hand, through frequent application of the will to the various organs of the body, primarily the organs of the respiratory system, it gives, over time, perfect control over the physical organism; on the other hand, and it is from this point of view above all that we have had to deal with it, it captures etheric (vital) energies from the atmosphere to benefit either the physical body or — to which we have applied ourselves — the astral body. Hatha yoga acquires great power over oneself, but, if misdirected, the processes it employs can lead, according to the *Markan-daya-Purana*, to blindness, muteness, deafness, mental weakness, and even black magic. It goes without saying that, in the above exposition of the processes of *Hatha*

Yoga, I have carefully eliminated all those that can lead to such unfortunate results; but it is no less true that the student is in danger. In a word, *Hatha Yoga* aims at the assimilation of the lower etheric and astral forces. *Râja Yoga* deals solely with higher energies, even divine ones: this is to say, this Yoga presents no danger; in these pages, however, we will not go that far and will limit ourselves to indicating the processes — adapted to the Western way of life — that can be implemented to assimilate the higher astral and mental forces.

Swami Vivekananda published a short treatise on *Râja Yoga* [148] that contains excellent instructions and which students would do well to absorb. It is this treatise that will serve as our guide in the following lines.

Râja Yoga is divided into eight successive stages that must be passed through one after the other and which are, with their summarized teachings:

1. *Yama* — comprises five acts: Absence of violence and cruelty (universal innocence), Loyalty, Honesty, Chastity, Selflessness.

2. *Niyama* — comprises five acts: Purity, Patience, Mortification, Study, Worship.

3. *Asana* — The study of postures.

4. *Prânâyâmâ* — The science of breathing (mastery of the vital and higher forces of the being).

5. *Prâtyâhâra* — Inner examination.

6. *Dhâranâ* — The concentration of physical, psychic, and mental forces.

7. *Dhyâna* — The science of meditation.

8. *Samâdhi* — Super-consciousness.

The first two degrees involve moral training that can be summarized as follows: — Above all, control one's personality, actions, and thoughts: free oneself from all desires, as well as from any attachments or hopes; engage in frequent meditation, concentrating them in the heart; love all living beings, and especially humankind; practice morality; take care of one's body and mind; devote oneself to study; impose deprivations on oneself; draw closer to the divine through meditation and prayer; in a word, practice goodness in all its meanings and in its full extent.

The third term is also of great importance, for each day one must perform a series of physical and mental exercises that are impossible in a bad posture. The theories of Yoga recommend certain postures, *Padmâsana* and *Gidhâsana* among others, which, while very familiar to Easterners, would be very uncomfortable in the West. It is therefore important to find a posture that one can maintain for a long time without physical or mental fatigue. The most natural position is the one to adopt, because one individual will feel very comfortable in a certain posture that would be untenable for another. Once, after study, one has adopted an attitude, this is the position one should *always* adopt for meditation or practice.

Here are some guidelines in this regard, however: — During study and meditation, the body works intensely (producing the nervous force necessary for the brain); it will also be necessary to shift certain nerve currents and give them a different direction. One will experience new vibrations, and it will seem that the entire constitution is transformed; but the spinal column will be the principal seat of this action, so it must, of necessity, remain free and vertical, keeping the chest, neck, and head in a straight line; the entire weight of the body will be borne by the ribs: this leads to a comfortable and natural posture, for it is easy to see that one cannot have lofty thoughts when one's chest is hollow.

After learning to sit in an upright position, it is appropriate to practice what the physiological philosophy of Yoga calls the *purification of the nerves*. This is achieved by blocking the right nostril with the thumb and inhaling as much air as possible through the left nostril; then, without stopping, exhale through the right nostril while closing the left; and, breathing again through the right nostril, expel the air through the left, and so on.

This exercise should be repeated *three* or *five* times in a row, for a minimum of *fifteen* days or a maximum of one month; at the end of this time, the nerves are purified. Special treatises indicate times for this exercise that are rather inconvenient to observe in the West; it will be sufficient to practice it four times a day: — in the morning, upon rising, — immediately before the midday meal [149] — immediately before the evening meal — and finally before going to bed.

The purpose of this exercise is to activate the magnetic currents *Idâ* and *Pingâla*, which circulate on either side of the spinal column, where the main nerve center after the brain is located: the spinal cord. It is essential, and only after practicing it for the indicated period of time can one, as we will do shortly, approach the fourth degree, *Prânâyâmâ*, the mastery of breath.

It should be noted, however, that two obstacles can be encountered that destroy its effect: illness and doubt; one should therefore only engage in it in a state of perfect health and with a disposition of mind that reflects faith: — one must first practice consistently, and practice will bring proof.

To this physical exercise, we must add another — a moral one — which consists, before and after the *purification of the nerves*, that is to say, while we are in the desired pose, in addressing to all of nature a thought of altruism: "May all beings be happy! May all beings be at peace! May all beings be blessed!"

Above, I defined *Prânâyâmâ* as the science or domination of breath or respiration; it is more accurate to say that *Prânâyâmâ* is the conquest of *Prâna*. What is Prâna? It is *Energy* itself, the primordial force, which, combined with *Akâsa*, the ether [150], the primordial substance, produces the physical universe. *Prâna* is therefore the vital principle that animates materialized *Akâsa*. How can one go about conquering *Prâna*?

We must first look around us and begin by learning to master what surrounds us. Our body is what is closest to us, and our thoughts are the thoughts that touch us most closely. The *Prâna* that gives life to our body and our thoughts is the one closest to us of all the *Prâna*. The small wave of *Prâna* that represents our own mental and physical energies is, of all the waves in the infinite Ocean of *Prâna*, the one that comes closest to us; we must therefore first master this small wave, and then we can hope to master, little by little, as many waves of *Prâna* as possible.

---

[147] Literally *royal union*.

[148] *Râja-Yoga, or the conquest of inner nature*, translated into French by S. W. — 1 vol, in-12, Paris, 1910.

[149] That is, at times when the stomach is as empty as possible.

[150] The ether penetrating us through breathing, carrying *Prâna* with it, we understand why *Prânayama* is commonly defined as the science of breath.

Prâna therefore constitutes the vital force of the body, and the energy specific to the mind: hence, if we can express it thus, two kinds of *Prâna* that are summarized in what we call the *Self*.

Material *Prâna* is energy in action. Modern physics demonstrates that the total sum of energies existing in the universe is constant, and that this total sum of energies presents itself in two alternative forms: in the potentiality of being, then in a state of rest; thus, energy evolves constantly throughout eternity: it constantly flows through us, and it is at this moment that we can capture and assimilate it in its two modalities of vital force and mental force. This being well understood, I come to the exercises of *Prânâyâmâ*, which concern *Raja Yoga*.

First, the most favorable position. — You must sit very upright: the spinal cord, although inside the spine, does not adhere to it. If you sit crooked, you displace it, and it is important that it be free of any pressure. Every time you try to meditate while sitting, bent over, and hunched over, you harm yourself. You must keep your chest, neck, and head in a perfectly straight and vertical line. You will achieve this with practice, and it will be as easy as breathing.

Controlling your nerves is the second goal to achieve. Rhythmic breathing is essential here, for we know that the nervous center, which governs the respiratory organs, has a kind of guiding influence on all the other nerves.

You must breathe rhythmically, [151] inhaling and exhaling, which will harmonize the system. After practicing this exercise for a while, it would be a good idea to add the repetition of a few words such as "AUM" [152] or any other sacred word that you emit naturally, while inhaling and exhaling in a rhythmic, harmonious manner; you will then notice that your entire body becomes rhythmic, and you will truly know what rest is: sleep is nothing compared to the sleep you will acquire in this way.

The first effect of this breathing practice will be to modify your physiognomy: hard features will soften; calmness of thought will give calm to the face. These changes will occur after a few months of practice.

---

[151] See above regarding rhythmic breathing.
[152] This sacred word will be explained later.

After practicing the first breathing exercise for several days, you will try a more complicated one. Slowly fill your lungs with air, which you will inhale through the left nostril [153], and at the same time concentrate your thoughts on the nervous current. In this way, you send the nervous current from the top to the bottom of the spine by striking violently on the last plexus, the basic lotus, seat of the *Kundalini* [154]. Keep the current like this for some time. Imagine that you are slowly drawing this current with your breath, to the other side, then exhale gently through the right nostril.

This exercise seems a little difficult at first. To make it easier, close your right nostril by pressing your thumb against it, and then breathe slowly through the left nostril. At this point, close both nostrils with your thumb and index finger; imagine that you are drawing the current down and striking the base of the *Sushumnâ* [155]; then stop pressing your thumb and breathe through your right nostril. Then breathe slowly through this same nostril while closing the other with your index finger, then close both as before.

------

[153] Corresponding to the Idâ current.

[154] Yogis call *Sushumnâ*a hollow channel that forms the center of the spine. At the lower end of this channel is what they call the *Kundalini Lotus*. They describe it as triangular in shape and say that it contains a power they call *Kundalini*. When *Kundalini* awakens, it seeks to force its way into the central channel (*Sushumnâ*); it progresses little by little, and as it rises, thought gradually develops, intelligence opens, and various insights and marvelous powers come to the Yogi. When Kundalini finally reaches the brain, the Yogi is perfectly detached from his body and his mind: his soul is free.

We know anatomically that the spine is constructed in a very special way. If we draw a *figure eight* horizontally (∞), we notice that it is composed of two distinct bodies that touch each other. Let's stack the *eights* on top of each other, and we will have the image of the chain formed by the spinal column. The superimposed bodies on the left constitute the *Idâ*; those on the right constitute the *Pingalâ* (the two nerve currents, corresponding to each of the nostrils and which we discussed above), and the hollow canal, the center of the spine, is the *Sushumnâ*. Where this ends near some lumbar vertebra, a delicate fiber descends, and the canal, through this very fiber, continues, but is much narrower. It is closed at its lower end, which is located near what is called the *sacral plexus*, and to which anatomy gives a triangular shape. The different plexuses centered in the spinal column can very well represent the different "lotuses" of the Yogi.

[155] See the previous note.

Westerners are not accustomed to controlling their breathing as Hindus do; it would therefore be wise to apply the following timings: inhale for *four* seconds; hold the breath for *sixteen* seconds; and finally expel the air for *eight* seconds [156].

As you engage in this exercise, concentrate your thoughts on the triangle (the sacral plexus), concentrate your thoughts on this center; imagination can help you enormously. The next breathing exercise consists of slowly inhaling, then immediately exhaling, and then remaining breathless for the same amount of time as before. The only difference is that in the first exercise, one holds one's breath; while in the second, one expels it. This latter exercise is easier than the first.

You should not overdo the exercise of holding the air in your lungs. At first, do it no more than four times in the morning and four times in the evening; later, you will increase this number with the duration of each exercise. You will find that this is possible for you, and you will develop a taste for it. Then you will increase it further, slowly and cautiously, basing your practice on your strength, and you will reach six repetitions of the exercise instead of four. But if you practice without method, you risk harming yourself.

This constitutes the *Prânâyâmâ* of *Râja Yoga*.

The procedures indicated above are neither dangerous nor difficult. The more you practice the practice of holding the breath for a while, the calmer you will become. Think of "AUM," and you will be able to practice while working on something else. If you practice assiduously [157], one day the *Kundalini* will awaken, all of nature will begin to transform, and the book of science will open.

Here, I am obliged to digress in this summary of *Yoga* to give a necessary explanation about AUM — or OM — whose name has just appeared for the second time under my pen. — What is AUM?

---

[156] In practice, you can replace seconds with the pulse rate you always have on hand.
[157] That is, every day and three or four times a day.

In Vedantism, this is the sacred appellation par excellence; it therefore corresponds to the *Yod-He-Vau-He* of Hebrew Kabbalah, but carries in itself infinitely more power to mystically symbolize the Divinity understood both synthetically and analytically.

Indeed, this word is graphically rendered by a single Sanskrit character; it comprises two letters (a [compound] vowel and a consonant, the basis of all language); and finally, it is expressed in three sounds: A-OU-M; it is therefore the representative sign of the Divinity understood simultaneously as unity, duality, and trinity.

But there is more: the pronunciation is, as I have just said, A-OU-M; the first of these three sounds is wide open; then it blends into the second, less sonorous, which itself ends in the murmur of M, which begins with a sound of its own becoming nasal, then null: the pronunciation of this word thus harmonizes with the entire range of all cosmic vibrations, in which anyone who pronounces it as it should be said participates, a fact which will be explained later. For the moment, I wish to convey the full mystical and sacred significance of this word, which has been repeated and venerated by generations and multitudes, from the most remote antiquity to the present day.

To avoid anthropomorphism, the Vedantin mystics represented the Divinity not by a name but by this formula which is neither masculine, nor feminine, nor neuter, but all three at once. The three sounds that compose it represent Spirit, Force, and Matter, or, if you will, Essence, Substance, and Existence, which result from their intertwining. *A* is Atma, father of all beings and source of all creators; *M* is Mulaprakriti, source of all things and mother of all creatures; finally, *U (OU)* represents Oueaohou, the Tibetan and esoteric name for the Word, that is, for the creative activity which, from emanation to emanation, becomes the various aspects of force. This middle principle participates in both extremes and is so intimately coessential to them that it is often identified with one or the other. In summary, *A* and *M* can be conceived as two mathematical points fixing the limits of existence, and connected by a lifeline, by a mobile quantity U, representing the whole of existence, the universe, the son between the father and the mother.

In the chapter *The Mystery of the Trinity* in *The Secret of the Absolute*, by E. J. Coulomb, one will find profound and illuminating considerations concerning the hieratic value of AUM, to which I am forced to confine myself here.

On the other hand, E. Bosc says somewhere [158] of this sacred monogram: — *Pranava* therefore contains at once unity (OM), duality (AU and OM), and the trinity (A, U, M); thus this syllable represents, like the number 3 and the triangle, the symbol of the triple aspect under which we try to form an idea of the *Absolute* or God: Infinity, First Principle, Supreme Principle. This syllable is extremely sacred; it is also considered the root of the Universe and of beings; this is why we cannot give the key to it, because if we did, it would reveal many occult correspondences that it is not permitted to reveal [159]...

Here finally is the summary of the meanings of the divine word as given by Dr. Th. Pascal [160] "*Aum* is the Being par excellence, the great human synthesis: the Beginning, the Middle and the End; Substance and Force; Intelligence and Spirituality: the divine Consciousness. It is the unfathomable Noumenon and the subjective Phenomenon; the Germ and the Flower; the root of all akasic [161], astral [162] and physical correlations. It is one of the aspects of the *lost word*. Superior triad: Atma, Buddhi, Manas [163], higher *Self*, it is All and Nothing. The Kabbalists would say that it is the Great Pentacle. Each of its letters has its own numerical, colored, etc. value, and those who possess the secret of its various intonations can bring powerful vibrations into the various planes of the surrounding nature."

I will give below the simplest and best known of these intonations; but first, I must warn the reader who might think he can replace *AUM* with the Hebraochaldaic *Yod-He-Vau-He* or with

---

[158] *Dictionary of Orientalism and Occultism*, 2 vols. duodecimo, Paris, 1896, art. AUM.

[159] The complete key to the word is given in India only to certain initiates, but what has just been said above is sufficient to understand the sacred value of this monogram.

[160] *Curiosity*, August 14, 1894.

[161] The *Akasa* is the highest principle, the spiritual, subtle, and super-sensual Essence that fills space, emanated by the Divinity.

[162] The astral forces are intermediaries between the akasic energies and the material forces.

[163] V. the chapter on the *Occult constitution of man*.

any modern divine appellation, that, while this substitution may give him some results on the mental plane, it would be of absolutely no value on the astral and physical planes, since it would not harmonize with any of the series of vibrations discussed above.

I now turn to the pronunciation, the *intonation* of the sacred word.

There are a number of them that are used in Vedantism, but the simplest, the easiest, the most accessible for Westerners, is that indicated by A. Caillet, and which I limit myself to transcribing as he describes it:

"The projection into verbal vibrations of perfect accord of the sacred word "AUM" is the most energetic means that we possess of raising the rate of our own vibrations in the Ether. This sacred word, chanted slowly on the notes *do-mi-sol* of the perfect accord, seems to contain the whole ascending range of creative sounds, and, by influence, carries all our own vibrations into waves of increasing rapidity. It symbolizes the set of all possible sounds, beginning, as it does, with the mouth wide open and ending with the mouth completely closed, in a purely nasal sound, after having passed through all the intermediate positions; we can say of it: it is the WORD... Thus, the vibrations of the sacred word, chanted on the notes of the perfect chord, determine a *vibratory ascension*, if one can so say, a gradual evolutionary elevation of all the vibrations constituting the being. To obtain its benefits, it is sufficient, after having fulfilled the conditions of general relaxation (which consists of suppressing all involuntary movement of both the body and the intellect, and mainly of producing calm in the ever more or less agitated mind) and preliminary recollection, to inhale a full breath, then to pronounce the sacred word during the exhalation, chanting it in a deep voice on the three notes of the perfect chord: do...mi...sol... — This exercise can be continued for three to ten minutes, depending on the effect produced. One will feel the vibrations take hold of the entire being, and a sensation of calm and spirituality reign with increasing intensity. Through prolonged practice of this type of religious chant, one sometimes succeeds in producing the strangest psychic phenomena."

To these very precise indications, I will add two others:

1. There are people who are distracted by chanting; now, the sacred word must be meditated upon at the same time as it is chanted; these people will therefore be able, and better still, to murmur the chant instead of chanting it.

2. On the other hand, there are circumstances and environments where one can hardly chant aloud; in all these cases, one can be content to chant *mentally*; but this mental psalmody will only be able to produce a real effect in people who, having devoted themselves for a certain time to the exercise of *real* psalmody, will have undergone its physical, psychic, and intellectual effects, and will have thereby made themselves capable of reproducing them well through a mental operation.

We see, from the detailed explanations above, that, from the point of view which concerns us, the sacred word AUM can hardly be replaced by the *Yod-He-Vau-He* of the Kabbalah, any more than by any other sacred invocation, which cannot correspond with the higher energies, and, consequently, make the various constituent elements of the organism of the operator participate in the series of cosmic vibrations which must act on him.

This long but necessary digression on the value and use of Vedantin AUM being finished, I resume my explanations relating to the practice of *Râja Yoga*.

The *Idâ*, the *Pingalâ*, and the *Sushumnâ* channel form three currents of action, but ordinary people only have the first two at their disposal: only the Yogi can use the *Sushumnâ*. When this channel opens, one passes into a state beyond the senses, and intelligence becomes supra-sensory and supra-conscious. The Yogi's goal is therefore to open this channel through the respiratory and mental processes we have discussed.

We still have a few words to say about *Ojas*. Of all the energies contained in the human body, *Ojas* is the most subtle, but also the one that dominates the others. It is stored in the brain; therefore, the more *Ojas* a person's head contains, the more powerful, intellectual, and spiritually strong that person is.

Ojas is quite difficult to define, and we can only cite certain modalities of its realization. It is, for example, the warmth of speech, the power of conviction, the magnetism of example, the assurance of knowledge, the feeling of virtue, etc. It is therefore, strictly speaking, a mental energy, but it is perhaps, as we shall see, that which is both the most necessary and, sometimes, the most difficult to acquire.

Humanity possesses a greater or lesser reserve of *Ojas*. All the *higher* forces that act in the body are transformed into *Ojas*, for it is only a matter of transformation. The same force that, externally, produces electricity or magnetism, is transformed into internal force; the same forces that produce muscular energy are transformed into *Ojas*. According to the Yogis, the kind of human energy that manifests itself through sex in the sexual function can easily be transformed into *Ojas*, if it is stopped, dominated, and, since all these functions depend on the lowest center [164], it is this one that the Yogi particularly monitors. He always strives, by the same means of meditation, will, and breathing, to collect all this sexual energy and transform it into *Ojas*. Only chaste men and women can make *Ojas* flow to their brains, and this is why chastity has always been considered the highest virtue; man feels that, if he is not chaste, spirituality abandons him; he loses his mental vigor and moral strength. This is the reason why all religious orders — in all high religions — which have produced giants in the spiritual respect, always insist on the obligation of absolute chastity. Perfect chastity, in thought, word, and deed, is essential. How, indeed, can one hope to become a Yogi if, while practicing Yoga in any form whatsoever, one leads an impure life?

I will say little about *Prâtyâhâra*, which is the mental examination to achieve mastery of the mind, and *Dhâranâ*, which is the concentration of forces through the will, these two degrees being very difficult to approach for a Western student. I will only note the primordial exercise of each of them, the most accessible, according to Swami Vivekananda.

The first lesson of *Prâtyâhâra* is to sit for a while and let your thoughts run wild. They bubble constantly and resemble a wriggling monkey. Let the monkey jump as long as it can: simply wait and observe. Knowledge is power, says the proverb: this proverb speaks true. As long as you are ignorant of the workings of thought, you cannot control it. Give it complete control; it may well welcome the ugliest ideas, and you will be surprised to have been able to conceive such vileness; but you will realize that, every day the wanderings diminish in number and violence; that thought calms down every day. During the first few months, you will notice a thousand thoughts within you; later, you will find only seven hundred; and, a few months later, the number will decrease again, until the mind is completely dominated. To get there, you have to practice daily...

When you have practiced *Prâtyâhâra* for some time, go a step further and tackle *Dhârana*, which is the concentration of forces by fixing the mind. What does it mean to fix one's mind on certain points? It is to force it to feel certain parts of the body to the exclusion of others; to try, for example, to feel only one's hand, to the exclusion of all other parts of the body. When the *Chitta*, or mental matter, is confined and concentrated in a certain place, this state is called *Dhârana*. There are several kinds of *Dhârana*, and when practicing it, it is good to leave a little play to the imagination. For example, one can force the mind to think only of a certain point in the heart. This is very difficult; but if one imagines a lotus at this point in the heart, the thing becomes easier. This lotus is bathed in a resplendent light. Fix your mind there. Imagine again that the lotus of the brain is luminous, or think of the different centers of the *Sushumnâ* that we have already discussed.

Speaking of the heart and the brain, Swami Vivekananda mentions the two main points where thought must be fixed; but it is good, in order to concentrate physical forces and — especially for the case at hand — psychic forces, at one point, to gather them, to *collect* them, if I may express myself thus, along their entire path; one must therefore fix one's thought on the main points of the spinal column where they are accumulated, going up little by little. So first think of your phantom, objectify it in a way before your eyes; then, when you *see it clearly*, locate it, center it by narrowing it [165], in the middle of the base of your body, between the anus and the perineum, a location that should appear to you mentally as a triangle of molten gold; then bring it up to the source of the urethra, which should be imagined as a red dot; then have it successively reach the Navel Plexus [166], which should appear yellow to you; the Cardiac Plexus [167], white; the Pharyngeal Plexus, black; the Cavernous Plexus [168], ruby; and finally the Pineal Gland [169], the great center of psychic forces, the brilliant color of the sun.

It must not be hidden from us that all this, already very difficult with Eastern education, is almost impossible in our West for anyone who is not armed with an iron will to overcome difficulties.

Thus, to overcome the following five obstacles: pain, sorrow, fear, loss of breath, and exhalation, the Yogi must renounce hatred, love, desire, hope, and finally accustom himself to holding his exhalation by fixing his breath on any point. This is how the Yogi attains the siddhis or supernormal powers; but he must also combat four enemies: the flesh, the senses, sin and pain, by acquiring the seven purities of the body: of morals, of intention, of belief, of judgment, of bodily and mental attitude and of intelligence; and this through spiritual benevolence, and the firm conviction that *Karma*, or Law of merits and demerits, governs our successive states; finally, he must have the intuitive perception of the Absolute, and detachment from what are called the goods of this world.

From all that has preceded it is clear what difficulties must be overcome if one wishes to go beyond the first stages of *Râja Yoga*.

I will therefore not go beyond this in this exposition of *Râja Yoga*; I will not address the higher degrees of *Dhyâna* and *Samâdhi*, referring those curious to pursue this study to the work of Bosc de Vèze and especially to the excellent — though brief — treatise by Swami Vivekananda, but with the very important and

---

[165] The living ghost only has its normal size when it possesses its odic double or etheric forces, its own or those of a receptive subject; reduced to the *astral body*, it is, according to sensitive seers and magnetic subjects placed in a state of clairvoyance, the size of a twelve-year-old child. Vedantic theories represent it to us, under the name of *Prana-Maya-Kosha*, or *Envelope Reflecting Breaths*, as having a height of ninety-six fingers (approximately 1.10 m) and possessing an *aura* that extends within a radius of twelve fingers (approximately 0.15 m). It is this aura that must be reduced to *center* the ghost at the indicated location.
[166] A *plexus* is an interlacing of nerves (or vessels). Nerve plexuses belong to the cerebrospinal system as well as to the sympathetic nervous system.
[167] Near the heart (below the aortic arch).
[168] Branch of the great sympathetic nerve that surrounds the internal carotid artery.
[169] Small nerve mass located approximately in the center of the brain, behind the third ventricle.

express remark that E. Bosc's work deals primarily with Yoga, that is, with the development of the lower etheric and astral forces and only incidentally with *Râja Yoga*, while that of Swami Vivekananda deals only with *Râja Yoga*, that is, with the training of the higher mental astral forces and, purely incidentally, with *Hâtha Yoga*: these two books can therefore only complement each other and not supplement each other. Indeed, in what concerns us in these pages, I believe I have achieved the proposed goal, which was to seek in *Hâtha Yoga* and *Râja Yoga* methods capable of energizing the higher elements of the Being — the astral body and the mental body — which constitute the principal parts, the basis, in a way, of the exteriorized living phantom.

Before closing this overview of the methods capable of bringing about the assimilation of mental forces in man, I would ask the reader to refer to what was said in the fourth paragraph of the first section of this chapter, relating to the use of the coloration of the surrounding environment to aid in the absorption of hyperphysical forces by capturing certain cosmic currents.

I will only recall here that the light yellow color leads to the development of mental energies, that, if a color combination is required, this combination must be based on the colors white, light blue, and gold, and that finally, shades of orange, green, and red must be prohibited, for the reasons explained in this passage to which I refer the reader, — everything said there, from the point of view of the coloring of the atmosphere, of the astral body and, consequently, of the currents of astral force, applies absolutely to the mental body and the capture of mental energies.

It remains for me to apologize to some readers for perhaps having held their attention too long on considerations that may have seemed a little nebulous to them, although I have made an effort to make them as easy to understand as possible.

Certainly, a person nourished solely by official science will only be able to shrug his shoulders at this exposition of a high science that is beyond him; I will, however, draw his attention to the dual fact that, on the one hand, without going as far as Yoga, and without proceeding as scientifically as it, certain contemplative religious orders in the West attach great importance to the respiratory gymnastics of chanting and to the position of the body in prayer and meditation, with a view to developing in their members certain faculties of asceticism; and that, on the other hand, Ignatius of Loyola, who was a brilliant trainer of men towards mysticism, and whose Order produced so many highly eminent individuals, surpassed all Yogas in the meticulousness of the material exercises that he imposed on his disciples with a view to placing, in them, all bodily forces under the absolute dependence of mental energy.

But it does not matter! The occultist will understand me, and I believe in any case that I have done the student good by putting within his reach processes — notably Yoga adapted to the necessities, conditions and habits of Western life — with the help of which he will be able, with application and perseverance, to acquire certain supernormal faculties.

———

CHAPTER IX

MATERIAL CONDITIONS

So far, we have examined the main subjective conditions of personal out-of-body experience: control of the will and appropriation of the astral body. It remains for us to say a few words about the objective, external and material conditions, whose influence on the outcome of the operation, although infinitely less than that of personal conditions, nevertheless plays a certain role in the conduct of the experiment, and, as such, must be mentioned here.

We saw above that, in the *laboratory* or training context, it was necessary to note the atmospheric, climatological, meteorological, etc., variations that could occur during this period: this is because all these elements, which superficial minds thoughtlessly disdain, have, in what concerns us, a relative importance, it is true, but one that the serious operator would be ill-advised to neglect.

I will therefore briefly review the main ones of these conditions. H. Durville says somewhere [170], regarding the *objective* exteriorization of the living ghost: "All the conditions necessary for studying out-of-body experience are not always easy to meet. It would be necessary: 1. that the atmosphere is never heavy or humid, that the air is not charged with electricity as when a storm approaches, and that the temperature is constant and relatively high; 2. that one is, if not in absolute darkness, at least in relative darkness; 3. that only a small number of witnesses are admitted to the study sessions, all sympathetic to each other,

----

[170] *The Ghost of the Living*, 1 vol. in-12, Paris, 1909, (Henri Durville).

interested in the research, but without passion or bias, and not always demanding to verify for themselves the reality of all the phenomena as they occur; 4. That the meetings take place in a room far enough from the street so that outside noises do not reach it, and that the greatest silence reigns, both inside the room and in those surrounding it. It is also necessary that this room always be the same, because the phenomena are obtained there more easily than in any other where experiments are never conducted."

What H. Durville says here about the splitting of a subject applies more or less, as is logical, to experiments in personal splitting. I will therefore say a few words about each of these conditions.

Humidity. — The phantom is a kind of coagulate of an electrical nature. Now, we know that humidity is the great solvent of electricity, which, finding a conductive substance in a humid environment, diffuses quickly there instead of remaining on the surface where it was created or accumulated. Exteriorization, on the other hand, does not occur instantly, but over a period of time that can last from a few minutes to several hours. This inevitably happens when operating in a humid environment: as it forms and is projected, the phantom substance becomes diluted in the surrounding atmosphere and cannot achieve sufficient condensation; the result is simply a weakening of the operator, who uselessly emanates his neural force without any external effect. It is therefore better from all points of view to operate in dry weather.

But what if the experiment is conducted in a dry environment (room, etc.) while it's raining outside? Here again, it's better not to attempt it except during the initial trials, when one is seeking pure and simple splitting without sending the phantom far away. Indeed, the phantom has, if not its own will (its will, in principle, is that of the operator), at least its own particular instinct, which warns it of all the causes of injury that may affect it; in such a case, it is essentially in the situation of a chilly dog that its master wants to send to the river: it resists the controlling will as much as it can. It is certain that when it is well condensed, it suffers little from humidity, given its rapidity of transport, but it is always less maneuverable. Therefore, in any case, it is better to operate in perfectly dry weather.

Precise experiments, carried out from this point of view, have established the following: — the astral body does not dissolve in water, except in certain medicinal waters; we can therefore affirm that atmospheric humidity has no effect on it; on the contrary, the etheric double dissolves very easily in any water and in a certain number of liquids (without, however, the experiment with various liquid substances having been pushed very far, but we are only concerned here with water in general); it is therefore very sensitive to humidity; now, it is a constituent part of the phantom at the moment when the latter is exteriorized; its sensitivity in this regard is such that, in the driest room, it appears influenced by the humidity from outside; it follows from this fact that the exteriorization of this double — and, consequently, of the phantom — is much more difficult when the external atmosphere is humid, and this results in a certain fatigue for the operation.

Therefore, as just said, dry weather is best suited to the experiment.

Atmospheric pressure. — From L. Lefranc's experiments, it appears that the atmospheric medium acts differently on the etheric double; when the barometer rises, there is a decrease in the mechanical action of its forces, but its luminosity increases; the opposite effects occur when the pressure increases: there then seems to be condensation of the etheric matter.

Now, let us not forget that it is through etheric force — its own or that communicated to it by the receptive subject — that the exteriorized phantom can act on matter. It therefore seems appropriate to advocate visibility effects especially when the barometer is above 760, and conversely, the production of mechanical effects when it falls below this average.

Atmospheric electricity. — This unfavorable influence can act in three ways: on the operator, on the operation, and on the phantom itself.

It must not be forgotten that the operator preparing for his out-of-body experience has, by this very fact, placed himself in a certain state of nervous imbalance; he is therefore extremely sensitive to external influences: we know how stormy times affect nervous people. Therefore, he is not in the calm conditions required to proceed with his own out-of-body experience. By natural consequence, this splitting will only occur with difficulty and fatigue, especially since the experimenter will then have a good chance of not being in full possession of either his will or his psychic powers, the sensitivity of which becomes extreme as soon as they are oriented toward mysterious things. Atmospheric electricity therefore influences both the experimenter and the operation.

But there is more: the phantom itself is subject to its influence.

Let us remember what has been said elsewhere, that the *aérosôme* is of an electrical nature. Now, one of the fundamental laws of electricity is this: electricity of opposite polarities attract each other, and electricity of similar polarities repel each other. Furthermore, any non-isolated body placed in an electrified medium electrifies itself in the same way as that medium. If, therefore, atmospheric electricity is +, that of the experimenter will be +, and, by forced consequence, that of the phantom to be exteriorized will itself be +. The result will be that atmospheric electricity will repel the astral body, that is, will obstruct its exteriorization, and the splitting of the operator will be most difficult. If, on the contrary, the latter, to obviate this difficulty, isolates itself in its environment and establishes communication with an electrical source −, it is certain that, the astral body then being of modality −, its exit will be facilitated; but it is no less certain that the electricity + of the atmosphere will combine, as it emanates, with the electricity − of the *aérosôme* in such a way as to return to the neutral state of equilibrium, and that the operator will tire himself out without any other result than to externalize a force which, as it is produced, will be, if not annihilated, at least neutralized.

In summary, the best condition for the operation, from this point of view, is the absolute neutrality of the atmosphere from the electrical point of view.

Temperature. — In cold, the living being contracts, withdraws into itself; in heat, it expands and expands; heat is therefore an almost absolute condition for the success of the splitting. But what heat? Since sensitivity in this regard varies infinitely from individual to individual, and even within a single individual depending on the seasons, the time of day, the health and general equilibrium in which it finds itself, etc., it is difficult to lay down a precise rule and fix a number of degrees *ne varietur*. Here, however, is a general indication on which one can base oneself.

It is a good idea to conduct the experiment in an environment whose heat can be easily regulated, for example, a room heated by gas, a bed covered with several blankets, etc. The heat, which is gradually increased, reaches, at a given moment, a certain degree that causes the operator perfect well-being; It is appropriate to go a little further, but be careful not to reach the point where the heat becomes a nuisance, because any bodily discomfort, whatever it may be, will necessarily hinder the experience.

It is for this reason that winter, or at least an average season, must be considered preferable to summer, where the ambient heat forces one to seek coolness and, consequently, places the physical body in conditions unfavorable to the emanation of neurological force and consequently to the final result of the operation.

Clothes. — This falls under the temperature conditions, since clothing is designed to permanently provide the human body with the temperature it needs; the clothing worn at the time of the operation must therefore be neither too hot nor too light, but, between the two, it must be warm rather than cool, so as to maintain the body at the upper level of those that constitute its well-being.

But clothing must also be examined from another point of view: it's fit.

As just stated, any bodily discomfort constitutes an unfavorable condition; therefore, one should not choose clothing that is too tight, that which squeezes the waist or restricts movement, but rather that in which the body feels free in all its actions, where the limbs move effortlessly, where breathing is easy, and which does not weigh on the shoulders, the lower back, or the waist.

Lighting. — Light, as has long been noted during spiritualist experiments, is a solvent of all ghostly substance. From a chemical point of view, light is an agent that is both very subtle and very energetic. Its action, observed in an infinite number of circumstances, is especially remarkable on silver salts, which it reduces; a similar phenomenon occurs on ghostly substance. But it is above all as a physical agent that light acts on the same substance. A phenomenon then occurs based on the same principle as that which makes a flame very indistinguishable in broad daylight. Its action in this regard, which appears to be both physical and chemical, makes light an agent to be feared in the circumstance that concerns us more specifically, since it dissolves the ghost as the physical body externalizes it.

Therefore, daylight, that is, sunlight, must be absolutely avoided.

But what should we think of artificial light?

This offers many different degrees of illumination, from the low blue flame of gas to the electric arc: there is therefore a choice to be made, although in principle, absolute abstention from all light, natural or artificial, is much preferable.

But since there are people — particularly nervous people — who cannot bear absolute darkness, who, even at night, could not fall asleep without a nightlight, I will say a few words about the type of lighting that *can* be used in a pinch.

The best light is that given by a small nightlight, with a very low flame, low enough to blur the outlines of all the objects it strikes instead of emphasizing them, which could distract the operator.

This flame must also be enclosed in a transparent glass globe. The ideal color for this glass would be dark red, which only produces safelight and, consequently, has less effect than any other in dissolving the ghost. But there is another element of the question that must be taken into account: red light has a very painful effect on sensitive and nervous people: there are even magnetic subjects whose action positively makes them scream. It follows that, under its influence, the operator — who, let us not forget, must possess highly developed neuritis — will always feel a certain discomfort, which must be avoided all the more since the aerosol emanating from him will contribute to this discomfort.

It therefore seems that the most favorable color is light blue; at least, it is the one that — used in the objective production, in the laboratory, of a living ghost — gives the best results. Light of this type is very soft, does not tire the eye, and tends to blur all nearby objects: it is therefore the preferred light.

It is understood that when using this light source, the operator should not position himself near it or under its direct radiation, but should move as far away from it as possible.

As a consequence of the near darkness required, the drapes in the room where the operation is taking place should not be light, but dark in color, and the room itself should, as far as possible, not contain any bright or shining objects that might attract and hold the eye, such as marble clocks, paintings, mirrors, etc. If the operation is taking place while lying down, the light should be placed as far as possible from the bed, the white sheets of which should be covered and veiled by a light, dark-colored blanket; In this case, it would even be a good idea to place a screen between the light and the bed, leaving the bed and the operator in very dark conditions.

Assistance. — A witness can always be a distraction, even unwittingly and despite their best efforts. It is therefore preferable to operate completely alone and without any assistants.

But there are cases, particularly in a household, where it is difficult to operate in complete isolation. On the other hand, one might rightly hesitate to undertake such an experiment without having at least one confidant who, in the event of an accident, would be able to provide the experimenter with the care their condition requires. I will therefore outline what the role of the witness should be in such a case.

In principle, the more this role is minimized, the better it will be fulfilled. This means that the witness should under no circumstances be a distraction. They should appear neither agitated nor unruly, but should remain occupied (reading, working, sleeping, etc.) in their chosen position. If they need to move around, they should slide quietly across the parquet floor. If one wishes to operate at night during sleep, the partner occupying the same bed must above all have a very peaceful sleep. In short, whatever the circumstances, the witness must adapt to them in order to be careful not to cause any discomfort, of any kind, to the operator. This means that the witness must always be warned of what is being prepared, and that, consequently, it would be, I do not say only illogical in the first place, but absolutely insane to prepare an astral projection in the midst of uninformed people, because, in addition to the fact that their presence would significantly hinder the operation, one must anticipate the disturbance and dismay in which the comatose appearance of the operator's body during the experiment would throw them, and the imprudence of all kinds that could result.

But the presence of a witness must be examined from another point of view.

H. Durville wrote: "There are individuals in whose presence it is always impossible to obtain the slightest phenomenon. These individuals are of two kinds: 1. Those who, strong and robust, are very willful, especially if this will is not disciplined, as in the case of stubborn people, because they radiate powerfully around them, without being able to oppose a brake to this radiation; certain harsh magnetizers who want everything to bend before them, and all those who, without anyone knowing why, are antipathetic to the subject; 2. A certain number of sensitive subjects, especially when they are very sympathetic to the subject of experimentation. — The former give off abundant effluvia which, projected with energy, repel those that the subject provides for the formation of the phantom; and the latter, repelled, tossed about, cannot condense sufficiently. The contours remain vague, the molecular vibrations barely appear, and the large undulations are tumultuous or barely outlined. The second individuals do little to harm the formation of the phantom at the beginning of the out-of-body experience, but it is impossible to exceed a certain degree of condensation and make it remain in place, because it is attracted to the sensitive witness and separates from it only to return to it again. — In both cases, the experimenter expends a lot of energy without being able to obtain any significant phenomena."

What this author says about objective out-of-body experiences is also true, to a certain extent, for subjective out-of-body experiences; one should not hope to achieve a serious result with a person whose will is disordered or greater than that which you yourself can muster, any more than with a witness who, for one reason or another, is unsympathetic to you.

Then remains the question of the "too sympathetic" witness. — It is obvious that if it is of a sensitive nature, that is, if it can play the role of a receptive subject, it will be valuable since it can, through its presence, assist in the out-of-body experience and then control the actions of the exteriorized phantom. If it cannot fulfill this other role, it will only be useful in the very first attempts, by facilitating exteriorization, but later, when the operator wishes to send his own phantom here or there, he will have to do so without the presence of a witness of this nature.

Silence. — It is obvious that, since any noise is a cause of distraction, absolute silence must reign around the experimenter; it is therefore advisable to operate in a place where echoes from the street or neighbors do not reach. A room with a thickly carpeted floor and heavy door and window curtains, so as to dampen external and internal noise, is the most favorable location. It goes without saying that no stranger, servant, visitor, etc., should be allowed into the room for the duration of the experiment.

I will again borrow the technical considerations relating to noise from H. Durville, for what he says, in this regard, about the objective phantom applies absolutely to the subjective phantom.

"The phantom, very well condensed, is disposed to action; a prolonged noise of a certain intensity, even a lively conversation, only in hushed tones between the witnesses, is enough for its contours to become less clear, for the large undulations to become tumultuous and jerky; it then trembles throughout its entire mass, becomes blurred, less luminous, less pleasant to the eye, and loses all aptitude for work. At this moment, if a sudden emotion occurs in it, as sometimes happens without any very appreciable cause, if an intense noise resounds, or if he is struck by a jet of bright light, like the photographer uses to take a snapshot in the dark, he abandons his place and goes to shelter behind the subject as if to make a shield of it. Often also it disintegrates completely and its elements return almost instantly to the body of the subject. The splitting is finished, and if one wishes to continue the experiment, one must redouble the subject; but then the phantom, which remains fearful, only advances with suspicion toward the place where the work desired of it calls it; in any case, a great deal of time is lost, and satisfactory results are rarely obtained afterwards. The sound vibrations therefore act with tremendous intensity on the phantom; and, as any movement is reflected from it to the subject, one can, by holding the latter by the hands, observe the sonic movements in it, as one observes them on the surface of a vibrating bell to which one lightly applies one's hand. These movements are even perceived by the phantom well before the noise has reached the ears of the assistants. A heavy car, for example, comes down the street at a certain distance; no one hears it, but the experimenter perceives the subject's agitation under his hands. This agitation increases, the car approaches, one hears it, and the agitation increases still further; the car passes, the noise stops, but the agitation persists for a few moments. The ghost is then more or less disorganized. The sensitivity to sound movement is such that by holding the subject by the hands, one can perceive the agitation produced in the ghost by the sound of the clock striking, which one can barely hear. — After this description, one can easily understand that any noise, even the change of position of a witness, and, above all, the introduction of a stranger into the study, must cause a more or less significant disturbance... "

From the above, one can conclude that it is important not only to choose a room where no accidental noise will penetrate, but also to operate at a time when the operation is most likely not to be disturbed by outside noise. This brings us to the question of choosing the most propitious hour.

Moment. — When dissociating a subject to make their ghost emanate, the most favorable time period for the operation appears to be from 3:00 p.m. until 11:00 p.m. This is certainly an indication, but it should not be applied rigorously to personal out-of-body experience, for the conditions are somewhat different, since, in the first case, it is the action of an external will that produces the phenomenon on a subject, whereas in the second, it is an automatic act.

The Chevalier de Reichenbach had observed that luminous phenomena, produced by a subject in a dark room, begin around mid-afternoon, reach their maximum around 10:00 p.m., and then decrease until the following morning.

This indication is more precise than the previous one, but it is still vague because Reichenbach did not see the reason for the maximum he indicated: I will explain it.

The astral body is both internal and external; there are times when the physiological work of the material body absorbs it, when it contracts in a way on itself to live mainly within the *sarcosôme*; there are others when thought, on the contrary, draws it outside; finally, there are times when, with nothing holding it within the physical body, it tends to escape from it: let's see what these moments are.

At the time when Reichenbach lived, life was generally normal as follows: one rose early; one ate the main meal around noon; in the evening, a simple snack, and one went to bed around 9 or 10 o'clock. What happens in this case, relative to the astral body?

In the morning, it presides over the normal resumption of vital functions; then the ingestion of food and the work of digestion require its control and regulation. When digestion is complete, then it is freer; thought, on the one hand, draws it outside; on the other hand, the *sarcosôme* needs it less since its inner life develops automatically; the evening meal, very light, calls it back and interrupts its exteriorization, which then resumes and increases until the usual time of sleep, during which all bodily functions continue unconsciously, mechanically. Then, nothing holds it back in the *aérosôme,* from which it escapes to a greater or lesser extent, sometimes even completely: hence certain dreams. When the time of waking approaches, it seems as if it regrets returning to its daily work or wants to take advantage of its last minutes of freedom, because, even at this time, one notices in it a push towards the outside. Then it returns to preside over the awakening and continue its task as physical regulator.

We see, therefore, that there are two moments each day when it tends to exteriorize itself in greater proportions than at others: the time when the physical body falls asleep (hence the desire to sleep when one is at the usual time) and the time when it awakens; the first moment (drowsiness) is much preferable to the other, since the tendency to exteriorize is greater there.

So, at least in principle, the moment when one begins to lose consciousness of oneself is by far the most favorable for out-of-body experience: it goes without saying that for the individual who is accustomed to taking a nap in the middle of the day (provided it is not a digestive nap), the beginning of this rest can also be chosen, although less favorable, than the one that inaugurates the deep sleep of the night when the mind is not worried about having to wake up soon, and when, consequently, the astral body feels freer.

But this is only an indication of principle, for there are individuals — I know some — who go to bed, for example, at 10:00 p.m. with the will and the ability to exteriorize themselves, and in whom out-of-body experience only occurs around 2:00 or 3:00 a.m. Is it, in this case, the will that only produces its effect at a certain time? Is it not she who acts, but the monoideism she created before falling asleep, and which needs time to gather strength? Is it finally the work of exteriorization that is slow? I don't know: perhaps these three reasons act simultaneously. In any case, the individuals in whom this delay occurs present an infinitely more complete exteriorization than the others.

In summary, the most propitious moment is the one when one usually falls asleep, in the evening.

On the other hand, is there a particular hour that is preferable to any other?

I had not yet addressed this question when I gave my first paper on the subject of personal splitting at the International Congress of Experimental Psychology in Paris in 1910. At the end of the session, my learned colleague, Pierre Piobb, well known for his scholarly works on scientific occultism, who himself has studied this question extensively, approached me and said: "If one operates at the hour of the Lord of the 9th House, the result is infallible." He has repeated his assertion to me several times since.

Although I have never yet had the opportunity to verify its validity, knowing my interlocutor's authority in such matters, I do not hesitate to offer some guidance in this regard.

To understand his words, it is important to know that in astrology [171], the zodiac comprises twelve *solar houses*, which are the position occupied on the astrological chart by each zodiacal sign, and each possesses its own meaning.

---

[171] I apologize for speaking of astrology here: this word will likely make more than one reader smile; I should have used the term meta-astronomy, which is more appropriate today; but to prevent any misunderstanding and to show that I am concerned in these pages with serious matters, and with serious treatment, it will suffice to say that in our time astrological studies are undergoing a veritable renaissance. It is certain that our times do not yet equal the great eras of Junctinus of Florence or Ptolemy of Pelusium, but finally, today the mathematical difficulty of these special studies calls upon high intellects, astronomers, engineers from the École Polytechnique, etc., as the signatures of several recently published works demonstrate.

As for me, I will be brief, and for good reason, having devoted little time to the study of this science.

The 9th House deals, among other things, with long journeys.

On the other hand, the *lord* of a *house* is the planet that occupies a predominant position there. It is obvious that the *lord* of the ninth *house* varies according to each person's horoscope, that is, depending on whether the establishment of this horoscope places a particular planet in a predominant position in the ninth house: in this regard, it would be prudent to consult a professional. But, on the other hand, if the establishment of the *genethliac chart* does not place any planet in this *house*, or if the planet located there is weak, the natural lord of this *house* is the planet Jupiter, which is, to use the technical term, *on its Throne*. Consequently, in many cases, it will be appropriate to operate during the hours of Jupiter, which are, from midnight, the following:

Monday	—	3rd, 10th, 17th, 24th.
Tuesday	—	7th, 14th, 21st.
Wednesday	—	4th, 11th, 18th.
Thursday	—	1st, 8th, 15th, 22nd.
Friday	—	5th, 12th, 19th.
Saturday	—	2nd, 9th, 16th, 23rd.
Sunday	—	6th, 13th, 20th.

It is explained that the hours in question do not correspond absolutely to the equal division of clocks, but vary according to the days and seasons, and are calculated as follows: Twelve equal hours of night beginning at sunset and ending at sunrise [172]; and twelve equal hours of daylight beginning at sunrise and ending at sunset — the first hour of a day being the one following midnight.

If one adopts this system, it is especially logical to choose one's time on the day of the master of the *house*, which, in this case, is Thursday.

I apologize for this brief incursion into a science that is almost unknown and which seems futile to many. I repeat, I have not had the opportunity to experiment with this system, which I only speak of by hearsay; but it is too curious and touches too closely on the subject studied here to be passed over in silence.

---

[172] Every complete calendar contains the hourly times of sunrise and sunset.

Position. — The best position for performing one's own unfolding is the one that least disturbs the physical body; it is therefore advisable either to lie down in bed or to stretch out comfortably in a large, low armchair. One should avoid tall or narrow armchairs that would hinder sleep, and chairs where the mind, while still fearing a possible fall, would not have complete freedom. One can, in a pinch, lie down on a wooden floor, but not on a bare one: the discomfort of such a position would prevent the body from completely resting, and, consequently, the mind from having complete freedom of action.

In summary, the position matters little, on the express condition that it does not cause any discomfort of any kind and that it does not disrupt the operation in any way.

Moral provisions. — Complete calm of mind is absolutely essential. It is therefore contraindicated to attempt the experiment if one has any material or moral concern, if any preoccupation ties your mind, if any boredom troubles you; even the anticipation, the imminent expectation of such an event constitutes an unfortunate condition; moreover, a great joy, whether experienced or expected, will prevent you from having the freedom of thought necessary for the act you are about to perform. The operator's mind must tend absolutely only toward the experience being prepared; consequently, any motive for distraction, happy or sad, past, present, or future — in short, whatever it may be, whatever its nature and even its importance — must be absent when preparing for this delicate operation of splitting, which requires precise restraint of the mind and great control of the will.

Bodily dispositions. — These dispositions result from all the preceding conditions: bodily well-being, calm of mind, comfortable posture, etc. However, I must add a detail that is important if we remember that the physiological work of digestion hinders the freedom of the astral body; on the day one wishes to attempt the experiment (as also on the days preceding it, so that the organism does not suffer any functional disturbance), it will be advisable to eat very sparingly, remaining largely within one's appetite at each meal. — This does not mean that one must fast, fasting being a cause of bodily and consequently astral weakening, but that it is good to be moderate in one's food, and, between two dishes, to choose preferably the one that contains the greatest quantity of nutritive substance in the smallest volume, so as to burden the stomach as little as possible.

————

CHAPTER X

PSYCHIC PREPARATION
For the initiated only.

This chapter, I hasten to say at the outset, is not written for the proponents of official science, who will be able to laugh at it at their leisure, as they doubtless amused themselves at the one above where the *capture of hyperphysical forces* was studied; it is addressed solely to occultists, and to those who believe that matter is not everything and that the scale of beings does not necessarily end at terrestrial man. But, having undertaken to indicate by what means the phenomenon of personal out-of-body experience can be realized, it would have been illogical for me to leave aside what relates to external aids.

In principle, out-of-body experience is a purely psychic phenomenon, that is, produced solely with the aid of forces that are an integral part of the human being and that are at the personal disposal of the operator, under the conditions we have studied so far, and those we will study later.

But it is no less true that the operation does not take place entirely on the physical plane; it does indeed have, as its starting point, a human being, that is to say, a material entity, to end in another human being, and yet the phenomenon is not, in its entirety, of a material order.

If, indeed, we refer to what was said above about the occult constitution of the human being, we will see that while, in humans, the *sarcosôme* and the etheric double live on the physical plane, the astral body (the basis of the living phantom exteriorized and sent far away) and the higher principles, constituting the human being, live on higher planes and notably on the astral plane. Now, my personal experiences to date have shown me beyond doubt that any operation on the astral plane arouses a struggle between the normal Entities of that plane, some being favorable to the operation while others, on the contrary, are hostile to it.

Why? To what end? We know nothing; but the fact itself is indisputable, and if one wishes to attempt the experiment with the greatest possible chance of success, it is appropriate to take it into account, even though we are completely ignorant of the role that Entities of the astral plane may play in the production of purely amimic phenomena.

It is to my knowledge that various out-of-body experiences, with which I am familiar, have been accomplished with the help of Intelligences external to matter, and supernormal; and, on the other hand, I know of *no* experimental out-of-body experience in which magnetic subjects placed in a state of clairvoyance did not report the intrusion of Astral Entities, some to assist, and others to obstruct it. [173]

We must therefore say a few words about the Entities that are encountered on the plane closest to the one we live in.

Whether they are disembodied human beings, as spiritualist doctrine teaches, or beings in involution (elementals) or in evolution (elementaries), as occultism asserts, or whether, according to theosophy, they are the remnants of an ancient humanity more evolved than ours, matters little. The essential thing is that they exist, that their existence can only be denied through ignorance or bad faith, and that by acting on their plane, one necessarily, fatally, enters into a relationship with them.

Now, their mentality seems, for anyone who has been in contact with them, to be substantially adequate to ours; but what particularly distinguishes them from living man is, on the one hand, that there are among them some who are formidably powerful both in terms of good and evil, and that many of them know how to manipulate matter on earth, in ways we will only know many centuries from now. Our natural or artificial seers [174] describe them to us as generally having a human form, but also generally enveloped in an aura tending towards red or blue [175], each of these colors designating Entities of evil (red) or goodness (blue).

— 234 —

Depending therefore on the goal that the human experimenter sets for himself, he will be helped by the former and hindered by the latter. A person who, for example, pursues the phenomenon with the aim of harming other people will have the Red Entities on their side, while the Blue Entities will strive to make it fail. A person who, on the other hand, pursues a higher goal, whether science or altruism, will be aided by the Blue Entities and will have to fight against the Red Entities.

Therefore, when engaging in this kind of experiment, it is a matter of conciliating the former and neutralizing the latter. How can this be achieved?

In principle, there is only one way: to practice kindness in all its forms, for it is especially true on the astral plane that the saying of popular wisdom holds true: Birds of a feather flock together. By developing within oneself only elevated feelings of altruism, science, and kindness, one calls upon similar Entities around oneself who will assist the operator. Later, when we study the hyperphysical dangers that threaten him, we will see that, for his personal safety, it is necessary for him to act in this way; here, I am only concerned with the help that can be given to him, in view of this experiment, by the Beings of Mystery.

An experimenter, whom I will discuss later, regarding a violent injury to the stomach that he had reported from one of his astral outings, one day asked the Entity of Mystery who guides him

---

[173] We will encounter facts of this nature in Chapter XV: *Practical study of a development.*

[174] Magnetic subjects artificially placed in a state of clairvoyance.

[175] Just as, as we now know, every sound corresponds to a color, so, on the astral plane, every feeling gives its possessor a particular coloration. Leadbeater and Annie Besant, in their work, *Thought-Forms*, established the range of the principal psycho-chromic relationships; we note, for example, that very light yellow corresponds to good intellectuality, light green to sympathy, bluish-gray to fear, etc. Now, within this range, the different shades of blue correspond to higher feelings: devotion, religiosity, affection, etc.; red or reddish colors relate to lower feelings: anger, pride, etc. All these colorations give each of these Entities a particular tone that makes any Entity on the astral plane whose feelings are imbued with kindness appear to the seers to be generally colored blue, more or less light, more or less dark, and those who experience base feelings, selfishness, hatred, jealousy, etc., more or less red. See in this regard the results of certain experiments reported in the chapter on the *Practical Study of a Development.*

in his experiments the following question: "How is it that, when one does not yet possess the awareness of one's direction, one is not injured more often during the experiment?" The answer was: "Fortunately, there is a God for the split; but what has just happened to you is nothing compared to what awaits you until you have acquired the power to direct yourself, and this power you will only acquire through practice and willpower."

This answer needs to be explored further.

"There is a God for the split" clearly means that when one is in this state, friendly Entities watch over the operator, direct their phantom, and prevent them from harm that could threaten them *as much as possible*. As for acquiring mastery of direction, this can only be achieved over time, through experimentation, through energizing the will in this direction, as we shall see later. Will, moreover, has a great influence, depending on its intended goal, on the Entities, good or bad, of the Astral... Always the implementation of will!

But this answer also throws us into a line of thought that, I repeat, I would have liked to avoid discussing, and to which I am led by force of circumstances. It was my intention, in beginning this work, to stay within the realm of experimentation, illuminated solely by the data of psychology and normal science, carefully avoiding any incursion into the domain of occultism — which some people regard as less than serious. Until now, I have deviated from this rule of conduct only on points where, lacking the guidance of normal science, I was obliged to resort to the teachings of Western or Eastern Occultism.

I find myself, even now, in a situation where current science no longer offers us any guidance because it regards all these experiences as so many dreams or mystifications: I must therefore rise above it and approach the immense area of occult science.

Readers of these pages who believe that official science is everything and that one can only go astray by crossing its boundaries will have to close this work here, the preceding chapters of which, in short, open up fairly broad horizons for them by offering them possibilities beyond the banal... Let them therefore be content to dissociate normally, relying on the "God of the split" to avoid possible harm or making the sacrifice of fatalism in advance to whatever may befall them! Provided they do not abuse their acquired faculties, so as to avoid as much as possible the bodily harm that awaits them, their attempt will at least have one good result: that of proving to themselves that in all I have said so far there is nothing impossible and that all the indications given are absolutely serious. It will be the same in these last pages, but, by their very nature, I have already said it and I repeat it once again, they will only be addressed to researchers determined to abandon the paths of official science, to go further than it, to climb higher than it, and to acquire supernormal faculties outside of it and above it.

It is therefore important above all, if one wishes to go further, to enter into relations with the Entities who protect the experimenter's exits, which will ordinarily present no difficulty since they are the very ones who are constantly, unbeknownst to him, in contact with him, and are always nearby; a simple but energetic mental call is enough to bring them back when they momentarily move away.

Two paths are open to those who wish to enter into relations with the Beings of the astral plane: the path of occultism, which leads human beings close to these Entities, which makes them penetrate their domain of the astral plane, and which is particularly easy for those who already possess the faculty of exteriorizing themselves, since all out-of-body experience is an exit to the astral plane; and the path of psychism or spiritualism, which brings the astral Entities to the physical plane. It is the latter that I would prefer to recommend because, if the indications one draws from it are less clear than those provided by occult procedures, since, unless the experimenter personally discovers an appropriate mediumistic faculty, they are given through the intermediary of a medium to whom recourse must be had, at least they are received by the person concerned in the waking state, which allows them to fully penetrate them and act with absolute awareness.

It is therefore advisable to seek out a good writing, auditory, or intuitive medium, and to enter, through them, into contact with the Entity protecting the exits, so that it may carefully follow the ghost and avoid, as far as possible, any dangerous mishaps. [176] The method employed is, in short, nothing more than a collaboration, for this specific purpose, between a human being and an Entity of the Mystery. Strange as it may seem, this method is very often used to achieve a number of goals, but most of the time unconsciously, I mean without the knowledge of the human being who is meant to benefit from it. Conscious collaborations of this nature also exist, but only, it goes without saying, within the reach of those who know how to organize them. [177]

Once one has succeeded, in this way, in entering into communication with the Entity who is best able to account for the way in which the splitting takes place and how the ghost behaves, the path to follow is very simple. One must first study coolly, without bias in any direction whatsoever, I mean without enthusiasm or disdain, the communications obtained in this way, in order to see if one is dealing with a frivolous and mocking being, or with a serious and elevated entity.

In the first case, one must interrupt all relations with the Being whose advice can only be harmful, and proceed, if one wishes to continue, with one's own strength alone, that is, by intensifying one's will toward the goal to be attained on the one hand, and, on the other, by renewing the splitting very frequently, to acquire a habit during which one can gradually become aware of what is happening during the outings: this is what we will see when studying further how one can acquire the awareness of direction.

In the second case, if the Being with whom one has entered into a relationship proves to be evolved and helpful, it is best to let oneself be guided and protected by it, at least for the first attempts; more than the operator, it knows the possible pitfalls of the route, and better than the operator, it is in a position to help the operator avoid them; better than him, finally, he knows his psychic and mental organization, as well as the processes and means which are most appropriate for him to achieve his *desideratum*: consequently, an astral Entity — that is good, it goes without saying — to whom your feelings of kindness have made you sympathetic, will always be for you the most effective protector, and the most appreciable guide.

---

[176] We will see later that this same method can be used, in many cases, to learn the most effective methods for each individual to acquire the awareness of direction.

[177] I mention a case of this kind, which is personal to me, in the final note of the work already cited: *Sorcery of the Countryside.*

The difficulty here is knowing exactly the nature of the Entity with which one enters into a relationship so as not to become, at some point, its victim. Also, just as when it came to training for the development of physical neuritis, the very serious advice was given to rely on enlightened advice to avoid any accident or nervous illness, so, in the present circumstance, the operator who wishes to resort to assistance from the Mystery will act very prudently, if he is not absolutely aware of these matters, by being accompanied, at the chosen medium's home, by a perceptive witness, familiar both with the generality of the Entities who respond in such cases and with the processes of out-of-body communication, and capable of discerning the traps that could be set for the experimenter's ignorance.

I apologize, once again, to the ordinary reader, for having written this chapter which will have seemed childish to him: it will seem, on the other hand, necessary — and it seemed so to me — to every occultist and to every psychic, as well, I think, as to all those who believe that, in cases where normal science remains silent, it is better to draw some light from outside it, rather than to remain struggling in the darkness.

———

PART THREE

———

PRACTICAL

CHAPTER XI

———

EXPERIMENTATION

So, you have carefully followed your own training in self-doubt; you have felt your will energize, take on an authority, a self-possession you didn't know it possessed; you have noted the progressive development of your neuritis and the degree of hyperesthesia of your sensitivity... you want to move from theory to execution, and transform your acquired knowledge and latent possibilities into action... How will you act?

Perhaps I should have included the chapter on the *dangers* of the experiment here so that the potential operator would be well aware of what he is exposing himself to. But I am sure that, among all the readers of these pages, there will not be one lacking enough common sense to attempt the adventure while ignoring the risks involved.

So, I assume these risks are known, as well as how to protect oneself against them, and I repeat: How will you act?

You must not believe that, from the first attempt, you will be master of the operation: if this is to be so, it is because you will have had in your possession an absolutely well-predisposed organism, and because your training will have been followed with mathematical exactitude, stopping just at the extreme point, — without remaining below, which would leave you with unused strength — without going beyond, which can produce organic accidents in you. Practice must therefore be nothing more than a series of attempts to achieve increasingly significant results, and only when you have reached the last one can you call yourself master of the operation; even then, success must not be fortuitous, but repeated a certain number of times.

I will therefore examine successively all the degrees that must be climbed with patient and tireless energy before reaching the last one.

A) *Preliminary tests.*

I strongly recommend, for the reasons explained above, that you carry out the first tests while lying in bed and in your first sleep: in this way, the act of splitting will be facilitated by the circumstance itself, and part of its operations will be carried out unconsciously, mechanically, automatically.

To this end, you should force yourself to go to bed every night at the same time — a little before the time you notice sleep occurring.

As soon as you are lying in bed, assume a comfortable position, preferably the one you are used to sleeping in, but avoid lying on your left side because, in this situation, the heart is always somewhat hampered by the weight of the surrounding organs. I believe the best position is lying on your back: this is the one in which breathing occurs most normally.

It goes without saying that all lights should be turned off if possible, and those outside should be as dimmed as possible; that one will have no worries, no worries on one's mind; in a word, that all the general conditions of the experience will be met.

As soon as one is lying in the chosen position and the sheets have noticeably reached body temperature, it is important to concentrate within oneself and direct all one's will toward this single goal: to exteriorize oneself. As sleep approaches, the mind tends to wander and touch upon all sorts of subjects: one must react against this unfortunate propensity, and fix one's thoughts solely on the proposed goal, so as to create the monoideism that will act when sleep has dulled the will itself. To this end, one must try to mentally picture the progress of the operation: the *sarcosôme* gradually becoming numb in a drowsiness that is first light, then increasingly deep, finally leading to sleep; the *aérosôme* emanating little by little, partly to the right, partly to the left, to then reunite on the left and form the phantom, etc. The test must be done several times — several consecutive evenings as much as possible, trying to keep, *wanting* to keep the memory of what will have happened during this astral outing, and which, at the time, will seem like a dream — admitting, which is very rare at the beginning, that one has it and above all that one remains aware of it.

These first astral projections are quite difficult to control, because for many people they leave no memory other than that of what is commonly called a leaden sleep. Others, on the contrary, wake up the next day with a more or less pronounced general fatigue — which in some goes as far as stiffness — as if during the night they had engaged in great bodily work, at least somnambulistic, because their memory has recorded no other memory of the night than that of a deep, continuous, and calm sleep. Some, finally, wake up the next day in a more or less pronounced state of nervousness accompanied by slight discomfort (headaches, etc.).

The physiological consequences of out-of-body experience vary depending on the organism, and it is only over time, through experimentation, that when one does not retain the memory of what was done during the out-of-body experience, one can realize whether one has truly exteriorized oneself.

The delicate aspect of these first attempts is that one has not yet found a way to verify their reality; one can, however, try to control these first attempts at exiting oneself, using the following procedure: — On the edge of a piece of furniture, place a very light object, for example a slightly bulky duvet, a sheet of cigarette paper, a match, and doze off with the intention of *wanting* this object fall; in this case, we will not only be content to imagine the progress of the splitting, but also the act that must follow, that is to say: the *aérosôme* sliding on the floor towards the piece of furniture where the object is placed, the internal efforts that one can make to make this object fall, either by pushing it with one's finger, or by blowing on it, etc.

In a word, at the moment when sleep grips the physical body, the act to be accomplished must be broken down into all its parts, so that the monoideism created by the operator preserves its details.

It is perfectly possible that this type of experiment will not succeed, any more than others of the same kind that one might have attempted: one should not conclude from this that the splitting does not take place, but that the exteriorized phantom does not yet have sufficient strength to accomplish the projected act; it is only later and with the help of another *criterion* that we will know whether or not the splitting takes place. This constitutes only a series of tests, preliminary attempts whose aim is to clarify things; for example, with regard to the will, if one feels that one is sleeping badly, that sleep is disturbed, it is because the will has been too violent, and that the monoideism created by it proceeds from exasperation and prevents rest, which should not be. The will put into action must be, as I have said elsewhere, clear, firm, but without abruptness, without jolts, without exacerbation — such as, to make an analogy, that which would have made you definitively set an early date for a long-ago journey: such a resolution does not disturb sleep, which does not prevent it from being very firm and from being accomplished on the appointed day.

When we have made several attempts of this kind, and as a result, we have reason to suppose that the exteriorization is operating normally, we will have to get in touch with a receptive subject.

B) *Choice of the receptive subject*

The best subject one can encounter is, without a doubt, one who belongs to the category of so-called *clairvoyant* mediums, because they exhibit all the qualities required from the point of view that concerns us: easy exteriorization of their etheric forces to assist the ghost of the experimenter who has reached them, and material discernment of ghostly forms. [178]

But, just as not every medium is clairvoyant, so not every clairvoyant is necessarily a medium: clairvoyance and mediumship are sometimes found in the same individual, but they are not necessarily concomitant. It is quite rare, moreover, to have a medium around them who is precisely a clairvoyant at the same time, or to be sufficiently connected with them to ask for their assistance in controlling a series of attempts at out-of-body experience.

---

[178] Mediumship, as we now know, is based above all on the subject's ability to exteriorize their etheric double.

But if one is lucky enough to know such a subject in their intimate relationships, it is with them and not with another that one *must* experiment, for they will be better able than anyone to observe the success or failure of the first attempts and to follow — profitably for the operator — all the successive stages of progressive development.

The best receptive subject that can be encountered after the clairvoyant medium is undoubtedly the good magnetic subject, also accustomed to exteriorizing their etheric double. But the choice of such a subject, unless they know how to place themselves in a state of sleep through self-magnetization processes, will lead to practical difficulties, because for each experiment, they will need to have a magnetizer at their side to put them in the desired state.

In any case, if he knows how to place himself there, he will provide roughly the same services as a clairvoyant medium — superior to him in some respects, since he can be brought, as it were, to a deeper and deeper hypnoid state, while mediumship is invariable; — inferior to him in other respects, since mediumship is persistent at all hours of the day and night, while the magnetic subject, in a normal state, is devoid of both clairvoyance and the possibility of exteriorizing himself.

I believe, having seen this type of operation, that the best mode of experimentation consists of using both kinds of subjects: the medium as the receptive subject, and the magnetic subject, near the operator, as a witness to the phenomenon; in this case, he either reports, as the operation progresses, what he is able to observe, or — provided he retains the memory of his perceptions in this state — he recounts, after waking, what he saw.

But, like the clairvoyant medium, the good magnetic subject is not necessarily in the ordinary relationships of everyone. It is therefore a matter of compensating for this by using any person, but one whose organism both approximates a certain required ideal and presents some facilities for the special development of certain of his faculties.

I will therefore explain what these faculties must be and how to go about developing them and bringing them to a point where the chosen person can become not a medium or a magnetic subject, but a good receptive subject for the experimenter, and capable of properly controlling his experiments.

The principal quality of a receptive subject is clairvoyance; but relatively few seers are aware of this quality; for most, it is a possibility that is only latent because they have lacked the opportunities to become aware of it. It is therefore unlikely that one has a true seer, a conscious seer, in one's immediate surroundings or even in the circle of one's acquaintances; but, on the other hand, everyone certainly has an unconscious seer around them: — it is a matter of discovering them.

If one has thoroughly understood what has been said previously about temperaments, one will recall that the basis for the production or perception of psychic phenomena is neuritis. Consequently, the receptive subject must be a nervous person; but precisely the nervous person is, of all men, — after the sanguine person — the most prone to hallucinations, which must above all be avoided in a subject whose faculty must be used for the purpose of control; the purely nervous person must therefore be discarded. A temperament that is mitigated by the nervous person must be found — but in what way?

The sanguine person is even more exposed to subjective hallucinations than the nervous person, and the lymphatic person is susceptible to almost no phenomena: these two classes must therefore be discarded. On the other hand, the bilious person is very adept at observing the existence of psychic phenomena: it is therefore appropriate to choose the receptive subject from one of the three categories below, listed in order of importance with respect to the desired goal:

1. Bilious-nervous;
2. Nervous-bilious;
3. Purely bilious.

The bilious-nervous person should be much preferred to any other. It goes without saying that if one uses a medium or a magnetic subject as a receptive subject, they must exhibit the same characteristics — and in reality, they do, since they are very generally of both a nervous and bilious temperament, which allows them to simultaneously perceive the phenomenon and assist in its realization.

But even then, it may be that the subject is neither nervous enough, nor, above all, bilious enough, and that they need to develop one side of their temperament — I will therefore indicate the procedure to follow to achieve this *desideratum*.

He must first follow the preparatory diet to bring his body back into balance, as the operator himself did; the formula has been given above: likewise, the formula for temperamental detoxification, if necessary, which is a very rare case because, to use it, one would have to deal with a purely bilious person.

It is therefore mainly the bilious side of the temperament that will need to be developed in certain cases.

Here is the formula for the diet that should be followed to achieve this result.

Food. — White meat stews; long sauces; fish in court bouillon; onions, leeks, garlic, cabbage, broad beans; melons, watermelons, bananas, very ripe oranges; medlars, corms, chestnuts; black and stale bread.

Drinks. — Cider, pear, wine, milk.

Habits. — Little sleep on a hard bed (six to seven hours), moderate intercourse. Occupations. Boring, absorbing, selfish, as much as possible.

Emotions. — Long-lasting and unpleasant, but not violent; gnawing worries.

Chemical stimulants. — Sweet alcohol (kirsch, rum, cognac, etc.) and certain liqueurs such as kummel, blackcurrant, anisette; yerba mate, coca infusion, tea.

Physical stimulants. — Lukewarm baths not exceeding fifteen minutes; dull, sad colors: gray, greenish-yellow, slate blue, dull violet, etc.

To be avoided. — Cordials: Chartreuse, Benedictine, raspail, etc.

These treatments should be followed as indicated above.

There is yet another reason why the subject must be endowed with a certain neuropathy capable of expressing itself to a relative extent. We know from experience that the astral body, reduced to its own forces, has no effect on matter: in order for it to be able to act on matter, that is to say, to materialize itself either partially or totally, it must possess etheric forces within itself, in addition to its own energy.

We know, moreover, that the etheric double moves only very little — a few meters at most, and sometimes less than a meter — from the physical organism whose material life it possesses, and that it returns to this organism as soon as the phantom moves away from it.

In the preliminary experiments indicated in the previous chapter, the astral body, acting near its *sarcosôme*, possesses within itself the etheric force of this *sarcosôme*. But as soon as it moves away from it, it is, by that very fact, deprived of this force, which is nevertheless necessary to act on matter. In this case, where can it draw this force that it lacks? From the receptive subject who, obviously in such an occurrence, must play the role of a true medium [179].

It is therefore appropriate that this subject be able to exteriorize itself to provide the operator with the etheric force that he may need, this etheric force being communicated with a certain ease.

But a bilious-nervous temperament and the ability to express oneself to a certain extent are not the only conditions that a receptive subject must meet.

He must also be:

1. Linked to the operator by a mutual sympathy, which will aid in the splitting. Indeed, warned in advance of the days and times planned for the experiment, he will himself send his thought — a reflection of himself — toward the experimenter, and this thought, a vehicle of sympathy, will powerfully attract the *aérosôme* to be emanated.

2. Favorable to the experiment. This goes without saying: an assistant hostile to an undertaking always causes it to fail, and in

---

[179] There is not only an analogy in the two cases, there is a perfect similarity. Indeed, in an experimental spiritualist séance, the Entities that present themselves, being devoid of physical bodies, possess no etheric force that would allow them to act on matter. They therefore borrow that of the assistants, and particularly of the medium, whose characteristic is precisely to be a veritable reservoir of etheric force. This is why I said that the best receptive subject would be a medium gifted with clairvoyance.

this case, the failure would be due to the opposing effluvia that his thought would bring with it.

3. Endowed with a certain composure in order to first carefully observe the phenomenon he will witness in order to then accurately report it to the person concerned, and to even be able to assist with his will, which will be of great influence throughout the entire course of the experiment. This composure, moreover, will allow him, in the event that the phantom is not yet visible (which only happens over time), to analyze his own sensations to deduce those that may be the work of the present but invisible phantom.

4. Possess a certain technical training, to usefully follow the phases of the operator's development, to know, in the event of the phantom being visible, which part of the experimenter he is dealing with (astral reflection or *aérosôme*), etc.

5. Furthermore, it will be a good idea, at least for the first attempts, for him not to live far from the operator; even if he can be encountered under his own roof (but in another room), this will only be better, for the reason that will be explained, this proximity should aid success.

Finally, which sex is best to choose as this receptive subject? Men, generally speaking, possess more composure, and women more sensitivity; but since the first quality is acquired more easily than the second, it is to be expected that a woman will respond better to what one has the right to expect from a receptive subject. — It goes without saying that, if one can find as subjects two spouses presenting the sensitivity of the woman united with the composure of the man, the experiment will have all the more chance of success.

Before moving on to the tests that can be carried out with the receptive subject, it remains for me to say a few words about a rather rare case, I believe, but which, at least, can arise: that in which the receptive subject, after having been developed, displays good qualities, but at the same time reveals himself exposed to hallucinations, which removes all his value as a subject; this can come from several causes in him, notably from his rich blood. It is therefore appropriate — recalling what was said above, that hallucinations have no effect on the lymphatic individual — to bring the subject's temperament back towards lymphatism, which is done quite easily by using the following regimen that I borrow from Marius Decrespe [180].

Food. — Sausages in moderate quantities; heavy vegetable foods, such as sauerkraut, corn and buckwheat porridge; few onions and other lilies; all starchy foods, potatoes, beans, lentils, split peas, etc.; rye bread in fairly large quantities; for drinks, plenty of beer, lots of milk, and pure water.

Habits. — Prolonged sleep (nine to ten hours) in a soft, fairly warmly covered bed; absolute continence; a very sedentary life requiring as little movement as possible; indoor occupations requiring no physical or intellectual effort, other than application and perseverance (do not overexert your patience, especially if you do not have much of it naturally); entertain yourself with simple but persistent, though not obsessive, ideas; carefully avoid emotions; accustom yourself to having a lot of order, especially in small things; maniacally applying oneself to always putting the smallest objects in the same place and, above all, within easy reach.

Chemical stimulants. — Snuff or smoked tobacco, and, to help one get used to sleep, very little chloral, and only in the early stages.

Physical stimulants. — Prolonged lukewarm baths (at least half an hour every other day in the afternoon); soft, pale colors.

C) *Test with a receptive subject*

When you have finally met the subject whose collaboration will help bring the out-of-body experiment to a successful conclusion, here is how you should act towards them.

First, you must warn them of the day and time the attempt is to be made, so that they can actively participate by sending their sympathetic thoughts to you at the appointed time. They must also

_____
[180] *Research on experimental conditions.* Messrs. Hector and Henri Durville, Editors.

want the operation to succeed and, to this end, they must set two objectives at their will: 1. the release of the operator's *aérosôme*; 2. the visit that the exteriorized phantom *must* make to them, while visible. But it is also important to be on guard against possible hallucinations that the subject's current awareness can create. They should therefore only be warned in the early stages, until they have repeatedly observed either a vision of the phantom or minor incidental phenomena from which they can draw the *certain* conclusion that the phantom has come near them. From this point on, the visits must be announced to him very imprecisely: "these days" or "next week," in order to keep him alert to the production of the phenomenon, but also to check, by matching times and dates, whether he is experiencing any unconscious hallucinations.

I return to the first attempt with the subject.

This will require the following little preparation.

I assume that, for greater ease, this subject lives near the operator or even under his roof. The operator will have to make the journey to his subject several times beforehand, walking slowly and carefully observing all the details of his path: draperies, furniture in the anteroom and corridors, if it is in the same apartment, shops, streets, signs, etc., if there is an exit, all details that must be precisely recorded by memory. He must then visit the future subject as closely as possible in the room he will occupy at the time of the experiment; note the topography of the apartment, the particularities of the rooms to be crossed, the overall layout and details of the room where he will be received by the subject; in a word, understand all the particulars of the path to be taken, in order to be able to carry it out mentally, at the very moment of the operation.

But that's not all, and it is now a matter of magnetizing the astral body, of guiding it, as it were, toward the subject, which requires further preparation.

We have seen that the astral body exteriorizes itself like a vapor at the level of the spleen to form, to the right and left of the operator, two half-ghosts whose union, usually on the left, constitutes the complete phantom. This is the general course of the operation reduced to a theoretical diagram; but if the fluidic vapor is emanated by the *sarcosôme* especially at the level of the spleen, this does not mean that it only emerges there; at the moment of sleep, there is a true expansion of the astral body which, until then enclosed within the physical body, seems to escape from it through all its pores, the exteriorization at the level of the spleen being only more abundant, and, consequently, more perceptible to the sensitives who are present at the experiment. So at this moment, the astral body forms a veritable *aura* around the material body: in this movement of expansion, it must enclose within itself the magnetizing agent that will guide it in its exit, the nature of which can vary infinitely: a letter (as recent as possible), a lock of hair, etc., coming from the receptive subject and which you will have previously placed under the pillow or which you will hold in your hand if the subject is a woman wearing her own particular perfume; a few drops of this perfume spread on the pillow will indicate to the phantom, by awakening its suitor, the direction to follow, etc.

In a word, it is important that throughout the entire duration of the work of dissociation, the *aérosôme* be in contact with a material object which, combined with the action of the monoideism previously created by the will, guides it in the desired direction. Once these preparations are made, one should go to bed at the usual time and direct one's will toward a dual goal: exteriorizing the *aérosôme,* and sending this exterior *aérosôme* toward the receptive subject. This will must remain fixed, firm, and immutable, but without violence, without distraction, without jolts, as long as drowsiness does not set in, so as to create, in full lucidity, in full possession of oneself, the monoideism that will act shortly. When one experiences the warning signs of resolution, when one notes the first symptoms of numbness, one must mentally travel the entire path to arrive at the place where the receptive subject is waiting, recalling as precisely and clearly as possible all the details of the journey: in a word, one must create in one's mind the landmarks that will guide the ghost in its exit. If sleep seizes the operator at the very moment he finds himself mentally in contact with the receptive subject, it will be perfect.

Now, once sleep has occurred, what happens? The astral body has begun to exteriorize itself from the beginning of torpor; outside the *sarcosôme*, it finds the thought of the receptive subject whose sympathy powerfully assists it in this operation, attracting it. But during this expansion, it is in a certain state of turmoil comparable to that of a man who awakens and who needs a few seconds to regain possession of all his faculties. It is during this period of expansion, where he remains undecided, floating, that he must encounter the magnetizing agent, a letter, hair, or perfume, which imprints an idea on him and gives direction to his nascent activity. On the other hand, as his state of confusion fades, he becomes aware [181] of the monoideism created by the will, which tends to send him to the very source of the magnetizing agent. The action of this monoideism is energized in him by the will of the receptive subject, whose effluvia he perceives, and which acts in the same direction by attracting him. Here, then, are three agents joining forces to lead him to the place where he is expected. He lets himself go, and it is then that all the points of reference that the operator mentally established before falling asleep come into play: the *aérosôme* recognizes its path, follows its route, and arrives at the desired location.

This astral projection could not be better compared than to the following example:

Two travelers are traveling by carriage to a country they know very little about, but where, before becoming theirs, their horse lived. Their ignorance of the place, at night, has caused them to take a path full of potholes where their horse stops, exhausted. Both dismount: one, who knows the place better than his companion, takes the animal by the bridle and pulls it forward; the other pushes on the wheel to help it out of the rough patch, and, in this way, one pulling and the other pushing, they arrive at a main road; but then the horse recognizes the path it has often traveled before; it thinks it is being taken back to its old stable, and, of its own accord, it goes to the place where it was intended to be taken.

D) *Development.*

It should not be assumed that the exteriorized phantom will appear, alive and luminous, to the receptive subject from this first attempt: visibility is one of the qualities acquired last. It may, of course, happen that the *aérosôme* is seen from the first attempt, but

---

[181] This consciousness of the exteriorized ghost is one of the subconsciousnesses of the integral being.

this is, and can only be, a very rare exception, and for this to occur, the experimenter must, from the outset, emanate torrents of psychic force.

But, it may be asked, if the phantom is not visible, how can we know if the experiment was successful?

Here, the percipient must use all their sagacity, all their powers of observation and analysis, as well as all their memory, to retain the memory of even the most minor incidents that may have marked the phantom's passage. For example, it seemed to them, among other things, that they were hit on the forehead or the hand; If, the next time, he experiences the same sensation, there is a good chance that it is the work of the ghost; if in the future he perceives the same sensation each time the release has been announced to them, there can no longer be any doubt for him — except that which must always arise from the possibilities of hallucination.

The example just cited is taken at random from among a hundred other possibilities; but it must be remembered that, during his first outings, the ghost is always quite weak because he is naturally fearful. And this is understandable: — confined, during normal daytime life in the physical body, he has acquired the habit of letting himself be guided by it, which is, in short, the first interested in not hurting himself; the result is that, outside the physical body — a fact amply emerges from H. Durville's experiments — he is remarkably clumsy in guiding himself; also, in the unconscious outings to which everyone is more or less prone, he prefers to go to the space where he feels freer and where the friends he has temporarily abandoned to incarnate attract him. Therefore, this clumsiness in guiding himself, which stems from his lack of habit, makes him timid and, as a consequence, robs him of his strength; consequently, it is possible that he may not even be able to make himself felt tactilely and that the only phenomenon announcing his presence will be a kind of oppression — more moral than material — that the receptive subject will experience. This is to say how meticulously the subject must observe, during these tests, all his sensations, both external and internal, in order to see which of them will be repeated during each of the experiences.

Indeed, it is important to note that the exteriorized ghost tends to repeat the same actions each time. A person I know intimately and who engages in these experiments has two receptive subjects whom his *aérosôme* usually finds at night during their sleep: one of them is generally awakened by feeling his hair pulled or by hearing his name called, the other by feeling his arm shaken. This repetition of the same acts stems, I believe, from the very timidity of the ghost, who constantly fears hurting himself; he has noticed that a certain act performed near a certain person does not harm him, and he repeats, on the next occasion, this act, which he knows from experience to have no adverse consequences to fear.

Regarding the act — always the same — to be performed near the receptive subject to manifest his presence, the operator can try to assist in its production by himself *wanting*, before falling asleep, for his *sarcosôme* to perform a previously defined act, of which he has first made known to his receptive subject. But one must be careful that the will that proposes multiple and simultaneous goals usually lacks clarity and, consequently, strength.

Now, when the operator acted alone, he proposed only one goal: to exteriorize himself; when he then joined an assistant, his goal became threefold: to exteriorize himself — to send his phantom to a certain place — to guide it on its path; this is already a lot. If, in addition, it is necessary to attach the order to perform a specific act when it arrives at its destination, there is a risk that the will, spread over four objects, will lose its strength and clarity, and that the result of the operation will be entirely negative.

This is therefore only an indication given, and not a rule to be applied; in such matters, it is up to each person to consult their willpower and see what they are capable of doing, taking care to note that the will to exteriorize themselves and send their *aérosôme* to a particular location must take precedence over all else.

In the case where one wishes to order a previously designated act, this act must *always* be chosen from among those pertaining to tangibility, for it is the physical quality that the phantom acquires before any other [182]. This is all the more so. Later, as it acquires visibility in terms of audibility, it sometimes precedes, sometimes accompanies, and sometimes finally follows visibility.

At first, therefore, one can only ask the exteriorized *aérosôme,* as an act indicative of its presence, for a phenomenon of tangibility, whether it must touch or grasp the percipient subject at a certain point in their body, or whether it must disturb or overturn a certain pre-prepared object.

Material proof of the presence of the phantom in the receptive subject can be obtained by using the law of repercussion, according to which any injury to the astral body inevitably reverberates on the physical body.

Naturally, it is useless to ask the ghost to injure itself: its timidity would prevent it from obeying, since it is very timid simply when it comes to possible things, — and moreover, even if it obeys, the injury thus obtained would present no conclusive evidence, since it could have suffered it elsewhere, and finally, nothing would prove that it was not the *sarcosôme* itself that personally suffered this injury. It must therefore be the percipient subject himself who injures the ghost.

It goes without saying that this injury must present no danger: it is therefore necessary to prohibit stabbing or gunshot wounds which could, by disintegrating the astral body, kill the physical body [183]. It is not, in fact, a matter of making a deep wound, but a visible and therefore undeniable wound.

This, I know, will distance from the experiment the merely curious, solicited only by the desire, without more, to carry out an extraordinary experiment... I will be delighted, because it is not to such people that I am addressing myself here, but to serious

---

[182] In spiritualist materialization sessions, one is very often touched without seeing anything; the sounds one perceives are the sounds of impacts formed by the collision of some object. When one patiently pursues experiments with the same Entity, this Entity, which one has first and repeatedly touched and felt, needs a certain number of attempts before being able to speak. Even then, in the early stages, its language is difficult to understand due to its inability to pronounce certain letters, and it is only over time that it manages to make itself clearly understood. Thus, an Entity I followed for a long time only managed to pronounce my name after five sessions; until then, it had said: *Hachin*. As for visibility, it only develops completely last, and sometimes after months of work, trials, and fruitless attempts. Since the living ghost is of the same nature and endowed with the same possibilities as the dead ghost, it is easy to draw analogical conclusions from one to the other and to believe that the same laws govern their physical development.

[183] See on this subject experiments conducted by the author or reported by him in *Sorcery of the Countryside*, 1 vol. octavo, Paris, 1910. Messrs. Hector and Henri Durville, Editors.

experimenters, those who have enough conscience to know that if, when operating on a foreign subject, it is necessary to surround it with the most learned precautions to spare it any harm, on the other hand, when experimenting on oneself, it is necessary, while surrounding oneself with the necessary precautions, not to shrink from the occasional risk of injury. So, here is the procedure that I will indicate: — When the receptive subject knows, without a doubt, that the operator's phantom is near him, he arms himself with a steel needle, the point of which will exceed his fingers by one or two centimeters, and he strikes the phantom with it, not normally, which would only cause a prick, but by sliding obliquely so as to make a long tear.

But a precaution must be taken. We know that any injury to an astral body affects its *sarcosôme*, but we do not know, since neither experience nor observation have ever been made, whether this is only in the form of trauma or accompanied by all its harmful elements. It would therefore be advisable, to avoid any chance of phlegmon for the operator whose phantom is injured, to first flame the needle with alcohol; but this can only be done in the presence of a strongly formed phantom, otherwise the light would dissolve it. However, one can get as close as possible to this method by first flaming the needle, which will then be kept in an aseptic environment until ready to use. In such cases, the simplest procedure is this: — Take a steel needle (copper needles, painted needles, etc., must be strictly prohibited) five or six centimeters long, and insert it, so that its point protrudes about two centimeters, into a stopper tightly sealing a small bottle itself filled with an aseptic solution (boric acid at 40 grams per 1000 grams of boiled water, — sublimated at 0.25 grams per 1000 grams, — or carbolic acid at 3 grams per 1000 grams). Once the needle has been flamed with alcohol, it is immersed in the bottle, which is sealed by the stopper, the liquid should touch the base of the stopper. When the time comes to act, one need only withdraw the needle by grasping the stopper, which then forms its handle.

It is sometimes difficult to injure the ghost, because as soon as it guesses the witness's intention, it moves away with surprising agility. To my knowledge, there is one case where, for twenty minutes, the receptive subject pursued the clearly materialized ghost across his room without being able to reach him: as soon as he approached, the other quickly slipped away and fled to the other end of the room. This is due to the fear a ghost feels of any injury, because it knows that it can be disintegrated immediately if it is too deep, and that in any case, the physical body would suffer. It is therefore necessary to injure it, as it were, unexpectedly, which is relatively easy when it is visible: I say *unexpectedly*, when it has no idea what the witness is planning [184].

But when it is invisible? One must then wait until the witness feels the ghost's hand rest on their arm, forehead, or elsewhere, and takes advantage of this to inflict the wound; under other conditions, success would be merely the result of a highly improbable coincidence.

In all cases, when the *aérosôme* is injured in this way, the *sarcosôme* awakens under the influence of pain if the splitting is only partial; if it is complete, the *sarcosôme* only becomes aware of it upon natural awakening the next morning. From what I am saying, I have had several examples.

When it is impossible to reach the ghost to injure it, another method can be used, certainly less convincing than an injury, but still offering certain undeniable guarantees. Here it is: — it is not only the lesions themselves that are transmitted from the astral body to the physical body: in principle, *everything* that affects the former is transmitted to the latter [185]. From this point on, one can prepare in the witness or receptive subject a solution of eosin or any other tenacious dye. If the operator and the percipient combine their will so that the ghost dips the tips of its fingers in this solution — which, in short, will not injure it — there is a good chance that it will obey, but then — and I speak from experience, having seen this happen — the repercussions only occur sometime later,

---

[184] It should be noted, however, that this condition is quite difficult to fulfill, since the operator having previously warned the subject, the phantom is, by that very fact, aware of the planned experiment. — In this case, the operator must be in absolute control of his phantom to *force* it, despite any fear on the latter's part, to run the risk of injury; this means that this type of control should not be attempted in the first few attempts and can only be attempted with any chance of success when the exteriorized phantom is well familiar with the receptive subject.

[185] This is why, although it is not yet known whether the toxins of an astral wound are found in the subsequent physical wound, it is recommended above to *flame sterilize* the instruments that may be used to act on the *aérosôme*.

sometimes even the next day, that is, when the astral body has completely reintegrated its physical body; only then does the operator see his fingers covered in the dye used.

There is still one case where material proof of out-of-body experience exists: it is the one where the receptive subject is *burned* by the touch of the operator's phantom; but since this case only occurs fortuitously and in conditions that we still know only poorly, I only mention it here; — since, on the other hand, it constitutes, when it occurs, a risk (not very serious in truth, but still a risk) for the receptive subject, it will be discussed at greater length in the chapter on psycho-physical dangers [186].

The day we obtain this proof of out-of-body experience, a great step has been taken in this direction — the main one, perhaps, since we have the certainty that we can exteriorize ourselves. But if this is enormous progress, in terms of individuals who are resistant to any attempt at dissociation, it is nothing compared to the results that remain to be achieved — and which, like this one and in the same way, are absolutely within the realm of possibility for those *who want them*.

Among these results still to be achieved, there are five principal ones that must be pursued above all, and which are, in order of importance: audibility, visibility, the accomplishment of a previously willed act, awareness of direction, and finally the preservation of memory, the most important condition because when it is fulfilled it provides powerful assistance in the accomplishment of those that have not yet been achieved. I have just indicated these conditions in their order of practical importance, but this order is not, generally, the same as that of development; therefore, I will say a few words about them by following this last step, which is, at least generally: the accomplishment of a previously willed act, visibility, awareness of direction, and the preservation of memory.

It will be noted that I do not mention audibility; this is because, as I said above, the mode of development of this physical quality is, at present, relatively little known; I think it should be considered as concomitant and parallel to that of visibility; consequently, there is no need to concern ourselves with it: it arrives at its own time, and if, by chance, all the other conditions were fulfilled except for this one alone, it would then be easy to pursue this last result: — when, in fact, one possesses memory and visibility, it is relatively easy to compel the ghost to speak.

It has just been said that the above-mentioned qualities are listed in their *general* order of development: there are indeed exceptions — and numerous ones: in one experimenter, a certain faculty develops very easily and before another, while, in a different operator, the opposite occurs; this disparity in results can be explained by the various aptitudes of the astral body, although there is no need to address them here. For example, I know an experimenter whose ghost, according to his subjects, possesses tangibility, audibility, and visibility, and who, despite all his efforts, has not yet been able to make his ghost perform a specifically designated act. It is therefore advisable not to attach too much importance to the order of development, which can vary infinitely depending on the aptitudes of each individual.

Finally, there is a degree of development that one can — that one must — achieve; and about which I must say a few words: it is out-of-body experience in the waking state.

Generally, this faculty is innate and reveals itself by chance in its possessor: several cases can be found in Durville's aforementioned work, *The Ghost of the Living*. But it can also be acquired with work and tenacity, because it is, in short, only the culmination, if I may express it that way, of the efforts made previously to achieve out-of-body experience while asleep. It follows that this stage should only be approached when one has mastered the process while asleep.

People in whom this faculty is innate exercise it as follows: — they become absorbed in themselves, in a deep reverie having as their object the place where they wish to send their ghost or the act it must perform there; and, when their degree of restraint is sufficient, the splitting occurs by itself, in a sort of mechanical way, without, at least for most of them, losing consciousness. — I do not hide the fact that, through training and practice, one can acquire this operational facility, although experience, while requiring certain precautions and special preparations, is perfectly within the realm of possibility.

---

[186] Chapter XII, section B.

Here is how it should be done:

After placing oneself comfortably in an armchair, on a sofa, or on a bed, in a position that can be maintained for a certain time without any fatigue, one abstracts oneself from the surroundings. This may seem difficult for someone in a waking state; this is nevertheless achieved by the following process:

Man relates to external things by means of the five senses: sight, hearing, smell, touch, and taste — it is not a matter of annihilating these five senses, but of suspending their exercise for a certain time.

Taste will not concern us since, during this entire time, there can only be the swallowing of saliva, which, in itself, has a neutral flavor that does not arouse any particular excitement in the taste buds, which are accustomed to it.

For the sense of smell, it will suffice if the room where one operates does not contain overly strong odors, for example perfumes or pungent notes, and that it only arouses in the sense of smell sensations to which it is accustomed, and which, consequently, will not arouse any particular attention in it.

The sense of touch is already more difficult to dull; But one can take advantage of the habituation that occurs with great ease in him to achieve this. It is therefore sufficient not to move, to remain in absolute immobility, and, once he has made contact with everything in the immediate environment that can have an effect on him, he falls asleep, waking only if any movement brings him into contact with new objects or with a new form of objects: therefore, to neutralize it, all movement must be avoided — the body must rest inert in the place where it has been placed.

To obliterate hearing, to make it insensitive to all external noise, it is sufficient to dab the ears firmly with cotton.

Sight, if the room where one is operating is in perfect darkness, does not require special preparation; but if it filters the slightest ray of light, if the prevailing darkness allows the outline of objects to be glimpsed, even vaguely, one should place cotton balls over the eyes, held in place by a blindfold.

All these precautions taken, one becomes absorbed in an intense desire to free oneself and go and perform such and such an act. Absolute immobility quickly leads, under these conditions, to a numbness which becomes increasingly profound and favors the production of the phenomenon. In the midst of this torpor, all thought must be annihilated and the mind concentrated on its sole will, in an intense, unbreakable will, I would say almost materialized, since, in the words of an experimenter I know, when, at times, in such a case, an instinctive surge of consciousness occurs in him that brings him back for a moment to reality, he feels only his will *passing through his head like an iron bar*.

When all these conditions are met, the splitting occurs quickly: the operator slips into a general relaxation, a kind of lethargy in which consciousness, without being completely abolished, remains inert like the body. The body suffers at times, especially if the work of digestion is not finished; this suffering is revealed by breathing, which is short, labored, and ragged, but which fails to move consciousness.

The return to the normal state occurs quite naturally, through the reintegration of the organism, but, unlike the splitting of the body in the state of sleep, the splitting of the body which occurs, as has just been said, in the waking state, leaves some after effects. First, at the moment of regaining consciousness, there is a profound dejection, a complete asthenia of the entire organism, which lasts for some time, and against which one must react by an effort of will; to use a popular expression, one must *shake oneself*; then, this first state is succeeded by another fact of feverish activity, of exuberance, of need for agitation; it seems that the body, deprived of movement for a certain time, wants to limber up; Finally, this phase is followed by another characterized by a sort of bodily aches, vague and general fatigue, and mental asthenia: any effort is painful, whether physical or cerebral: here again, one must react and not listen to *oneself*; this weariness disappears in a short time; however, it can last a few hours; I even know of a case where it persisted for two days; in short, it disappears completely at the moment when the reintegration of the being is fully achieved.

There are circumstances where one is led to perform this experiment in front of assistants: this is the worst of conditions. One can, it is true, use their presence to a certain extent by asking them to add their will to yours to strengthen it, but how few people *know how to want*! On the contrary, despite themselves, despite all the best dispositions, they bring an instinctive feeling of selfish curiosity, and, consequently, emanate fluids that singularly hinder the release of the phantom. I cannot repeat it enough: the presence of assistants is the worst possible condition, because in order to control the fluids emanating from them, the experimenter must deploy an intensity of will that exhausts him and makes him ill, while on the other hand, the fraction of will directed toward this objective remains completely unused from the point of view of the main operation; it is even harmful to the production of the phenomenon, since it singularly and unfortunately complicates the initial monoideism.

There is another process of out-of-body experience in the waking state, which, instead of momentarily annihilating all the senses, uses some of them as adjuvants to bring the operator to a certain degree of hypnosis favorable to carrying out the experiment. Personally, I have never seen it used; I therefore do not know what results it might bring about; nevertheless, I will mention it here.

In this process, the body, taste, and touch are affected, as stated above: only sight, hearing, and smell are retained, which are used as follows. Near each ear, a watch is hung, the monotonous ticking of which produces a sort of lulling of the senses, while, in the complete darkness of the room, at a certain distance from the operator, a small alcohol lamp is lit, burning ordinary alcohol, but in which a large pinch of hemp flowers per liter has been previously macerated for twenty-four hours. The light obtained by this means, both flickering and fascinating, diffuses very mild narcotic emanations; moreover, before the operation, the room has been fumigated with incense intended to act on the brain. It is under these conditions that the will creates the monoideism that will lead to the production of the phenomenon.

I have never seen, I repeat, this process used, but it seems to me to be quite logically designed, according to the principles of self-hypnotization, to be able to bring the organism into a state conducive to the realization of the phenomenon; it even seems to me to provide greater ease of action through the use of these various adjuvants. And yet I would rather urge the operator to abstain from it, here is why: — In principle, willpower should be sufficient when it activates a suitably prepared organism; now, the dynamization of the will has never harmed anyone, and the well-conducted training of the organism towards a reasoned neurification presents no danger; I cannot say the same of these physical agents which act on both the sensory organs and the brain; their use can lead to the manifestation of certain functional disorders for the eyes, the ears and general cerebrality. Now, I believe that in such experiments, if one has the right, I would even say the duty to be wisely audacious, one does not have the right to alter — or even ruin — an organism, even one's own.

This study of development would not be complete if I did not say a few words about the ultimate level it involves: I am referring to *astral projection* itself, that is, the operation that consists of sending one's previously exteriorized phantom, no longer toward a receptive human subject, or toward the accomplishment of a material act, but onto the astral plane, to live one's astral life there completely.

Here, I will be very brief and very cautious; firstly, I do not have the right to write certain things which, if thoughtlessly disseminated among the public, could become a kind of danger, and secondly, in beginning this work, it was only in my mind and in my will to make it a special study of technical physio-psychology.

Occultists will understand my caution in this regard: it is not good for certain subjects to be addressed. However, those who know can be put on the right track by various teachings scattered throughout these pages, which they will be free to put to good use if it is their intention to study the astral itself. I will give here only one indication that may be useful to them: — Astral Entities, devoid of material bodies, do not, therefore, possess an etheric double [187]. The exteriorized human phantom can therefore enter into a relationship with them much more easily than with a human being, for whom, in order to act on matter, it needs etheric forces. I will say no more.

E) *Accomplishment of a previously intended act.*

I examine this fact first, because it seems to me the simplest to achieve, since it is, in short, only the result of the extension and

---

[187] In earthly immunity, the etheric double itself dies a few days after the physical body.

precision of a will that ordered the dissociation of the personal being — and that made itself obeyed.

It goes without saying that before tackling this next stage of development, the experimenter must have become established in the exteriorization of his phantom and its direction toward the receptive subject: it is only when his splitting is somewhat automatic and he is fully assured that his phantom always follows the prescribed direction that he can consider continuing his development. It is therefore appropriate that before going further in this experiment, he should have been perfectly sure that the percipient subject has not been the plaything of hallucinations that are always possible; To this end, he worked with him, after the first attempts, for which he gave him precise advance warning, first without precisely indicating the moment of his astral exit, then, at the end, unexpectedly. When there is perfect concordance between the accomplishment of the phenomenon and the relationships of the receptive subject, only then can the hypothesis of hallucination be discarded, and one can proceed further along the path of development.

The accomplishment, by the exteriorized phantom, of a previously specified and willed act is, like the orders of ideas that will follow, like any hyperphysical fact in general, the result of a will firmly directed toward a determined goal. Therefore, one must *want*.

But we have seen, regarding the direction of the phantom, that there are special means to lead it to the desired location: in the present case, it is necessary to use these means or other similar ones as material aids for the accomplishment of the given order: I will discuss them below. But first, I have to present a very important observation.

We still do not know the strength of the exteriorized phantom, since there is still no dynamometer specifically applicable to this use. It results from the experiments I had the opportunity to follow, at H. Durville, that the same phantom, I mean the phantom exteriorized by the same subject, exhibits enormous variations in strength: sometimes it can barely tilt the pan of a balance whose other pan is loaded with a few grams (to the point that one is obliged to establish an electrical contact to be sure of the disruption of balance), and sometimes, it violently throws a person to the ground in the full vigor of life. These excessive differences in the intensity of the force deployed come from a thousand causes (humidity of the atmosphere, state of health of the subject, heat of the room, etc.), many of which are certainly still completely unknown to us. It is therefore advisable to always act with the phantom as if it were extremely weak; otherwise, one could impose an effort on it of which it would be momentarily incapable, and the failure of the experiment could lead to doubt as to the reality of the splitting.

It is therefore a very unfortunate reasoning to say to oneself: — "Yesterday, of its own accord, the ghost shook a bell weighing 500 grams; therefore, today, it will be able to knock over, at my command, this inkstand that weighs only 100 grams." Indeed, yesterday, the ghost could have been more exteriorized than today or, for some reason that no longer exists, be more vigorous. On the other hand, it should be noted that, very generally, ghosts perform better the work they themselves have conceived than that which is suggested or imposed on them.

Therefore, in any case, if we do not want to expose ourselves to disappointment in these delicate experiments, we must start from this principle: — We do not know the exact strength of the ghost; we must therefore consider it very weak and act with it accordingly. Moreover, in such a case, it is not a question of more or less, but of affirmative or negative, and a being, whatever it may be, will prove its presence in a place just as well by changing the position of a penholder as by a cut stone.

The mechanical act whose accomplishment is imposed on the ghost must, consequently, require, at least at first, as minimal an expenditure of force as possible. Later, when it has become accustomed, one can act differently and impose real physical exertion on it: for the moment, for the beginning, it is only a matter of imposing one's will on it and determining whether it has accomplished it.

I will use an example already given above. — We *want* the exteriorized ghost, returned to the receptive subject, to throw onto the floor a light feather, a match, or a sheet of cigarette paper placed on the edge of a piece of furniture.

The operator must, *himself and at home*, place a feather or a piece of cigarette paper on the edge of a piece of furniture, and repeat the following procedure over and over again: he imagines himself to be his own ghost, approaches the piece of furniture, makes the appropriate gesture, and throws the object onto the floor. The more often he repeats this act during the day, the greater the chances of success.

Even if he can carry out this preparation under the conditions in which the act must actually be performed by the ghost, that is, in the home of the receptive subject, and on the piece of furniture that will be used, it will be all the better.

In the evening, he goes to bed at his usual time after placing under his pillow the object he used to prepare the experiment. Then he directs his will toward his own unfolding and toward sending his ghost to the subject. Since, having reached this point, after a certain amount of practice, the splitting occurs in some way automatically, mechanically, this effort on the part of the experimenter has nothing that can exhaust his will, which is sufficiently wholehearted to, at the moment when the prodrome of drowsiness occur, direct all of his energy toward the act to be accomplished.

The expansion of the astral body outside the physical body then occurs during this expansion; during the first moment of disturbance, the astral body encounters the object that must guide it and the monoideism created by the will; it goes to the percipient subject with the idea of what he must do there. There, he finds the object he must overturn prepared on the edge of the piece of furniture; but at the same time his hand has retained the memory, in some way physical, of the movement that during the day it has repeated many times with the material hand; in turn, and alone, it repeats this same gesture and causes the object to fall.

But doesn't the ghost have enough strength to produce the desired effect, and has the object remained in its place? Then the monoideism of the operator's will comes into play, supported by the subject's combined will: *the act must be accomplished.* We know, from experiments on the ghosts of subjects, that the astral body can, under certain conditions, materialize or fluidify at will; driven by this dual will that commands, it materializes its hand more fully, gives it greater strength, repeats the gesture, and the pen falls: the order is accomplished.

When one has succeeded in such an experiment, it must be varied, which is infinitely possible, — but never by ordering labors of force, which, in truth, could be executed, but could also not be, which would leave a doubt, always to be avoided, about the reality of the splitting. One can send the ghost to a particular part of the room, or make it strike a piece of furniture, or make it leave a fingerprint on a dusty spot, etc., etc., all of which require little expenditure of force, for one must not forget this: The astral body, removed from its *sarcosôme*, in fact possesses no etheric forces allowing it to act on matter other than those it has been able to absorb from its current environment (particularly from the receptive subject) and assimilate [188]. However, we do not know under what conditions this capture and assimilation of etheric force takes place.

I have just spoken of fingerprints on a dusty spot: — this leads me to say a few words about a particular means of identifying the exteriorized living ghost, a means of identification which is none other than the application of anthropometry or splitting.

---

[188] There are, however, cases where it borrows part of its strength from its own *sarcosôme*, when, as we saw above, it is not far from it, because then it possesses its own etheric double. — On the other hand, I have been informed of certain cases where the astral body, although distant, seems to draw the energy necessary for physical manifestations from its own material body at a great distance, because the synchronism of the movements of the fluidic body and the organism demonstrated the intimate connection existing between them at that moment. In this case, the fluidic cord connecting the double (ghost) to the physical body acts as an energy conductor, like an electric wire connecting two stations. Under these conditions, the operator would be his own medium. But the fact must be extremely rare, since (and this is understandable) the etheric double, being the holder of physical life, *cannot* abandon the *sarcosôme* — especially given that the observer could have made a mistake in mistaking for physical effects what, in reality, was only a simple transmission of sensation, perfectly explicable in itself since the astral body is the repository of the subject's exterior sensitivity. In any case, these are still little-known things, where, so far, only one fact has been proven: that the phantom, removed from its physical body and, consequently, devoid of the etheric forces that are proper to its personal organism, and which are nevertheless necessary for it to act on matter, takes these same forces from the living beings in its current environment, and assimilates them without our knowing even approximately the conditions under which this capture and assimilation take place.

In a series of experiments conducted in 1912 at the *French Institute for Psychical Research*, the fingers and hands of living, objectively exteriorized ghosts were placed on mirrors covered with a light layer of talc, producing prints that could then be easily identified using Dr. Bertillon's methods. To my knowledge, no such experiment has yet been conducted with a subjectively exteriorized ghost, which would provide irrefutable proof of the reality of the phenomenon obtained. In such cases, it is recommended not to use charcoal powder, lampblack, or any other dark powdered material, which, for some unknown reason, seem to inspire a certain repulsion in the living ghost.

Since, from the point of view of identifying the exteriorized living ghost, the application of this procedure can be of great importance, I think that it is appropriate to give in detail the necessary explanations both about the process of the operation and from the point of view of the means of identification and some anomalies that may arise.

A) *Preparing the control plate.* — Take a glass slide the size of a standard photographic plate (9x12 or 12x18); shake a small bag of thin cloth over it, containing talcum powder. Each shake causes a very light cloud of talcum powder to fall onto the glass, and the entire surface of the glass should be shaken equally. The layer of talcum powder does not need to be very thick: it is sufficient for the entire surface of the glass to turn white.

This layer of talc, it should be noted, is extremely fragile (which allows it to record the slightest print), and a simple breath is enough to blur or even destroy it. However, there are circumstances where prints need to be preserved: in this case, here's how to proceed.

Take a sheet of gelatin-bromide photographic paper the size of the glass plate. Expose it to sunlight, which blackens it. Then, immerse it for a few moments in a water bath to soften the gelatinous layer. Then, after placing it under a sheet of blotting paper to dry the surface, apply it flat and in a single movement, so as not to blur the print, over the previously impressed layer of talc. Then press firmly over the entire surface: the talc adheres to the gelatinous layer and becomes one with it, preserving all the impressions it has received. The paper is carefully removed and finally left to dry flat. From then on, the impression, although still requiring some precautions, is much less fragile and can be preserved indefinitely [189].

For the anthropometric elements necessary to know in the case at hand, as well as for the anomalies that may arise, I will borrow the following indications, published in the February 1912 issue of the *Psychic world*, under the signature of L. Lefranc.

B) *Description of dactyloscopy in living beings.* — This term refers to the reproduction of the highly varied patterns exhibited by the anterior, palmar, ends of the fingers. These patterns are, in terms of their form, entirely fixed in the same individual and extremely variable from one individual to another. They therefore constitute an excellent characteristic of individual identity. We present here (*figs.* 56, 57, 58, 59) four typical fingerprints to be used for classification. The drawings represent: 56, the *external loop*; 57, the *internal loop*; 58, the *oval* or *whorl*; 59, the *arc*.

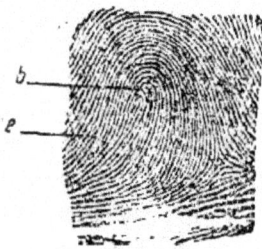

Fig. 56
Fingerprint type:
external lace

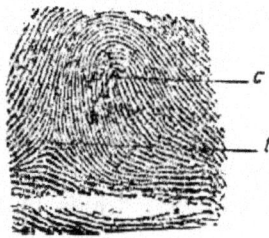

Fig. 57
Fingerprint type:
internal lace

Fig. 58
Fingerprint type: oval,
circle, spiral, scroll

Fig. 59
Fingerprint type: Arc.

[189] It should be noted that under these conditions, the image is inverted: a right hand appears to be a left hand, etc.

Here is the method to follow to identify a print:

Square method, as described by Forgeot:

1. Squares are drawn on an enlargement of the prints, as painters do when reproducing a sketch; thanks to identical squares, drawn on a drawing enlarged to the same scale as the print to be compared, we have exact reference points for noting the location and outline of the particularities of the two prints.

2. Examination of the bifurcations of the papillae (*b, fig.* 56).

3. Examination of the stops and restarts of the loops (*fig.* 59).

4. Examination of the segments (*d, fig.* 58).

5. Examination of the doubling of the loops (*d, fig.* 58).

6. Examination of the islands (*i, fig.* 58), which the prints present in very large numbers.

For identity to exist, the placement of these details must be exactly the same on the description used for comparison and on the resulting print. It is not so much the shape as the respective position of the details that will allow a conclusion, since the shape may be slightly altered by impasto or a lack of brushstroke.

The scars placed on the anterior part of the phalanx cause a very visible interruption in the outline of the loops, which, far from being detrimental, greatly helps speed identification.

In particularly rare cases where the visible details are not sufficient in number to provide absolute certainty, this is compensated for, for the general shapes (*figs.* 56, 57, 58), by counting the number of loops separating the central point from the triangular or delta point.

Indeed, in the shape (*fig.* 57) we notice a central point *c* and a triangular or delta point *t* placed on the left; in the shape (*fig.* 56) the same phenomenon occurs, but the triangular point (not indicated by a letter) is on the right. In the shape (*fig.* 58) (ovals, circles, spirals, volutes) there are one or two central points and two triangular points, one on the left (not designated by a letter) and the other on the right (*i*).

If a fingerprint is recognized as accurate, one can attempt to push the level of identification further by taking a print of the entire hand, which may be narrow or wide, short or long, thin or fat (chubby); knobby, hairy fingers; tapered, square, spatulate fingertips, etc.; the hand from which the print is obtained must therefore belong to one of these types mentioned and be identical to the operator's hand. But such clear clues are not always found in prints; therefore, we will indicate how one goes about it, where appropriate, to achieve identification.

C) *Procedures and anomalies.* — When a subject is split into two, his phantom (etheric body) is exteriorized; it can produce material phenomena at a distance [190]; but we were unable to obtain any fingerprints of his fingers despite a number of repeated sessions. We had to change our method; instead of exteriorizing the entire body, we were only able to exteriorize the phantom's left arm [191]. On the first attempt, an impression was obtained: we were on the right track; on the third attempt, an impression (comprising: the third phalanx, the second, and a third of the first) was given, with which we were able to perfectly identify the phantom as follows:

The imprint materialized at first glance represents an index finger (*fig.* 60); the third phalanx is devoid of papillae; on the other hand, the second phalanx is better formed: two longitudinal folds of skin can be distinguished; moreover, this index finger presents a deformation: the first phalanx curves to the left.

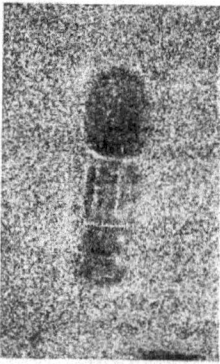

Fig. 60.
Fingerprint produced by the exterior
ghost.

Fig. 61.
Imprint of the subject's left index
finger.

Fig. 62.
Imprint of the subject's right
index finger.

On examination, we find by comparison with the two index fingers of the split subject (*figs.* 61 and 62) that this imprint materialized belongs to the right index finger: 1. by the resemblance of these longitudinal folds of skin to the subject's right index finger; 2. by the aforementioned compared curvature.

The measurement shows that the length of the second phalanx of the materialized index finger is the same as that of the second phalanx of the subject's right index finger: the second phalanx of the left index finger is two to three millimeters longer, and several of its folds are oblique. The measurement of the third phalanx should not be taken into consideration, because it varies depending on the subject's finger or the materialized finger's more or less firmness on the talc-dusted glass; it is noted that the contours of the materialized index finger are blurred compared to the subject's index finger. In summary, this imprint is so perfect in its resemblance that one might think it was obtained by trickery, in a moment of inattention on the part of the inspectors.

One curious thing should be noted: the obtaining of the *right* index finger, while we had duplicated the subject's *left* arm, an anomaly that we have not been able to explain; The same phenomenon was observed by Dr. Ochorowicz, with his subject, Miss Tomczyk, in her X-rays of fluidic hands. Here is an excerpt from the account of the aforementioned phenomenon [192].

"Seeing that the entire hand tends to be X-rayed, I open a 13x18 box, and we perform a new experiment, a little differently; I hold the plate perpendicularly in the air (remaining seated opposite the medium, about a meter from her right hand). The red light is barely enough to distinguish the white spot of her blouse. Despite this, the sleepwalker tells me:

— "I see the shadow of a hand detaching from my right arm... The fluidic arm is very long and it advances towards the plate... against the red light, it appears transparent... and her hand, which appears on image [193], is much more opaque... but it's

---

[190] At a short distance from one's own organism; we saw above that to act at a distance, the ghost is obliged to find in its environment the etheric forces of a receptive subject or any living being capable of exteriorizing these forces from its own organism.

[191] This shows that, in the case of subjective out-of-body experience, if the entire ghost does not have the necessary strength to materialize and act on matter (give imprints, etc.), one can out-of-body only a part of oneself (hand, finger), which, in this case, will have more strength to manifest itself.

[192] *X-ray of the hands*, by Dr. Ochorowicz, in the *Annals of Psychic Sciences*, 1910-1911.

[193] On the photographic plate, Ochorowicz had the print placed not on a glass slide covered with talc, but on the sensitive side of a photographic plate.

funny, it seems to me that it's a left hand, even though I'm holding out my right." And it seems she was right, since the image that appeared resembled part of the left hand..."

In his experiments, Dr. Ochorowicz made several observations, including three that we will note:

1. That the hand of the double can be imprinted much larger than that of the subject. — This is true: we made this observation when the ghost's hand is in the process of materializing; but when materialization is complete, the hand does not differ from that of the subject;

2. That a left hand can emerge from the right arm. — This is correct;

3. That the unipersonal etheric body of the subject, his double in short, behaves absolutely like a "Spirit."

To this last remark, we will respond that the materialization *process* of a double (ghost) of a living person is entirely different from that of a "Spirit." Thus, the double takes about five minutes to materialize, while it takes twenty to twenty-five minutes for the "Spirit." For the subject's double, a fairly thin, crude-looking fluidic arm forms below the subject's arm; the fluidic fingers appear elongated and are fed, in order *to materialize*, by a fluidic current starting from the tip of the subject's left shoulder blade, running down the left arm, and by another current starting from the crease of the left elbow and going to the digital extremities of the materialization. The subject exhibits no fatigue after the experience, except for slight pain at the point where the fluidic currents emerge, whereas, for the materialization of a "Spirit," alongside the fluidic double of the medium's arm, a second fluidic arm belonging to the "Spirit" is formed; the arm is very large, as is the hand, and its formation elicits cries of pain from the medium; the medium exhibits no fluidic current; the materialization is long, laborious, and leaves the subject, after the séance, in a state of profound prostration. In any case, since these various modes are partly subjective phenomena for the participants, except for clairvoyant subjects, they only become secondary after the identification process using the digital papillae has been used. Dr. Ochorowicz's various remarks cannot in any way elucidate the question of "Spirits."

A final experiment should be attempted with the ghost of the living, from the point of view of the following objection: to determine whether the action of the subject's thought would not produce an effect, and whether it would not modify the *shape of the fingerprints* of his own ghost. To this end, we have conducted a few experimental attempts, and we have recognized that it is impossible for him to produce a normal fingerprint.

Finally, quite recently, in a séance held on January 12, 1912, in the presence and under the supervision of Colonel A. de Rochas, our honorary president, and Father N..., on a mirror covered with a light layer of talc, according to the technique recommended above, we obtained the imprint of a ghostly index finger, which these gentlemen themselves very easily identified, using commonly used anthropometric methods, with the index finger of the subject from whom, under their supervision, the ghost had previously been exteriorized.

Such a result, obtained under these conditions, is absolutely convincing and allows us not to dwell on this subject further.

The preceding conditions concern the objective phantom; but they also apply, it goes without saying, to the subjective phantom, which can, like the other, produce fingerprints, and, by this very fact, allow those concerned to identify it. I will therefore add a few words to explain the current state of the question, which has progressed considerably since then.

Figure 60 shows the right index finger of our subject, Mrs. Lambert. For a time, in fact, only isolated fingers were obtained. But since the above lines were written, significant progress has been made.

For a time, I say, the prints obtained were limited to index fingers. But, by always working with the same subject in such a way as to accustom him to his external phantom, it was possible to obtain both the index finger and the middle finger — increasingly clear. Figures 63 and 64 reproduce, in this regard, the first successes and the latest results: each of them represents, at different periods of these studies, the right index and middle fingers of the same subject (remember that transferring them onto paper reverses the original position of the fingers).

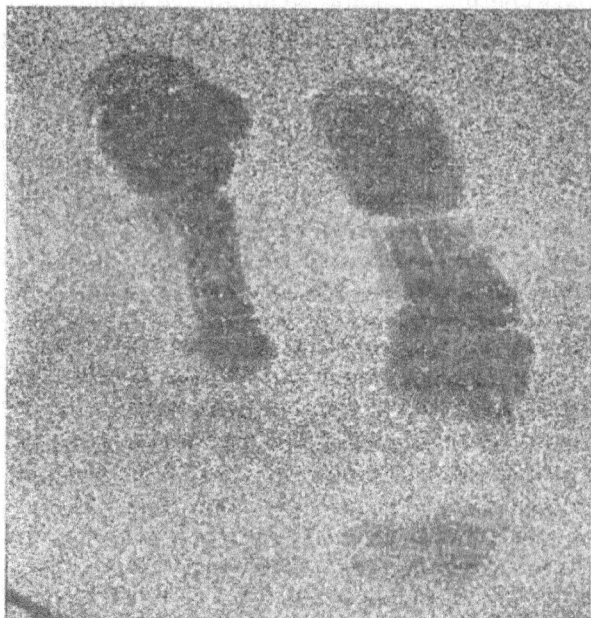

Fig. 63. — Simultaneous impression specimen (first results) of an index and middle finger of a living external ghost.

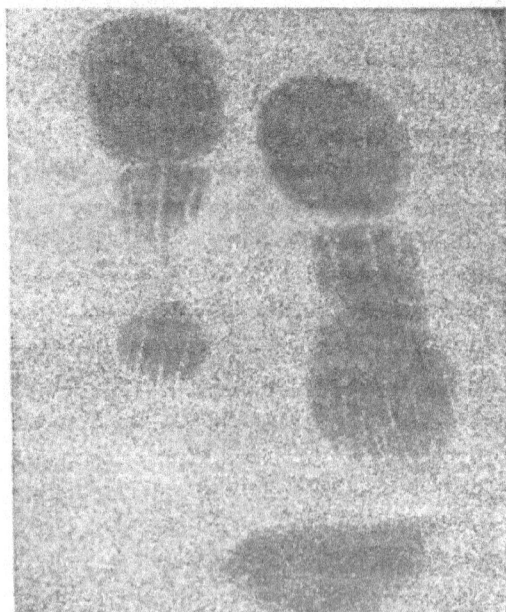

Fig. 64. — Simultaneous impression specimen (latest results) of an index and middle finger of a living external ghost.

Obtaining the simultaneous imprint of two fingers already facilitated identification; but they did not stop there, and, by continuing the attempts in the same direction, and always with the same subject, the hand was obtained, first partial, then finally complete (*fig. 65*). From then on, the identification of the phantom was easy: it is sufficient, in fact, when the imprint of the phantom's hand is obtained on a talc-coated mirror, to compare it with the physical hand of the subject imprinted in the same way on another talc-coated mirror.

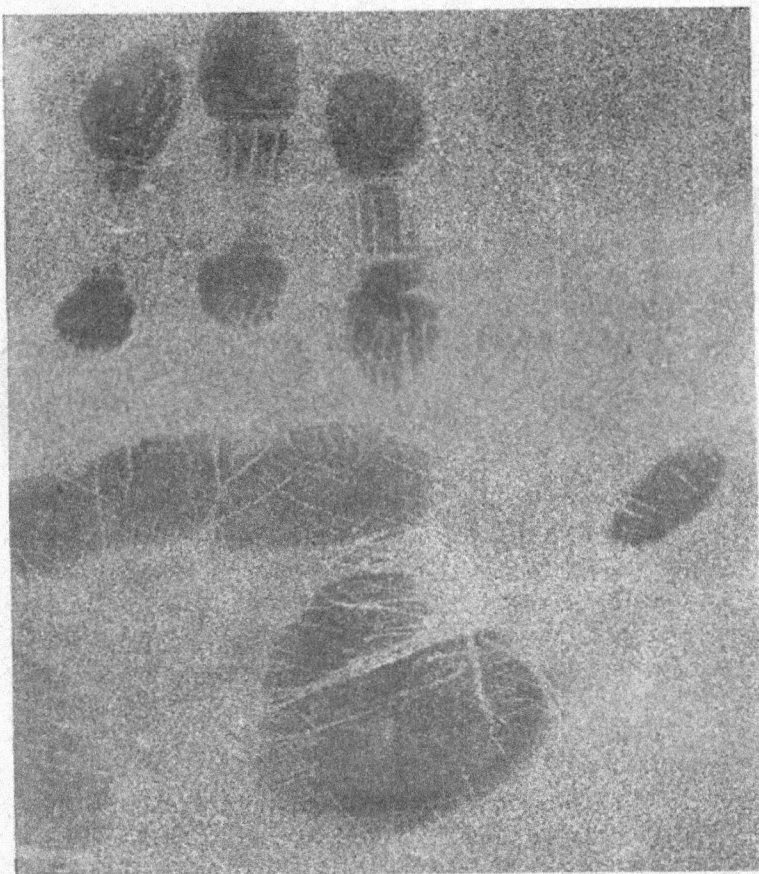

Fig. 65. — Imprint (reduced to 2/3) of a living ghost's exteriorized hand.

But the use of this process soon gave rise to a major objection arising from the very method of control and identification. And this objection is this:

"Certainly, the result is undeniable for the experimenters present who verified these facts for themselves; but what proves to the public, who did not witness the experiment, that it was not the physical subject who himself placed his material hand on the one and the other talc-coated plate?"

The objection, it must be recognized, had great force, and it was therefore necessary to seek a procedure such that its use would be both easy for a ghostly hand and impossible for a material hand.

After numerous attempts in this direction, Mr. L. Lefranc managed to solve the problem by the direct use of a special photographic plate on which the ghost's fingerprints are clearly marked (*fig. 66*), whereas the application of the living hand produces only coarse stains. This result was achieved on June 28, 1912. — At present, only index finger prints have been obtained using this process, but experiments continue, and it is very likely that the same thing will happen with the photographic plate as happened with the talc-coated ice: when the exteriorized ghost has acquired the necessary habituation, it will produce prints of its entire hand.

A curious observation should be made regarding the use of this particular process. — While as stated above, the living hand placed on the plate produces only stains due to the reduction of the silver salts, the imprint of the ghostly finger is revealed by a very fine, brown, powdery material, the origin of which is still unknown. These powdery traces are transferred to photographic paper using the same procedure as described above for preserving prints on talc-coated glass. As experiments continue in this regard, I will say no more on this subject; the indications given above should, moreover, be more than sufficient for experimenters in personal out-of-body experience to, over time and with the familiarity of their own ghost, leave undeniable traces of their own passage wherever they send their *double*.

We see from the above that if a fingerprint of the exteriorized living phantom can be obtained, objective, material, and scientific proof of the splitting will be provided by identification using anthropometric methods. But this fingerprint can only be obtained, I repeat, after a few attempts — more or less numerous — because the desire to achieve this result must unfortunately complicate the initial monoideism.

In any case, once we have entered this phase of development where the exteriorized living phantom can act on matter, the experimenter must bring to it a great deal of judgment and perseverance.

Judgment — because we must never ask the phantom to do something it is incapable of accomplishing, either due to a lack of training or strength, or because carrying out the order given would be repugnant to its nature or prudence; First of all, one must be sure whether he is capable of carrying out the given order without detriment to himself.

Perseverance, because it would be a recipe for successive failures to modify the given order at each test; in fact, he would hesitate between yesterday's order and today's, perhaps contradictory for him, and in any case given with a weak will, since it is variable; each time a failure occurs, one must seriously weigh the value of all the obstacles that may have produced it, and, if one of them seems, after reflection, too difficult to overcome, it is appropriate to choose another type of test that avoids or lessens that obstacle; on the other hand, if the major obstacle does not appear upon reflection, one must, at the next attempt, maintain, with great energy of will, the previously given order. The constant repetition of the same order, with each new attempt, stores up, ultimately accumulating such a power of volitional dynamics that the order ultimately leads to its more or less complete accomplishment: one must persevere, repeat the act until it is performed in a way that absolutely conforms to one's will.

On the other hand, there is a progression to be established between all the successively ordered acts: one must move from easy to difficult, from simple to complex, from less to more. It would be a waste of time — and energy — to impose a series of acts that differ little from one another: for example, flipping a card, then a domino, then a skittle, etc. It is important to fully grasp the idea that these exercises, for that is what they truly are, have no other goal than to train the phantom toward the actual realization of all its possibilities. When, in gymnastics, a child knows how to climb a rope, he is not wasting his time and acquired strength using the rope ladder.

The exteriorized astral body must therefore be gradually brought to execute all the orders it has left its *sarcosôme* in possession of, or which it receives, during its exit, from the will that commands it. Its training must therefore be, above all, logical and progressive. Furthermore, it will be made easier if, during the preceding phases of development, the phantom has already received — and executed — orders relating to its exteriorization, the control of its passage, etc. But this should not be regarded as an absolute rule, since, I repeat, I have had the example around me of an experimenter who dissociates himself completely, who sends his visible, audible and tangible phantom towards this or that subject (he has not yet tried to reveal himself to blind people, wanting to first achieve a more complete development), and who has not yet been able, despite repeated attempts, varied in every way and conducted as judiciously as possible, to make his phantom perform a certain desired act. What is the reason for this bizarre exception? I do not undertake to explain it and am content to record it, leaving the reader to draw whatever deduction he pleases.

F) *Acquisition of visibility.*

We are here approaching the study of a series of phenomena that can only occur through repeated attempts, patiently and tenaciously, and through sheer willpower. It is in vain to attempt to indicate a course of action: there is none. Sometimes visibility reveals itself spontaneously and without anyone doing anything to acquire it (there are even cases, quite rare, at least relatively speaking, where, under the influence of a violent emotion or for other ill-defined causes, the phantom is, from the first attempt, completely visible); and sometimes, on the contrary, it is acquired only with great difficulty and through sheer tenacity; there are even individuals who are absolutely resistant to it: — a matter, in principle, of special organization, no doubt, but also of more or less complete exteriorization and, no doubt also, of greater or lesser willpower. — It is therefore up to each experimenter to conduct their own tests in this direction and see for themselves which ways and means give them the best results.

But if no specific development process can be given, there are, on the other hand, certain notions and indications that operators must possess to guide them along this path.

If the phantom is visible, it is not, like other bodies in nature, because it reflects natural or artificial light, but because the substance, the immatter of which it is composed, is itself luminous.

I have spoken elsewhere, and at length, [194] of this particular substance that composes the astral body, and of the special luminosity with which it is endowed, which appears to me to be more or less condensed *Vital force substance*. I analyzed my experiments in this regard; I will not return to them here, contenting myself with quoting a passage from H. Durville (loc. cit.) which provides valuable information in this regard.

"As Reichenbach observed some sixty years ago, and as I demonstrated in my *Magnetic Physics* [195], sensitives in the waking state see, in the dark, the human body shining with a more or less bright light depending on their degree of sensitivity and training in this kind of experimentation.

"All bodies, even those considered inanimate, appear to the most clairvoyant as if they were alive, for they are the seat of luminous vibrations, of more or less perceptible movements that seem to communicate themselves by undulations to the surrounding environment. At every moment, they receive effluvia from this environment, and return others to it, in such a way that direct observation allows us to observe, through the sense of sight, a continual exchange of forces that build, destroy, reconstitute, only to destroy again and always transform. Molecular movements, which do not fall directly within the physicist's sense of sight, are perfectly distinguished even by ordinary sensitives.

"Living bodies, from the tiniest animal to the most evolved man, exhibit the phenomenon of polarity, as observed in electricity, in the magnet, and in terrestrial magnetism. There are bodies that only show traces of organization, such as crystals. This polarity is not only appreciable as a force, through the attraction

---

[194] *Sorcery of the Countryside*, ch. of the *Astral Body*, 1 vol. in-8, Paris, 1910, Messrs. H. and H. Durville, Editors.
[195] *Magnetic Physics*. Paris, 1895-1896, 2 vol. in-18. Messrs. H. and H. Durville, Editors. This work is essential for all those who wish to learn Magnetism, from an experimental or therapeutic point of view.

that poles of opposite names and the repulsion of those of the same name exert on each other, but these poles are perfectly visible in the form of colored light. The positive or southern pole, which is formed by the right side of the human body, shines a beautiful blue that ranges, depending on the subjects observed and also according to the eyesight of different sensitives, from pale blue to indigo; and the pole −, negative or boreal, of an orange no less beautiful, complementary to blue, which goes from light yellow to the confines of red, passing through strong yellow.

"Like electricity, this light, which is colored matter, more subtle than that which falls under the senses of each of us, can be observed in two forms: a dynamic or moving form, circulating inside the body, and giving rise to currents which, following certain directions, go from one end of the organism to the other and even beyond it; a static or resting form, on the surface of the skin. The latter constitutes around us a fluidic atmosphere from which effluvia continually escape, appearing to start from the pores of the skin and move perpendicular to it, up to a distance that is not easy to evaluate, because the more developed the sensitive (the observer), the greater this distance. For certain rare, highly trained subjects, it extends to about 2 meters, while the less clairvoyant can no longer distinguish it beyond 3 or 4 centimeters. It is more active at the extremities and in the vicinity of the sense organs; the eyes are particularly active. This is the aura of the Theosophists' etheric double, which can be photographed...

"This luminous manifestation is described by all sensitives as being remarkably beautiful; but it is even more beautiful in the out-of-body experience: the colors are lighter, more transparent, and the nuances more numerous, finer, and more delicate. The sight of ordinary sensitives then reaches the confines of the physical plane, ready to discover the even greater beauties of the astral plane: that of the best sensitives already contemplates them....

"With out-of-body experience, a simple yet remarkable phenomenon occurs. During waking, and even during the various states of magnetic sleep, the subject's body is seen as luminous and colorful, both by themselves and by other sensitives. As soon as the work of out-of-body experience begins, the luminous matter contained in the physical body tends to disappear, passing into the ghostly form that begins to take shape. The splitting being complete, the phantom has not only become luminous, but it appears with the subtle colors and delicate nuances observed in the subject before the operation. The physical body is thus truly separated from its etheric double. It is at the same time separated from its astral body, since the latter is the seat of sensitivity, and sensitivity, like luminous matter, is now located in the phantom.

"That's not all. As we seek to further analyze the double and the split before us, we must recognize that the splitting is much more complicated than initially supposed. Here, the phantom visibly formed by the etheric body appears to be animated only by a more subtle force. It is obvious that this force is there, that it comes from the astral plane, and that it in turn constitutes another body: the astral body, the seat of our sensations....

"But there are cases where it appears dazzlingly white, incomparably softer and more beautiful than sunlight or any artificial light, and without any colored nuances, at least to the eyes of ordinary sensitives. Thus, in her spontaneous out-of-body experience, Madame Lambert saw her ghost as entirely white. The [living] ghosts we have been visited by were also white, and the same is true of the ghost of the dead, who are forever freed from their etheric double....

"The etheric body rarely strays far from the physical body, for, being the giver of earthly life, if it were to wander too far, death would soon follow. Therefore, if the ghost moves away to a certain distance and for a certain time, it leaves the etheric double at its post to fulfill its usual function: it is then constituted only by the astral body. But the latter would be inert if it were not animated by a more subtle force coming from an immediately higher plane: the mental plane, the seat of thought, judgment, and will. The mental body is truly the higher principle that animates the ghost, for we realize that the latter, despite the difficulty it experiences in acting outside its organs, is the exclusive seat of consciousness...

"Everything I have said refers to the ghost formed near the subject, and from which little or no physical work is required.

"To produce physical phenomena: weighing on the scale, striking the table, moving it, and other phenomena requiring a greater or lesser expenditure of what we call muscular strength, the ghost needs some kind of force. It possesses this force, and if it lacks some of it, it can easily draw it from its surroundings. But every force requires a sufficient point of support for it to be transformed into work; and this point of support, the ghost can only find within itself. To do this, it must borrow matter from its surroundings to materialize its body, making it denser and more resistant. In this state, it generally ceases to be as luminous and transparent as it was at rest. Thérèse presents this phenomenon to us at a very high level. When her ghost is able to act, either to strike the table or to move it, her hands, which are placed above it, either in contact or at a small distance, become opaque enough that she, like the sensitive witnesses, no longer sees the table through it. When the ghost is standing, the subject no longer sees the shelves of my library through the upper part of the ghost's body.

"This phenomenon, which seems very natural to me, was widely noted by the Clairvoyant of Prevost, and Dr. Kerner, not a historian, expresses himself thus on the subject: 'The more obscure a ghost, the louder its voice and the more power it seems to possess to produce all kinds of noises and other physical phenomena.'

"When the ghost, well condensed, is disposed to action and does nothing, it possesses a certain amount of strength that it cannot maintain for long. This force suddenly escapes from the most condensed parts in the form of effluvia and even luminous jets, launched in different directions, and which, after traveling a distance that can vary from a few decimeters to 1 meter and even 1.5 meters, disappear into the surrounding environment. These luminous jets, which in no way resemble lightning or an electric spark, are often seen by all those present: they can be photographed..."

From this series of very judiciously established observations, we can draw the following conclusions, the application of which will serve, in the visibility tests, to achieve the desired goal:

A) The main force of the exteriorized phantom emanates, at the beginning of the operation, from the physical body. Therefore, the better prepared the physical body is, the greater the phantom's strength will be, and the greater its chance of visibility.

B) The phantom during operation assimilates forces taken from the environment or from the bystanders (receptive subjects), but we know little about the process of this phenomenon.

C) The phantom, in the vicinity of the *sarcosôme*, is rather colorful; it is rather bright when seen from some distance, and *always*, when seen from afar: the percipient subject must consider this as an absolute rule, to avoid certain hallucinations.

D) The material work of the phantom is done at the expense of its luminosity, and, consequently, its visibility. Consequently, the day one enters this phase of development, it must be pursued only to the absolute exclusion of all others. The astral body must leave the *sarcosôme* with the sole monotheism of making itself visible, or, in other words, of being as strong, as condensed as possible; its outings during this period must not include any other goal, even a very incidental one, even in the complete absence of visibility. In a word, he *must* be seen — nothing else.

E) It carries with it the mental body; that is thought, judgment, will, and consciousness, of which the mental body is the seat. It is therefore necessary, at the moment when preparing for the out-of-body experience, to imprint the will for a strong push towards visibility upon the phantom.

F) Finally, when the astral body is charged with force, this force escapes from it in the form of luminous effluvia visible even to the blind, and even more so to the sensitive. This detail must be carefully noted by the receptive subject, who will be able to deduce, from the production of the phenomenon, the assurance that the phantom is near them, seeking to make itself visible.

This brings us to the monitoring procedures that the percipient subject can employ to determine whether the phantom, which comes to find them, I suppose, periodically, is making progress toward visibility.

On this subject, I would ask the reader to refer to what is said above (Chapter II) about the N rays emitted by the living ghost and the way in which these rays act on screens made phosphorescent with calcium sulfide acid.

These screens are prepared as follows: a sheet of *matte* black paper is glued to any cardboard (so as not to give off reflections if operating in only relative darkness) on which small areas of calcium sulfide [196] are scattered. The object is then exposed to sunlight for a few moments, then, after exposure, it is kept in relative darkness until ready to use.

At this point, the screen must be placed on a sofa, couch, or rug, where the operator will send his phantom to the receptive subject with the order to lie down on it [197]. In this way, the prepared screen will be in the middle of the phantom substance, and after a short time (about half a minute, depending on the strength of the phantom), the percipient subject will see the screen illuminate under the action of the N rays emitted by the astral body. The greater or lesser degree of illumination of this screen will show the progress or the stationary state of this *aérosôme* on the path to visibility.

Furthermore, a record of each test can be kept, to compare the results, or based on the fact that the light stored in phosphorescent screens has a very strong effect on photographic plates, *even when they appear completely extinguished*. It will therefore be sufficient to leave the phosphorescent screen in the ghostly substance for the same desired time each time, then to photograph it after a strictly equal time for each attempt: the subsequent comparison of the photographs between them will show if there is progress and if this progress is noticeable.

G) *Acquisition of direction awareness.*

In many out-of-body experiences, a bizarre fact occurs: the operator has the will to dissociate and send his phantom to a certain subject; he splits himself into effects and his astral body goes to the indicated place where his presence is noted. But when,

---

[196] This is the process indicated by H. Durville. Personally, I have used screens that are much less delicate to handle and prepared as follows: — On a fairly rigid piece of cardboard, glue a thin, matte black fabric, like lustrine, onto which, using a brush, spread a fairly liquid paste made of phosphorescent calcium sulfide powder and white copal varnish. It is then allowed to dry for twenty-four hours. — This type of screen is perhaps a little less luminous than those where calcium sulfide is used pure, but it is much easier to handle and less fragile, since the composition is, in a way, one with the fabric.

Glass slides or wooden boards can also be used, but the composition adheres less to them than to the fabric.

[197] I always assume the operator is working in bed and during sleep. The ghost, as long as it has no action to perform, automatically assumes the position of the *sarcosôme* from which it emanates: it will therefore tend to lie down.

after his exit, he has reintegrated the physical body, the latter is covered with bruises, scratches, bruises and even sometimes wounds, without it being possible for those who have not yet acquired the ability to retain the memory of their exit to know where and how the *aérosôme* received all these lesions which were then reflected on the *sarcosôme*. I have cited elsewhere the case of an operator who, after an astral exit, woke up in the morning with a "black mark" measuring fifteen centimeters by twelve centimeters on one side of his stomach, without even being able to conceive the idea of the circumstances in which he had found himself...

This phenomenon is, at first glance, inexplicable; however, upon reflection, two causes can be attributed to it: the first is that, when the astral body moves away from the physical body to reach a given place, it follows its path in a straight line as much as possible and without regard for obstacles, at least if its route has not been previously mapped out for it; in this case, when it has a certain distance to travel, it rises to a sufficient height to avoid encountering anything; but at the point of departure as at the point of arrival, it always has obstacles to overcome or circumvent: hence, collisions; — the second reason is that, as stated above, the astral body, deprived of the physical body and obliged to act alone, is supremely clumsy in its movements, which it does not know how to adapt to material obstacles.

But there may also be other causes for these lesions. For example, in the aforementioned case of the experimenter wounded in the stomach, he later learned, by questioning an Entity of the Mystery with whom he is in frequent contact, that he had accidentally found himself involved in an Apache battle where he had been struck by a truncheon in passing; the location indicated, at the fortifications of Paris, was in fact very precisely on the straight line connecting the small town where the experimenter was located, to the number ... of the Avenue de l'Opéra where he was going. One may wonder what his thought, his judgment, his will and his consciousness were doing in such circumstances, which, in the mental body, were an integral part of the ghost. Did the material sleep of the operator react on these moral elements to cloud their lucidity? Do these moral parts of the being, in the event of a split, split to leave a fraction of themselves with the *sarcosôme*, and, thus divided, do they no longer have their normal power? Was it, finally, mere chance that caused a blow from a truncheon to fall precisely at the place and moment the exteriorized *aérosôme* was passing? I can't say, but these misadventures to which one is exposed during an astral projection demonstrate the importance of acquiring the awareness of direction, so as to skillfully avoid obstacles along the way, to see the possible pitfalls, and to extricate oneself from the dangers into which one may find oneself thrown against one's will.

Now, make no mistake: acquiring this particular faculty is one of the most difficult there is, and it is only in the long run, after repeated attempts, that one can achieve it.

Indeed, as shown above, the basis of any *wanted* astral journey is this: — to create a monoideism that dominates the mind after the body has been made capable of out-of-body experience. This monoideism will include the disengagement of the astral body, its dispatch to a designated location, the act it must perform there, and — if applicable — the route it must follow to get there: all things that are easy to predict or prepare in advance; in this case, the ghost conforms to the monoideism that directs it. But if a fortuitous incident arises, an unexpected obstacle, and monoideism is silent on this point, the ghost finds itself left to its own devices, and, aided by its clumsiness, it is likely to suffer some harm.

We can therefore see the benefit of being constantly in control of one's direction.

I have questioned several experimenters on this subject; Their unanimous responses boiled down to this: it is already enormous to be able to dissociate and send one's ghost to a designated location; to its direction, for the care of avoiding obstacles and dangers, it is to it that one must rely! — And yet there are, I know, individuals who possess this faculty. How then did they acquire it?

There are two ways to avoid the pitfalls of the road that necessarily accompany the sending of the exteriorized phantom far away: either to rely, as was said in Chapter X, on the *Psychic Preparation* of the experience, on the guidance of a friendly astral Entity who guides the operator and helps him avoid possible dangers, — but this is only a stopgap, so to speak, and is completely outside the consciousness of direction since, with such a way of acting, one is forced to rely on an assistant, just as in a mountain excursion one has a guide to help you avoid unknown precipices — ;or to rely only on oneself to personally judge the difficulties of the path and find the means to avoid them — and then it is the acquisition of the consciousness of direction that is required.

This is, moreover, what results from the response, which I quoted above, of a Mystery Entity to an operator who had been injured and was surprised that it was not more often during the experiment: "Fortunately, there is a God for split individuals; but what has just happened to you is nothing compared to what awaits you, as long as you have not acquired the power to direct yourself, and this power you will only acquire through practice and willpower!"

In practice, I believe that the two processes — astral assistance on the one hand, and personal consciousness of direction on the other — can and must be used concurrently and simultaneously, and that the first, in the absence of the other, is indispensable; but finally, since it is good to be able to direct oneself and watch over one's own safety, this ultimately brings us to the question already posed: — how can one acquire the consciousness of direction?

All the operators I have had the opportunity to question on this subject have given vague answers from which it is impossible to infer anything: — they do not know... they do not remember how they act... Some regard this condition as natural, as inherent in the very production of the phenomenon, without being able to analyze the ways and means of its realization... others perfectly remember finding themselves at the place, near the receptive subject where they wanted to go, remembering in every detail what they did there, but without being aware of how they got there: for them there is a gap, a hole in their memory, between the moment they fell asleep and the moment they found themselves at the desired place; the same is true for the return, — and this is very general, but in a very understandable way: — indeed, for the outward journey, the ghost guides itself by the artificial means that have been explained above; it advances only cautiously, one might say step by step, and by force of energy, of will towards the goal that has been assigned to its exteriorization; whereas, for the return, it is guided by the fluidic link that connects it to its *sarcosôme*, and it only has to follow [198]; if we remember that the exteriorized ghost, when it acts on the material plane, is endowed with an intense timidity caused by its distance from the physical body by which it lets itself be guided in the ordinary circumstances of life, it will be easily understood that, except for particularly trained individuals, the return to the *sarcosôme*, the reintegration, must be accomplished with great speed — perhaps instantaneously.

On the other hand, there are operators who, along the way, retain all their judgment, as if in a waking state; I was told of one who, when, in two, wanders through Paris, sometimes takes the wrong path, and this consciously: there are, as it were, however strange it may seem, two wills within him, one that sends him where he intended to go, and the other that makes him take a path that will lead him elsewhere, which he is aware of, but then he obeys what is for him like a higher impulse even though he knows it to be erroneous; this strange situation usually ends in the following way: the more he is aware of moving away from his goal, the more the first will, the one that leads him there, gains strength, and there comes a moment when, within his heart, a sort of conference takes place between the two wills, following which they agree on the path to follow. It would have been very interesting, for the study being pursued here, if this operator could provide some information on how he acquired such a developed awareness of direction. Unfortunately, he is one of those who regard this faculty as natural; he does not remember not having possessed it; from his first attempt, which took place fortuitously, *it was so*; consequently, he does not remember ever having had to make any effort to acquire it, although it seems that, to reach this point, even if we admit that the germ was within him, this germ must have been at least developed by some process — application of will or exercise.

For, in summary, it seems to me that these must be the two primary factors of the problem.

---

[198] Specific experiments conducted on subjects in this regard have demonstrated that the translation speed of the externalized phantom increases, on the way out, with the distance to be covered, but that the return, in all cases, takes place with at least double the speed.

Willpower, obviously, must play a certain role in all this; the difficulty is that, as soon as one wants to put it into practice, one encounters an obstacle, always the same: — complicating the initial monoideism by *wanting* to account for the difficulties one will encounter along the way weakens, by that very fact, this monoideism, which must, above all, be created as simple, as easy to execute, as possible, failing which, *especially during the first attempts*, one runs to failure.

This perhaps, in short, is the solution to the question; for the first attempts, one can rely on the "astral guide" mentioned above, and, when one is sufficiently in control of the phenomenon of exteriorization, one can attempt to complicate the initial monoideism by adding to it the *will* to account for the incidents along the way; then comes the repetition of the exercise, which gradually frees this faculty from the matrix in which, in principle, it remains obscured.

Moreover, since all organisms are far from possessing the same psychic organization, one can, by operating as stated in Chapter X of *Psychic Preparation* — that is to say, I am addressing myself solely, in this, to psychics and occultists — enter into a relationship with the Entity protecting the out-of-body experiences, to ask it to indicate the processes (which differ at least in detail for each individual) for acquiring the awareness of direction.

This seems to be, at least, the best path to follow to acquire the exercise of this faculty.

But for the experimenter who, out of fear, disbelief, or any other reason, would not like to use the "astral guide" and who could not, for whatever reason, use the procedure indicated above, or who has failed in his attempt, I will, in the following paragraph, indicate another, based on the hidden but undeniable relationships existing between the consciousness of direction and the preservation of the memory of the acts accomplished during the out-of-body experience; but I must say that this other procedure is much more difficult to implement, and certainly more random as to its results.

H) *Preservation of memory.*

This faculty is in some ways the corollary of the previous one, for it is obvious that if there is no awareness of direction, there can be no preservation of an absent thought. It is therefore by the same means that this special memory can be acquired. I would therefore have classified this phenomenon under the same heading as the previous one if practice did not show us that it is absolutely distinct from it and if it did not give rise to the examination of a particular phenomenon which is this: — if there are a large number of subjects who, in the state of splitting, act very normally, following all the laws of reasoning, and despite this cannot retain the memory of what they have done and said in this state, absolutely as if there were two memories within them, one relating to normal life and the other special to exteriorized life [199], on the other hand, there are subjects — infinitely rare, but there are some — who are incapable of directing themselves in the state of splitting, who only exteriorize themselves and are carried here and there at random, but who, having returned to themselves, faithfully preserve the memory of everything their exteriorized phantom has done and seen. This is a bit like dreams, but in inverse proportion; many people, unable to give direction to their dreams, remember very well, upon waking, the smallest details of their dreams, while others believe they are dreaming only very rarely because, when they return to the waking state, they cannot remember them, their special memory being abolished. Although psychology accepts that there is no dreamless sleep, which is why the theory of dreamless sleep has long prevailed, this is due to the extreme difficulty one experiences in remembering a long series of dreams: remembering only the last ones, without being able to go back to the first hypnagogic period which had served as their starting point, it was believed necessary to conclude that the first sleep is dream-free, which is an error [200].

---

[199] A similar phenomenon is found in hypnotic subjects placed in a trance state: they do not remember, once they have returned to their natural state, what happened to them in the trance state, where one is obliged to place them when one wishes to obtain some clarification from them in this regard.
[200] It should be noted that in magnetic or hypnotic sleep, images appear in the brain from the very first moments.

Moreover, since a certain number of dreams are nothing other than astral projections, we will be able to deduce from their mechanism valuable indications regarding the preservation of memory. Here is the account of a remarkably well-reasoned dream taken from *Dreams and the Means of Directing Them* [201]:

"In another dream, in which I believe I am riding a horse on a beautiful day, the awareness of my true situation comes back to me, as does the question of whether the free will of my imaginary actions belongs to me in my dream or not. Come now, I say to myself, this horse is only an illusion, this countryside I am traveling through a setting; but if it is not my will that evokes these images, it seems to me, at least, that I have a certain control over them. I want to gallop, I gallop; I want to stop, I stop. Here now are two paths, which lie before me. The one on the right seems to plunge into a dense wood; the one on the left leads to a sort of ruined manor. I feel that I have the freedom to turn right or left, and consequently to decide for myself whether I want to create associations of ideas, images related to these ruins or to this wood. I first turn right, then the idea comes to me that it would be better, in the interest of my experiences, to guide such a lucid dream towards the turrets and the keep, because by trying to remember exactly the principal details of this architecture, I might perhaps, upon waking, be able to recognize the origin of these memories. So I take the path on the left, dismount at the entrance to a very picturesque drawbridge, and, for a few moments while I am still asleep, I examine very attentively an infinity of details, large and small, ogival vaults; sculpted stones, half-eaten ironwork, cracks and alterations in the wall, admiring with what precision all this is painted before the eyes of my mind. Soon, however, and while I consider the gigantic lock of an old, dilapidated door, the objects suddenly lose their colors and the clarity of their contours, like the figures in a diorama when the fireplace moves away. I feel that I am waking up. I open my eyes to the real world: the brightness of my nightlight is the only one that illuminates me. It is three o'clock in the morning."

---

[201] No author name (by Hervey de Saint-Denis) Paris, 1867.

Several interesting deductions can be drawn from this account.

First, the will is never absent from dreams; it simply loses its effect on the muscular system; as for the rest, it directs — at least in many cases and for those who do not allow themselves to be carried away, inert, by the chance associations of ideas — in one direction in preference to another; but it is enough to want in a dream to produce this or that muscular movement, for example, walking, for the subsequent effort to occur, increasingly pronounced if the will is firm and repeated: this process will bring about awakening in the middle of the dream, and, consequently, will allow the memory to be preserved [202]. But it is necessary, as much as possible, to produce this effort at the culminating point of the dream, that is, at the moment when the events that take place there are of the most interest if one wishes to retain a sufficiently clear memory of them; otherwise, if one brings about awakening during a period of the dream when the events lack relief, the memory will be confused and clouded — if it even persists. This is how it happens to many people who never remember their dreams, sometimes awakening abruptly in the middle of a nightmare; they felt they were falling into a precipice or were the victims of an assassination; the instinctive effort they made at the critical moment to escape brought the muscular system under the control of the will and caused a sudden awakening that left them with the memory of their dream.

This muscular effort is therefore, whether it is a simple dream or a split-second experience, a valuable aid in producing either the awakening or the sudden reintegration of the astral body, leaving the memory intact, if it was made at a high point of the dream or the astral outing; with practice, and gradually, by bringing the awakening to less and less crucial circumstances, they

---

[202] It was stated above, speaking of the will, that the action of this faculty on the organism, although dormant like it during sleep, can nevertheless be exerted under the impulse of a vigorous effort. The will can, for example, in the middle of a dream, make an imaginary character kick, and the movement of this kick, executed in reality, brings about a sudden muscular relaxation that is enough to awaken the sleeper. This fact is well known to people prone to dreaming while half-asleep, who take advantage of this means to escape a nightmare or to wake up at the end of a pleasant dream whose memory they wish to preserve.

will manage to preserve the memory of everything that struck their minds during sleep.

This naturally only applies to the relatively few people who are aware of dreaming, and who can therefore easily acquire the habit of a sort of mnemonic gymnastics. But what about the others, those who don't believe they are dreaming because they have never — or at least very rarely — retained the slightest vestige of their dream? Since the best way to preserve the memory of their out-of-body experience is first to preserve the memory of their dreams, we must *help them* first to dream, and then to recall, once they return to the waking state, the subject of their dream.

What I have just said will at first seem paradoxical since nothing is more personal than a dream. But before concluding that it is paradoxical, we must remember that a dream never occurs of its own accord; it always has an external origin, whether it be an act performed during the day, a memory brought to light at the moment of dozing, an incident occurring during sleep, etc. In short, a dream is always the result of auto- or hetero-suggestion. It will therefore be sufficient to have an assistant nearby who will suggest the object of the dream to the sleeper and then facilitate its recollection. This assistant may be the chosen receptive subject, but he or she does not need any of the special qualities of a subject: it will suffice for him or her to understand the mechanism of dreams and to know how to intelligently adapt the suggestions he or she produces to them.

I will give two examples of this procedure, which must be used at any stage of sleep, but naturally without warning the person concerned so as not to create within him or her a current of ideas that would disturb his or her drowsiness and distort his or her normal sleep.

The assistant silently approaches the sleeper and begins a song, first in a very low voice, which he gradually raises so that he can be clearly heard by the sleeper, but without exceeding a very moderate pitch, for fear of waking him. Then, towards the end of the song, he gradually softens his voice, ending in a whisper. He then wakes the sleeper: — "Were you dreaming?" — "Me?" "I never dream." — "Yes, indeed! You were talking... you seemed to be approving or blaming a singer." — "Oh, that's true! I thought I was at a concert." — "Well! Remember... Was it a concert at Mrs.

X's?" — "No, I remember… it was in a large hall with galleries… a theater or a concert hall, I don't remember." — "Make an effort to remember: were you with someone? Were you interested in the play? What was its subject?" etc., etc.

Or, sometime later, or even immediately after, when the sleeper has resumed his slumber, the assistant returns to him, and, using the same voice system, first quiet, then a little louder, but without ever waking or even disturbing the sleeper, and finally ending in a whisper, he pronounces clearly, imitating a brief commanding tone: — "Carry… arms! Arms on the right shoulder! To march… forward… march! One… two… One… two… one… two…" And the voice weakens into a whisper. A minute later, the sleeper is awakened. — "Weren't you dreaming?" — "No." — "Come now! Remember." — "I'm sure I wasn't dreaming." — "Think carefully… Didn't you see any soldiers?" — "By the way… yes… I think so… I was watching a review… but it's so vague!" — "Try to remember." Where was this review taking place? Was it a company? A regiment? An army corps? Was there cavalry? Artillery? Etc.

The first few times the test is attempted, the sleeper will remember little: one will have to force his memory, so to speak, then this memory will become easier, and finally, through repeated attempts, he will be able to recall the entire dream on his own.

Then he will no longer be awakened immediately afterward, but one, two, or three hours later; and when he has finally proven that he has indeed retained his special memory, only the next day will he be asked to recount what he dreamed. Then he is at the level of the other subjects I mentioned above: he remembers the details of his dreams.

I found in the *Journal of Magnetism and Experimental Psychism* (March 1912) [203], relating to this study of dream provocation, a curious article by Dr. G. Durville, from which I will quote a few passages, among those that interest us most regarding the subject treated here, and from which the reader will be able to benefit most.

In Greece, there were sanctuaries called *Manteions*, where people came to sleep. The priests of these sanctuaries had "charms" to evoke the gods in dreams. Porphyry tells us on this subject how dreams were created in the temples of Hecate (personification of the moon): "Carve a statue of well-planed wood, as I will teach you. Make the body of this statue with wild rue, then adorn it with small domestic lizards; crush myrrh, styrax, and frankincense with these same animals, and leave the mixture in the air during the crescent of the moon; then address your wishes in the following terms... (formulas not preserved). Do things carefully; you will build me a dwelling with the roots of the self-grown laurel, and, having addressed fervent prayers to the image, you will see me in your sleep."

We see in this sentence from Porphyry what knowledge of psychology the priests of Hecate already possessed: to create dreams for those who wanted to see the goddess, they sought to vividly capture their attention, for they knew that we dream of what preoccupies us; it is undoubtedly for this reason that they imposed rather absorbing preparations on those who wanted to see Hecate; they knew the effect of sensory excitations on the production of dreams, since they recommended the use of "mystical" odors, such as styrax, myrrh, and frankincense.

I myself was able to observe several laws of the effect of incense on a subject magnetically asleep. Madame Kintzler thus experienced mystical dreams under the influence of incense vapors.

All experimental research on dreams was very vague and imprecise until Maury. Maury was one of the first to explore, in a truly scientific manner, the curious question of the experimental provocation of dreams. The work of Hervey de Saint-Denis, Havelock-Ellis, Calkins, Mourly-Vold, Clavière, Sanotis, and finally Vaschide completed the question.

The methods employed by these psychologists for the experimental study of dreams are of two kinds; in the first, the psychologist himself is the subject of the study; it is on himself that he studies the progress of the dream, he is himself the dreamer; this method can be called the subjective method. In the second method, the psychologist studies the dreams of others, creates artificial ones, and directs them; this is the method that can be called objective.

---

[203] MM. H. and H. Durville, editors.

Subjective method. — Maury deserves the credit for the first methodical experiments; let's leave it to him to explain his method himself.

"I observe myself, sometimes in my bed, sometimes in my armchair, at the moment when sleep overcomes me; I note exactly what state of mind I was in before falling asleep, and I ask the person next to me to wake me up, at moments more or less distant from the moment I dozed off. Awakened with a start, the memory of the dream from which I was suddenly torn is still present in my mind, in the very freshness of the impression. It is then easy for me to compare the details of this dream with the circumstances in which I placed myself to fall asleep. I record these observations in a notebook as a doctor does in his journal for the cases he observes.

"Observation by a partner is almost always indispensable, because, before the mind has regained consciousness of itself, psychological facts occur whose memory can, no doubt, persist after waking, but which are linked to manifestations that only another person can observe.

"Thus, the words one speaks, whether asleep or in a restless dream, must be heard by someone who can relate them to you. Even gestures and attitudes are also important. Finally, what makes the assistance of a second person necessary is the impossibility of waking you up, at a given moment, by a mechanical process, as you do with the help of a willing hand."

Vaschide, in his beautiful study, *Sleep and Dreams* (p.86), rightly says that the method employed by Maury requires a very special education, a habit of analyzing oneself and one's dreams. Moreover, the experimenter must have an intense dream life.

Objective method. — This method was aptly named by Sante de Sanctis, the *indirect introspection method*, in addition to the previous one, which he calls the direct introspection method.

It is easy to induce dreams in sleepers; all that is required is to create any sensory excitation, whether tactile, auditory, olfactory, gustatory, or visual. These excitations, reaching the brain, will excite groups of neurons that will evoke memories, which will be linked together by association of ideas.

Maury conducted some fine experiments on this subject, as did Prévost (Geneva, 1834).

Here are some experimental dreams that I believe I should reproduce verbatim [204].

I. — His lips and the tip of his nose are tickled with a feather. He dreams "that he is being subjected to a horrible torture; that a pitch mask is applied to his face, then suddenly torn off, tearing the skin on his lips, nose, and face".

II. — The back of his neck is lightly pinched. "He dreams of being given a blister, which awakens in him the memory of a doctor who treated him in his childhood".

III. — A hot iron is brought close to his face, held far enough away so that the sensation of heat is slight. He dreams of "chauffeurs entering houses and forcing those inside, by putting their feet close to a brazier, to declare where their money is".

Dreams provoked by auditory excitement. — A pair of tweezers is vibrated some distance from his ear while steel scissors are rubbed against it. He dreams that "he hears the sound of bells; this sound of bells soon becomes the tocsin: he imagines himself in the June Days of 1848".

The words *Asor*, *Castor*, and *Leonore* are whispered in his ear; awakened, he remembers "hearing the last two words, which he attributes to one of the speakers in his dream".

Dreams induced by olfactory excitation. — He is made to smell eau de Cologne, and he dreams that "he is in a perfumer's shop; he is in Cairo, in front of extraordinary storefronts".

Dreams induced by visual excitation. — A light surrounded by red paper is passed several times before his eyes. He dreams "of thunderstorms, lightning, and the entire memory of a violent storm he had experienced on the English Channel fills his dream".

Hervey de Saint-Denis also conducted excellent research on the experimental production of dreams.

Professor Vaschide is also one of those who have contributed the most to clarifying this question of experimental dreams.

---

[204] Cited by Vaschide: *Sleep and Dreams*, pp 92 and 276.

Here is one of his experiments:

"After an hour and a half of sleep (deep sleep), we play a gramophone in a room where the subject is sleeping. A pad placed in the instrument's bell considerably dampens the sound. At the same time, we abruptly awaken the subject by shining a strong light on his eyelids. He jumps up in bed, saying, 'You're hurting me,' and, to our question, 'Did you dream?', after a discourteous remark that dream experimenters might expect from their subjects, he replies negatively and begins to fall asleep again. We prevent him from doing so, and he wakes up slowly and completely. While rubbing his eyes, he vaguely searches his memory, and, as he is a psychologist himself, he strives to provide as complete an observation as possible. Four minutes pass without any recollection. We then speak to him of an expression of beatitude that his face had taken on before waking, and we say to him verbatim: 'It seemed that you were listening to pleasant music.'

"Concentrating his attention, he then replies: 'Yes, it's true, I now remember hearing distant music; and, strangely enough, I have before me the following dream which returns more intensely as I speak, and here it is: it seemed to me that I was with you in the laboratory and that we were dancing with women under the moonlight; I also remember a state of such great calm that I dozed off as if into a delicious sleep to the rhythm whistled by hundreds of people. It's very curious that I remember all that...' — Here is a case in which the subject claims not to have dreamed. However, by asking him more precise questions, by, so to speak, turning his thoughts back, by engaging his attention, we managed, to his great surprise, to evoke dream images whose veracity we could verify using this criterion: acoustic excitation... What is also very interesting in this dream is that we found the rhythm of whistling associated with the dream images. Indeed, the tune we had played on the gramophone was the *Waltz of the Burglars* by "Francine's Dad", and we ourselves had allowed ourselves to accompany it by whistling."

From the preceding examples, the reader can see by means of which procedures it is possible to induce, study, and recall dreams. But to avoid errors of judgment, it is appropriate to warn the experimenter unfamiliar with this special chapter of psychology of a very remarkable peculiarity: that, in dreams, time does not exist; a fact, tiny in itself, will occupy hours, while entire series of events can unfold in a few seconds.

I will limit myself to citing a single example relating to the sometimes prodigious speed of dreams:

"We will recall, in this regard, the story of the sleeper who dreamed that he had been arrested, tried, and condemned for a crime attributed to him. He had experienced the horrors of prison, had been taken from his cell, led to the guillotine, and guillotined. He had woken up terrified, having received his canopy on his neck. All these images had been conjured up by the mind between the moment the canopy fell and the moment he perceived this sensation of falling. All this time had not taken a single second [205]."

By using all these varied processes, the experimenter can gradually become aware of his dreams, which, by a natural and logical sequence, will lead him to become aware of his out-of-body experiences and to retain the memory of them.

There is no denying that this way of operating is extremely painful, since it interrupts normal sleep and transforms into fatigue what should constitute an element of rest. But where is the training, whatever it may be and in whatever subject, that is done without difficulty? Can one learn to draw or swim without exerting oneself? I believe that I am addressing myself here to experimenters who *want* to succeed. If the path seems too difficult to them and the learning too hard, let them close this book; it is not written for them.

But I suppose that the operator has overcome all obstacles and that he is master of this special memory: it is up to him, then, to apply this faculty to his out-of-body experience.

The first few times, he should not forget the thought of the

---

[205] PAPUS (Dr. G. Encausse), *Reincarnation*, 1 vol. in-12, Paris, S. D. (1912). — In this case, the transmission of sensations occurring at a rate of 34 meters per second, if we assume a maximum distance of twenty centimeters between the nape of the neck where the canopy had struck in its fall, and the cerebral location of the perception of sensations, this entire succession of events which, in reality, would have occupied a duration of several months, took place with its multiple details in a duration of time which does not exceed *one hundred and seventieth of a second.*

muscular effort (discussed above: sudden relaxation of the muscles by an energetic act of will) to be made in a culminating phase of his out-of-body experience: this effort, by recalling his will and consequently his astral body, will bring him back to normal life, and he will remember the event which, in his astral out-of-body experience, immediately preceded his awakening. He should gradually become accustomed to returning to himself during increasingly less significant periods of his out-of-body experience, before making the effort of will necessary for his return to normal life; then, when his memory is no longer restive, he should await the logical and natural conclusion of his out-of-body experience: little by little, he will become master of his memory, and the memory will remain in him of what he did or saw during the out-of-body experience.

On the other hand, an important fact to note is that the memory of events and the consciousness of direction are united by links that are still poorly defined, but undeniable. This is a remark that can be put to good use by the experimenter who does not wish to resort to hyperphysical means, such as those I noted in the preceding paragraphs, to acquire the consciousness of direction. He can therefore, having reached this point of development, instead of aiming first at the acquisition of the consciousness of direction, for which, I repeat, normal science offers us — and for good reason — no guidance, no point of support. He can, I say, take advantage of what we know about dreams and the teachings resulting from the numerous experiments conducted on this subject to first acquire the memory of dreams, which should then lead him to the memory of out-of-body experience. The fact that memory can only preserve what has previously been in consciousness will lead it — for longer, with more difficulty than using the hyperphysical route, granted — but ultimately will lead it to acquire awareness of its actions in a state of out-of-body experience, — and the sense of direction will come naturally afterwards.

In fact, in such matters, it is unclear what the basis of memory rests on. All the subjects studied by my colleague Pierre Piobb [206] have a special memory of their actions in a state of out-of-body experience; almost none of those I have studied retain the memory of the actions they performed in this state, and, when they do retain it by chance, this memory is so vague, so confused, that one wonders if it is not the result of auto-suggestion prior to the out-of-body experience.

Is this difference due to the fact that Pierre Piobb's subjects operate at an astrologically favorable time? [207] I don't know.

It seems, at least in my opinion, that this possibility of remembering, after splitting, is due to memory in general, to its normal strength, to a greater or lesser extent, and that by developing general memory, one must achieve some results with regard to the special memory we are dealing with here. I am led to conclude that by developing his general memory, the experimenter in personal splitting is called upon to reap technical results; he can, moreover, use this method concurrently with the others I have just indicated.

There are a certain number of procedures aimed at strengthening and developing memory; they can be found in special treatises on mnemonics. I will describe here only five exercises, which seem to me to be very effective and which are taken from the *Treatise on Yoga* by E. Bosc de Vèze; they are, therefore, of Hindu origin and little known in the West.

1. — One should begin counting from *one* to *ten*, and one should not allow anything to enter one's mind other than this. As soon as one has completed this counting, one's mind will be in a receptive state: it will be ready to receive all the impressions one desires.

One should then concentrate one's mind on this idea:

"My memory is improved, my memory is perfected" [208].

One should practice this exercise for an hour and a half each time, as often as possible.

2. — One should choose nine or ten figures that one will represent to one's mind during the day. One should firmly imprint them on one's mind; then, one should recall them at least once a day for a whole year. Each day, one should imprint a new figure on one's mind, while not forgetting the old ones. If, however, one has forgotten some of the old ones, then one should not concentrate one's mind on new ones until one has firmly fixed all the others in one's mind.

This is a most interesting exercise.

3. — Practice adding different totals, starting with a single-digit number and increasing with a two-digit, three-digit, four-digit, etc. number. Practice remembering the numbers and also their total. These numbers should be present in your mind from day to day, and, in order to progress, the student should learn a new sum each day.

4. — You must concentrate your mind on a tree or shrub and keep it firmly in your mind; practice this twice a day. Each time, you must add (in your memory) a tree or shrub (seen) in a new location, then think about them each day, keeping all this firmly in your mind.

5. — Every night, after going to bed, at the precise moment you are about to doze off, say, "My memory is progressing; my brain is in a receptive state to receive any impression whatsoever; I can rely on it. I have absolute control over my mental faculties; I can remember a great number of things. My memory improves every day; every day I also now notice a great change in my mental qualities. My thoughts progress with great speed; my brain is in good health, and I firmly desire to progress more and more every day" [209].

If these exercises are performed daily, even for a very short period of time, one greatly develops memory. When one observes and can verify this development day by day, one acquires great patience; whereas someone who has a bad memory in principle loses confidence in himself; but if he realizes that with the preceding exercises he obtains results, he suddenly improves the poor conditions in which his memory finds itself.

Although these procedures may seem bizarre, they are no less good for perfecting memory; we can therefore only encourage our readers to practice them, but assiduously and without any discouragement.

It seems certain that ordinary memory, thus strengthened and

---

[206] See his work: *The Evolution of Occultism*, MM. H. and Durville, editors), in which one will find a practical method for studying Astrology, Magic, and Alchemy which can lead, according to the author, to their complete elucidation.
[207] V, chap. IX, *Material Conditions*, § *Moment*.
[208] This exercise is based on the theories of auto-suggestion.
[209] Like #1, this exercise is based on auto-suggestion.

energized, will be more able to record and preserve the memory of events that occurred during a period of out-of-body experience.

I) *Use of an ordinary receptive subject.*

At the point we have reached, I assume the experimenter to be in possession, if not of all the secondary faculties of out-of-body experience that I have just examined in succession, then at least of all those that he is capable of developing within himself; for there must be no mistake, the totality of these faculties, and especially the latter, are acquired only after a long series of painful efforts and continuous trials; only exceptionally gifted subjects succeed in this from the outset, but how rare are they? I do not know if I am not exaggerating in saying one in a thousand. So I will leave this exception aside to deal only with the majority, that is, with all those who are capable of expressing themselves in an average way, and these are legion: it is me, it is you, it is anyone who possesses some neuricity and the patience and willpower necessary to develop this neuricity according to the system I have just indicated, or any other that his instinct or his studies have shown to be more appropriate to his organism.

Having, at his discretion, sufficiently operated with his sensitive subject, he wishes to go and find, by way of splitting, any other person he pleases...

Here, the first recommendation, the sovereign recommendation that must be made, is, above all and in all, to act with the utmost prudence. And the primordial act of this prudence is *never* to go and find anyone without having warned them.

I hardly need to say that, to do this, it is absolutely necessary to have acquired *visibility* and *tangibility* to a fairly pronounced degree, otherwise noting will result, obviously. But these two faculties constitute a double source of danger if one goes to find an unwarned correspondent, the first for the correspondent himself, the second for the operator.

Indeed, many cases can arise in such an occurrence that were impossible to foresee. Let's quickly examine the main ones.

In the middle of the night, you wake someone unexpectedly; one of two things can happen: either this person recognizes you, or they don't, — and, suddenly roused from their sleep, there's a good chance they won't recognize you; in either case, a host of complications can arise. Suppose, for example, that this person has, without your knowledge, or even without their own knowledge, a heart condition; you could have their death to blame on you. If, on the contrary, they are of a weak or tormented mind at that moment, will you be sure not to bring on an outbreak of madness, a frenzy of the brain, a nervous illness, or something else? — But I admit that your correspondent is a man of vigorous intelligence, healthy in body, and instantly entering into possession of all his faculties upon waking... If he does not believe in ghosts, what can he think of the individual he finds in the middle of the night in his own room, except that he is a criminal? Suppose, as is logical to think, that he has a weapon near his hand and that he uses it: it could mean the brutal dissolution of your ghost, and, as a result of the repercussions of the injuries on the physical body, death for you. On the contrary, he believes in ghosts? Is he aware of the experiments you are conducting? Who tells you that he believes in this incredible phenomenon because it is inexplicable to someone who has not observed it and has not studied its special theories? Who's to say that, to teach you a lesson, simply to see what will happen, he won't brutally harm your ghost?

So, we must start from the principle that an experiment of this sort, tried on an uninformed subject, presents dangers of all kinds, of which I have just briefly indicated only the main ones; consequently, I repeat, we must *never* act on someone we have not previously informed, and *who has consented*; otherwise, that is to say, if you act despite their refusal, you may find yourself in the presence of a person who, unnerved, will not be in control of their actions, and, for you, the danger will be the same as in the previous cases.

But we must also not make such a proposal to just anyone who comes along. Just as, to begin, you had to resort to an appropriate sensitive, so, to continue, you must resort to a person chosen as judiciously as possible.

We have seen, in fact, above that habituation plays a major role in the actions of the phantom; it may therefore be that it only shows itself in its full visibility to the ordinary sensitive because it is accustomed to materializing before them; if, therefore, you send it to a "correspondent" to whom it is not accustomed, there is a good chance that it will lack the strength to make itself seen. On the other hand, if bilious temperaments are more apt than others to perceive hyperphysical phenomena, this is likely due to the fact that these temperaments provide them with the strength necessary for their manifestation.

It is therefore appropriate that, when you change receptive subject, your exteriorized *aérosôme* encounter in the new one conditions of action similar to those it found in the old one, although pronounced to a lesser degree. It is therefore advisable to always choose, at least initially and for the first substitutions of subjects, temperaments that are more or less bilious-nervous, but in whom this quality is always present. In a word, one must take advantage of the fact that habituation plays a major role — still unexplained, but observed in many diverse cases — in the development of *aérosomatic* forces and their external manifestations, to, first, accustom the phantom to the change of subject, and then accustom it to revealing itself in temperaments that are less and less bilious; this is again a kind of training, easy to follow for those who have acquired the habit of splitting themselves effortlessly.

In all cases, one must avoid taking as subjects children whose intellectual development could be disturbed; young girls and overly nervous people, of a pathological neuritis, in whom the observation of the phenomenon could lead to a cerebral exaltation whose effects cannot be measured, the sick whose mind would run the risk of being affected in an unfortunate way; the elderly whose declining faculties would be likely to receive a deplorable impulse; people whose religious beliefs, more pious than enlightened, are based on an irreducible belief in the existence of the devil, and whom the observation of the phenomenon could throw into an unhealthy mysticism, etc. We see, from this rapid enumeration, how numerous are the categories of individuals for whom such an experiment must be rigorously prohibited.

It is therefore appropriate to choose one's subjects only from among people who are absolutely robust in body and mind, whose intelligence is not only above average, but also shows no aversion to studies of this nature. In short, one must apply the same meticulous care to this choice as a surgeon forced to immediately and urgently perform a major operation far from any medical assistant and with makeshift aids; he seeks, among those present, those who will not be disturbed by the sight of blood or the emotion inherent in the first spectacle of an operation; he will preferably choose men in the prime of life, energetic women, etc. The same *criterion* must be used when it is a question, for an experimenter of out-of-body experience, of knowing near which person in his entourage it is appropriate to operate, so that no harm can result either to the chosen subject or to himself.

Only later, when numerous successful trials with different subjects have shown him beyond a doubt that he can manifest himself near the most diverse temperaments, but also when he has imperturbably acquired the awareness of his direction, will he be free to slightly soften the strictness of these rules; in any case, he must *never* act with someone for whom an experience of this nature could be a cause of material, mental, or moral harm, and this, in the most absolute manner. One must not believe that this is a simple matter of conscience (which, in some people, especially when it comes to acts unknown to the law, is often too elastic), but be firmly convinced that this way of acting can be a source of dangers not only objective, but — which will especially strike the broad consciences I have just spoken of — subjective. I have mentioned a few of them in the preceding lines: I will have to return to them and list others in the next chapter. But first, I have a few words to add about the change of subject.

It may be that the manifestation of the phantom that occurs well with one subject only gives a completely null result with another: this may only come from a lack of habituation on the part of the exteriorized *aérosôme*; it is therefore better to persevere for a while, rather than change "correspondent" too quickly: repeated changes can only confuse the phantom, and prevent it from acquiring strength, if not take away those it already possesses.

If, despite everything, we observe the persistence of the nullity of the results, it is appropriate to study the subject employed even more scrupulously, to realize whether, without being hostile to such experiments, he does not experience some boredom, some moral constraint, — to know, in a word, whether he is or is not one of those who frankly give all their strength to help achieve success, or whether he is one of those others who, in the presence of all that, for them, is the unknown, the mystery, withdraw into themselves in an instinctive feeling of refusal, stronger than they are, superior to all the assurances they may have given to willingly lend themselves to the control [210]. There are sometimes very delicate reasons for these failures, personal to each subject, and which, for this reason, it is impossible to enumerate here. It is up to the experimenter to see, to find out... In any case, if he is forced to change the subject again, it would be good for him to return for a while to the first one, near whom he developed, to find out if this unsuccessful attempt has not harmed the very act of splitting and, consequently, the strength of the exteriorized phantom.

Moreover, the first few times one moves from one receptive subject to another, it will always be useful to return once or twice to the first subject, which should constitute, from this point of view, a reservoir of psychic strength, or rather, of habituation, and near whom the ghost will experience a sort of rest after its previous attempts, a rest that will at the same time be a kind of comfort, since it will find there both the usual environment in which it developed and the subject that always welcomed it, during its development, with a reserve of psychic energies that it assimilated.

This second phase, with different subjects, must therefore evolve around the first subject like a rotating machine around its pivot.

It goes without saying that one must always proceed with as much logic as caution; otherwise, a misstep could cause the ghost to lose some of the previously acquired strength. Consequently, one should avoid starting with a new receptive subject at the same point as one left off with the previous one. On the contrary, for each of the first four or five receptive subjects, it will be appropriate to run through, under their supervision, the entire range of operations performed with the first, more quickly, or perhaps less meticulously — or perhaps even more so! But ultimately by starting from the very beginning the series of successive developments.

---

[210] Experimenters who are not averse to occult studies and those who have already used the services of a medium to acquire the consciousness of direction may fruitfully use this intermediary again to learn, through his means, from Entities familiar to the experimenter, what the obstacles are preventing him from any success with this or that subject.

Only then, when the operator is absolutely master of his effects, can he abandon the beaten track and inaugurate new experiments: until then, it is prudent for him to regard himself only as a bird that must learn to fight against the wind, otherwise, if he wants to fly beyond his strength, he will feel his wings broken.

CHAPTER XII

———

DANGERS OF EXPERIMENTATION

I now come to a chapter that is to be my apology for having written the preceding ones. I earnestly beg the reader to read it with supreme attention, and to fully grasp the fact that, if I place this chapter before them, it is not with the childish idea of dramatizing for pleasure an experience of a higher order, but with that of exposing what is, in an absolutely positive way, as it is, without exaggerating anything and also without hiding anything.

While I was stating, at the beginning of this work, the conditions that must be met in order to achieve self-doubt, I was thinking to myself: "I will have two kinds of readers, *those who know* and *those who do not know*, or, in other words, those who have experienced it and those who believe it is all a joke. So, two kinds of critics will welcome the reading of this work: some, the first, will find that I get lost in idle details because of being useless, that I make a lot of childish, not to say naive, recommendations; why? Because, for those who have studied, who have experimented, all this goes without saying and must be naturally familiar to anyone who undertakes to engage in an attempt of this nature; and nevertheless all this had to be said to be known to those who, having never opened a book on occultism, feel within themselves, either because chance has revealed it to them, or because they want to verify if they really possess it, the possibility of splitting themselves. The others, those who believe in none of this, who live a purely animal, not to say vegetative, life, regarding dreams as a sort of momentary madness, as a temporary illness of the brain, who are content to eat, drink, and sleep without observing anything around them, considering life as something lamentable or grotesque — depending on whether they have digested poorly or well —, without tiring their petty cerebral nature searching for its causes, those finally who believe only in what strikes their senses, who eat an omelet without thinking that it constitutes a miracle of nature since no one has ever been able to explain how and why the same degree of heat liquefies butter (a solid) and, on the contrary, solidifies albumen (a liquid), who have, in a word, never studied anything, never observed anything, these, on the contrary, will shrug their shoulders and push the book away, exclaiming: "What Joke!... The author must be mentally unbalanced to think that a reader could ever take him seriously!"

Now, at this moment when I undertake to show the dangers inherent in the experiment, I see these two kinds of criticism rising up before me once again: — What's the point, some will say — those who know — what's the point of this chapter? It is obvious that the human body is not made to dissociate, and that if it splits into its constituent elements, it can only be at the risk of its existence: two lines would have sufficed to note this danger. Others, on the contrary, the ignorant, will exclaim: So here at last is the answer to the riddle! The author isn't as crazy as we thought... on the contrary, he's a very cunning fellow who, after devoting four hundred pages to making us believe in an unrealizable phenomenon, now undertakes to guard himself against any denial of the facts by preventing us from attempting the experiment by displaying dangers as imaginary as the experiment itself!

I will answer the former: You know, but others don't know, and they must be educated. I will answer the latter with a silence that I leave them free to take for confusion: that's of no concern to me. But I owe it to myself, I owe it to the serious readers who have followed me so far with the thought of making at least one attempt; to make them see the dangers to which they are exposed, not to make them abandon their project, but so that they only carry it out with full knowledge of the facts; that is to say, both with the awareness of the danger and with the knowledge necessary to avoid or ward it off.

So I will talk about the dangers presented by personal out-of-body experience; but these dangers are so multiple and of such different kinds that I will resort to a special classification in their enumeration. I will therefore divide them into two categories relating to: 1. the preliminary training; 2. the out-of-body experience itself, and in this last order of ideas I will speak of the dangers: *a)* — material; *b)* — intellectual and moral; *c)* — psychic; *d)* — hyperphysical.

A) *Dangers of training.*

The reader will recall that during this work, two methods of energizing the will were given, and, for that of the astral forces, a dual regimen: one preparatory and based on vegetarianism to bring balance to the temperament, the other intended to activate nervous excitement; training the will and balancing the temperament offer nothing dangerous and can be practiced by anyone, under any circumstances. The same cannot be said of the neurification of the being, which can lead, if one is not careful, to all forms of neuropathy. It must therefore be absolutely forbidden to any individual who is already excessively nervous on a regular basis, as well as to anyone who, due to particular circumstances, finds themselves momentarily afflicted with excessive nervousness.

On the other hand, almost no one knows their own temperament exactly, and an error in diagnosis in this regard can lead to the most deplorable consequences: a candidate for splitting, who knows themselves insufficiently and believes themselves capable of undergoing neurification training, must not end up unconsciously overstimulating their nervous system to the point of illness.

It will therefore be an elementary precaution for anyone wishing to undergo this type of training to first consult their *regular* doctor, that is, the one who best knows their constitution and temperament, to obtain a serious definition of the latter's composition. At the same time, they would do well to tell them why they are requesting this consultation, to explain their purpose, and to outline in detail the regimen they intend to follow. If the doctor, whom I assume to be a man of conscience and knowing his client perfectly, sees the slightest contraindication in him (heart disease, neurosis, etc.), he will warn him; he will likewise steer clear of this experiment if the patient seems too weak or too young to endure it. Finally, by studying the indicated regimen with him, he will make any modifications that he deems necessary for the patient's physiological state.

Only after this consultation can the training be safely carried out, provided that the limits set by the doctor are observed. To this end, it will be advisable not only to assiduously and regularly take one's own biometric formula to monitor its variations, but also to return periodically to see the doctor, who will make the necessary observations to ensure that the operator's health does not become the price of the phenomenon.

This is the physical danger. But there are others.

The sensitivity of astral forces becomes extreme in any individual who directs their thoughts toward mysterious things; this results in an abnormal state from the point of view that concerns us, and with which excessive caution must be exercised.

Finally, the anticipation of the experience must not degenerate into a fixed idea that would quickly lead to fatigue and even cerebral overwork.

By taking care to maintain one's calm, with appropriate distractions, whether in amusement or in work, one can easily avoid these two causes of future danger; but the other, the first, is more immediate, more intense as well, and the most elementary prudence dictates that one begin and continue training only with the proper advice of a doctor.

B) *Dangers of out-of-body experience.*

These dangers, as I have just said, are varied and can be classified into several categories which I will examine successively and succinctly.

1. *Material dangers.*

It would be truly childish to discuss in detail whether, when there is a dissociation of the elements of being, there is, or is not, mortal danger. This is so obvious that I will limit myself to showing precisely what, in the case of out-of-body experience, is the exact situation of the physical body; the basis and foundation of all normal being.

The very beautiful and convincing experiments of H. Durville [211] have demonstrated that at the moment the out-of-body experience begins, the human body is abandoned by all its higher principles, as would be the case with a corpse: the mental body has taken with it intelligence; the astral body, sensitivity; and the odic body, life. However, one cannot say, strictly speaking, that it is a corpse, since it is united to its phantom by a fluidic link that transmits to it physical life and the orders of the nervous-sensitive system; one could better say of it that it is an automaton, or, even more precisely, a puppet whose strings are pulled by the phantom. In a word, of all the constituent principles of being, only the material part and the mechanical life remain, that which presides over unconscious physiological functions; yet Rochas's experiments have demonstrated that in certain cases the heartbeat can slow down.

The experimenter is therefore, in the case of exteriorization, like the human being who finds himself subjected simultaneously to chloroform, which abolishes his sensitivity, to curare, which destroys muscular strength, and to some narcotic, which suspends cerebral functions.

Does this mean that the *sarcosôme* then lives a purely vegetative life? Not even that, for the plant possesses the sensitivity that no longer exists in the split being. The life that remains in him is nothing more than unconscious mechanical life, which is more like non-death than life, so close does it come to lethargy when the phantom (intelligence — sensitivity — life) orders no movement: it is indeed he who carries true life, and if he did not transmit it to the *sarcosôme* through the fluidic link that unites them, the latter would pass in a few seconds into the state of a corpse that nothing could revive. And it is easy to see what accidents this fluidic link is at the mercy of.

So much for the splitting of the body itself; let us now see what happens when the exteriorized phantom is sent far away.

As long as this phantom remains near the *sarcosôme*, it carries within itself the odic body (that is, life) with which it can move within a radius of a few meters. But when the ghost is sent far away, a split occurs within it: the odic body, the bearer of life, separates from the ghost and returns to the *sarcosômatic* body, which, deprived of it, would quickly die. Just as the odic body is united to the *sarcosômatic* body by a fluidic link transmitting life, so the ghost itself (astral body and mental body) is united to the odic body by a fluidic link, transmitting orders and sensations. Now, these two fluidic links, which are veritable umbilical cords connecting the expelled fetus to the mother, become increasingly thinner, in direct proportion to the distance. The *odic-sarcosômatic* cord thins relatively little, since the exteriorized odic body always remains close to the *aérosomatic* body. But the odico-astral cord is liable to reach enormous lengths, when, for example, the ghost is sent to Dakar or Noumea. How tenuous must it become then? Now, if we understand all the accidents to which a link of a few meters is exposed, it is impossible to calculate all those that can damage a tenuous thread of several hundred, several thousand kilometers.

It is important, however, to appreciate things precisely and not to consider this connection as a material thread, silk or cotton. If this were the case, any experience of this kind would be fatal. It is fluidic, that is, constituted by an immatter that one could say is endowed with immeasurable elasticity if this term did not evoke a purely material idea: this is not, therefore, where the danger lies, but in the fact that, as I have already said, this immatter is electrical in nature, that is, subject to the dissolving power of points like atmospheric electricity, and instantly disintegrates through sudden and violent trauma such as that of a gunshot, as is lightning in its globular state. We see that the risks of damage, however minor they may be, nonetheless constitute a formidable source of hazard.

There's no denying it: any serious injury, any partial disintegration suffered by the ghost, by the odic body, or by the fluidic bonds that unite them, is death without sentences, instantaneous, brutal. At least that's the best that can happen to the imprudent, for we will see later, when discussing hyperphysical dangers, that something even more lamentable can happen to them; similarly, in the article on psychophysical dangers, we will examine what happens to the more minor injuries suffered by the ghost.

---

[211] See his work *The Ghost of the Living*.

2. *Intellectual and moral dangers.*

If there is one quality that is absolutely essential for anyone undertaking out-of-body experiences, it is undoubtedly mastery of the intellect and full possession of reason. Anyone who has ever felt, through the blows of fate or for any reason whatsoever, their intellectual capacity waver, anyone who has ever experienced, even accidentally, a clouding of their thinking, anyone, in a word, who does not have, to use a popular expression but emphatically expressing what it means, their brain firmly screwed into their skull, must rigorously and absolutely refrain from touching the things of the Mystery, under penalty of feeling their intelligence sink at the turn of an experience and their reason crumble to shreds under a wind of madness.

Therefore, such experimentation must be strictly forbidden: — to children — young girls and young women — to men and women who have not reached the full maturity of their moral, intellectual, and physical strength — to the sick — to the elderly, unless they have acquired the habit in the prime of their life and there has not been too long an interruption of these experiments — to individuals of delicate or fragile mentality — to weak and indecisive characters who could, at the first semblance of success, find themselves fundamentally upset — to the ignorant, who, at the first misunderstood incident during the trials, would be distraught and panicked; in a word to all those who do not have the acquired energy, composure, knowledge, intelligence, and reason to be able to immediately ward off all the adverse events that this type of experimentation entails.

And I beg the reader to believe that I am not painting a gloomy picture for the sake of it, with the aim, as some may think, of diverting attention from the occurrence of a phenomenon whose possibility this work demonstrates; but that the dangers indicated are far from fictitious — without however being exaggerated. Indeed, I have so far shown that splitting is a very accessible operation for many, since many engage in it unconsciously during their sleep; but for me, it is a haughty duty of conscience to enlighten the imprudent and the feeble-minded so that they may know that if the fact itself does not present a danger beyond human strength and resolve, it is at least surrounded by multiple and multiply perilous circumstances against which it would be foolish not to take precautions — and, for the author personally, it would be execrably dishonest and odious not to warn the reader.

Now, among the risks inherent in this experiment, intellectual and moral perils occupy the first rank. I will not detail them in detail; the subject would be too vast and would exceed the scope of this work alone; it is enough for me to point them out, so that everyone, however little they reflect, can grasp them in some way. But certainly the mental danger far outweighs the moral peril, for, let us not hide the fact, it is bordering on an abyss of madness to engage in an attempt so far removed from any normal life conditions, and only those who have the knowledge, energy, and strength of character necessary to achieve success will be able to approach it. For those who risk falling along the way, what good is a paltry attempt whose most obvious result will be to bring confusion to their minds?

This experiment must be like certain others — in chemistry, for example — whose dangers are such that only teachers realize them by surrounding themselves with an excessive luxury of precautions; as for the students, even those who, no longer being students, do not have the absolute need to operate personally, they are content to read the reports, to study the procedures theoretically, and to judge whether the announced results correspond well to the goal of the operation. As for the rest, they leave to those stronger, more learned, more resolute than themselves the task of carrying out practical research and experimenting with things in reality.

However, since individual freedom must be taken into account, even if directed towards a harmful goal, and since these pages may fall into the hands of readers who nevertheless wish to put their teachings into practice, it is appropriate to give a rule of conduct here whose application will have the effect of mitigating, at least to a certain extent, the mental peril of the undertaking: that is, if one insists, to follow the progression as indicated in the preceding pages, the training, tests, etc., but by breaking down the final goal into a number of secondary and partial goals; the final goal is too high, too immense: it would crush poorly prepared mentalities; whereas it is open to everyone to try successively, for example, what the dynamization of the will or the astral body will produce in them, then to make a few attempts, the simplest, most natural, of out-of-body experience, but with the firm resolve to give up if they fail, not to persist, and never to move on to a more serious attempt before having successfully completed the preceding one several times — with, also, the firm resolution to abandon everything as soon as they experience the slightest fatigue or the slightest cerebral exaltation. Under these conditions, and if they rigorously apply this line of conduct, they have a good chance of preserving their mentality intact.

There is, moreover, another point to which it is important to draw the experimenter's attention, for it is a matter of their own safety.

They must, from the very first attempts, determine whether, in their case, after the experience, reintegration is taking place correctly and normally. If this reintegration is difficult and poorly accomplished, he is warned of this by a general fatigue that is primarily cerebral; a sort of aches grips his body, and he feels a certain emptiness in his head.

In this case, he is recommended — and very urgently — not to go beyond the level he has reached, but to begin the same experience again under identically similar conditions, and to repeat it several times, until this particular fatigue has completely disappeared.

Only when his subsequent reintegration is accomplished normally, that is, without bringing with it the slightest discomfort, is he free to move on to another experience of a different order and higher degree.

3. *Psycho-physical dangers.*

These dangers are based on the law of repercussion, which can be formulated as follows: any injury to the astral body has repercussions on the physical body. As things stand, we do not know whether the repercussion is immediate and occurs through the fluidic link, or whether it only occurs at the moment of the ghost's reintegration of the *sarcosôme*; but however it occurs and however it is explained, however incredible, even inexplicable it may seem, repercussion is a fact that has been observed many times and undeniably established. A few examples have already been given in previous chapters, and I have personally observed other, most bizarre cases during my experiments. I will cite only two, whose bizarre nature shows that the phenomenon of repercussion obeys very extensive and complicated laws, although we are generally unaware of them.

— During a session (1910), H. Durville, busy magnetizing his subject (Mrs. Lambert), whom he was facing, heated by his efforts at magnetization, took off a piece of clothing and threw it abruptly behind him while half turning around. In doing so, he struck with his arm a phantom that I had brought [212]. This trauma had repercussions on the then exteriorized phantom of Mrs. Lambert, and then, ultimately, on herself. The explanation I have since been given of the phenomenon is this: — Every act, produced on the astral plane and emanating from the physical plane, must fall back by successive repercussions on the physical plane. The shock had occurred on the completely astral phantom; it had immediately rebounded on the living phantom (that is, the mi-astral, mi-physical) with whom the other was in relation at that moment, and, from there, either immediately or after the reintegration of the *sarcosôme* by the phantom, on the physical body of the subject.

— Another time (1911), with the same operator, the exteriorized phantom of Mrs. Lambert was endowed with such strength that it successively took two receptive subjects, Mrs. C... and Mrs. L..., by the waist and threw them onto the parquet floor [213]. In this fall, Mrs. C... suffered a severe bruise on her knee, which the subject, Mrs. Lambert, also suffered on her own knee. The explanation, requested later, was as follows: — A lesion is transmitted not only from the astral to the physical, but on all those who are fluidically linked. Mrs. C... had emanated her phantom, on which the bruise on her knee was transmitted; this phantom was fluidically linked at that moment with that of Mrs. Lambert: the latter was also injured, and, from it, the injury fell back on Mrs. Lambert's physical body.

These two facts show how complex the laws of the phenomenon of repercussion are. It is therefore possible that the experimenter who has performed his out-of-body experience finds himself bodily injured not only by the traumas and injuries received by his exteriorized phantom, but by all those that affect the people — and in particular the receptive subject — with whom he is in fluidic relation.

But what he has above all and above all to fear, it hardly needs to be said, are the injuries affecting his own phantom; now, the latter is exposed to an incredible number of hazards, as a result of the out-of-body experience itself, and as a result of his own clumsiness in conducting himself. I have explained elsewhere where this clumsiness comes from: the astral body, accustomed to letting itself be guided in its movements by the physical body to which it is united and to which the habit of moving in matter has given a certain skill in avoiding shocks and clashes, lacks this skill by itself; the result is that it runs into all obstacles [214] and that the *sarcosôme* suffers from its clumsiness; and, in a state of splitting, opportunities for injury abound for the phantom. Let us study them a little.

At the very moment of exteriorization, the causes of injury are nil, unless there is an unforeseen incident: the fall of some object, etc. But as soon as it is made to move, it collides with the furniture in the room [215], the walls, even the ceiling, because, being weightless, it can rise very easily [216]. And if it is made to go outside, the experience is even more likely to be more uneven,

---

[212] A ghost from the Beyond. For me, it was a question of bringing together a living ghost and a ghost from the Mystery, to study certain reactions of one to the other.

[213] It was, as far as I remember, during this same session that the exteriorized ghost of Madame Lambert disturbed the seats of the assistants, as shown in Figure 30. We see from this that with the exteriorized ghost, there are cases where the danger is purely physical.

[214] In certain cases of experiments with an objectively exteriorized ghost, when one wanted to make it pass through a door, it preferred to dematerialize completely and pass *through the wall* (even if it meant rematerializing in the other room) rather than go through the door, where its clumsiness caused it to violently bump into the doorframe, which, as a result of transmitting the sensation of trauma to the subject, made the latter scream.

[215] This is why the experimenter has been recommended elsewhere to carefully visit the room where it is to manifest itself to familiarize itself with all the furniture and objects there.

[216] This occurred during certain experiments by H. Durville, and the sleeping subject felt the impacts of its ghost against the ceiling. (See *The Ghost of the Living*, by H. Durville, Paris, 1909).

because outside, everything is an opportunity for injury for the ghost — clumsy in guiding itself —, especially since when no path has been prescribed for it to arrive at a desired place, the one it takes is always the one that comes closest to a straight line. Also, it has the habit, as soon as it is outside, of rising to pass over all obstacles; but finally, when he approaches the assigned goal, he has to come back down to earth, and then everything is a cause of injury to him, from the passer-by who bumps into him [217] to the corner of a street which he clumsily skirts.

But that's not all: truly improbable accidents can happen to him along the way. I mentioned above the case of an experimenter wounded by a violent blow to the stomach after finding himself, out of body, and without knowing how or why, in the middle of an Apache battle: I will have to come back to this later; this is an operator who always acts prudently and takes all the necessary precautions, so he rarely returns injured. But, on the other hand, I know a mediumistic subject whose limbs and body are constantly covered in bruises, contusions, scratches, and even more serious wounds, all resulting from his multiple astral outings. So I only have to look at his arms, and when I notice the existence of lesions more recent than the others, I say to him without fear of being mistaken: — "Last night, you went for a walk outside yourself!"

It is certain that the one who splits himself and sends his ghost outside must expect a series of misadventures, because it is rare, very rare, that one reintegrates the *sarcosôme* without a wound or a bump, the result, I repeat, of the clumsiness of an astral body deprived of its natural guide, the physical body: these are the minor inconveniences of experience [218].

---

[217] A subject split in magnetic sleep is sent home: as his ghost climbs the stairs, he says to his magnetizer: — Someone is coming down; he's going to hurt me as he passes. — Move aside to let him pass. — I can't... Oh! He crushed my foot... — After the session, the subject's foot was bruised.

[218] Usually, upon waking, one notices the existence of a painful "blackness" on some part of the body.

When the split occurs unconsciously, the operator, who is not warned, wonders with surprise, upon observing the situation, how he could have hit himself with such force in his bed... — This case occurs very frequently, and there is perhaps no one who has not been a victim.

But all this is generally not serious as long as the ghost only collides with inert matter. It is different when he finds himself in the presence of a human being who, out of malice, stupidity, simple lack of composure, — or less than that, out of incredulous, stupid curiosity, wanting to see what will happen following a stab or a revolver blow, wounds the ghost. Serious cases of this kind abound, many of which have resulted in fatal outcomes [219]. It is therefore extremely imprudent for someone who has succeeded in splitting himself into two, to send his ghost to just anyone without first warning the person: in such circumstances, one has enough opportunities to be wounded, even seriously, without creating further opportunities that could be avoided. Many people, in fact, only fall asleep with a weapon within reach: now, what thought can come to them when, suddenly roused from their sleep, they see a shadow wandering around their room? They only think of the presence of a criminal, and their first impulse is somewhat instinctive: to use their weapon. There is a typical observation in this regard, called the Bojanoo case, which can be found in the *Initiation* of April 1893: in the story, the woman — a witch who was splitting into two — was struck by a saber and died.

Excessive caution in such matters cannot therefore be recommended too strongly; especially since, while we know in which cases repercussion can be said to occur, there are many others where it occurs by virtue of laws that are completely unknown to us. I cited two observations at the beginning of this paragraph, which, if they had not caught the fact in some way in flagrant act of production, would have seemed incredible and inexplicable. And in how many other circumstances does the phenomenon of repercussion occur, of which we are ignorant, of which we cannot even suspect!

I provide here several photographs of lesions made to the astral body, in certain experiments, and repercussions on the physical body.

The first three present the development of a hyperphysical burn occurring in the following circumstances:

---

[219] Cf. the somewhat classic case of the miller Bigot.

One evening in April 1911, Mrs. Lambert was split by Mr. H. Durville. The phantom, fully exteriorized, was sent by the experimenter towards an experimental table to knock over a designated object.

As she was about to knock down this object with her left hand, her forearm was seized by an enormous hand, the subject said, a monstrous hand that twisted it. The subject cried out in terror and it was with difficulty that the operator managed to get the invisible adversary to release its grip. Then, once the subject had been reconstituted, she was left with an intense contraction on her left forearm that disappeared only with difficulty.

Upon waking, the subject no longer feels the pain and goes home; but the pain returns when she goes to bed, and she does not sleep all night.

The next day, we observe:

1. the increase in volume of the left forearm; the measurement taken 9 centimeters below the epitrochlea gives 24 centimeters on the left and 22 centimeters on the right, i.e. 2 centimeters of increase (*fig. 67*);

2. a diffuse redness extending from the crease of the elbow to 5 centimeters from the wrist joint; 9 centimeters from the epitrochlea and on the antero-external surface of this left forearm, we notice a more accentuated redness measuring 7 centimeters in diameter, accompanied by a multitude of blisters the size of a pinhead, as shown in the photograph (*fig. 68*) taken the day after the accident; passing the hand over the rest of the forearm, we can feel innumerable blisters in the process of forming, but very tiny to the eye.

On the second day of this accident, the diffuse redness increased; the tiny blisters on the rest of the forearm increased slightly in size; the aforementioned pinhead-sized blisters opened, oozing serosity similar to that of a second-degree burn; the edema of the forearm had now invaded the dorsal surface of the hand (*fig. 69*), and, as a result, flexing the fingers became slightly painful.

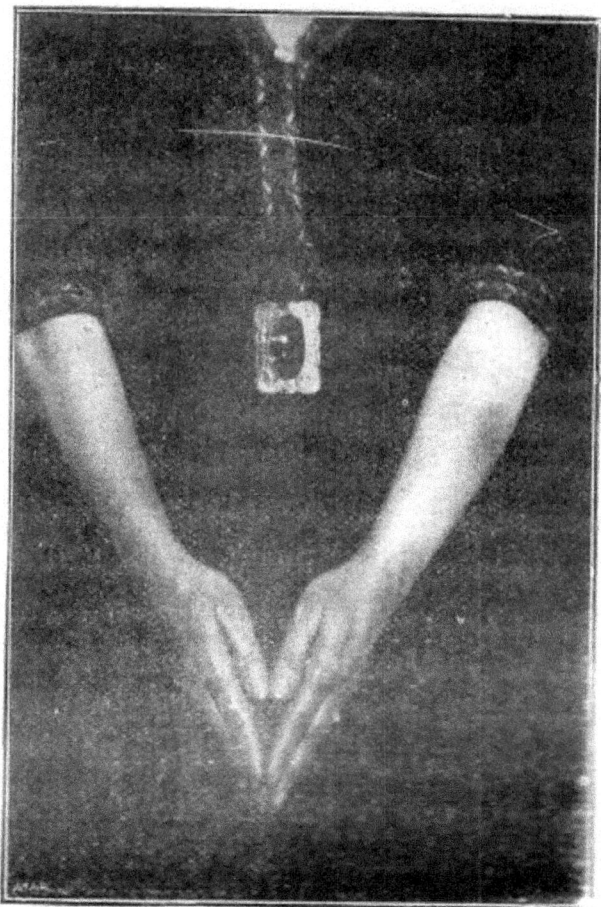

Fig. 67. — Hyperphysical burn received during the splitting,
A) photograph taken the day after the accident
(comparison of the two arms).

On the third day, the tiny blisters had dried without opening; those that had opened seemed to dry, forming a crust; the edema of the left hand still persisted; there was a slight decrease in the volume of the forearm; the pain diminished under the influence of appropriate treatment (magnetized water compresses). In summary, around the fourth day, this unusual burn was healing. Although the effective cause of this burn has remained rather obscure, it is undeniably a lesion that affected the exteriorized living ghost, and then had repercussions on the physical body.

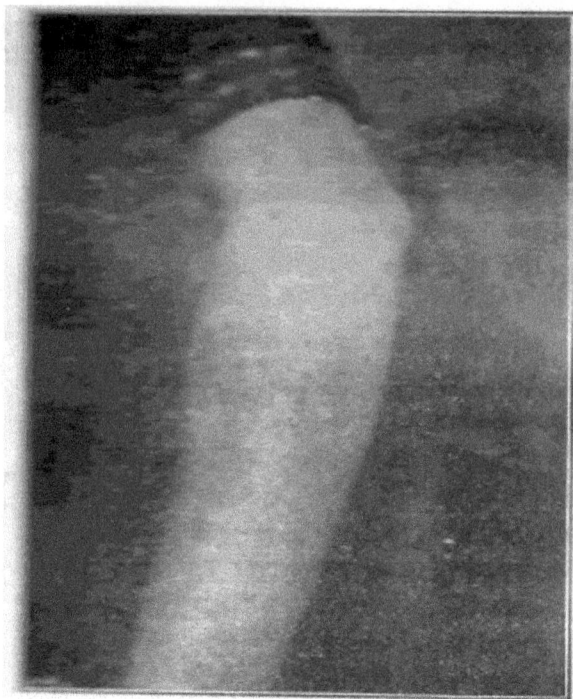

Fig. 68. — Hyperphysical burn.
B) photograph taken the day after the accident
(detail of the injury).

Therefore, the experimenter who splits himself must fully grasp this idea: his ghost is called upon to move in a mysterious environment, where pitfalls will take on all forms for him, without him having any compass, no guide to help him avoid all the risks he will inevitably encounter.

It will be objected that these risks are not so dangerous that no one has ever been seen returning from an astral projection... Okay! But they do exist, I have provided proof of this, and, as such, I had to point them out to urge all operators to be cautious; only fools believe that prudence is the negation of courage and resolution; on the contrary, everyday experience teaches us that the bravest people are generally the most prudent: there is a sailor who holds several life-saving medals, that is to say, having undeniably risked his life in the middle of a storm, without hesitation, to save his fellow men, who would never be sent out to sea for a walk when, in his opinion, the weather is unsafe.

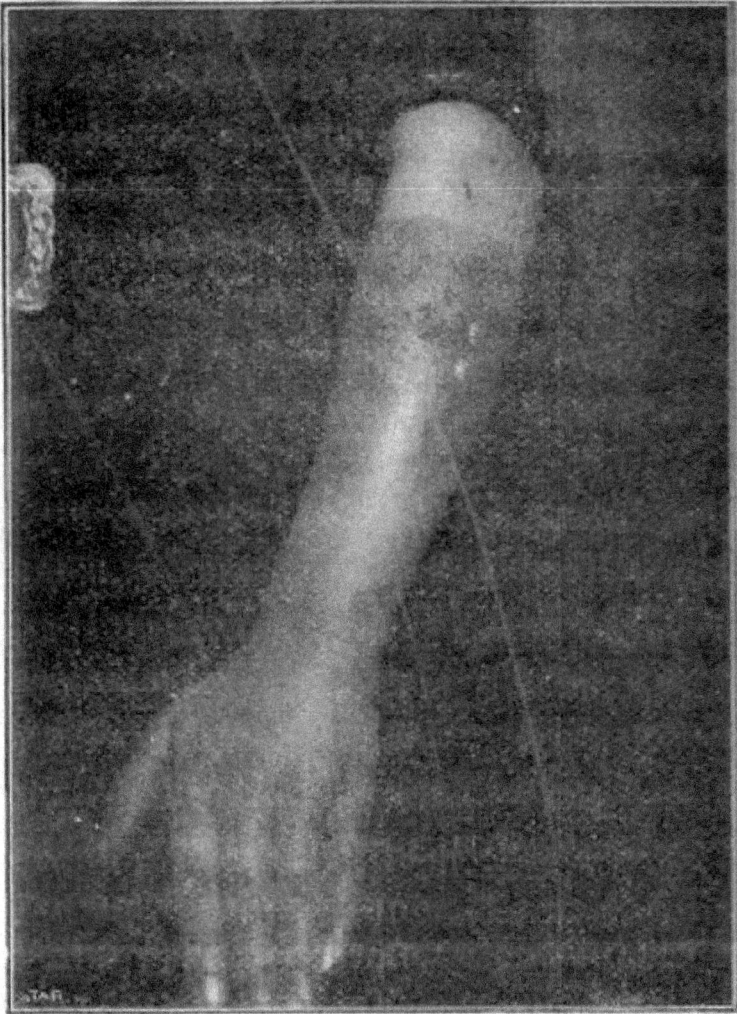

Fig. 69. — Hyperphysical burn.
C) photograph taken two days after the accident.

In out-of-body experiences, the same must be done; to inquire about possible danger in order to arm oneself with precautions against it is the characteristic of the experimenter truly worthy of the name, who thinks that a known danger is a danger already half avoided.

During these astral projections, one should therefore be careful not to approach the first person who comes along without first knowing what kind of reception awaits them; this is precisely why it has been recommended to choose as a receptive subject a person of calm and incapable of losing their composure in the presence of an apparition as extraordinary, even if foreseen, as that of a living ghost. I know of a receptive subject who, although warned in advance of the strange visit he was about to receive, and to which he had agreed, was so impressed by the realization of the phenomenon that he could only find one sentence to say as he sat up: "Is that you, Mr. X? *Sit down!*" It is obvious that this subject was deeply troubled at the time; suppose that his disturbance, instead of being expressed by this out-of-the-ordinary phrase, had manifested itself in an instinctive gesture of defense, what would have happened?

Therefore, caution is recommended above all. But when all logical precautions are taken, the resolute man approaches the experiment by trusting in the words once spoken to me: "There is a God for split individuals!"

There is another type of psychophysical risk that I must discuss here, although it does not threaten the operator, but because the receptive subject can be a victim of it, I have mentioned it elsewhere, during the study of development, because its occurrence provides clear proof of splitting: these are cases where the phantom *burns* the receptive subject by its touch.

This case is rather exceptional, it should be stated immediately; but ultimately, it is only relatively rare, and I have had to observe its occurrence several times; as such, it is important to devote a few lines of explanation to it.

In reality, we know of its existence, but we are completely ignorant of the conditions under which it occurs, and we know only one thing about this phenomenon: that it is not constant; to give just one example, I will cite an experimenter who burns some of his receptive subjects, having them touched by his external phantom, and does not burn the others.

This burning, I hasten to say, generally will present very little severity, but there are also a few cases where, without being very significant in intensity, it nevertheless presents a rather serious appearance: I give a specimen (*fig.* 70), which represents a case of a burning received during an out-of-body session.

Fig. 70
Burn received by Mrs. T..., during an out-of-body experience.

How does such a phenomenon occur? Here again, we are reduced to hypotheses. I suppose, for my part, that the fact occurs not directly on the material organism, but on the exterior *aérosôme* of the subject, from where it is reflected on the physical body, and this, as a result of a theory which is personal to me, which, naturally, I only give under the most express reservations and which is this: — From certain particular experiments, it seemed to me to be able to conclude that "when two astral substances are brought into contact, the one which is the purest reacts on the one which is closest to matter, in the manner of a caustic on living cells. When the affected substance does not belong to a physical body, we are unaware of the consequences of the reaction; when, on the contrary, it is attached to a living body of material life, there is a repercussion of the lesion of the astral body on the physical body in the form of a burn which, as we shall see, is of a particular type not found in any degree of normal burning."

According to this theory — and naturally admitting its accuracy — the phantom of the experimenter, well exteriorized, that is to say, well freed from materiality, would be astrally superior to the phantom, less exteriorized, and consequently, charged with materiality of the receptive subject; and the reaction would produce a sort of burning then reflected on the material body of the latter; or again the astral body of the subject would be, by itself and by its own constitution, formed of more or less pure fluids, which would explain why the same operator could burn some of his receptive subjects while leaving the others unharmed. I repeat, there are certain very obscure factors here that escape us.

On the other hand, if I describe the injury that occurs in such circumstances as a *burn*, it is because the outward appearance of this injury, as well as the pain it causes in the subject, seem to classify it among what is ordinarily called so.

But a thorough examination generally reveals in this type of injury particularities that are not found in any degree of normal burn; that is, coming from instruments, vapors, caustics, etc.; among these particularities, I will cite in particular a desquamation of the epidermis circumscribing the wound, and a bristling of the skin (goosebumps) itself circumscribing the desquamation indicated above [220].

---

[220] A detailed description and discussion of a similar lesion found on an experimental subject can be found in a final note in *Sorcery of the Countryside* by the same author. I reproduce here (*fig.* 71) the photograph taken during this burn.

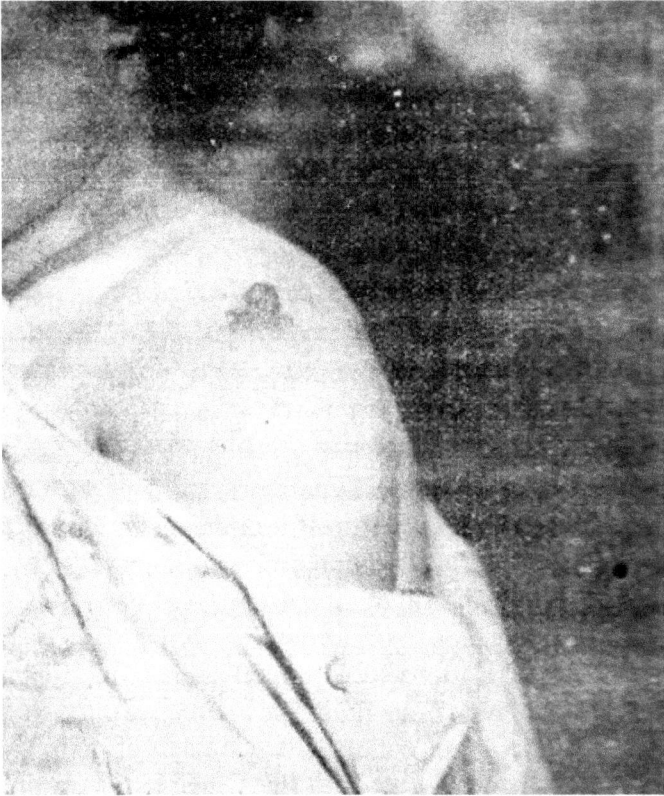

Fig. 71.
Hyperphysical burn, received during a doubling
experience by the subject's exteriorized ghost
and reflected on his physical body.

Moreover, burns as deep as those similar to the lesion represented by Figures 67 and 71 very generally leave scars behind; in no case is this the case with the types of psycho-physical burns with which we are concerned here.

Finally, I will have said everything about them when I add that they are very easily cured in a few days with applications of magnetized water; I do not know, due to a lack of tests in this direction, the effect that ordinary remedies, such as applications of oleo calcareous liniment or picric acid, could produce on this type of burn.

4. — *Hyperphysical danger.*

I stated above that it was my intention to complete this study without addressing, as much as possible and only when the insights of normal science were absolutely lacking, the hyperphysical side of the question, which, in short, can be resolved by staying not on the ground of ordinary science, which, in this respect, has only given us indications, but on that of technical observations.

On only rare occasions during this work have I been forced to speak of occultism, but only when forced to do so by the very nature of the subject at hand (capture and assimilation of energies from higher planes, psychic dispositions, etc.).

At the point I have reached, I must still speak of occultism. The reader who doesn't believe in this will have to shrug off these pages, but it's not by hiding the hyperphysical danger that one can neutralize it, and whether one affirms it or denies it, I know perfectly well that it exists: I am therefore, willingly or not, obliged to say a few words about it.

We have spoken above of the Entities of the Mystery with whom we enter into relations either directly, when our organism provides us with the necessary fluids, or indirectly, through the intermediary of individuals endowed with an appropriate organization. This is not the place to study their nature or their reason for being: they exist and interfere with our actions, sometimes with our knowledge, and sometimes — most often — without our knowledge: that is enough.

For spiritualism, they are the disembodied spirits of our dead, high or low, good or evil, frivolous or serious, presenting, in a word, all the series of intellectual and moral development that we encounter in humanity.

For occultism, they are evolving Beings — *Elementals* — already reached a higher degree of development, immortal, endowed with intelligence and responsibility, and in charge with the management of the world [221]; or else, involuting Beings — *Elementals* or *Larvae* — very inferior to humanity, mortal, and, consequently, hungry for life, endowed only with instinct and without responsibility, charged with moving the elements under the direction of the Elementals: the latter represent the animality of the astral plane, while the former, in a way, form humanity.

These two doctrines being the most widespread, I will not concern myself with the others which, in this respect, are more or less similar.

In any case, we are undeniably surrounded by Entities, good or bad, some of whom help us, whether we are aware of it or not, and others are on the lookout for every opportunity to cause harm: — either, according to spiritualism, which sees them as former human beings who lived in wickedness, to continue the evil that was the essence of their lives; — or, according to occultism, which regards them as beings hungry for life, to take their share of our existence by committing the evil that is the only thing within their reach and which, moreover, they do not know how to distinguish from good.

Now, it must be recognized that, when we pass onto the astral plane, we are inevitably disoriented there, due to a lack of habit; we move only clumsily there; we are, in a word, in a state of absolute inferiority, compared to the Entities who normally live there. We are therefore prime prey for the wickedness of the lower Entities, to whom we deliver ourselves, as it were, bound hand and foot if we do not first take certain precautions.

On the other hand, it should be noted that, in our normal state, the harm that the evil Entities of the astral plane can do us cannot exceed certain limits — very limited if our lifestyle keeps them away; very extensive, on the contrary, when we give them a free hand or call upon them. But the very fact of our splitting places us in a particularly dangerous situation with them: — on the one hand, the higher part of our being, sent to the astral plane, moves there awkwardly, hampered by the fluidic bond that attaches it to its material body; and, on the other hand, the *sarcosôme* left inert, abandoned and defenseless on the physical plane, is exposed to all attempts without being able to resist them; and it offers too easy prey to all astral appetites that want either to revive in order to continue doing evil, or to prolong their own lives by stealing ours. Therefore, as soon as a living being exteriorizes its ghost, that is to say, as soon as it abandons its physical body defenselessly, this physical body is immediately open to attacks from Entities of the Mystery who would like to lodge there; in other words, when the master of the house is absent, the burglars feel free to operate — and they use it.

When the *sarcosôme* is prey to a *material* attack, it quickly recalls its higher elements by means of the fluidic link that unites them to it [222]. But this fluidic link is precisely composed largely of astral matter; consequently, he finds himself exposed to the enterprises of astral Entities. I do not believe, to tell the truth — and without having any certainty of what I am putting forward, which is simply my personal opinion — I do not believe, I say, that these Entities have the power to completely break this link, basing myself on the fact that the breaking of the link would be death for the experimenter and that there seems to be a higher law prohibiting astral Entities from interrupting a human existence; but at least they have the power, with the help of certain actions, to so distend this link, to interpose such obstacles, that the re-entry of the *aérosôme* into the *sarcosôme* is made virtually impossible. Then they install themselves in this body without a master — and it is madness!

We can state in fact that in all cases where there is madness without cerebral lesion, this madness is caused by the intrusion of a larva or an evil spirit. — Madness is gentle when the intelligence that has abandoned its *sarcosôme* recognizes the impossibility of returning to it and resigns itself; it is, on the contrary, furious when there is a struggle between the thief and the rightful owner: this explains why, among the demented, the agitated present a greater chance of recovery than the others; their latent will to recover their organism helps the care of mental therapy.

And note that the Spiritist doctrine explains all kinds of insanity: the intrusion of a spirit who, during his lifetime, was ambitious or powerful, leads to delusions of grandeur; if the spirit is that of a murderer, the madness will be bloodthirsty, and so on. We can therefore see, moreover, and without my needing to dwell on it further, how terrible the hyperphysical risks presented by an astral projection are: — snares for the ghost on the one hand — attacks against the *sarcosôme* on the other. And if there were no way to prevent them, we can confidently say that the splitting of a living being could only present two outcomes: death or madness.

---

[221] Sometimes, however, according to this very doctrine, it is the disembodied souls of living people who manifest themselves to us.

[222] In case of injury or trauma to the physical body, this recall occurs instantly.

Fortunately, — without which any experience of this nature would be absolutely impossible — there is a process for protecting oneself from these two terrible eventualities.

I have just said that the Entities of Mystery are constantly involved in our actions, and that they are, from a moral point of view, good, neutral, or evil. Every living being therefore has around it a sort of gathering of these Entities, with one of them predominating (which occultist doctrine calls the *master*, spiritualist doctrine the *guide*, and Catholic doctrine the *guardian angel*) whose mission is to watch over the incarnate being, and to give rise in it impulses toward good.

But how is this group of astral Entities that surrounds the living being composed? *As the living being itself wanted!* — The proverb: *Birds of a feather flock together* is even truer in the afterlife than in our world; a man accustomed to vile acts and criminal thoughts quickly surrounds himself with vile and criminal Entities; on the contrary, the good man, the just man, creates an entourage of Beings of justice and goodness. The strength developed by the living being in this regard is such that it can even influence its own guide, who ends up being neutralized or removed when the surroundings are too powerful in wickedness, or by being replaced by a superior Being when the living being's progress in the ways of morality requires a *guide* of a superior essence.

Now, in any splitting, the *guide* ordinarily follows the phantom, and it is the surroundings that guard and defend the abandoned *sarcosôme*.

If, then, the experimenter is a good man, having known how to group around himself, through his previous life, through his actions and daily thoughts, Entities of high morality; if, on the other hand, he is guided in his attempt at splitting only by higher motives of science, progress, and charity, he will be free to depart without fear: he leaves behind faithful guardians who will jealously watch over his inert and abandoned *sarcosôme*, and will return it to him intact at the time of reintegration.

If, on the contrary, the experimenter is a pervert, having until then attracted near him by his daily actions and thoughts only Beings of evil; if he wants to conduct this formidable experiment for the sole purpose of harm, malice, or simply selfishness, he is to be pitied: the Entities he leaves behind will be the first to attack the defenseless *sarcosôme* and divide its spoils among themselves; — it has been observed that many people who engage in witchcraft and goetia end up in the hut of a madhouse: these are those who have sought to use the phenomenon of splitting to serve their appetites and passions.

This must therefore be clearly understood: — Anyone who has a life behind them that is not of absolute purity, anyone who has lived until now according to the rules of a flawed morality, anyone who has never, in their thought or conduct, given preeminence to altruism over egoism, and who wishes to undertake this experiment for a purpose that is not of a higher essence, such a person, in truth, would do better to abstain. This advice may make the frivolous, incredulous, and ignorant sneer, for whom nothing exists except what falls under their senses, and who draw from their very ignorance the right to mock everything that exceeds the lowest level of their understanding, — I don't care! Those who *know* will realize the extent to which I am right to act thus.

Besides, there is a formidable danger here, unsuspected by most: it was necessary for me to bring it into full light; it was necessary that after having indicated the ways and means of the experiment, after having given all the possible facilities for attempting it, I draw the attention of today's reader who may be a daredevil tomorrow, to the perils inherent in such an attempt, and that I insist particularly, not on the physical dangers of which the first comer can realize, and measure the extent, but, particularly on those which, unsuspected by many, are all the more formidable — and hyperphysical dangers are among these.

I beg the reader, if he is not familiar with these ideas, not to believe that I am pushing the dark, that I am exaggerating through dilettantism in this misplaced: he must understand that his attempt, if it succeeds, will make him live, for its entire duration, in a world which is not his usual and normal world, and that this other environment which he will penetrate will present its own risks which he will be able to avoid only by conforming to the line of conduct which I have just indicated and which I summarize in two words: to have behind oneself only a pure life — to have before oneself only a high goal.

CHAPTER XIII

TECHNICAL DIAGRAM

Having reached its completion, this work appears to us to be full of imperfections, caused, it is true, by the very nature of the subject.

Some chapters dealing with subjects of lesser importance, but more difficult to understand, have acquired considerable scope, while others, more important but more easily assimilated, comprise only a few pages.

On the other hand, there are special and technical considerations that, to be fully grasped, required very extensive development.

In the midst of this whole, which may, at first glance, and despite all the care taken, seem disproportionate, confusing, and complicated, it is possible that the central idea, the Ariadne's thread that should guide the reader through the subject's twists and turns, has, on several occasions, escaped him.

It therefore seemed appropriate to provide an overview of the operation, in which the reader will be able to summarize everything they have learned, and which will show them the details they may have overlooked, details whose precise study will be easy to refer to in the body of the work.

At the same time, during this general summary, some particularities will be noted that were not addressed in the preceding chapters.

The phenomenon of personal out-of-body experience consists of dissociating one's own organism and leaving the material part here or there, while the higher elements of the being are sent elsewhere.

This phenomenon, which is usually considered very rare, is, on the contrary, very common. The reason for its apparent rarity is that, most of the time, it occurs unconsciously in the agent, and manifests itself near subjects who, not being in a state of receptivity, are not affected by its manifestation; on the other hand, when they are aware of it, they see it, due to the agent's unconsciousness, only as the result of a dream or a hallucination.

To be able to study this phenomenon experimentally and no longer by simple and rare observation, it is therefore sufficient that the agent be in a state of consciousness, and the recipient in a state of receptivity, which, as we will see later, presents no insurmountable difficulty, because, on the one hand, it can be affirmed that there is no individual who does not possess, *in principle*, the faculty of splitting himself, and, on the other hand, the choice and training of receptive subjects are relatively quite simple; in practice, personal splitting and receptivity are matters of temperament and special training; we will first examine these two conditions.

I. *Temperament.* — The experiments of Messrs. de Rochas, Baraduc, Durville, etc., show us that the substratum of the exteriorized living phantom is composed above all of neurotic force, since the astral body [223] is the repository of individual sensitivity — which amounts to saying that the more neuroticity is developed, the easier the dissociation of the being becomes.

---

[223] The phantom of the living has been experimentally broken down into three main parts to date:

1. The *etheric double*, the repository of physical life, and never departing from the material body; it forms the support for the phantom evolving near the physical body, to which it returns as soon as the higher elements of the Being depart from it.

2. The *astral body*, the repository of sensitivity (neuric force); it constitutes the fluidic support of the phantom far from its physical body, and can materialize in certain cases when an etheric double (its own or that of a third party) provides it with the necessary substance.

3. Finally, the *mental body*, the repository of intelligence.

The first element always has a human form; the second most commonly possesses it, but can in certain cases modify it — hence the phenomenon of zoanthropy. These two elements give rise to its phantom form. The third (mental body) constitutes an aura that envelops the entire phantom and is particularly bright at the top (Dr. H. Baraduc's *mental ball*).

This brings us to the subject of temperament, which is too often confused with character, and which I will define as: "A physiological state determined by the predominance of an element, organ, or system" [224].

It is known that there are four commonly counted temperaments: — Nervous — Bilious — Lymphatic — Sanguine — although some physiologists deny the existence of the bilious temperament, which they simply regard as the onset of a pathological condition of the liver.

On the other hand, my personal observations have shown me that nervous individuals are the most likely to actively produce psychic phenomena; — bilious individuals are the most likely to passively experience them; — sanguine individuals are the most predisposed to hallucinations; — and finally, lymphatic individuals are the least likely to generate and experience these phenomena, but also the least predisposed to hallucinations. — All these factors must be taken into account in the formation of the percipient agent and subject.

On the other hand, temperament is very rarely absolute, but rather of a composite order: nervous-sanguineous, bilious-lymphatic, etc.

Based on this, is it possible to modify a temperament? — Yes, under certain conditions and to a certain extent.

Temperament is the result of two causes, one which seems specific, innate, characterized from the birth of the individual, and which depends on his anatomical and physiological constitution: this cause, constitutional and organic, is outside our action and we can do nothing about it. — The other, perhaps dependent on the first, lies in the variety or type of performance and functioning of the human machine: it is the coefficient of activity of organic exchanges; over this other cause, we have a real influence, and we can modify it to a certain extent by an appropriate regimen which, in this case, must be naturally directed towards the neurification of the organism.

---

[224] Physiologically, temperament is no longer considered today as summarizing a type of organism, or rather it is considered as relating to types of different classification (see what is said on this subject in the course of the work); but, to be better understood by the reader, I examine it here in its old meaning, which has not ceased to be in use among the public.

I have described elsewhere this regimen, which encompasses diet, ventilation and climate, hydromineral treatment, and nervous stimulation; suffice it to say that it is capable of developing neuritis even in lymphatics, who are, however, the most lacking in it.

Theoretically, the pure nervous is the temperament best suited to splitting; but I would never recommend the personal practice of this phenomenon, and even less temperament training, to the pure nervous: it contains within itself too many seeds of various neuropathies, which these actions would inevitably develop. Therefore, the temperaments best suited to first supporting training and then experimentation are, above all others, the bilious-nervous, then the sanguine-nervous with a strong predominance of neuritis: these are the most capable of producing the psychic force on which the realization of the phenomenon will rest.

Another consideration must be examined.

This special training must be closely monitored and controlled by the operator himself, as it would be somewhat imprudent to undergo it without knowing where it should lead: the best of regimens, pursued excessively, can lead to an imbalance in the body. It is therefore advisable for the operator to carefully track his own daily progress towards neurification.

There are a number of instruments designed to measure the emission of psychic force, among which Dr. P. Joire's sthenometer and Dr. Baraduc's biometer occupy the first place; I will only speak of the latter, with which I am more familiar. It is known that it marks, on the right and left, attraction and repulsion, that is, the absorption or emission of psychic force.

Theoretically, it seems that the best biometric formula proving the ease of personal splitting is double repulsion, on the right as well as on the left. In practice, this is not the case, because the formula *Repulsion/Repulsion* must have been preceded, in the person concerned, by an almost completely opposite formula: it therefore indicates a very poorly balanced organism, subject to enormous oscillations. This means that, for the agent presenting this formula, the process of personal splitting will present disadvantages, if not even danger.

In principle, the well-balanced organism is one that presents the same degree of attraction and repulsion: it is therefore a matter of reducing the degree of attraction to a certain extent, and, on the contrary, increasing the degree of repulsion as much as possible. This will be achieved by developing neuritis using the regimen indicated above.

The training in question must be twofold. We have just seen the part of this training that concerns the astral body. But it must not be forgotten that all psychic and hyperphysical operations are based on will; therefore, while the neurifying regimen puts the bodily instrument in a state of proper functioning in preparation for its future dissociation, it is appropriate to develop the agent's Will at the same time.

II. *The Will.* — There are a number of works specifically relating to the development of willpower, but these works only deal with willpower in the waking state, and splitting can only take place, except for highly trained individuals, in the sleeping state; I must therefore say a few words about the functioning of willpower during sleep.

Sleep, from a physiological point of view, is a period characterized by the rest of the organs serving the life of relationships, and by a redoubled activity in the functions of inner life.

The will, therefore, has an infinitely lesser effect on the organs of relationships during the sleep period, and one could say that it itself becomes drowsy.

Now, there is a remarkable correlation, from the point of view of sleep, between the functions of the body and those of the mind. Just as, during this period, there is a weakening of the organs of relation and, on the contrary, a doubling of the vital, internal, and passive forces of the human body, favored by the suspension of the expansive forces of action, so there is an increase in power and intensity in what one might call the passive intellectual forces, for example, memory, imagination when it is left to itself, etc., while, noticeably weakened, attention and will, these expansive forces of the soul, can no longer be exercised without effort.

The *process* of the operation therefore seems entirely appropriate: it suffices to replace the normal will, which is falling asleep, with the memory that is awake, or, in other words, to replace the will's own action with that of a special monoideism, which, entrusted to memory, will act while the will itself remains asleep.

In practice, this result will be achieved by firmly wanting to split oneself before falling asleep, especially before being overcome by the numbness that immediately precedes sleep, that is, while the will still possesses all its energy. As for the period of numbness prior to sleep, I will explain later how it should be used.

I mentioned above that there are many works dealing with the development of willpower. But there is one point that I have not seen addressed in any of them, and which I will discuss because I find in it a way to double the energy of training. Willpower can be broken down into four elements: — Possession — Deliberation — Determination — and Action — which are interdependent.

Now, it should be noted that possession, or self-control, generally subordinate to the will, reacts upon it in many circumstances; it follows that one can have a dual means of action to energize the will: direct action on the will itself and indirect action on self-control.

Everyone knows direct action: it is based on auto-suggestion. The person who constantly repeats to himself, fully imbuing himself with the meaning of "I have willpower! I have energy!" and who, on every occasion, knows how to put this formula into practice, will energize his will; but also the person who acquires perfect self-control will succeed in hyper-energizing his will.

There are several methods for acquiring self-control: I believe the main one, the most effective, is that which consists of mapping out one's daily schedule every morning, down to the smallest details, and deviating from it only for higher reasons. Self-control, thus obtained, in turn reacts on the will, instilling enormous energy in it: this is indirect action.

There are, in short, two methods of action that can be employed simultaneously: this is why I felt it necessary to note them down.

The will, thus hyper-energized, will easily create, before falling asleep, the monoideism that will be stored in memory during sleep. This monoideism is the order to dissociate, which the organism will obey if it has itself been prepared for splitting by the aforementioned regimen.

In summary, at the point we have reached, training has given the individual both the appropriate instrument, that is, an organism capable of dissociating, and what we can call the lever of the phenomenon, that is, a will capable of making itself obeyed. In other words, the agent is ready for the split.

But before dissociating, and to do so usefully, it is important to protect oneself from a percipient subject.

III. *The percipient subject.* — The true receptive subject, in such a case, is the clairvoyant medium; immediately after him comes the good magnetic subject who can be put into a state of clairvoyance; failing these two main types, it is appropriate to use, as the percipient subject, the sensitive gifted with clairvoyance; but, nine times out of ten, this subject is unaware of himself, and it is a matter of discovering him.

If we refer to what has been said about temperaments, we will see that the bilious person is more suited than any other to the perception of psychic phenomena: we will therefore have to choose this subject from among the bilious, and it would be from among the purest possible bilious people that it would be appropriate to choose him if his role were to be limited solely to the perception of the phenomenon.

But it is also necessary for the receptive subject to be able to assist the agent in the process of doubling (at least for the first attempts), and to attract him in some way towards himself. Under these conditions, its role is half passive, half active, and must be able to express itself to a certain extent; it will therefore be appropriate to choose it from among individuals with a bilious-nervous temperament, and, as much as possible, slightly lymphatic, namely: — the bilious element to perceive the phenomenon — the nervous element to assist — and the lymphatic element to avoid hallucinations.

There are methods for developing the bilious or lymphatic side of a temperament as well as for accentuating its neuritis; I will simply recall them without dwelling on describing them in detail.

In short, it is sufficient to take a subject presenting the appropriate physiological characteristics, which one will develop to the necessary extent; but above all, one must avoid choosing the receptive subject from among temperaments of even the slightest degree sanguine, since any sanguine individual is exposed to objective and subjective hallucinations.

The percipient subject must, in addition, meet certain specific conditions which are:

1. Be linked to the operator by mutual sympathy;
2. Be entirely favorable to the experiment;
3. Be endowed with a composure allowing him to seriously analyze his sensations;
4. Be possessing a certain technical training;
5. And finally, if possible, not live too far from the agent, at least for the first attempts.

Furthermore, which sex is most suitable? Men, in general, possess more composure, and women more sensitivity; since the first quality is acquired more easily than the second, women should be preferred, — or better still, one can, if possible, take two subjects, the husband and the wife.

IV. *The conditions of the experiment. = Humidity.* — Since the phantom is a kind of coagulate of an electrical nature, humid weather and environments should be avoided. Humidity has a particular effect on the etheric double, which it can prevent from releasing.

Atmospheric electricity. — For the same reason, one should avoid weather and environments impregnated with electricity, as this electricity can affect the operator, who is in a state of nervous imbalance; — which will present more difficulty for the operation; — and finally the phantom, who will personally suffer from it.

Temperature. — Heat promotes the expansion of the astral body; therefore, the environment where the out-of-body experience is being prepared must be kept at a temperature slightly higher than that of the physical body, or at least such that the operator feels perfectly comfortable.

Clothing. — Any clothing that is uncomfortable in any way should be avoided; it should be warm rather than light.

Lighting. — Since light dissolves all ghostly substances, complete darkness is preferable to even dim, artificial lighting.

Assistance. — It is best to act alone; but if one is forced to have a witness, if, for example, one is married, the witness must be informed of the experiment so as not to be alarmed by the possible consequences, and must arrange to pass as unnoticed as possible, avoiding any cause for distraction for the agent.

Silence. — The room where one wishes to operate must be sheltered from all outside noise, which could only be a cause for disturbance; it must therefore be isolated, furnished with drapes and rugs, etc., in a word, as quiet as possible.

Time. — The most propitious moment for self-exteriorization appears to be, at least for the first attempts, between 11 p.m. and 3 a.m.; this is both the time when it is easiest to achieve silence and darkness, and the time when, as a result of habitual sleep, the astral body has the greatest tendency and ease to escape from the *sarcosôme*.

Position. — The best position for the agent is to be lying in an armchair or on a sofa, or better still, in his bed where he will fall asleep as usual, but as much as possible on his back or on his right side, so as to avoid compression of the heart.

Moral Dispositions. — Complete calm of mind is of absolute necessity. It is therefore a formal contraindication in cases of illness, simple discomfort, worries, annoyances, or even vague apprehensions. The mind, in a word, must have no motive for distraction that would prevent it from creating, by its will, the monoideism that will lead to the production of the phenomenon.

Bodily Dispositions. — These dispositions must result from all the preceding conditions: bodily well-being, calm of mind, comfortable posture, etc. Furthermore, it is advisable to eat very sparingly on the day of the experiment (and the days preceding it), not by fasting, but by controlling one's appetite so as to avoid any digestive discomfort.

V. *Experimentation.* — With all this carefully observed, and the dual training of will and nerves having produced its effect, we will now examine the procedure.

I will pass over the preliminary tests that can be performed alone, for example, by trying to throw to the ground a light object, a sheet of paper or a match, previously placed on a piece of furniture, in the very room where one is splitting into two [225].

I will come immediately to the first tests with a receptive subject.

Before disengaging, some preparations must be made to facilitate the operation.

First, the agent will have traveled several times from the room where he is to disengage to the one where he is to manifest, carefully observing and memorizing all the details of the route. Similarly, in the room where he will be expected, he will note the arrangement of the furniture, the place where the percipient subject will be waiting, etc.

It goes without saying that the percipient subject will, at least for the first attempts, be informed of the day and time (which should be the time when the agent usually falls asleep), and that this receptive subject will wait for the exteriorized phantom at the indicated time and place, in as complete darkness as possible.

Furthermore, before going to bed, the agent must prepare for the subsequent magnetization of his astral body, for example by placing objects, letters, or other items emanating from the percipient subject under his pillow, or, if the latter habitually uses a characteristic perfume, by sprinkling a few drops of this perfume on his pillow, etc.

Then, he goes to bed 20 or 30 minutes before the time he usually falls asleep. He turns off the light, and, as long as the temperature difference between his body and the bed keeps him awake, he *wants* to — firmly, but not violently — continuously and smoothly go and find the percipient subject; the will deployed must be such that it acts in a regular, measured manner, and without bringing with it a restless sleep that would hinder all experience. The agent must thus create, energetically but calmly and continuously, the monoideism that will keep watch in his memory after his will has slumbered.

When he feels himself invaded by the numbness that precedes sleep, the monoideism must be created. The agent then only concerns himself with the subject he wants to find: — he thinks that he himself is getting up; his thought opens the bedroom

---

[225] In experiments with a receptive subject, it is the subject's *etheric double* that provides the agent's phantom with the substance it needs to materialize more or less, and without which the astral body would have no effect on matter; for experiments conducted by the isolated agent, in the very room where the out-of-body experience takes place, the phantom, not moving away from the physical body, possesses within itself the agent's own *etheric double*, which allows it to act on matter.

door, crosses the antechamber, crosses the threshold of the apartment, goes down the stairs, finds itself in the street; there, aided by memory, it retraces the entire journey, recalling the minute details of the route; it enters the receptive subject's home, heads toward his room, whose details it reviews, where it is awaited... During this series of mental operations, sleep has come. What happens then?

The receptive subject, having been warned, has sent his own thoughts to the agent, along with his desire to carry out the operation. An atmosphere of sympathetic scents is thus created around the agent, which will powerfully aid the out-of-body experience.

At the moment when sleep invades the agent, his astral body expands outside his *sarcosôme*. He is initially in a certain state of turmoil, in which he is not yet self-conscious, but in which he feels drawn outside the *sarcosôme* by a sympathetic atmosphere. His state of turmoil diminishes as sleep becomes deeper, and he radiates more. During this radiance, he encounters the objects that must magnetize him in the desired direction: the subject's letters, his perfume, etc. When he has taken complete possession of himself, he finds himself in the presence of the monoideism previously created by the agent's will, which watches over his memory. He knows that he must go towards the percipient subject. Where is this subject? To find out, he has only to go back to the source of the effluvia emanating from the letters or the perfume; he finds other effluvia in the environment, emanating from the sympathetic thought of the receptive subject: he has only to let himself be led, as it were, by the hand.

Let us not forget that, during sleep, memory is awake: now, memory shows him the whole way, and the journey is made, so to speak, automatically.

Arriving at the source of the effluvia, that is, near the receptive subject, what will he do?

Here, it is impossible to lay down any rules: he will act according to his strength at the time, also according to the thought that is particular to him, the occasions, the circumstances, etc. I personally know an operator who, when he arrives near a subject, has only three ways of manifesting himself: either he calls him, — or he pulls his hair, — or he shakes his hand. But it must be said that this operator has, as receptive subjects, only highly nervous organisms, which, easily exteriorizing their psychic strength, communicate it to the ghost and give it the necessary vigor. It is especially in this respect that it is beneficial for the subject not to be merely of a bilious temperament, but rather bilious-nervous.

Nothing can therefore be said about the way in which the exteriorized ghost can manifest its presence, and it is up to the receptive subject to exercise their sagacity of observation in this regard.

If the ghost is either visible, audible, or tangible, nothing could be simpler for the receptive subject to control its presence. But if the *aérosôme* possesses none of these qualities, does that mean we are deprived of means of control? No. This control will then be more delicate and difficult to apply, but it can be organized as follows:

H. Durville's experiments have proven that the living phantom emits N rays [226] in great abundance, even if it is not visible. Furthermore, it is known that N rays illuminate calcium sulfide previously exposed. Therefore, the receptive subject need only surround himself with screens filled with calcium sulfide, to judge by their illumination — and also by their subsequent photography, since calcium sulfide remains under the influence of light for a long time — whether the agent's *aérosôme* has come to find him.

It is true that one can use the repercussion of the astral body on the physical body for the same purpose, either through trauma or artificial coloring, by having the receptive subject strike the phantom, or by having it covered, for example, with eosin or any other tenacious coloring agent; but these methods are not

---

[226] An explanation is necessary here. Everyone knows that N rays, discovered — after Paracelsus, who had pointed out their existence — by Messrs. Blondlot and Charpentier, were first observed everywhere and by everyone, and were then the subject of unanimous denials: action, reaction — excess in one sense as in the other. I do not have to take sides; I simply note, in what is the subject of this study, that the calcium sulfide, previously exposed to sunlight, illuminates in the vicinity of the phantom, as a result of the rays emanating from it, and which appear to me to be N rays; but the name matters little; the fact alone is of value in what concerns us, and the fact is this: the living phantom emits rays of a particular nature, whatever the name, which act on the calcium sulfide.

recommended, the former being dangerous for the operator, and the latter being too random. The agent may also, in a pinch, *want* his *aérosôme* to dip his hand in a prepared eosin solution at the site of the manifestation; but, apart from the fact that the phantom (always fearful by nature until it has become accustomed) may refuse this test, the use of this procedure would undesirably complicate the monoideism that is the basis of the phenomenon and which, for the first attempts, must be created as simple as possible. It is therefore better, from all points of view, to stick to the use of calcium sulfide.

It is only when the external *aérosôme* has proven its presence near the percipient subject that the agent can consider bringing about the progressive development of the phenomenon.

VI. *Development.* — When an operator has succeeded in manifesting his presence near a sensitive subject well-endowed from a neurological point of view, there are certain degrees of development that he reaches very quickly, and others, on the contrary, whose possession is only asserted over time and with difficulty.

But before proceeding with this development, he must acquire a certainty on which his own security is based: — that the reintegration of his being, after each splitting, occurs normally and effortlessly. This is, it must be said, the most ordinary case; but if there is some difficulty in the operation, the agent may be warned upon waking by a more or less severe fatigue, which is mainly cerebral. It is therefore necessary to continue the tests until this particular fatigue has disappeared, which will also serve him in that he will acquire the necessary habituation, and his exteriorized phantom will condense better and better there.

Only then can it continue its development.

Tangibility and audibility are usually the faculties that manifest first; visibility comes only later; however, this is not absolute. To acquire these faculties, there is no need to complicate the basic monoideism: with repeated attempts, the phantom condenses better and acquires them almost mechanically.

When the exteriorized *aérosôme* has acquired tangibility or visibility, the receptive subject can attempt to injure it slightly, so that the repercussions of the injury on the physical body undeniably prove the splitting.

The other degrees of development are acquired with greater difficulty, and only through both practice and will, that is, through the complication of the initial monoideism.

The first degree is the ability to perform, in a state of splitting, a previously desired act; it also provides evidence of dissociation by forcing the ghost to dip their hands in a coloring solution or to leave their fingerprints on a mirror covered with a light layer of talc [227]. It should be noted, in this regard, that while the repercussions of injuries are immediate, which is likely due to the fact that the trauma forces the *aérosôme* to reintegrate the physical body as quickly as possible, that of the dyes only occurs over time, after several hours, sometimes even the next day, when the organism is completely reintegrated.

The second faculty to acquire is directional awareness, which is very useful, because without it, the exteriorized *aérosôme* is exposed to numerous road accidents that the agent could not have foreseen and which the ghost's clumsiness does not allow him to avoid. An operator I know was similarly wounded in the stomach during a split, by a violent blow from a club received in a battle with Apaches who were on his right path and from which he had been unable to move.

Finally, there is the memory of what was done during the split, which is perhaps the most difficult skill to acquire; it seems to be attainable only through special memory training, and above all through practice and willpower.

It is only after having mastered all these diverse possibilities that the operator can think of sending his *aérosôme* towards people other than his ordinary subjects [228]; but even then he must only do so with supreme prudence, and by warning his possible correspondents, because his astral body may find itself at the mercy of a determined man who takes the ghost for a criminal: there are examples of death caused by this practice.

---

[227] Avoid lampblack, as well as any powdery body of black or even dark color, for which experience seems to have shown the ghost to feel repulsion.
[228] It is well understood that he will receive from them or find in their environment the substantial force necessary for the material manifestation of his own ghost.

VII. *Dangers.* — I have spoken in detail above of the multiple dangers that this experiment can pose, and I have indicated the precautions that must be taken to guard against them. I will limit myself to listing them succinctly to draw the attention of any prospective participant who might believe that reading this chapter alone can replace the study of the book.

These dangers are of several kinds:

Material dangers. — I will surprise no one by pointing out their existence: the dissociation of a being into its constituent parts and the sending away of some of these parts present an obvious peril.

Intellectual and moral dangers. — These exist especially for weak characters and faint-hearted people: for anyone who lacks complete self-control, a solid intellect, and a large fund of specialized knowledge, such an experiment can only be advised against.

Psycho-physical dangers. — These are caused by road accidents which, due to the repercussions of injuries from the astral body to the physical body, can seriously injure the latter.

Hyperphysical dangers. — Occultism teaches us that any living body left to abandon its higher principles is immediately targeted by evil Entities: it also teaches us how to defend ourselves against them.

In summary, to engage in this experiment with any chance of success and to avoid the dangers that surround it, one must combine extensive technical training with great caution, a firm character, absolute composure, and self-confident moral strength.

In all this, I have only intended to summarize the work to give the reader an overview of the operation; but they would be mistaken if they believed that these lines were sufficient; only one fact should result from their reading; the possibility of personal duplication inherent in each of us since it is a matter of neuricity and will, and since there are processes for neurifying even lymphatic temperaments and for endowing the will with the necessary energy.

I have only one word to add: I believe in the effectiveness of the processes presented throughout the book, because I have personally seen them produce positive results in several practitioners, one in particular, whom I have followed closely, who has not yet, in truth, reached the last three degrees of development, but who is applying himself to them, who, in any case, through the use of these processes, has acquired all the preceding stages, and who does not, for that reason, have the vanity of believing himself to be constituted differently from ordinary mortals... Therefore, what he has done, others can do, and these others are you, me, everyone...

———

PART IV

———

APPLICATIONS

CHAPTER XIV

———

SOME FACTS

Cases of conscious out-of-body experience are far from rare; what makes us generally tend to regard them, if not as hallucinations — for after all, they often carry with them objective and material proof of their reality — at least as simple anomalies, is that this phenomenon has been little studied to date; there are very judiciously recorded collections of facts (*Phantasms of the Livings Telepathic Hallucinations, etc.*), but the general theory has been little addressed until now.

And yet, cases abound. Even official higher science is forced to deal with them: it understands nothing about them, moreover, since, inevitably, the theory escapes it, and it places them in the very elastic category of *dreamlike delusions*; in this regard, we will find the study of a most characteristic case, under the signature of Professor Gilbert Ballet, in the *Medical Bulletin* of November 4, 1911, a case remarkable enough to be analyzed here:

Last December, a 28-year-old girl, a teacher, Miss D., presented herself to the department of Professor Gilbert Ballet, complaining of curious disorders. She admitted a sort of split personality, the feeling of which caused her to experience a pronounced state of anxiety. At the very moment when she told us about her anxieties, she had the impression, and at least in appearance, the conviction, that her *self* was absent, that it was wandering through the world, that the person who was speaking to us was a sort of envelope without real mental life, the true personality having detached itself and being elsewhere. The result was a state of mental suffering and acute anxiety...

In her family's home in Saint-Germain, she began to experience unusual feelings of being split in two, which have since become more precise. For a year, she had sensations of "emptiness" throughout her body. A little later, around the age of 25 or 26, she sometimes had the feeling in the evening that her life was slipping away; she felt very tired [229]. Around that time, she had the impression that she was split in two... Later, this feeling of being split in two became more pronounced. Here is what she recounted in December 1910: — For four years, she has been split in two by G.P. [230]. She saw herself in America, in a large square where cabs were passing: there was no mistaking it. They brought her back in June 1910. When she returned, she was on a boat; she saw herself in her bed; her mouth was open, and *she came back in through it*. On July 6, they tried to take her back; G.P. even took her back, because she is with him now. It's not she who is here at the moment, it's another person whose "fluidic double has been made to enter her".

Other people have taken it too; her brother-in-law, who is in contact with Pickmann, the magnetizer, took it fluidly. A magnetizer, D., did the same. She is currently being seized by a little invisible man every night.

She has visions of several kinds... These visions have determined strange convictions in her: *she senses things from a distance by telepathy; once, for example, she guessed that her sister had no money; she sent her some: the fact is correct* [231]. Also, in her home, she is called the witch.

She has already had several lives [232]; she doesn't know when, because time doesn't count for her...

She has multiple doubles that correspond to her various present personalities, because she has several personalities, at least three... [233]

---

[229] This is, in fact, the sensation produced by the very act of doubling in *all* subjects (C.L.).

[230] A young man with whom she appears to have fallen in love.

[231] The double, living partially on the astral plane, finds there the vision of "astral images": this is what we will see, more explicitly, in the study of the Rousseau case that follows this one (C.L.).

[232] When, in our hypnology laboratories, we conduct the so-called "memory regression" experiment on a split subject, we always arrive at this result. (See *The Successive Lives* of Col. De Rochas.)

We saw her several times a week, complaining of being split in two. She came to beg us, here or at our house, to bring back her double; because she is still, currently, split in two...

She still feels like she's split in two, that "her entire physical and moral self has been split in two", "that most of it is absent", that what remains, that is; the present *self* that speaks to us, [234] is incomplete. Her true *self* left when she was at Beaulieu, then returned, and left again [235].

She touches, hears, sees, tastes, and smells normally. She represents things visually and aurally. However, when questioned about this, she says that the impressions seem "distant" [236].

Moreover, they vary from day to day. "There are two of us, says the patient, pulling at the same life; sometimes it's one and sometimes it's the other of the *selves* that prevails [237]." "When I eat well, I gain more strength; it seems to me that my other *self* benefits even more than I do [238]."

She is anxious because she cannot live without her true self [239]. She saw the latter's profile on the curtains [240], he seemed as if he had suffered. She would rather die because *perhaps* her other *self* would die with her and neither of them would suffer any more.

---

[233] There is a particular memory disorder here: what the subject calls "his personalities" is constituted by various modalities of splitting (C. L.).
[234] This subject splits himself in a special hypnoid state that is almost a waking state (C. L.).
[235] Effects of successive splits (C. L.).
[236] For anyone familiar with the phenomenon, this expression is perfectly understandable. The astral body, which holds sensitivity, is exteriorized: sensation, to be perceived by it, is obliged to travel a certain distance, which is doubled to return to the *sarcosôme* (C. L.).
[237] This sensation of two *selves* obviously comes from the two states of splitting and wholeness, which give the subject the impression of two different *selves* (C. L.).
[238] This is also very understandable, as the physical body only benefits from the production of material forces, while all others (neuric, etheric, astral, and mental) double.
[239] Without being reintegrated (C. L.).
[240] What she calls her true self here is in reality her *double*, which she sees like many subjects in similar cases. If she calls it "her true *self*," it is because she feels it is missing to constitute her wholeness (C. L.).

On May 1st, she arrived in the ward in the morning and said to me: "I know everything. My double is going to have a child. I know this because I have a stitch in my left side. There are things I can't put into words. I've known this for a month. It's him [241] who makes me think of this." Then I saw it in his face when I glimpsed him in my curtains. He's not far from here, in Paris. Since G. P. is the father of this child, I'll go to court [242]".

Professor Gilbert Ballet's conclusions seem rather embarrassed: "By its coherence, its relative consistency," he says, "this delusion unquestionably belongs to the group of systematized delusions; here, there's nothing reminiscent of the flight of ideas of maniacs, nor anything resembling the secondary explanations, the ideas of self-accusation or ruin that we observe in melancholics..."

Ultimately, he sees it as a "systematized dream delusion in a dubious woman".

In the notes that followed step by step the preceding summary, I endeavored to restore the reality of the facts which is summed up in this: — It is, in this case, an observation made by a scientist of high value, certainly, but which, ignoring the existence of the duplication phenomenon, is naturally carried to put its manifestations in one of the many classes of delirium; And this observation was made on an unconscious subject which, ignoring not only the great frequency of the phenomenon, but even its possibility, and, all the more so, its conditions of being, does not realize its partial life on a neighboring level and confuses, in its distraught understanding, the astral visions with reality.

I now approach another case which offers great analogies with the previous one, but in which the subject, being aware, analyzes all his sensations and realizes what happens. We will see what sharpness differentiates it from the previous one.

---

[241] Her double (C. L.).

[242] Already, previously, the subject saw herself in a ship's cabin, ready to give birth. This is not delusion, as Professor Gilbert Ballet believes, but a confused perception of the astral snapshot of a mediate future that the subject has related in the first case to the past, and in the latter to an immediate future. We know that the great difficulty, as far as viewing astral images is concerned, even for experienced clairvoyants, is to differentiate what relates to the future and what relates to the past (C. L.).

M. Rousseau [243], born in 1855, a commercial representative in Versailles, splits himself very easily, sees his ghost, and sometimes becomes aware of some future events.

Since his childhood, Mr. Rousseau has had the strange faculty of splitting himself spontaneously, and sometimes to feel, see and hear at a distance, in a word to know, not an event that takes place at the very moment, but which will be fulfilled in a period of time which can vary from a few days to several years [244]. In a very short time, four to five minutes at most, he becomes fully aware of all the details of this event, its immediate or distant consequences that will take days, months, years to be fully accomplished. Here are some examples.

Being a child, it sometimes happened to him, in the morning when he got up, to not only know what subjects were going to be dealt with at the school he frequented, but also the smallest details, such as, word for word the questions that the teacher would ask the different students, as well as the answers, word for word, that would be given; and even the resulting impression in the students in general as well as each of them in particular [245].

He sees the demonstration of the Reuilly barracks with all the smallest details that preceded him, accompanied and followed. He sees the arrest of several politicians and in particular their leader, a man of high size, demonstrating his excitement by sententious words, supported by great gestures, a man whom he does not know personally. He sees the trial investigation, the meeting of the Senate, transformed into a high court of justice, the conviction and the exile of those accused, their return and the end of their political careers.

Three months later, he learned from the newspapers the realization of the first part of his vision, and, on the illustrations, he recognizes Toutléde for having seen him at the head of the demonstrators.

---

[243] Cases extracted from the *Ghost of the living*, by H. Durville, already quoted.

[244] Effect of partial life of the double on the astral plane where he has the vision of "astral clichés" (C. L.).

[245] To understand the nature of the links which unite these two kinds of apparently very dissimilar phenomena, it must be remembered that clairvoyance is *very generally* only the result of partial duplication (C.L.).

The events which were the final consequences showed him the accuracy of his vision. Before the day of Reuilly, Mr. Rousseau shared this event, which seemed close to him, to a few friends, seriously, convinced of the reality of this faculty. One of them, an artillery captain in Versailles has realized it, and the hero of this story has confirmed it since.

A few years ago, he saw that his young son, who was then very well, was going to fall very seriously ill. He sees all the phases of the disease, the despair of his wife, the successive crises that will occur, the embarrassment of the doctor ending up by declaring that the child is irrevocably lost, a host of small details that it would be too long to report here, and finally convalescence.

After fifteen to twenty days, the child falls ill, the doctor is called who soon declares that there is absolutely nothing to do; finally, everything happens absolutely as Mr. Rousseau saw previously.

In 1897, he saw that the bishop of Versailles will soon make a series of conferences at the municipal theater, on a special subject which is not exclusively religious. Nowhere was there talk of these conferences, when, two months later, three or four conferences of the bishop are announced. They take place, as he had seen, at the municipal theater, with the program that he knew and in front of spectators he had also seen.

These phenomena of early vision and almost mathematical knowledge of what must happen during the course of a future event, generally occur in the evening, at around 10 to 11 p.m., when he is in bed or is about to get into it.

He then sees variously colored, blue, white, reddish fluids which escape from all the parts of his body, but especially from his hands. He then experienced a slight tremor of the whole body, accompanied by a pleasant or unpleasant impression, depending on the feeling he will experience. These fluids condense above him and take the form of his body. It's his *double*, he said. This double, this ghost thus exteriorized no longer obeys him, and soon leaves through the walls. He goes to the place or on the premises where the event must take place, and there he sees all the optical, hearing and other details that must perform there.

A very important observation is placed here. There are events he must attend in person, and others he will not take any part. In the first case, it seems to him that, when the ghost leaves, *all his physical and moral personality, his conscious self,* leaves with him, and he is only aware that his physical body is there, lying in his bed. He then sees all the smallest details that he will see by attending the achievement of the event; this is what happened relative to his son's illness. In the second case, that is to say when he must not attend this accomplishment, as it took place for the day of Reuilly, he realizes that something of him goes to the place where the event will happen, but that his conscious self remains with his body, in his bed, and that he is entirely, physically and morally, completely awake and fully conscious. He then appeals to be really in two places at the same time: in his bed first, and then in the distance, in place where the event will occur. He thinks he could get up, come and go, but he prefers to stay in bed. In both cases, he does not realize when and how the ghost returns to take its place in the physical body.

I just said that these doubling phenomena "generally occur in the evening, from 10 to 11 p.m."; but, although very rarely, they also occur during the day, with the same tremor. In the latter case, the impression is always unpleasant; and, without having any sorrow, he shed tears for a few moments.

For many years, this duplication only occurred spontaneously; now, when he wants to be informed about a change of position, about the result of a case, or any other fact to come, he only has to strongly fix his thought on the fact which he wants to take note, and splitting almost always occurs by providing him with the desired knowledge. A particularity is to be reported. While seeing the fact of being accomplished, he never knows the date of his accomplishment [246]. He knows that this fact will occur in such or such place, in such or such conditions, and in such or such establishment, if he knows beforehand one and the other; but if he has never seen them, he can only designate them without naming them. Thus, he wanted to know if he would withdraw from business, and, in this case, if he would remain in Versailles.

---

[246] I recall here what I said elsewhere, about dreams: — on the astral plane, time has no value.

He *knows* that he will live in a small town which does not seem very far away. He does not know the name of this town, but he has the most absolute certainty that the first time he crosses it, he will recognize it perfectly; because he noticed his small town hall simply built in bricks, and all the details, topographic and others, are deeply engraved in his memory.

Mr. Rousseau is a man filled with common sense. For a long time, he did not believe in God or the devil, any more than in the survival of the soul beyond the tomb; but these phenomena, to which he only attaches little importance, made him think that *something of us* could well survive after death. Despite this, he never wondered if it was the double that, in the latter case, survives the physical body. He does not believe in religion, at least as the priests teach and practice it; nor does he believe in the phenomena of spiritualism which he has sometimes seen. He is not a medium because he has never obtained mediumistic phenomena; on the contrary, he realized that, when he is by chance at a spiritual meeting where it is said to be easily obtaining phenomena, he bothers the medium enough so that they can no longer obtain anything. He has never heard abnormal noises at home, as mediums often hear, such as unusual crackles in furniture, knocks or objects moving.

Cut like Hercules, very strong, very robust, Mr. Rousseau, who is of a nervous-sanguine temperament, has never been sick. Auto-suggestion is not to be feared at home, because without enthusiasm, there is no illusion; neither does he allow himself to be suggested; because he dominates rather than allows himself to be dominated. It is certainly for this reason that in his presence mediums are reduced to helplessness.

Here is the story of an experience made by Mr. H. Durville with Mr. Rousseau: I extract him from the same work.

With the knowledge of the subjects used for my experiences, Mr. Rousseau is suitable enough with me that on Tuesday, March 3, 1908, he would go to bed (at his home, at Versailles) around 9:30 pm in the evening, and that at 10 p.m. precisely he would send his ghost to my session. He would show himself and seek to see what is going on. For this, an armchair must be prepared for him towards the window of my work office, next to the office. A phosphorescent screen, accusing the presence of N rays, will be placed on the back of the chair, and the ghost will do everything possible to illuminate it. After ten to twelve minutes, he will get up, advance towards the door, look at us, will send us a greeting, and he will withdraw by crossing the closed door.

Tuesday March 3, 1908, at 9 p.m., everything is ready as I just said for the reception of the ghost. Two experienced subjects, Mrs. Lambert and Léontine are there, as well as Mr. Dubois. MM. Doctor Pau of Saint-Martin and Haudricourt attend the session as witnesses. The latter are informed of what must happen; but Mr. Dubois and the subjects, I have already said, know absolutely nothing. We are in the dark, and the scale is arranged on the table, as if to see the weight of the ghost. To note the extent of the field of action of the expected ghost, a phosphorescent screen, previously insulated, is fixed on the back of the chair by means of a pin; other screens, also insulated, are placed: one on the fireplace, about one meter from the chair; another on one of the shelves of my library, about two meters; and finally two others, on the same radius, about three and four meters...

I split Mrs. Lambert; Mr. Dubois seeks to split Léontine. The ghost of the latter must remain as a witness of the phenomena that I will seek to obtain the ghost of Mrs. Lambert. This is placed at the bottom of my cabinet, and Léontine is towards the fireplace, on the side opposite the table.

I pray Mrs. Lambert's ghost to go to the table, to announce its presence there by a hit, then get on the scale to put the electric ringtone in activity; and, to avoid any mental suggestion, I energetically fix my thought on these phenomena that I would like to obtain while waiting for the appearance of Mr. Rousseau's ghost.

Mrs. Lambert is uncomfortable. Her ghost goes to the table under the influence of my will; but there, distracted, it makes no effort, returns to the subject, and no phenomenon occurs.

Léontine is barely split; she is pissed off, worried, and does not want to see anything that is going on. She is uncomfortable, undergoing, she said, a strange, unpleasant influence, which does not hold to any of the assistants.

At half past 9 p.m., Mrs. Lambert is also worried and becomes more nervous. It is very surprised to see towards the window, near my office, precisely in the place occupied by the chair, a vaporous, slightly luminous column, which floats as if it were agitated by a light wind. She has not yet observed a similar phenomenon. I am trying to divert from this vision the attention of the ghost and I insist energetically so that it returns to the table and manifests its presence there. It comes back there, but its distraction and its concern are such that it does not stay there, and that it even comes to take refuge behind the subject as if to hide.

At 9:55, Mrs. Lambert, frightened, rushes on me by exclaiming: "But it is a ghost who is there; it's the ghost of a man!" I try to reassure her by telling her that the visit of this ghost was expected, that she already knew him and that she was not afraid of it, because he is not animated by bad intentions. A little reassured, she agrees to observe it: "He is quietly seated in the chair; he looks at us." After a while I can assess eight or ten minutes: "Oh!" she said, "he gets up, he walks, he comes here." At the same time, she gets up, very upset, and says that she is violently attracted to him. To prevent her from moving forward, I have to grasp her between my arms, and go against her, by severely giving her the order to stay there. After a time that seemed to me very long: "The ghost withdrew," she said. She agrees to sit down, and, after two to three minutes, pushing a long sigh of relief, she exclaims: "Ah! Finally ... he leaves; he's near the door, he looks at us ... he left ... I like that better!"

Meanwhile, agitated and trembling, Léontine was barely mastered by Mr. Dubois, who, disconcerted himself by what was going on, kept asking him what was the cause of this unexplained terror. He could not get from her other answers than this: "It is a ghost ... I don't want to see it!"

We are doing everything we can to calm the subjects, and we only get there. After a few minutes, I check the screens. That of the armchair on which the ghost sat is very well illuminated; I can distinguish it at one meter at least. I take it and give it to the witnesses. That of the chimney is also, but to a lesser degree: I can barely distinguish it at a distance of thirty centimeters. The one on a library department, about two meters from the chair, is still a bit; but I need to know where it is to put my hand directly on it. The other two are by no means illuminated. I present them all to the witnesses who do not distinguish the last two; but which very well between them recognize the difference in brightness that the others present.

We flash the room, and we wake up the subjects as slowly as possible, to allow them to resume their exteriorized forces. We return to them to wake them up again. Finally, at half past eleven, that is to say about an hour and twenty after the departure of Mr. Rousseau's ghost, the subjects, calmed and comforted by a snack, can withdraw in fairly good physical and moral conditions.

It should be noted that Mr. Rousseau's ghost did not observe, at the session, all the conditions heard in advance, since he should not advance towards the subject.

The same evening, in the presence of witnesses, I wrote a few words to Mr. Rousseau, praying that he give me his impressions. I told him that the subjects believed that he had seen him, without giving him any detail of this vision. He replied the following:

Versailles, March 5, 1908.

My dear Sir,

I hasten to reply to your letter. I will tell you that I saw and felt nothing. I did as I usually do, wanting my double to come and find you, to sit in the armchair you indicated, and to do his best to illuminate the screen. It seemed to me that my double left at that moment, but I didn't see him. After a moment, I ordered him to go towards the subject, at the back of the room, and, if necessary, to mingle with his double, if possible.

I held on for about fifteen minutes; and suddenly, without experiencing the slightest weariness, I felt as if a mechanism had stopped. I assumed that my double had returned at that moment.

Yours faithfully, etc.

There are some important observations to be made about this apparition, adds H. Durville at the end of his report.

— First, the subjects put into sleepwalking and questioned independently of one another, after recalling the memory of the out-of-body experience, declared that they had also had, at the beginning of the session, a presentiment that something abnormal was going to happen. They then saw the vaporous column float for a time, the duration of which neither of them could estimate; then, suddenly, in its place, they saw, with all its minute details, the phantom appear, as if it had passed through the window, without experiencing the slightest obstacle. They saw it standing in front of the armchair arranged for it; then they saw it sit down very calmly and look at us. Then they both saw him advance to the back of the room, heading towards Madame Lambert, but he was stopped by opposing *wills*. On his way there, he passed close to Léontine and brushed against her dress. This brush impressed her enough that she immediately fell into a state of shock. Finally, both subjects saw, in the same way, the ghost withdraw towards the door, look at us again, and disappear instantly. Madame Lambert, who had seen M. Rousseau at a previous session, recognized his ghost perfectly. Léontine had never seen him.

— What could this floating column have been like that preceded the ghost's appearance?

If we refer to the theosophists' theory, we find a hypothetical but rational explanation for this phenomenon, which would consist of the following: Before sending his ghost, M. Rousseau certainly seriously considered putting himself in the right conditions to succeed in the experiment; and it would be his thought, considered as a mental force clothed in astral matter [247], which would have taken, not his resemblance, because this matter was not condensed enough, but a crude form which, by condensing at the moment of apparition, would have contributed to the formation of the ghost.

— Since both subjects have often seen their own ghost, they should be accustomed to enduring the sight of another ghost without emotion.

It should be noted here that fear always seized Madame Lambert when, spontaneously split into two, she saw her ghost floating above her physical body. Although this emotion was not as intense in Léontine, she was always afraid at the sight of hers.

---

[247] Thought, taken in isolation, is material, not of the coarse matter that falls under our senses, but fluidly material; otherwise, we would not be able to explain either mental suggestion or the destruction of brain cells, as physiology teaches us, by the very elaboration of thought, for we could not conceive of a purely spiritual thought destroying physical cells. Moreover, it has now been proven that thoughts have their own forms and colors. — C.L.

If subjects are usually afraid of their own ghost, it is not surprising that they are even more afraid at the sight of a stranger's [248], especially when it presents itself to them in such unexpected circumstances.

We see, from the two preceding examples, the whole difference that exists between an unconscious splitting and a conscious splitting.

Here, on the other hand, is a fact which is quite poorly known, which leads me to give the account of it as written by Captain E. Volpi, of the Italian army.

These are the conditions in which the unconscious splitting of the future wife of this officer, who at that time did not know her any more than he was known of her, was recorded on a photographic plate, the reproduction of which I give below (*fig. 72*).

Fig. 72. — Double of Captain Volpi's future wife.

---

[248] This seems to be a matter of simple habituation, for two years, in 1911 and 1912, that is, three years after the previous experiment, I experimented with Mrs. Lambert without noticing this fear of her own ghost; but I always saw her moved by the presence, during the session, of a foreign ghost. — C.L.

On December 17, 1879, toward the evening, I obtained this photograph in the presence of Lieutenant Colonel of Artillery Baron Daviso and the medium Anna de Cornélis, accompanied by her husband, at the home of a photographer in Rome. No one, not even the photographer, could tell me what this woman was who, so extraordinarily, presented herself to us. It should be noted *that she was not seen by any of the assistants during the pose.* That same evening, Anna de Cornélis was put into a distinct sleep.

My first wife, who had died almost eleven months earlier, came to tell me that she wished to speak to me through the medium.

I then asked her what this last female bust was that appeared in the photograph in question.

She replied: "You knew her in other existences."

D. — What does she mean by this hand resting on the back of the chair and indicating precisely, with her index finger, the seat of the same chair, while she stares at me?

R. — She marks the future.

D. — What is her name?

R. — Réna.

The name Réna was nonsense to me.

Baffled by this name, which I had never known, I remained in doubt for the rest of the communication. However, I was certain that this woman in the photograph was a spirit; this is what I had just said at the Paris Congress of 1889.

After two and a half years, almost in 1882, I had just met a young woman with whom I fell deeply in love.

I married her. She was living about six hundred kilometers from Rome when I obtained the photograph in question [249]. Her name was Iréne; I was far from thinking that her name could be Réna, and it never occurred to me to compare it with the aforementioned photograph.

It was only after the Paris Congress in 1889, when I returned to my family, holding the print in my hands on the one hand, and looking at my second wife on the other, that I found a perfect resemblance between the two.

I said to my wife: Don't you know that this photograph looks very much like you?

— "That's true," she replied, examining it; I see myself as I was a few years ago when my photograph was taken, especially because of the position of my head, which is raised and high, etc.

(As for me, I've never seen in other women this head position that she so clearly described).

---

[249] She did not know Rome, and had never been there.

So I replied, half furious: But we can't trust sleepwalkers since Anna de Cornelis told me that this apparition was called *Réna*!

At these words, somewhat surprised, she said to me: What! In my country, everyone, including my mother, calls me *Réna*!

I was completely astonished by this fact and very pleased with what I had just heard.

And to think that in no case had it occurred to me that *Réna* could be a corruption of the name Iréne!

All sorts of doubt were now gone. It was a great joy.

While thanking God, to whom I had addressed myself during the pose, I understood that it was my second wife who had come to mark the future with her hand on the back of the chair, staring at me, and thus indicating that she would one day come and sit beside me, becoming my wife. She also told me that she remembered very well having been ill, on December 17, 1879, with an apostema on the left side of her jaw; and that during this illness she remained almost always drowsy from the force of the illness that tormented her. As for having known her in other existences, I would have to cite some rather interesting and lengthy spiritualist facts that, for the present, I believe it superfluous to report in this letter. I am, however, certain of having lived in other existences, which explains the present case...

ERNESTO VOLPI

Personally, I have had quite a few occasions to meet individuals, professional or otherwise, who practice out-of-body experience; I could therefore cite a certain number of cases, either among those that have come to my attention and that I have reason to regard as authentic, or among those that I have observed myself. Among the former, I will cite only two: I extract one from a letter written to me some time ago by a naval doctor to whom I had the opportunity to point out the existence of the phenomenon.

November 30, 1911.

Sir,

"... Moreover, I was aware of the matter, because one of my comrades who has been following these studies with interest for years told me three months ago that he was able to appear near his wife, who was separated from him by great distances.

This officer, whose good faith I cannot yet suspect, proceeded, I believe unconsciously, as you recommend, by educating and developing his will. He was first able to dissociate, then appear to his wife, in the same room, then in an adjoining room. Then, after these successful experiments, his ship was abruptly sent to Portugal during the recent political events; at that time, without warning his young wife, he succeeded in appearing to her several times.

I only have his statements, but, on the other hand, one of his companions, incredulous, apparently noted the days and times when he told him he should attempt to dissociate; however, it seems that these days and times coincided with a slight time difference [250].

I have never had to study this officer, who must have interrupted these experiments, the danger of which I believe he does not fully understand; but nevertheless, he seems to me eminently disposed for a complete development...

A physiologist, sir, I mean a student of official science, cannot accept these facts; therefore, the great number of physicians who study and follow courageous research of this nature are forced to reject from the outset the greater part of the teachings of psychophysiology. For my part, I never treat a patient without seeking to penetrate his mentality and sensitivity. Now, I must recognize that this is not how we have been taught to care for our fellow human beings. I am therefore convinced that your studies and those of minds sufficiently free from official prejudices will broaden our means of therapeutic action..."

The other case is also taken from a letter from a doctor, Dr. T., who wrote to me about his personal experiences; I quote it from the point of view of the self-observation that it constitutes.

Paris, October 16, 1912.

Sir,

I have carefully read and reread the brochure on Personal Out-of-body Therapy that you were kind enough to send me... The struggle for life, and especially my poor health, have made me overly sensitive for several years, which makes me very unhappy. I have also been magnetizing a lot for years, which must have further developed my unfortunate tendencies toward externalization. The fact remains that there are days when I feel all my vital force draining away from me, and this vital force is absorbed not only by my patients, which I do not regret if they are doing well, but by people in flourishing health, no doubt with absorbing powers, who, by their presence, exhaust me to the point that I must take very serious precautions with some of them.

---

[250] Probably coming from the difference in meridian.

A poor, very sensitive woman, Mrs. M. M., sometimes comes to my house and tells me that I go to see her at night, that she sees my ghost sitting on her bed, that I care for her, that I advise her. I always shrugged my shoulders when I heard her talk like that, but I haven't laughed since yesterday, since I read your brochure. It's possible that I exteriorize myself at night without realizing it, since according to you it's possible. I also have, in the midst of stupid dreams, as we all have from time to time, a strange dream of clarity, of lucidity, and, reflecting, I tell myself that, during my sleep, my ghost perhaps sometimes wanders around a receptive subject, or that of a transmitting subject who has become receptive in my home...

I could cite other cases of the same nature; it seems preferable to me, not wanting to lengthen this work excessively, to take a single subject, one of my friends, whom I was subsequently able to observe personally, follow quite attentively, and whose progressive development will form a study not devoid, it seems to me, of interest because it shows the phenomenon in some way caught in the act. This person shared his notes with me, with permission to use them, and provided me with all the additional explanations I requested, but formally wishes not to be nominated in order to continue his research, protected from untimely, indiscreet, and embarrassing curiosity.

A detailed study of his case will be the subject of the next chapter.

CHAPTER XV

PRACTICAL STUDY OF A DEVELOPMENT

X... is a man now about 60 years old, quite strong, having suffered, since a rather delicate childhood, only one serious illness around the age of 28; in short, good health, and a nervous-bilious temperament with a strong predominance of neuroticism. Morally, he is a very calm, very settled individual, whose life has passed amidst intellectual, scientific, and other pursuits. He believes in neither the marvelous nor the supernatural, putting into practice what has been called Hamlet's principle: "Everything is possible," but only admitting what is demonstrated to him.

Some thirty-five or thirty-six years ago — the exact date eludes him — he had the opportunity to become acquainted with works on occultism that piqued his curiosity. The theories relating to the astral body seemed very acceptable to him because they conformed to the reality of things. He read about cases of out-of-body experience, and one day the thought came to him to test on himself whether this phenomenon was truly within the realm of possibility.

He knew from his reading that any hyperphysical operation (and he then regarded the act of out-of-body experience as such) must be preceded by special training of a certain duration and based on vegetarianism; on the other hand, considering the exteriorization of the astral body as a phenomenon due to the organism's neurological capacity, he concluded that this training must also aim to develop its neurological capacity. As we can see, there was both truth and falsehood in his reasoning.

Consequently, he created a largely vegetarian diet, deprived himself of sleep, subjected himself to electricity sessions and deep meditations on the intended act, and consumed coffee and other stimulants; He regularly went to bed at 1:30 in the morning, spending the late evening thinking, in the dim light of a dimmed lamp, etc.

As he was married, a father, and did not want to tell anyone about his plan for fear of being deflected, he could not strictly follow the diet he had set for himself, for fear of provoking comment, but he came as close as possible to it. As luck would have it, the neuroticism that dominated his temperament was easily adaptable and developed during this lifestyle, however imperfectly it was followed. But on the other hand, a different, random motive compensated for the imperfection of this regimen: to be more certain of its success, he had likened this planned splitting to one of the great hyperphysical operations that require forty days of training: the prolongation of the regimen compensated for its irregularity and brought about, in a way, the desired result, which occurred, one might say, despite himself.

Indeed, every evening for forty days, he meditated deeply on his plan, until one-thirty in the morning, then he went to bed with the firm resolve to free himself in *so many* days.

At first, everything went well, and his willpower suffered no weakening; on the other hand, at certain signs, he felt his nervous sensitivity increase: all was therefore for the best.

But as the appointed deadline approached, the enthusiasm of the first days gave way to serious reflections; the danger of the experiment became apparent to him, with all its extreme consequences, and a fixed idea took hold of him: "What if I wasn't going to be able to return to my physical body?" As a result, the day before or two days before the end of the training, seized by an anxiety greater than himself, at ten o'clock in the evening, he "sent everything to hell," as he put it, and went to bed with a nagging regret: that of having done everything to prepare for an experiment that he was abandoning at the last moment.

It is noteworthy that, unbeknownst to him, and inevitably, one might say, he had just placed himself in the most favorable conditions for the success of the test: his nerves exasperated by both his fear and the disappointment of abandoning his project. This dual thought bothered him for a long time, drove away the sleep he was craving, and only allowed him to fall asleep at the usual time: one-thirty.

What happened next? He doesn't quite know. Here are the terms in which he recounted to me what he called his mishap:

"I don't know how long I had been asleep, perhaps two minutes, perhaps hours, I don't know. I became aware of myself in a sort of dream; I was walking around in the middle of the night in my room, where, despite the darkness, I could clearly distinguish the smallest objects and details. I felt a sense of well-being within me, a surprising lightness; it seemed to me that with each inhalation my body rose, as it descended with each exhalation; in short, it seemed to me that I was floating in the atmosphere. At that moment, I had no doubt that I was experiencing a lucid dream. But what was I doing, and as a result of what hypnagogic conditions did I find myself wandering like that in my own room? A dream usually has its goal, toward which it moves with a velocity that sometimes makes you live years in a few minutes... here, nothing like that! I saw my wife sleeping placidly, and the thought came to me that I shouldn't wake her. I then thought of my daughter, whom it seemed perfectly natural to see instantly in front of me, although her room was separated from mine by two partitions, all doors closed. I thought again of my wife, whom I saw again. But near her, I saw someone... who?... I don't know... a sleeping human body... suddenly, the thought came to me that this body occupied my place, that *it must be mine!* Then, in a flash, I understood everything: it was my body lying in the bed... and me... I was either dead or I had been exteriorized!... And a terror seized me, that of not being able to reintegrate my body, a terror further energized by the thought, if I were dead, of all the unfinished tasks I had left behind. And I felt a pang of despair with the intense, mad desire to return to my body... Here, I no longer remember... I found myself standing on the bed [251], trying to escape, while my wife, awakened with a start, clinging to me, called me, tried to hold me back, because the living room was being repaired, our room was cluttered with furniture: notably there was near the bed a pair of pointed bronze andirons, on which a fall could have caused me

---

[251] The shock of reintegration must have been so violent that it had made the suddenly revived *sarcosôme* leap upright.

dangerous injuries. At the time, I remained in a deep daze, motionless, not knowing what I was doing; the cold completely took possession of me, and I went back to bed mechanically, murmuring: 'I must have had a nightmare!'

"The next day, I woke up tired. My wife joked with me about my nocturnal escape, the real reason for which I was careful not to reveal. I promised myself I would never repeat such an escapade again.

"However, over time, my memories, initially scattered, began to coordinate. And I wondered how it was that the thought of my daughter had made me see her herself sleeping, motionless, in her bed? Was it my thought alone that led me to her, or had I really seen her through the two partitions that separated us?

"This idea haunted me, more and more tenacious, at the same time as the terror of the first moments faded. After all, the reintegration had been simple, very easy... Why not repeat the experiment — just to see if it was only my thought that acted in such a case, or if my astral body was really carried away following my thought?

"And the idea becoming fixed, I resolved to attempt a new and final test, solely to become aware of this detail that haunted me.

"I resumed my training for a few days, and one evening, I went to bed with the firm determination to escape and visit my daughter in her sleep.

"Again, I cannot remember the first moments of my out-of-body experience. I found myself in complete possession of myself, without knowing how it had happened, standing by my daughter's bed, watching her attentively. Then I realized that I was indeed in her room, where I could see all the furniture. I still felt a certain fear, but in a vague way, and the dominant feeling in me was rather, curiosity. I remember carefully examining the furniture to make sure that I was in reality in that room and that it was not my memory of the objects that made me see them: in a word, they were indeed objectively, before my eyes, and not subjectively in my brain. Afterwards, the thought came to me that, all the same, the experiment was dangerous and that I would do well to end it. I energetically *wanted* to return to my physical body — and from that moment on, I remember nothing.

— 378 —

"The next day, I woke up with a very clear memory of what had happened...

"I thought I would no longer have to repeat this experiment, which, despite its happy outcome, I persisted in finding dangerous, when, upon reflection, a question mark arose in my brain: 'How, by what process, had I managed to reintegrate my physical body?' I could not, in fact, remember anything about this operation. Moreover, I had read in certain works that the ghost is connected to the material body by a colored link... I had noticed nothing of the sort. — This thought, in the long run, became imperative, and I resolved to attempt the experiment again, promising myself in the most absolute way that this time would be the last.

"I subjected myself once again, for a few days, to my training system, and one evening, after much hesitation, I went to bed with the will to free myself.

"Then, as on previous occasions, and without realizing any more than on previous occasions how much time had passed between my physical drowsiness and my astral awakening, I regained consciousness: I was close to my physical body, but in two. The central idea that was the cause of this third astral outing appeared to me: I looked between myself and my body, and it was as if my attention had brought into being the object that I had not yet observed; the fact remains that, upon looking attentively, I saw a sort of connection, a large intestine, which emerged very clearly from the side of my material body and which, upon arriving near me, widened into an innumerable quantity of luminous and colored beams that enveloped me entirely as in a vast net. They were like successive rings of a yellowish or light or bluish red which, while being motionless in the chain, seemed animated by a very rapid vibratory movement: something like striations which form in a Geissler tube when an electric current passes through it. I considered this connection with curiosity: it seemed to me that if I had not *wanted* to see it, it would have gone unnoticed by me: I then examined more attentively my physical body which appeared to me, under the covers, as translucent, but in a rather vague way; this memory itself is a little confused with me, however it seems to me that if I had wanted to see all the internal organs functioning, it would not have been impossible for me. But I looked around me where I remember seeing what looked like circular fluidic movements: something analogous, but on a larger scale — and above all faster, more confused — to what one sees when one mixes an essence with alcohol and shakes the bottle; these fluids were diversely colored, of harmonious shades; at the same time, I *felt* them traversed by countless beings, but here again my memories are fluid and unclear, which I attribute to the fact that, wanting to see two things at once — my physical body and my surroundings — I saw neither one nor the other well. Moreover, I didn't dare move; it seemed to me that the bond uniting me to my material body was drawing me towards it and that I would have experienced pain if I had tried to stretch it by moving away. For I *felt* that it was elastic. In any case, I yielded to the attraction that he seemed to exert on me and I *re-entered* my body through the place where he came out of it, but in a particular way: it was not as if I had penetrated it through a specific opening, but as if the beams of light that enveloped me as they came out of the fluidic bond had amplified in such a way as to absorb him himself, and as if, as a result, there had been a fusion of the two bodies into one.

"I then felt a rapid numbness, and only awoke the next day, having some difficulty recalling the experience, the details of which only gradually, with effort, came back to me. This was indeed my last attempt of this kind, for I have never repeated it since: the terrifying thought of all the obstacles that can prevent the reintegration of the physical body has always prevented me from starting again. And it was only years later — one day when my wife recalled the strange start that had marked my first reintegration — that I admitted the true cause, all the more frankly because I had never repeated the experience and had not the slightest desire to repeat it."

Whatever the author of this self-observation may think, it seems to me that he must have engaged in astral projections more than once since then, but unconsciously from a subjective point of view, and objectively, either without returning — during this out-of-body experience — to the physical plane, or by returning there only near people incapable of perceiving his presence near them.

Indeed, this faculty, so curiously awakened in him, remained latent. He had proof of this years and years later, when, recently, a young woman he knows, who possesses quite developed mediumistic faculties, and, consequently, great sensitivity, said to him during a chance encounter:

— Ah! Mr. X…, you pay me strange visits!

— What do you mean? What visit have I paid you?

— Three nights ago, you — not you, but your ghost, your double, whatever! You came to my house.

— Me? You were dreaming!

— That's what I thought at first. I was only half asleep. I felt my hair being pulled. At first, I thought it was my husband, sleeping. I looked at him by the light of the nightlight: he was fast asleep, curled up in the alley, his back to me. However, my hair was *still* being pulled. I turned away and saw you: you were standing by the bed, and it was you who were pulling my hair. Astonished, I sat up and looked at you: then you burst into silent laughter, as if you were happy to have woken me up. I immediately called my husband to let him know you were there, but then you disappeared."

At this account, X…, at first incredulous, argued for the possibility of a dream or a hallucination. But faced with the receptive subject's very clear statements, he thought the matter was worth clarifying, and he announced that he would make an effort to go and see the subject on some of the following nights, which he did not designate for testing.

He deemed it pointless to resume his training system: since he could (assuming there had been no dream or hallucination) dissociate without special preparation, he thought it unnecessary to subject himself to a troublesome regimen; one of two things: either the perception had been real, and he had nothing to do to try to repeat it; — or there had only been a visual hallucination of this young woman, and he did not want to submit to the troubles of special training in order to resume experiments which he had long ago and deliberately abandoned.

Now, several times thereafter, this young woman informed X… that she had seen him again under the same conditions; sometimes he spoke to her, and other times simply appeared without saying a word. Most of the time, he woke her by pulling her hair, clear proof that the ghost was indeed condensed and materialized. And always the dates corresponded exactly to those when X... had wanted to attempt the production of the phenomenon by a simple exercise of his will.

Because, for him, the conditions of the test had been excessively simplified: all he had to do was *to want*, before falling asleep, to go and find his correspondent, for the phenomenon to take place — not every time, however, because on average there was failure every other time, which seems, in view of the successes, to be attributable to accessory conditions of temperature, atmosphere, etc., which also appear to have modified the results, because he appeared more or less visible, more or less alive, etc. Perhaps these differences in degrees of success also stemmed from differences in the intensity of the willpower that produced the phenomenon, for there were evenings when X... was more or less alert or tired.

In any case, one fact was certain: the evenings when his correspondent announced seeing him coincided well with those when he had wanted to split himself, on very irregularly spaced dates, for the purpose of the test, and, on average, two or three times a month.

But the phenomenon presented a particular oddity: although occurring with relative ease, much greater than during the first attempts, the out-of-body experience left no trace in X's memory. He was only aware of the accomplishment of his will in a rather fleeting and difficult-to-appreciate detail: a state of slight fatigue in which he found himself upon waking and which disappeared at the moment of rising [252]. He therefore wanted to resort to a serious check of the reality of his out-of-body experiences, using the now well-known phenomenon of the repercussions of injuries from the astral body to the physical body.

To this end, he asked the receptive subject to keep a strong needle within reach and to scratch and injure the phantom with it at the first opportunity, as much as possible on the arms.

A few evenings later, he activated his will in the direction of splitting; the day after, Mrs. X... received a letter from her husband's correspondent, which he shared with me, from which I excerpt the following passages:

"That night, from Wednesday to Thursday, I woke up feeling oppressed, and Mr. X. was next to me. I was in pain and wondered at the time if I was really awake. As it [the vision] persisted, I got up, took a pin, and then went to my nightlight. Mr. X... seemed distressed and very sad [253]. I wanted to prick him, but it was impossible to get near him! I went to him: he would run away to the other end of the room, and this was the whole time, for four minutes. It was 1:25 a.m., and Mr. X... seemed afraid of my pin. I was annoyed at not being able to reach him: as soon as I was near him, he was somewhere else. Suddenly I turn around and see S... [254] laughing — with the look of Mr. X... I think. And as he was coming towards Mr. X..., he disappeared very quickly..."

In this letter, the facts are clearly stated: — X...'s correspondent, to be sure that she is awake, gets up, takes a pin, goes to her nightlight, notes the time her clock marks at the beginning and end of the apparition, walks towards the ghost and chases it around her room to scratch it with her pin. It is very difficult, it is impossible in this case, to argue that it was a hallucination or a dream!

Moreover, X..., who is interested in the occult movement, the validity of which his personal experiences have shown him, attends psychic gatherings from time to time. Around this time, finding himself in such an environment, he asked the Entity that manifested itself to examine him and tell him if he was made to split himself easily. The Entity strongly urged him to persevere in this experiment, and concluded: "You don't know how much, with perseverance, you could achieve in this endeavor." — The interview in question took place in front of five people whose names I know.

Regarding X...'s outings, one detail should be noted: the actions of the day preceding the split generally influence it. In the aforementioned case where X... appeared heartbroken and very sad, it seems certain to me that, although he doesn't remember it, X... must have had some worries before splitting himself.

---

[252] This lack of memory most likely stems from the fact that, in these new circumstances, X...'s neuritis is no longer heightened as it was during his first experiences by a long retreat and mental exercises.

[253] X..., when questioned on this subject, does not recall any reason for sadness that could have given him an air of affliction.

[254] I have said that X...'s correspondent possesses mediumistic faculties: S... is an astral Entity who visits him most often.

On the other hand, sometime later, he appeared on the same subject, dancing, jumping, and fooling around, in such a way as to make him laugh: this outing had taken place on the evening of a day spent with his family, where X... had enjoyed himself greatly after enjoying a lunch washed down with fine wines. — It therefore seems certain that the influences under which the experimenter's morale was placed in the period of time immediately preceding the split had an effect on the nature of the splitting experience.

However, X... wanted to obtain certainty of the reality of his astral outings, not because he had suspicions about the veracity of his correspondent who had no interest in misleading him, but to give himself the satisfaction of knowing if he was like certain experimenters who can only manifest themselves to a single subject and who fail with others, or if it was possible for him to send his phantom to other people: the success of the experiment should bring him the desired certainty, which the repercussion, on his *sarcosôme*, of a deliberately inflicted injury to his exterior *aérosôme* had not yet been able to provide.

To this end, he contacted another person whom he knew to be very nervous and who had previously told him about certain *visions* she had from both sleep and the past: he therefore thought he would find in her a good, receptive subject, and asked her not to be alarmed if, one night, she saw him appear before her. Here again, the success rate was, on average, one in two attempts.

The first time the phenomenon occurred in this other subject, the latter, very disturbed — one would be, at being thus awakened by his strange visitor — had only this to say to him: "Is it you, Mr. X...? Sit down!" — And the ghost sat down.

Another time, as the percipient subject did not wake up quickly enough despite his repeated calls, the ghost seized his right arm and, shaking it vigorously, forced him out of his sleep. He then spoke to him about things that interested them both, and then vanished into a rather thick smoke [255].

---

[255] Undoubtedly a knot of the coagulated astral matter, constituting the ghost, which had been violently disintegrated by the ghost striking a piece of furniture. — See in this regard the so-called Cideville affair: the ghost of the wounded shepherd Thorel vanished amidst such thick smoke that those present were forced to open the windows.

All these details, of course, are provided by the receptive subjects, since X... now remembers nothing of what happened during his out-of-body experiences; but he is currently practicing acquiring this special memory, as well as the other elements that constitute the complete astral projection that he still lacks. To this end, he is working to perfect his out-of-body processes in order to achieve as complete a result as possible, and he engages in his experiments fairly regularly.

This is not to say that he has not experienced some disappointments, and even that he has not picked up a few wounds and bumps during his outings, because he does not yet possess, despite his efforts in this direction, what I have elsewhere called the awareness of his direction, and he has had, in this regard, a few misadventures, the most curious of which is the following:

In June 1910, he was in a small town in Normandy. One evening, he had the idea of exteriorizing himself and going to find a receptive subject, Miss A..., who lives in Paris, on the Avenue de l'Opéra, but without remembering afterwards whether this was a simple wish on his part or a fixed idea in the period of numbness that precedes sleep. The next morning — I remind you that he retains no memory of what his *double* did during the splitting — he woke up with a rather severe pain in the right side of his stomach, very close to the iliac bone. Upon verification, a circular bruise ten centimeters in diameter, with localized swellings, completely black, occupied the painful area.

Highly intrigued, X... questioned his memories, but in vain; he did not recall having received, either the day before or during the night, a shock violent enough to have caused such an injury; the blow must have been strong enough to have gone unnoticed either while asleep, or, even more so, while awake.

He was therefore very perplexed and didn't know what to think when one of his friends, aware of his experiences, asked him: Could it not be a shock received during an out-of-body experience?

And, in fact, he could only see explaining the painful enigma in this way.

Indeed, shortly after his return to Paris, I had the opportunity to take him to a place where, with the help of the *Ouija* board, one has very curious communications with the Mystery.

X... approached the operators, explained the facts, and asked if they could explain them to him.

— Wait, let me see? replied the Entity, which was then communicating.

And, after a few moments, no doubt devoted to examining the injury, the following strange conversation began, transcribed as the lines came and went:

— You had gone to run away, said the Being, and you received a good blow, but it wasn't meant for you.

— A blow from what instrument?

— A blunt "thing" (sic).

— What else? Please specify. Cudgel? Hammer?

— Neither cudgel nor... a well-aimed blow from a truncheon.

— But under what circumstances?

— You found yourself in a battle, and you could have had worse!

And as someone laughingly points out to the operator that, during his astral excursions, he keeps deplorable company:

— Mr. X... is innocent.

— Since my split was unconscious, I can't explain how I could have found myself in such unpleasant company.

— By going on an escapade.

— But who were these people? Where did I end up?

— Among the Apaches.

— So, in this battle, I could have been killed?

— Almost.

— In such cases, accidents must often happen that cannot be explained?

— There is a God for the split.

— Who were these Apaches fighting?

— Two men, three women, and a large dog.

— You just spoke of risks taken by me... What were these risks?

— A large club grazed your head.

— You just said it was a blow from a truncheon that hit me...

— The blow from the truncheon was intended for the one wielding the club.

— Splitting shouldn't subject you to so much danger!

— Why, when leaving your home, do you sometimes get hit with tiles?

— And what chance prevented me from receiving the blow to the head?

— It was one of the women who held the arm of the owner of the big club.

— Explain this to me: The pain must have been intense; why, then, when it reverberated through my physical body, didn't it wake me up?

— Because you were very well split.

— And where did this scene take place?

— In your neighborhood, on the "fortifs."

It is certain that X...'s neighborhood in Paris is on the straight line that connects the town in Normandy, where he was, to No. 1 Avenue de l'Opéra, where he had wanted to direct his double; it is no less certain that X..., two weeks after this hyperphysical mishap, still had a yellowish swelling that was not very painful at the time [256] but which had been inky black, very large and very sensitive, and whose existence can be attested to by reliable witnesses; it is, moreover, certain that he did not know to what normal cause to attribute the lesion from which he had suffered; it is finally certain that X... exteriorizes himself easily; without, however, retaining the memory of what his double does during these astral excursions.

Moreover, X... has since had another Entity of the Mystery questioned to verify the preceding explanations.

I am transcribing this second communication as it was presented to me.

"You can tell X.... that the explanations provided are absolutely true, and that, moreover, he will receive further blows from the truncheon. He is surprised, he says, not to have been awakened immediately... there are several ways for the physical body to receive marks made on the astral body: when one is very well split, one does not always wake up; when one is only half asleep, a prick on the astral body can be enough to awaken the physical body..."

---

[256] That evening again, he had its existence confirmed by a witness.

I have just given the two communications received in this regard, and presented the observations relating to the material reality of the fact. I will refrain from any comment, leaving the reader to imagine what he will if the preceding explanation does not suit him. For my part, I cannot take sides: the reality of this explanation not having been materially demonstrated to me, the explanation itself can only be accepted in the absence of another... — But this other one, I do not conceive of it. So, what?

Such misadventures, as long as they are not more serious, constitute the ordinary risks inherent in any experience of any kind; X... is the first to laugh at them and, on the contrary, finds in them a reason to want to acquire, as soon as possible, full awareness of what he is doing during his projections.

Some time ago, I advised him to mechanically give way to his ghost, as it were, by placing under his pillow, before falling asleep, a letter from the person near whom he wished to manifest himself: the astral body, as I explained above, was supposed to encounter this object during its expansion outside the *sarcosôme*, and consequently find there a fluidic link to the source for which it would naturally return.

On August 28, 1910, X... followed my advice and warned his wife that in the evening he would try to free himself to go and meet a correspondent who was currently staying with her family near Langres. He went to bed after placing a letter from this person under his head, and fell asleep, *wanting* to exteriorize himself. The next day, he awoke with a certain fatigue that led him to assume he had succeeded — and he waited for events to unfold.

Two days later, he received a letter, which he shared with me, from which I have extracted the following passages:

"I am hastily sending you these lines while my memory is clear. You write pretty ones, Mr. X, for example! Last night, I was awakened, along with my husband, with a start, by a terrible noise. It took us a second to get up in bed, and who do I see? Mr. X... in the middle of the room, with his mocking face, looking at us. Then I cried out to my husband: 'Oh! Mr. X...! That funny face' (I repeat verbatim). My husband said, 'Well! What could he have dropped to make such a noise? If we could have pricked it [257]?'

"But it's likely that the effort you made had taken all your strength, because you collapsed, and I never saw you again.

— 388 —

Immediately afterward, I got up and noticed that a wooden darning ball, which had been in a display case near my bed, was no longer there."

Details follow, noted as the correspondent recalled them, and I place them in their logical order:

"I had used it [this ball] that same evening and had put it back in its usual place [in the display case], which had remained open. Now, this ball was under some chairs [facing the bed] in which you were in front of. As far as I'm concerned, you took the ball and threw it against the wall, under the chairs, to wake us up — and you succeeded.

"On the other hand, my husband told me: 'I dreamed that something was going to happen.' Indeed, something did happen. — As for me, I wasn't sleeping soundly and I thought [258] that my covers were being pulled back, but I can't be sure, because, without being asleep, I was numb: that's the only word I can find...

About every other day, I feel you in my sleep, and since I'm a heavy sleeper at the moment, it's likely that you don't like it and that you thought of waking me up in another way. What a leap we've made, my husband and I!... I ask you to start again.

"I asked C... [259], because she was there, if it was you who had produced this, she replied: 'He was helped, but the greater part was done by him. He will do even better, because he is very good at it.'"

.   .   .   .

During September 1910, X., who was staying with me, deep in Brittany, undertook a week-long experiment with this sensitive subject who was then in Haute-Marne: that is to say, there was, between the experimenter and the subject, a distance of approximately one thousand kilometers.

Consequently, on September 1st, he wrote to her to be ready from Sunday the 4th, ten o'clock in the evening, until Monday the 11th, six o'clock in the morning, asking her to place each evening

---

[257] With the needle held in reserve for this purpose, according to the previous recommendation.

[258] That is to say: "I had the sensation."

[259] I recall what was said above: this correspondent is gifted with mediumistic abilities, and C. is, like S., mentioned above, one of the astral Entities who habitually visit her.

a piece of paper and the wooden ball [260] on a seat at the bottom of a glass shelf that he knew existed near the subject's bed: his goal was to be able to throw this sheet of paper or this ball onto the floor, depending on his strength at the time. Furthermore, he did not intend to experiment every evening, but only on Tuesday the 6th, Friday the 9th, and Saturday the 10th, so as to see if his presence would be properly noted on the days he wanted to split himself.

Now, on Friday the 2nd, he did not intend to conduct any experiment, as that day was not included in the designated week; but that evening, as he went to bed, he reflected that his correspondent must have been warned since the morning; moreover, by a natural association of ideas, he was led to think of the small glass shelf at the foot of which he was to operate; and he wondered whether it was placed at the foot of the bed — which he knew occupied a corner of the room — or opposite it, fearing that his ignorance of the local topography would cause the experiment to fail, and regretting not having asked for an explanation in this regard.

It was under the obsession of this idea that he fell asleep, and although he did not intend to free himself that evening, although he had made no preparations for this eventuality, the dissociation took place automatically and unconsciously within him under the influence of this fixed idea.

Indeed, he received a letter shortly afterward in which his correspondent told him that she had received her warning on the 2nd, and that she had been very surprised — since she was not supposed to be ready until the 4th, and that, consequently, nothing had been prepared for the experiment — to see him on the night of the 2nd to the 3rd. "At 11:10, you came; I was asleep. On a sideboard a meter from my bed, I had placed, in a small basket, a small lamp and a doll's candlestick that I intend to take to Paris. You took these two objects and threw them on the floor. I confess that my husband and I are astonished; if I hadn't seen it, I wouldn't believe it. You collapsed [261] four times, which proves that you had used all your strength to pick up the objects.

---

[260] A wooden ball that had been used for previous experiments.
[261] Fainted by collapsing towards the floor.

"The fifth time you said to me, without me thinking of speaking to you, 'I'm experimenting and I'm not doing badly, aren't I, Madam?' And as I was thinking to myself, 'My friend, you should remember what you just did!' your face immediately changed, and you said to me, 'I don't know how it is, but I haven't remembered anything yet; but I'm studying it right now. So, the other evening when I came...' Then, you didn't finish what you had started; you collapsed, and I didn't know what you had meant."

This release, having taken place outside the prescribed period, is reported here only for documentary purposes, because it was completely involuntary and brought about solely by circumstances; as for the doubling of the indicated period, this is what happened.

The Operator's Side. — As I said above, X... intended to split himself, not on each of the fixed days, but only, for control purposes, on Tuesday, Friday, and Saturday.

Now, during the night from Monday to Tuesday, X... did nothing but cough, unable to close his eyes; on Tuesday, he got up, with the flu, aching, and unable to experiment. On Wednesday, it was the same, and he was wondering if he shouldn't write to the receptive subject to inform her of the situation; but, in short, the fixed period wasn't over, and after all, he would see what would happen if he didn't voluntarily split himself.

He used Thursday to take medication, and by Friday, he found that his flu was over: he therefore decided to operate that same evening, on Saturday, and on Sunday.

On Friday evening, X.... went to bed at nine-thirty, after having scattered all the letters he had from his correspondent under his pillow; he exerted great energy of will to go and find her; as he dozed off, he mentally ran through the path that separated him from the nearest railway station, followed the track to Paris, crossed Paris from the Montparnasse station to the Gare de l'Est, followed the railway track again... Sleep then overtook him; a deep and continuous sleep. He woke up at eight o'clock in the morning, very tired bodily and mentally, but unsure whether to attribute the cause of this fatigue to his nocturnal dissociation or to his discomfort of the previous days; in short, he did not believe he had split himself, not having yet recovered from his indisposition [262].

On Saturday night, he went to bed under the same conditions at 9:45 p.m. after the same preparations, and with an intense desire to succeed. He mentally retraced his steps and fell asleep around 10:15. He woke up around 11:30; a brief bout of insomnia ended between 11:50 and midnight. Then, he slept continuously, calmly until around 8:00 a.m. A feeling of fatigue, especially cerebral. He believed he had split his mind, but his insomnia around 11:30 p.m. left him with some doubts.

On Sunday night, he proceeded the same way: he went to bed at 9:30. He fell asleep at 10:30, at first deeply, then restlessly. He awoke several times, interrupted by drowsiness, until around 5:00 a.m., then a heavy sleep until 9:00 a.m. He felt generally tired. He didn't believe he had split his mind.

Receptive subject's side. — Every first day of the week, up to and including Friday, there was no result. On Saturday evening, the splitting occurred. Here are the correspondent's accounts:

"This Saturday night you came at a quarter to one [263]. I had left the display case open and had put a glass ball and a sheet of white paper on the first tier of the display case, which also contains some of my notebooks and some of your books. (All week I had put these two objects on a folding table in front of the display case, but that day the folding table was occupied by a dog who would not sleep anywhere but in my room. I wonder if it was not he who prevented you from coming all week, and if only today you are used to him.) Finally, as the wooden ball had been lost by this dog, I took the glass ball and put it in the open display case, first tier down. So, at a quarter to one, you came; you took the ball and threw it, so that it broke into a thousand pieces; you left the sheet of paper but you took a book by Phaneg (*Psychometry*) and you threw it on the floor too; then you bent down and said to me, swinging yourself: 'But, Madam, is it no longer the same ball?' So, you knew that this ball was there for you. We turned off our night light; my husband wanted to try to see you, but he saw nothing. I called you; you came closer to the bedside rug; we were going to speak to you, but you fainted. What surprises me most is that my dog said nothing, *nothing at all!*... I am very surprised by

---

[262] Since he was not seen that night, it is likely that, given his state of health, he lacked the strength to make himself known.

[263] That is, after his brief period of insomnia of 11.5 hours.

what you did; but my idea is that you did not come on the day you wanted [264]; I think you should do this in front of other witnesses".

— During the month of November 1910, X... was attending one evening, at the home of Mr. L., a magnetizer, the experimental splitting of a magnetic subject. For a minute, to facilitate the operation, the gas was turned off. When the light was restored, Mrs. L., who was attending the experiment, at some distance from X... and who is a sensitive and seeing subject, affirmed that she had been touched, in the darkness, by X...'s double; the latter initially denied the possibility of this fact, because he had remained awake, and, until then, he had only ever carried out the experiment while asleep; he believed that Mrs. L. had made a mistake and that she had confused some projection of the experimented subject with her own ghost; however, he had to admit the reality of the phenomenon when the magnetic subject, put into a somnambulistic state, declared that it was indeed the exteriorized ghost of X... who had struck Mrs. L. This was therefore a new stage of development for him, since he was now splitting himself in the waking state.

To gain certainty in this regard, X.... agreed with Mrs. L. that, during a new period of darkness that was about to occur, he would make an effort to free himself and send his double to strike her on the *right* shoulder. After the experiment, Mrs. L. claimed to have been struck on the *left* shoulder and the leg, and, in this last point, hard enough to require a few magnetic passes from her husband in order to return to his normal state. Here again, the fact was certified by the magnetic subject put into a state of somnambulism: it was undeniable, for X..., that he was now splitting himself in the waking state, and consciously.

Somewhat surprised by this unexpected progress, he questioned the magnetic subject, asking if he needed to undergo any training to increase his experimental strength, either in terms of neuritis or willpower.

The response was: — "There is nothing to be done regarding neuritis; the astral body is absolutely at the required point to disengage easily. On the other hand, there is some progress to be made in the area of willpower, which must acquire greater energy: this is where your efforts should be directed."

---

[264] We saw above that this exit was, on the contrary, wanted that day.

A few days later, X. repeated the experiment with Mrs. L., who was touched as before. But, a strange thing! Mrs. L., each time she was touched by X., experienced a particular burning sensation that her other receptive subjects had never before mentioned. Is this due to a particular disposition of her own organism? Is it due to the waking state in which X. operates with her? Only further experimentation will be able to provide the key to the enigma.

Very recently (January 11, 1911), X... conducted a public experiment, in a circle composed solely of occultists and psychics, with the aim of experimentally determining whether it was possible for him to dissociate in an atmosphere that was not hostile, but rather unfavorable because it was formed by the fluids emanating from the undeniable curiosity of those present.

This experiment took place under the following conditions.

X. was to strike a receptive subject seated in the audience [265], while two magnetic subjects, placed to his left and placed in a state of clairvoyance, were to describe to the audience all the phases of the operation. Furthermore, several natural clairvoyants (the Marquis de G., Mrs. V., etc.) were to monitor the magnetic subjects' statements.

To neutralize, as far as possible, the unfavorable fluids due to the curiosity of the audience, X. asked them to unite their wills and direct their beams in the direction of the phenomenon's realization. Finally, he resorted to another means of control drawn from metapsychism.

"In such a case," he said, "I know that there is a struggle around me, that I am surrounded by Entities of the Mystery, some of whom come to my aid and others, on the contrary, want to prevent me from succeeding; among those who come to my aid, there is one in particular who must be close to me; I have described it on a piece of paper that I am giving in an envelope to Mr. L. who, as magnetizer of the two seeing-subjects, will have to direct the experiment during my state of annihilation; he will ask these two subjects to describe the Entities they will see helping me; the description of the principal one among them must correspond to the one I have put in an envelope and which, only then, will be read publicly."

Then, after making his preparations (blindfold over his eyes, cotton balls in his ears, etc.), so as not to be distracted by any external cause, he absorbed himself in the intense desire to free himself, calling for help from the Mystery Entities who, it seems, assisted him in accomplishing the phenomenon.

Shortly after, the magnetic subjects reported seeing luminous and colored vapors emerging to his right and left, the union of which, to his left, formed the phantom, which quickly condensed. From then on, the seers in attendance had a visual perception of this phantom. Mrs. V. reported seeing a luminous ball appear above the operator, a fact that was confirmed by the magnetic subjects [266].

They then declared: — The operator was surrounded by red Entities [267] who formed a circle around him, and wanted to prevent the ghost from moving away from the physical body. But, almost immediately, bright, bluish Entities [268] approached him, among whom they noted, among others, a man of powerful build, with energetic but unattractive features, with crew-cut hair, who seemed to be in command...

When, then, the envelope containing the description was opened, it corresponded absolutely to that of this Entity.

This Entity broke the circle of red Beings — again according to the statements of magnetic subjects — and made way for the operator's *aérosôme*, which moved away from the physical body and circulated in the free space provided in front of the assistants, among whom those who were clairvoyant noted its presence and its movements in agreement with the two magnetic subjects.

This phantom moved toward the receptive subject, to strike him as agreed. But it was around him that the circle of Red Beings had re-formed, as if to defend his approach. The other Entities of the Mystery had left, or at least were no longer visible.

---

[265] At the last moment, there was a slight modification: since the ghost is usually very fearful, since, separated from the *aérosôme*, it always fears being injured, it was preferred to place the receptive subject outside the audience, about three meters away and to the right of the operator, so that the space separating them would be free of any obstacles.
[266] It was, very likely, the mental body that was emerging.
[267] Red is, on the astral plane, the color of evil entities.
[268] Blue is the color of good entities.

Is it to this circumstance that we should attribute the fact that the receptive subject was not struck by the exteriorized living phantom? Was it not rather for this other reason that three ladies present — who saw the experiment only as a curious phenomenon, unaware of its scientific significance — continued to chatter throughout the entire course of the experiment? We don't know. But several times, the Marquis de G. was obliged to call these clumsy assistants to silence, and to note that there was not, among the audience, the indispensable unanimity of will.

In any case, the ghost circulated before the spectators for some time without aim, and, consequently, without being able to reintegrate the physical body; it was only after about a quarter of an hour that reintegration could take place.

One detail should be noted: X. intended to conduct the experiment with a blue gas flame, that is, in such a way that everyone could see his presence in their seats for the entire duration of the experiment; but from the beginning, this light, although faint, bothered the two magnetic subjects, who simultaneously saw it as an obstacle to the operator's astral body being released, and requested its extinction. Consequently, the experiment took place in complete darkness, and the light was only restored — very faintly and momentarily — to read the description placed under the envelope. It was not completely redone until X. had regained control of himself.

As a conclusion, all evening he felt his mind empty and his body tired, and only the next day, upon waking, was he himself again, that is, in full possession of all his faculties. According to him, of all the out-of-body experiments he had attempted until then, none had tired him so much — which, in my opinion, was due to the difficulty that he had to overcome which stemmed from the unfavorable atmosphere.

— On March 18th of the following year (1911), a new experiment took place under the same conditions and in the same environment, with the same receptive subject; only one of the two magnetic subjects, intended to be put into a state of clairvoyance to describe the phases of the phenomenon, had been changed: other natural clairvoyants were in attendance. The goal of the experiment had not varied: to attempt to strike the receptive subject placed approximately 2.5 to 3 meters from the operator; but an additional goal had been added, as follows:

X. had thought of attempting to knock over a light object placed balanced on a table not far from the receptive subject; but, upon examination, a difficulty arose: on the one hand, if the object was too heavy, the double might not have the necessary force to act on it; on the other hand, if it were too light, it could be knocked over by an external cause (vibration of the wall by a car passing in the street, shaking of the floor or furniture by the unconscious movement of one or more assistants), etc. In short, the result could be inconclusive.

At the last moment, Mr. F…, who had learned of the attempt that was about to be made, appeared carrying two glass plates coated with lampblack, and asked if X. could have his double's hands placed on them so that the fingerprints could then be studied. This solution to the difficulty was immediately accepted by X., and the two plates, placed on the end of a desk behind the receptive subject and approximately 1.5 meters away, remained in the custody of the person who had brought them.

As soon as darkness fell, the splitting began, much faster than the previous time (which would show that the ghost was becoming familiar with the environment) and described in its general phases by the main magnetic subject.

X. had warned, as before, that there would be a hyperphysical struggle around him, and had given the general secretary of the group where he was operating the description, in an envelope, of the Entities he was going to call, and who, he believed, would help him.

There was indeed a struggle, for as soon as the seeing-subject announced that the phantom, formed on the left, was preparing to leave X. to go to the right in the direction of the percipient subject, he saw a *red* Being appear, opposing the passage of the double against whom he engaged in a struggle. But then, a *blue* Entity — the same as the last time, and whose description was found in the envelope prepared by X... — intervened and separated the living double from the astral Being. The latter, furious, threw himself on the seeing-subject and attempted to strangle him. The latter, terrified, screamed and tried to flee into the darkness. The magnetizer had some difficulty seizing him, bringing him back, and calming him down. There, the struggle continued between the seeing-subject and the red Being, who grabbed the latter by the wrist: the seeing-subject felt a violent burning sensation, then managed to get rid of his hyperphysical adversary.

During the entire time this scene lasted, little attention had naturally been paid to X's double, who had been momentarily lost sight of. When calm was restored, the seeing-subjects acknowledged its presence to the operator's right, and in front of him, the receptive subject declared that he saw someone approaching him, then, almost immediately, announced that the ghost had just touched his right hand. The double continued on its way to the office, where the lampblack-coated plates were located; once there, it remained for a few moments, as if undecided, and then returned to X.

The experiment had lasted about ten minutes; the magnetizer deemed it sufficient and awakened the seeing-subjects, one of whom — the one who had fought with the red Entity — was showing particular signs of agitation. The operator had some difficulty reintegrating himself, and it was necessary to use cold breath on him.

The results of the operation were then checked.

The seeing-subject, who had suffered a burn on his wrist during his hyperphysical struggle, pointed to the area where a burn was indeed observed: the skin was red in places [269].

Similarly, the receptive subject pointed to his right hand, where a burn [270] was also visible, but lighter than on the seeing-subject.

The patches were then examined: one of them bore certain signs that at first it was unclear to what cause to attribute it: either to a very light touch or to an accidental cause.

---

[269] The particular nature of these hyperphysical burns has been detailed elsewhere.

[270] It was explained above that when X... touches this subject, he burns him, without yet knowing whether this phenomenon comes from the subject's particular organism, or from the fact that the operator's release takes place during wakefulness, the force deployed is greater than that brought into play during sleep.

X. informed Mr. F. that if he had actually touched the patch, patches of soot would be transferred to his own skin when the reintegration was complete, that is, the next day or the day after.

For the next two days, X. constantly and meticulously examined his digital extremities, but without finding any trace of soot. He informed Mr. F. of this by letter, and consequently regards this part of the experiment as completely fruitless.

Complete reintegration took even longer than the previous time; the splitting had taken place on Saturday evening, and only on Monday morning did the operator find himself in his normal state.

In short, there was progress. The double, more familiar than before with the environment in which he had to move, had succeeded in touching the receptive subject, which he had been unable to do during the session of January 11. As for his failure in touching the plates with the aim of leaving his fingerprints, X. considers it purely accidental; he declares himself confident of success at a subsequent session, since he is aware of having previously performed, in this state, acts that required a greater deployment of strength than simply placing a hand on a plate.

This partial failure can, according to him, be due to three causes:

1. The struggle that the double had to endure at the beginning of the release, which certainly weakened him.

2. The presence of three ladies, the same as at the previous session, who he was later told had not stopped chattering among themselves, instead of helping him with their will, as he had requested of all the assistants: this resulted in opposing fluids that neutralized part of his deployed strength.

3. Finally, the exteriorized phantom is always very fearful; perhaps he was afraid of the new act that was required of him, and, consequently, evaded the will of the operator [271].

----

[271] It also seems that the material used to dust the ice may have had a negative influence. — Indeed, the same experiments subsequently repeated with a subject, that is, with an objectively exteriorized phantom, showed that fingerprints of this phantom are easily obtained on talcum powder, but *never* on lampblack.

— On January 20, 1912, a new public experiment in out-of-body vision was attempted by X. in the same circles, composed solely, as we have seen, of occultists and psychics. The technique was slightly modified under the following conditions:

1. The control plate, instead of being sprinkled with charcoal powder which some experiments seem to have shown to be a repellent to living ghosts, was covered with a light layer of talc and left, just as the previous time, under the care of Mr. F., for which he had come specifically.

2. The receptive subject, instead of being placed between the operator and the control plate, was placed beyond this plate, so as to attract the ghost, forcing it to pass close to this plate.

3. The magnetic subject, placed in a clairvoyant state, instead of being placed to the operator's left, was joined to the receptive subject, with a view to doubling the attractive force (the operator's phantom having in other experiments shown that it was familiar with this subject) which was to bring this phantom close to the control plate. X. had carefully trained himself, in the days preceding the experiment, in such a way as to produce maximum results.

Before the attempt, although very nervous from his preparatory training, X. gave the audience — among whom were a number of doctors — a lecture on the mode of production of the phenomenon, solely to show that if his organism was in a completely abnormal state, the brain within him was absolutely lucid and in possession of all its faculties. After having momentarily and as much as possible annihilated within himself each of the five senses that connect us with the environment, after having called for help from the Astral Entity that protects him in such cases, X., gathering all his will, dozed off in the kind of annihilation particular to this experience.

The seeing-subject successively indicated all the phases of the disengagement and described the phantom; very large, very strong, clearer than ever, according to him [272]. As soon as the phantom was disengaged, to the left of the operator, he slowly began to walk towards the subjects; but then a red Entity formed in front of him, to prevent him from crossing the door of the room where the receptive and seeing-subjects, and the control apparatus were located. There was a sort of struggle between X.'s phantom and this hostile Entity. During this struggle, another Entity revealed itself, which appears to be the one assisting X. in his experiments. Very tall, very strong, she remained until the end to the left of the operator, on whose shoulder her right hand rested, and was thus seen by several people in attendance.

Finally, the ghost of X... succeeded in pushing the red Entity away and crossed the threshold of the adjoining room, where it remained for a few seconds near the control panel, over which it extended its right hand; then it moved toward the subjects, pulled the hair of the receptive subject, and struck the seeing-subject on the arm.

During all this time, several non-seeing assistants, among whom was a personal friend of X., Mr. Paul H., saw a series of luminous trails, similar to phosphorescent vapors, moving and intertwining around her physical body.

Frightened by the sight of this phenomenon, a young woman, Mrs. T., who, although very nervous, had wanted to witness the experiment, fainted screaming.

The general secretary of the society where these events were taking place, standing near X., ready to give him any magnetic treatment his condition might require, raised his voice in the darkness to reassure the bystanders, shouting in turn:

— Don't be afraid! Don't be afraid!

This double cry brought X. out of his torpor. His ghost reentered his physical body, and the light was turned back on. X. remained there for some time before completely regaining consciousness, and for the rest of the evening, until his departure, he remained in a state of prostration. As for the young woman whose unfortunate weakness had put an end to the experiment, she soon regained her senses, thanks to the care given to her, but she was burned on the cheek... by what?... how?... (*fig.* 70).

The control plate was then examined. It did not bear, as the operator had wanted and attempted to do, a fingerprint that could be identified, but in the middle (in the horizontal direction) and at the bottom, there was a particular mark like that of a blow: over a slightly curved length of 0.025, and over a width of 0.003, the talc was clearly removed; this trace was attributed to a rather violent fingernail strike from the materialized ghost [273].

But then something eminently regrettable occurred. Mr. F., who had wanted to monitor the experiment and who had consequently been entrusted with the supervision of the control plate, was questioned about it, and could not say yes or no whether this mark, although clearly visible, had been on the control plate at the time he took charge of it. He simply said that he could not say anything specific, which is already bizarre for a controller. But then, pushed to the limit by the precise questions of the secretary general, who was certain that the mark in question had been made during the experiment, he argued that, since the two subjects, the receptive and the seeing, were not very far from the plate, one of them could have accidentally touched it. Now, it should be noted that by placing these two subjects beyond the plate, the secretary general had asked Mr. F. if he had any objections to the placement of these subjects, and Mr. F. had stated that he had no criticism to offer.

The conclusion of the incident is that one can judge with some severity an inspector who does not know in what condition the inspection instrument was delivered to him, and who disapproves, after the experiment, of the arrangements he had previously approved. And it is regrettable that an inspection worthy of the name requires qualities that are not everyone's prerogative.

To conclude this experiment, here is the letter that a clairvoyant witness, the Countess of C., wrote to the Operator a few days later and at his request, in order to have a precise account of the experiment.

---

[272] A habitually receptive subject of X, who was present at the experiment, nevertheless told him afterwards: "You were indecisive in outline and lacking clarity; your phantom is infinitely clearer, more luminous, and more visible when we do the experiment in private and, leaving your home alone, you come to find me alone at home." — This proves how much the presence of the assistants is an obstacle to the production of the phenomenon.
[273] Subsequently, by repeating the experiment with the phantom of an objectively disengaged subject, a similar mark was obtained; the subject, questioned about the mode of production of this mark, said that it came not from a fingernail stroke from his phantom, but from a fluidic filament emanating from his hand and which had touched the plate. It is likely that the same had been true in the personal out-of-body experience.

January 26, 1912.

Dear Sir,

I am pleased to send you the information you requested, if it can be of any use to you. I will try to be as precise as possible.

I. — At the beginning of your splitting, I saw nothing. I was kneeling on my chair, looking down at my neighbor's hat, and I was watching with the greatest attention.

II. — After 4 or 5 minutes, I distinguished whitish vapors above your head, not very distinct, but enough to see them, oval in shape and about 40 centimeters high.

III. — When Lambert [274] described your arrival at the talc-coated plate and your half-struggle with the red ghost, I saw *absolutely nothing in the doorway where the incident must have taken place*. On the other hand, while I was only looking at *this doorway*, my eyes were suddenly drawn to a shape white enough to stand out against the deep darkness, a shape that was standing to your left, and therefore very much to my right. I was almost facing the door, I was only looking at it, and my eyes were drawn to your left, that is to say, to my right [275]. I say *drawn*, because I didn't think at all to look in your direction, convinced that your double was in the doorway where Madame Lambert described it. So the shape had to be quite precise, quite vivid, for me to suddenly turn my head to the right, saying to myself in a low voice: "Hey! What's that?"

So I looked with all my might... the shape was very tall — at least 1.80 m — strong, VERY IMPOSING. She seemed to have her arms (or arm) slightly forward, and was standing motionless, perfectly CALM AND STRONG (my sensations on this point are absolutely clear); she must have had her right arm resting on your left shoulder. Then, mentally, I prayed to this being: "Oh! yes, protect him! Make sure no harm comes to him!..." I thought this forcefully, and that's when I *saw*, at the peak of the form, two shining eyes turn towards me. And I cried out in shock and my arms twisted in fear... I cried out aloud: "Oh! those eyes!" [276].

At that moment, said Madame Lambert, you were going to come back. You, *I didn't see you*. But, above your head, a rush of white, indefinable things, almost ceiling-high, with brilliant flashes, rushed from the door you came from into the corner where I was, rolling above you and your protective Entity. I screamed again (this time, my teeth chattered). And the lights came back on....

I'm not talking about the double, brilliant points (eyes, perhaps?) that I saw here and there, appearing, then immediately going out; for they look so little like eyes! They only resemble them in the approximation, that is to say, I see them two by two, at a distance from human eyes. But they are more like sparks. Is this retinal fatigue? Is this real? Your Entity's eyes were, however, on reflection, of the same nature, but more visible, a little duller perhaps, and I saw them for four or five seconds — five centuries for my fear!

I say fear, but note well that I was not afraid of Him! I loved this ghost. I was simply afraid of what I saw....

Now, dear Sir, will you allow me to share with you something I do not understand. — There were fifty of us there. Among these fifty, there were at least three clairvoyants, Mrs. Lambert, Mrs. L., and Mrs. A. Finally, me, who is lucky enough, the happiness of seeing something. Well! how is it that the four of us did not all see absolutely the same thing? Mrs. Lambert was describing your double and the red ghost. Besides, where she was, I believe she could not see in the room [277]. Mrs. L. saw very well what Mrs. Lambert saw [278] and this is logical, since the "drama" was happening near them, around them.

In the room, Mrs. A. saw you and did not see your protective Entity [279]. Me, *I did not see you* [280], and I saw this Entity, and I *felt* that it was brave, that you had nothing to fear; it seems to me finally that my soul felt the feelings of her soul...

How can this be explained? Isn't everything that moves in the beyond of the same fluidic nature, that some fluids are perceptible to some eyes, others to others? Could my eyes perceive the brilliant fluid of your Entity (I use the words I feel, without knowing if they are exact), without perceiving yours, of a different nature?

---

[274] The seeing-subject.

[275] The witness attached a small explanatory sketch to her letter, which could have been removed here by slightly modifying this explanatory sentence.

[276] This form is that of the astral Entity protecting X. during her experiments.

[277] This is mainly because, by putting her into a special state of sleep to allow her to *see*, the secretary general, who was her magnetizer, had ordered her to focus all her attention on the actions of the ghost of X., whose examination formed the main goal of the experiment: she therefore did not concern herself with describing the incidental facts.

[278] Note that Mrs. Lambert was in magnetic sleep, while Mrs. L. was awake, in a normal state.

[279] There is a slight error here. Mrs. A. had apparently been asked if she saw the Entity in question. Since she thought that Mrs. Lambert would, as had been agreed before the experiment, describe this Entity in detail, she feared, she later said, that she would influence the description that she thought Mrs. Lambert was supposed to give. Under these conditions, she preferred to reply that she could not *see*. After the experiment ended, she corrected the facts, but in a group that did not include the signatory of this letter, which explains this lady's error.

[280] The witness speaks of the exteriorized ghost.

And vice versa, for Mrs. A.? What do you think? [281].

What mysteries! Since the presence of several people, in good faith, who *see* something, cannot serve as a control [282].

With my apologies for this long letter, and hoping to find you completely recovered and fit, please accept, dear Sir, etc.

Following this session, I was given to understand to what extent the practice of occultism disconcerts certain — otherwise intelligent — people and causes them to commit the worst blunders from a scientific point of view.

Several doctors were present at this experiment, one of whom I had met by chance shortly afterward, and to whom I asked: What do you think of the out-of-body experience that you witnessed? He replied verbatim: But I saw nothing, therefore, for me, it is all fictitious! — So you thought you saw the ghost that is invisible to normal eyes? — Lady! [283]

In the naivety of this response, one can see the vanity of normal science, or rather, that of its proponents. This doctor did not seem to suspect that, to see something precise under a microscope, one must have undergone special microscopy studies; that to understand something at the beginning of a disease, it is important to have taken a course in semiology; that, finally, to

---

[281] Therein lies the solution to the enigma that intrigues the signatory of this letter. Besides the fact that on the astral plane there are many fluids of completely different natures (odic or etheric, astral, mental, etc.) that can be perceived by some and not by others, each type of fluid presents numerous varieties. It is, for example, evident that the astral substance that constitutes the basis of the phantom of the living is much more charged with materiality than that which constitutes the phantom of the Mystery: these two ways of being of the same substance make it, so to speak, two different substances that can influence a given living sensory organ and go unnoticed by the same organ in another individual. Are there not, in our material world, eyes that see better from afar than up close, or vice versa, others that fail to perceive this or that color, etc.?

[282] We see from the preceding explanatory notes that this opinion is erroneous.

[283] When he was three years old, H. Durville gave an experimental lecture on the ghosts of the living, which he made the mistake of making public. Ninety-nine percent of the audience expected that the ghost would be presented to them on a plate!... The *minus habentes* should be excluded from these kinds of studies.

visually understand the results of an autopsy, it is important to have some knowledge of anatomy and physiology.

In his scientific unconsciousness, this doctor was once again overtaken by one of his colleagues who, sometime before, had said to me in very real terms, "I cannot accept that another person sees what I cannot see!" He would no doubt have been very surprised to learn that not everyone has the same visual acuity as his neighbor; that there are myopic people who see better than him up close, presbyopic people who see from afar what he cannot see, color-blind people who see colors differently than he does, and he does not even suspect that, to acquire all its acuity, an organ must undergo a certain training, and that it is by subjecting the eye to this sort of training that one becomes clear-seeing. In short, what he was saying was exactly as logical as if he had stated: "I don't understand how there are people who know how to play the violin, when I don't know how to play the violin." He might have been surprised if he had said to this doctor: "I can't believe you know how to treat patients when I don't know how to do it myself!" It is likely that in such a case he would have replied, with a pitying smile, if not a shrug of the shoulders: "By Jove! You have to have done special studies and have acquired practice!..." But it never for a moment occurs to him that, to know anything other than what he knows, or to acquire faculties that are closed to him, one must have studied, practiced, in a word, submitted to training that he doesn't even suspect could exist. I have indicated elsewhere [284] how and by what method of training one can acquire the faculty of clairvoyance; I will simply refer the reader to it without dwelling on it further. But all this shows how certain men who call themselves *scientists* are absolutely and irreducibly anti-scientific! These men may have been good students during their medical studies; they learned their lessons wisely and, in life, they repeat them like docile students for whom nothing exists outside the *magister dixit* that the School instilled in them; but they do not have the soul of discoverers: it is a waste of time to tell them that there is a science outside of them... they think they know

---

[284] *The Beyond and Its Problems* (Composition of Magic Mirrors, Scientific Theory of Vision, in the Beyond, Practical Method, etc.) 1 vol. duodecimo, Paris 1907. Messrs. Hector and Henri Durville, publishers, 23 rue Saint-Merri, Paris.

everything! It is terrible to think that the obstacle to progress posed by the ignorance of the masses is nothing compared to the barrier of inertia formed by the semi-learned who think that nothing can exist beyond what they have learned! All this is truly pathetic... Let's move on!

— What follows is a study of the phenomenon produced by the same operator, but unexpectedly, as it were, and without any participation of his will, which shows how easily the organism can become accustomed to acts that, at first glance, seem completely abnormal and contrary to the nature of being.

On Sunday, February 18, 1912, X.... awoke with an intense fatigue that kept him overwhelmed all day. Around him, his family and close friends teased him repeatedly, telling him that he must have wandered the previous night. X.... did not think that his fatigue was due to a splitting experience; he attributed it rather to the restlessness of his sleep, but without being sure of anything, since his normal memory does not yet record the memory of what he did during his periods of dissociation. However, faced with the jokes he was subjected to, he reflected that if his state of fatigue really stemmed from an involuntary splitting of the mind, he would have to react in the future against a phenomenon whose automatic production subsequently left him in such a state of dejection. He therefore went to bed early with a view to resting, but could not help but reflect on the means by which he could avoid the production of the phenomenon in the future without his knowledge or will.

Sleep quickly seized him, and the next day he awoke completely refreshed and full of energy: all fatigue from the previous day had disappeared, and he went about his usual activities until evening; he was, in a word, in an absolutely normal state of physical and mental health. So he was not a little surprised when the last mail of the day brought him, in a single envelope, the following double letter, from one of his most habitually receptive subjects and her husband.

February 19, 1912.

Dear Mr. X....

My husband tells me he's going to write to you, but I prefer to send you my note as well.

Last night, I was awakened by my husband (at 4:50 a.m.) saying to me: "Don't you hear that noise?" He got up and showed me two ring boxes and a small lamp that he picked up from the wooden floor. He asked me: "Where were these objects?" — I replied: "In the library," and, my eyes still full of sleep, I *half* fell asleep again, while my husband went back to bed.

After about five minutes, I jumped up in my bed because someone was calling me (the bedroom door was only pushed open and a nightlight was burning behind it); hearing nothing more, I completely buried myself under my sheets. Immediately the same thing happened. So, I sat up completely in bed, and behind the door, I only saw your head.

Think how I looked! And you said to me: "Do you recognize it, M.'s [285] little lamp? I threw it on the floor; there's something else, under the chair, near the window."

It was dark, and we couldn't see.

You said to me again: "I've damaged the bookcase." Then again: "Your light is much too strong, madam, I'm going, but I'll take this shard of glass with me [286]."

My husband got up and went to look under the chair indicated: there was what one might call a doll's fruit bowl, which was missing part of the stem that you took away; and even then, I'm very angry with you, because I got it from a grandmother.

So you weren't afraid of cutting yourself? I imagine you may have the piece at home; don't throw it away, you'll give it back to me.

Then my husband went to see the library, which had nothing, except that an English book, a box of powder, and a box of beads were lying on the rug. I wonder how you had the strength to take all these objects from the library where they always are, one on top of the other. It's true that the library is never closed, but that doesn't matter: when you come, you'll see how these objects are usually arranged.

---

[285] This is a doll's lamp that X.'s *double* had thrown to the ground eighteen months earlier, while he was deep in Brittany, experimenting with Mrs. A, then to M., in Haute-Marne.

[286] Questioned further, the subject added that the ghost of X.... showed her a piece of glass which was, as we shall see later, the fragment of the foot of a small glass cup. — See the story of this experiment, page 392.

In any case, I wasn't the one who gave you these glass objects to touch; you did it yourself. I even noticed that you seemed very cheerful!

This is all very funny! You see, there's no need for spirits to be a *poltergeist*.

Come on! When you come back, don't break anything! What amuses me is that you recognized M.'s lamp.

See you soon, Mr. X., and please accept, etc.

Here is the testimony of Mrs. A.'s husband, who witnessed the phenomenon (Mr. A. is not gifted with clairvoyance; he therefore did not see the ghost, he only saw the production of the physical effects of the phenomenon).

Dear Sir,

A few words for myself.

Mr. X., you are as strong as the Mahatmas [287]! This time, was like the first time I found myself at M., in good conditions for observation.

Here are the conditions under which the phenomena you produced (for, there is no doubt, it was indeed you who produced them) took place.

It was about a quarter to five in the morning, and I had just awakened suddenly, without apparent cause.

This awakening has often occurred in my home, almost always preceding some psychic phenomenon.

I jumped out of bed almost immediately to find out what time it was: the hand of my watch showed a quarter to five or twenty to five. I went back to bed immediately without waking my wife, but I could not get back to sleep.

I had been back in bed for about ten minutes when I heard a very loud noise, coming, it seemed to me, from several objects falling to the floor in the middle of our bedroom, and having broken.

I rushed out of bed again, lit the lamp, and saw, in the middle of our room, near a small table, a small porcelain lamp and two ring boxes lying on the floor.

I woke my wife, who hadn't heard anything, and showed her the objects. She seemed surprised, still half asleep, and didn't seem to attach much importance to them.

So I went back to bed. But, at that moment, I saw her staring at a darker part of the room (for I had left the lamp lit). So I asked her what she saw; she answered me: "It's Mr. X. Mr. X," she added, "says that something has fallen under the chair again..." And she pointed at a chair.

---

[287] Higher entities but living human life, according to the Theosophy doctrine

Then: "that he damaged the bookcase."

So I got up a third time and went to pick up, from under the chair I indicated, a small glass saucer with a broken stem, and from which a piece was missing — quite a large one, in fact. Then I went into the next room, where I found, lying on the floor, at the foot of a small bookcase, two small cardboard boxes and an Anglo-French dictionary.

My goodness! Mr. X., I admit that these are beautiful phenomena, very convincing for us. You're getting stronger and stronger, and if you actually took that piece of the cup with you, that's even better!

If I were you, I would mention this experience in a special journal, or rather, would it be better to wait until I can reproduce it with receptive subjects other than ourselves?

This phenomenon, produced unconsciously and without the knowledge of its author, calls for some reflection.

A. — It seems likely that since X. was not at all thinking about splitting himself that evening, it was the thought of seeking ways to overcome the unconscious production of the phenomenon, a thought with which X. fell asleep, which, by creating a special — very powerful — monoideism, brought about the splitting.

B. — The exteriorized ghost of X. must have been looking for the subject to whom he was going to visit. Now, in Paris, the subjects with whom X. primarily experimented were three in number; one had just experienced a very painful bereavement and was certainly not in a state of receptivity; the same must have been true of the second for some unknown reason; therefore went to find Mrs. A., who is, of all his receptive subjects, the one with whom X. has the most experience, the one, consequently, with whom he is the most familiar, and finally the one who, as a result, communicates to him the greatest amount of etheric force.

C. — A fact that is difficult to explain is the carrying of the piece of glass; it is appropriate to analyze it.

We know that the living ghost is composed of: 1. the etheric double or odic body, holder of physical life, never straying, for this reason, more than a few meters from the *sarcosôme* from which it emanates; 2. the astral body, which can go anywhere, but which, by itself, cannot materialize nor, consequently, act on matter if it does not receive communication of the etheric or odic force coming from a double, its own or that of another person, of the receptive subject in this case; 3. of various higher principles that need not be mentioned here.

Now, in the aforementioned case, the receptive subject lives about a kilometer and a half from X.'s home; it was therefore not from X. that the ghost received the necessary odic force, but from Mrs. A.'s etheric double, the receptive subject. It is perfectly understandable that, under these conditions, it was able to act on the matter in Mrs. A.'s environment, that is, to throw and break relatively light objects, and to hold a fragment of glass in its hand. But did it actually carry this fragment away as predicted? For this to happen, the ghost would have to be able to retain for itself, for a certain time, and by moving away from its source, at least part of the etheric force that was communicated to it precisely because it was in the immediate vicinity of the receptive subject. Is this possible? This cannot be denied *a priori*, but this possibility seems to be invalidated by everything we know *experimentally* about the etheric double which *never* moves more than a few meters away from the physical body to which it belongs; there would therefore be a sort of dissociation of the etheric forces, which is not at all demonstrated, on the contrary [288].

On the other hand, X. has made a serious search at home for this fragment of glass, if it is there; but although the difficulty of finding this fragment in an eight-room apartment is considerable, it is presumable that the piece of glass will not be found there. Now, what could have happened since it could not be found in the apartment — much smaller and easier to explore — of Mrs. A.? This, very likely: — The ghost announced that he was taking the object away... Perhaps he thought he could do it, or perhaps he was joking, which seems more likely. He could certainly have left the house keeping this small fragment, but, eight or ten meters from Mrs. A., the subject's etheric force abandoned him, and the piece

---

[288] However, according to G. Delanne, we can have some reservations about this, because there are well-documented cases where the *double* of the living has clearly drawn the energy necessary for physical manifestations from a great distance, from its own material body, because the synchronism of the movements of the fluidic body and the organism, demonstrated the intimate connection existing between them at that moment. The fluidic cord connecting the double to the physical body had the effect of conducting energy, like an electric wire connecting two posts. In this case, the subject is its own medium.

of glass must have fallen into the street.

In any case, just as Mrs. A. keeps the broken object, so X. searches at home for the missing piece. Bringing the two parts together would, in fact, provide experimental proof of the existence of a hitherto unknown phenomenon. In order to find it, to know its whereabouts, two methods seem likely to yield some results: — 1. Interrogate an astral entity on the day one is in communication with it; — 2. Interrogate the ghost of X. when it manifests itself again near Mrs. A., provided it is convenient for him to respond, for it is known from numerous experiments that the exteriorized ghost possesses a will of its own that is difficult to control.

In any case, these two methods of investigation were employed as far as possible.

Indeed, as far as he was concerned, in the following nights, X. tried to free himself to send his double to the receptive subject for interrogation. The first attempts were unsuccessful, probably due to the excessive energy expended, which led to restless sleep, that is, the condition most contrary to the production or phenomenon.

Finally, on February 24, X. received the following collective letter from Mr. and Mrs. A., which, although not providing the expected solution to the problem, marks a new and unexpected step in the development of the phenomenon.

24-2-12

Dear Sir,

You'll never imagine how exasperated I was with you last night.

My husband woke me up, saying, "Can't you see anything? The little lamp has just been thrown onto the floor!..." I see nothing and I heard nothing.

I still feel like I've been twitching for a few minutes. I could feel sleep overcoming me... Bang! A slap!... Stunned, I sit up and see you falling to the floor [289]. I lie back down... Bang! A harder slap!... I was angry. I sit up and see you fall to the floor again. — I lie back down... Bang! A *resounding* slap!... *That makes three!...* And I can still see you with your mocking face, falling to the floor.

And each time, you fell!... It's a shame, because I would have liked to talk to you.

I'll pass the pen to my husband.

Mr. X...

As my wife says, the smacks (for they are smacks rather than slaps) were very loud: I heard them every time, as well as a singular noise that occurred in the room, on iron or glass, as much as it seemed to me.

Finally, you are becoming stronger and stronger; I have not given up hope of seeing you materialize in a session that would be of great importance.

To which Mrs. A. adds:

My husband forgets to tell you that he heard the lamp fall, as well as a shell coming from the bookcase, no doubt thrown by you.

This letter requires two remarks.

First, it is certain that, on the one hand, Mrs. A., being a very powerful mediumistic subject, possesses a great capacity to exteriorize her neuritis, and, consequently, can easily communicate it to X.'s ghost; and that, on the other hand, this ghost materializes closer and closer to Mrs. A., to the point of losing, upon contact with her, the shyness that is characteristic of any exteriorized living ghost. — These two considerations are sufficient to explain the increase in this ghost's strength.

On the other hand, the production of slaps or smacks is not very easy to explain, because, truly, this is a reprehensible familiarity, for which X. initially apologized to the patient. But there's more: since he had never, ever, even been touched by the idea of assault against his receptive subject, he initially doubted that it was his exteriorized ghost who had resorted to such eminently regrettable methods; and he wondered — Mrs. A., I repeat, being gifted with powerful mediumship — if it wasn't an external Entity who had taken form near this subject, for some as yet unexplained purpose. But the mocking look on his face that Mrs. A. noticed led him to believe that it was indeed he who, unconsciously — I remind you that he has not yet acquired control

---

[289] Collapsing, disappearing into the floor.

of his actions in such an instance — had resorted, to methods not yet accepted by the manuals of civility, to attract the attention of the half-asleep receptive subject. But is *astral* civility the same as human civility? It seems, based on a number of previous facts, and of which we find many examples in the *Phantasms of the Living* by Drs. Gurney, Myers, and Podmore, that, on the related plane, reprehension only begins to be exercised in cases of actual lesion and injury. This is, moreover, a very obscure chapter of experimental psychology, and only the future will elucidate it.

— Finally, here is the account of a later experiment that will show what can be achieved by exercising this faculty at the level of development we know, when it is put to use consciously, but without prior preparation.

On December 14, 1912, X. was in the same environment where he had already experimented three times in public; he was asked to make an impromptu attempt. He accepted, eager to carry out this impromptu experiment, not for the benefit of those present, but for himself.

Indeed, public experimentation in such matters constitutes the worst possible conditions, in that, although, in order to utilize the strengths of the audience, they are asked to firmly and jointly *want* the phenomenon to occur, there is always a feeling of selfish curiosity to be reckoned with, which makes *everyone* present wonder: "What will happen?" and which produces adverse fluids that surround the operator, which he can only control through the intensity of his will.

Furthermore, whenever X. knows he must perform his splitting act in front of an audience in the evening, his daily *curriculum vitae* is as follows: — He gets up around 9:00 a.m., so as not to be tired from his morning, and until lunch, he searches through the morning's minor events for all the most trivial causes of irritation, accumulates them, exaggerates them at will, so as to exacerbate both his mentality and his nervous system.

Lunch is, for him, very moderate, so as not to overload his stomach. After this meal, while he avoids causes of irritation so that the mental body, well balanced, is in full possession of itself and increases as much as possible its power of domination over the material organism, he also seeks every means of irritating himself, through the random incidents of the day, in order to put himself, by the evening, in that state where, as he puts it, *one feels the need to break something*. At the evening meal, he simply takes a few spoonfuls of broth, very slowly absorbed, and which are simply intended to deceive the stomach, so that the demands of this organ do not cause him any trouble during the evening. In a word, he organizes his daytime existence so as to arrive at the moment of the experiment with as empty a stomach as possible, with a will sure of itself, and with an absolutely exasperated nervousness.

But on that day, nothing of the sort.

Old friends had come to lunch at his house, and, aided by conversation, he had eaten more copiously than usual, without, however, overindulging. The afternoon had then passed for him in conversations of a certain gaiety; finally, in the evening he had dined as usual, that is to say, moderately, but to his satisfaction.

He was therefore, at the time of the experiment, in the most unfortunate conditions imaginable: his mind completely untrained, his nerves absolutely normal, and his stomach in the midst of digesting.

He saw this as a special experiment to be attempted for himself personally, in order to find out if, under these conditions, he would obtain any results, and resolved to risk what, for him, was a real adventure.

He first warned those present of the unfavorable conditions in which he found himself, so that there would be no disappointment in the event of failure. Then, without any training, without any preparation other than that which consists of bringing about the momentary annihilation of the five senses, lying in an armchair, he proceeds to his splitting.

A single magnetic subject was present, who was to serve as both seer and receptive subject, and whom the operator intended to strike on the left shoulder. Placed in magnetic sleep, this subject declared that the operator's phantom was exteriorizing itself, but without moving away from the physical body, probably due to insufficient strength. He was brought closer to the operator, but, under these conditions and due to the absolute lack of prior training, the phantom was unable to perform any act, and after a few minutes, the operator and the subject were awakened.

A clairvoyant woman, T., who was in attendance, declared after the experiment that, as the magnetic subject had reported, she herself had seen the exteriorized phantom to the operator's left, but dull, poorly condensed, and without force.

In any case, this experiment demonstrates that X. is capable of splitting himself even in the most unfortunate conditions, unexpectedly, and without any preparation, but that, on the other hand, he cannot, in this state, achieve any effective results without prior preparation; this is what he wanted to know by making this attempt, and the reality of the fact is clear to him. By continuing his training, however, and through repeated attempts, he hopes to succeed in giving his exteriorized phantom the strength it still lacks in this sort of improvised experiment. Only time will tell if this is possible.

Thus, at the point X has currently reached, he possesses more than half of the elements that constitute a perfect astral projection:

— His body has acquired the ability to dissociate.

— He knows how to deploy the will necessary to achieve out-of-body experience [290].

— He can send his phantom to a predetermined location [291].

— He possesses tangibility, visibility, and audibility.

— He reintegrates his *sarcosôme* with satisfactory ease, and in a way mechanically.

However, he lacks three special faculties:

— The ability to perform, in a state of disengagement, a previously desired act [292].

— Awareness of his direction.

— The memory of what happened and what he did during his periods of exteriorization. This is what he is currently trying to acquire by submitting to a series of scientifically conducted attempts, under specific conditions that this is not the place to detail, because that would only be repeating what was said above

---

[290] His successes show, by the very force deployed by the ghost, that he is very well condensed and that failures must only come from external conditions, a defective state of the atmosphere or environment, etc.

[291] Even if it means encountering a subject capable of exteriorizing his own etheric force and communicating it to him to allow him to manifest his presence, and endowed with the perceptive faculties necessary to see or feel him.

[292] However, as we have seen during the preceding experiments, he begins to be obeyed by his ghost.

in the special chapters relating to the development of the general faculty of exteriorization.

Since that time, X. has had no public experience: they exhausted him. But he has shown himself to several people, and — this is his main progress — he expresses himself very easily unexpectedly and without any preparation.

Fig. 73. — Splitting a priest.

Photo taken by an amateur photographer, a priest himself, who is sure he did not take two poses on the same plate, while the person photographed is sure he did not move.

Fig. 74. — Doubles of two little girls.

Photograph obtained by Commander Darget in Tours, by photographing
Mr. Pinard's two children, previously magnetized. The pose of the
children — who have not moved — is completely different in terms of
the physical bodies and the ghosts; they do not have the same pose, and
the bouquet held by one of the little girls is not in the hand of the double.

Fig. 75. — Accidental splitting observed in Lyon.

There are many photographs of splitting, obtained very generally by chance: we give one (*fig.* 76) which is among the most remarkable.

Fig. 76. — Double of Mile B…, following a serious condition of
chloroanemia that lasted three years.
Photograph taken by the convalescent's uncle, whose double we see is
emaciated, aged, and sick.
The ghost, smaller than life, has just emerged.

Fig. 77. — Another double of Miss B...
Second shot, taken immediately after the other and under the same
conditions.
The double is life-size: the exteriorization is complete.

Fig. 78. — Conscious splitting of Mr. Sigurd Trier, editor-in-chief of the Danish magazine *Sandliedssoegeren*, consciously photographed in London by Mr. R. Bournsell, 13, Richmond Road, Shepherds Bush.

Mr. Trier very easily exteriorizes his double, which is audible and visible. On November 13, 1906, he had the above photograph taken. — A small detail unfortunately takes away part of the value of this shot: Mr. Trier, absorbed by the exteriorization of his double, mechanically carried under his nose, at the moment of being photographed, a bouquet of violets that he was holding in his hand and which adds to his physical face an appearance of mustache.

CONCLUSION

CHAPTER XVI

PUTTING THIS METHOD INTO PRACTICE

The author wrote this book in full awareness, based on the scientific data currently available on this subject, and based on what he was told by people seriously practicing their own out-of-body abilities...

Does this mean that anyone who comes across this treatise will be able to achieve an out-of-body experience at their first attempt? It would be unfortunate to entertain such an opinion.

First, it has been stated previously that a certain number of people (young women, children, the sick, etc.) should carefully refrain from such experimentation, which is only suitable for individuals endowed with sufficient physical and intellectual strength to withstand the ordeal without weakening.

But there is more.

Even if we consider only the category of individuals capable, by their physiological and mental conditions, of engaging in this experience, there is a selection process that is necessarily made by the very nature of temperaments. I recall that there are four types of temperaments (nervous, bilious, lymphatic, and sanguine) which combine with each other but, taken absolutely, divide human beings into four different classes.

Now, it is enough to refer to what has been said about these temperaments to know that the nervous ones in particular are suited to this kind of experiment, the bilious ones being more likely to provide receptive subjects; as for the sanguine ones, they will have difficulty achieving their splitting, which will be absolutely barred for pure lymphatics.

Since training can only succeed if the material is susceptible to it, at least a good third of individuals find themselves *ipso facto* excluded, for although in principle each of us possesses this faculty in a latent state, we must take into account the insurmountable obstacle presented by certain categories of organisms: it is quite obvious that the best violinist cannot make himself heard when he lacks an instrument. And the others, those who have the necessary instrument, the appropriate organism?

Remember the parable of the sower [293].

"A sower went out to sow. And it happened that some seed fell along the path, and the birds came and devoured it all. Some fell on rock, and, having no root, it withered. Some fell among thorns, and the thorns grew and choked it, and it bore no fruit. And some fell on good soil and yielded fruit that sprang up and grew..."

In its naive form, this parable is profoundly true and applies to all intellectual seed.

How many of the readers of these pages will have perused them with curiosity, then, having reached the end, will turn away, thinking: Charlatanism! Does official science speak of all this [294]? — The seed has fallen by the wayside.

Others will reflect, upon finishing this reading, that indeed, there is some logic in all this, and that after all, there would be a certain curiosity in attempting the adventure; they will confide in friends, some of whom, strong-minded because they have never studied anything, will mock them for their credulity, and others will tell them to beware of Charenton... and, not wanting to appear foolish or insane, they will shrug their shoulders — a clear sign, for them, of their superiority. — The seed has fallen among the stones.

Still others will think: Yes, we know, all this reflects the reality of the theories we believe in; but really, do we have the time, with professional or worldly duties, to follow such meticulous training? And then, can we really, when we go to bed

---

[293] Mark, IV, 3 seq.

[294] These are comparable to those ignorant peasants who, when told that a century ago our country dominated all of Europe, respond placidly: — That's not possible, because after all, if Napoleon I had existed, *it would be known!*... What can one say to such a denial!

after three hours of intensive music or bridge, have the willpower necessary to express ourselves? — The seed fell among the thorns.

Finally, a few — the last, those in whom the seed fell on good soil — had faith, alive at first, but faltering as trials accumulated, as difficulties piled up. And, out of a hundred who began with the robust ardor of a neophyte, how many will have the courage necessary to reach the goal, without succumbing to the partial failures inherent in any undertaking, without being sidetracked by material concerns or simply by the distractions of each day? A number may be infinitesimal.

And yet there are some, since I myself have encountered them.

These, it will be said, were specially organized... agreed! But does that mean they had no obstacles to overcome, no difficulties to overcome, no fears, even to surmount? No. These are simply characters better tempered than others, who, perhaps of wax in the face of life's ordinary difficulties, have shown themselves to be of brass in the face of the obstacles special to this experience...

These pages are therefore addressed to solidly tempered individuals, to those who, having studied the theories, realize that nothing among all that precedes is in opposition to the reality of things, and who, arming themselves with energy, know how to *will* and direct their will toward the goal to be achieved. Only this book can be useful to this elite. Whether others regard it as a deceptive fantasy, as an unhealthy lucubration, is of great indifference to me: I do not know them; I address myself only to energetic characters, to wills that know!

The sphinx of ancient Egypt is an eternal symbol for us, whose teachings we can, in this respect, practice: — its human head shows us that we need, above all, the study that leads us to *Science*; its lion's claws indicate that to reach the goal, one thing is necessary: *Audacity*; its bull's flanks, hardened by the continuous digging of a refractory soil, teach us *Will*; and finally its eagle's wings, folded in on itself and enveloping it, command us *Silence*: these are the four qualities required of any candidate for the tests of Mystery; he must *know* in order to undertake with a chance of success; he must *dare* in order not to be stopped from the start by obstacles; he must *want*, since success is only through will.

Finally, one must *be silent*, so as not to unleash against oneself the mob of fools and envious people, the pack of the ignorant, the timid, the weak, and the loudmouths....

But these pages are also addressed to another category of readers.

Although written along a path hitherto unexplored, although established in accordance with the latest teachings of theory and experimentation, they do not have the foolish pretension to establish the barrier beyond which no researcher may venture; every day, science advances, progresses, evolves; every hour brings us new knowledge — and this especially in studies relating to the Mystery, and which have received such a lively impulse in our time. Soon, tomorrow perhaps, this study will seem childish and backward, and investigators will arise who will be seduced by the desire to do better than their modest predecessors: I call upon them, I desire them, I extend my hand to them, even if the attempt I am making crumbles to dust behind them!... Their descent into the arena will mark the vigor of these studies, and the higher level of a new task to be accomplished; I have fulfilled mine in my own time, trying to do well in a path hitherto untouched by any practical exploration: they too will come, in their own time, the workers of tomorrow, to fulfill a new task, to place more correctly the milestones that I have established, to show better than I what I have only imperfectly taught: in this, I will be happy, thus exceptionally giving the lie to the words — profoundly true, moreover — of du Potet: "All truth useful to men is born of pain!" I will be all the happier because I remember the great thought of J.B. Biot: "In science, there is nothing as simple as what was found yesterday, but nothing as difficult as what will be found tomorrow."

And, if I may conclude this work with a quote from the Master to whom it is dedicated, I will conclude this study by reproducing here a passage from a letter that Colonel de Rochas did me the honor of sending me in recent days, during the printing of this book, and which, in absolute conformity with my thoughts, sums up its spirit well, although my eminent correspondent did not yet know its content:

"Explorations in these unknown regions are carried out by isolated individuals driven, like you and me, by the desire to know;

and it is only when they are thoroughly explored that officials arrive with all their equipment to study the details. It is by writing a major thesis on the nervous system of the flea that one arrives at the Institute."

Menez-Ellen, July 1910.
Paris, October 1912.

———

Glossary

A

Abulia — Lack of will, drive, initiative for action, speech or thought.

Aérosôme — The Astral body.

Amimic — Unable to express oneself using gestures.

Animality — Animal nature.

Annalists — Chronicler of yearly events.

Apostema — A filled abscess.

Apparition — A ghostlike image of a person.

Astral body — The repository of sensitivity (neuric force); it constitutes the fluidic support of the etheric double far from its physical body, and can materialize in certain cases when an etheric double provides it with the necessary substance. Vehicle used on the Astral plane.

Anabiosis — A bringing back to consciousness.

Astral Entities — Inhabitants of the Astral plane; including those both helpful and harmful.

Astral projection — The intelligent and semi-material part of the being leaving the physical body and projecting itself onto the astral plane.

Auto-suggestion — The influencing of one's physical or mental state by thoughts and ideas that come from oneself.

B

Bicorporeality — A subject possessing two bodies, each of which may be seen in two places (a body in each place).

Bilocation — The simultaneous presence of the same person in two different places (the same awareness in each place).

Biometer — An accurate instrument used for measuring neuro-psychic vital force by Dr. Baraduc.

C

Causal body — Beyond the mental body, appears to hold the highest faculties of the soul, such as memory, and seems to correspond to the higher Manas. Located above the mental ball, a sort of flame whose summit appears surrounded by a brilliant halo. Since it has never yet been possible to isolate and photograph it, we are reduced to hypotheses about it.

Chloroanemia — Possibly associated with gastric ulceration and poor diet.

Christophany — An appearance or non-physical manifestation of Jesus after his ascension.

D

Desideratum — Something that is needed or wanted.
Dynamization — Act or an instance of dynamizing, to give power or energy to something.

E

Effluviographies — Images of human radiation such as fluid around the hands and fingers.
Elementals — A lower class of non-physical entities.
Etheric Double — A non-physical body that is holder of vital energy for the physical body, maintains the life functions of the physical body.
Exteriorization — The process of "splitting".

F

Fluidically — An energetic bond between two subjects.
Fluidity — The flowing of fluid energy.
Fortifs — Part of the Fortifications of Paris.

G

Goetia — Books containing information for performing magical practices.

H

Hâtha Yoga — (Hindu) Assimilation of lower etheric and astral forces.
Hematosis — The formation of blood.
Hetero-suggestion — Influencing of one's physical or mental state by another.
Hyperphysics — In Lancelin's day, what was magic, and is now science.
Hyper-dynamized Will — Advanced form of energizing the Will.
Hyper-dynamization — An advanced, increased form of dynamization.
Hypnoid State — A splitting of consciousness, a double conscience.

I

Immatter — That which is not material, immaterial.
Intersigns — Communication from someone close who is dying.
Involuting — To return to its former condition.
Involvating — Including something that is a necessary part.

J

Jiva — (Hindu) Vitality.

K

Kama Rupa — (Hindu) The Animal soul.

L

Linga Sharira — (Hindu) Also the Astral body.

Lycanthropy — A supernatural condition in which men assume the physical form of werewolves or other animals.

Lymphatism — Enlargement or swelling of the lymphatic tissue, due to lack of lymphatic circulation.

M

Manas — The Human soul.

Magister Dixit — Latin for "Master Said". The teacher's final say.

Materialization — The appearance of matter from the non-physical.

Melancholics — An emotionally sensitive or depressed person.

Memtrams — Sanskrit; also Hebrew-Chaldaic invocations, Greek or Latin prayers.

Mental ball — The bright orb above an apparition's head photographed by Dr. Baraduc.

Mental body — Seat of intelligence, beyond the astral body.

Metapsychism — Beyond the sphere of ordinary psychology.

Metaphysiology — Beyond the sphere of ordinary physiology.

Monoideism — A prolonged preoccupation with a single idea.

N

Neuric or *neurotic* or *neurological force* — Sensitivity.

Neuricity — The principal constitutive force of the Astral body.

Neurification — Developing neuric force for use by the Astral body.

Neuritis — The Astral Body.

Neurologicality — Pertaining to a person's neurological force.

Neurosity — The amount of neuric force of an organism.

Neuroticity — The force that constitutes the astral body.

Ne varietur — The principle that something cannot be altered or changed.

O

Occultism — The study of knowledge from antiquity hidden from the mainstream of society, may also include esoteric religious traditions.

Odic body — Also the Etheric double.

Ojas — Sanskrit term meaning "vigor".

Ogival — Pointed.

P

Phantasmatophany — Seeing an exteriorization.

Phlegmon — A localized area of acute inflammation of the soft tissues.

Périsprit — Also the Astral body.

Prâna — Energy in action.

Presbyopic — When the eyes have lost the ability to see things clearly up close.

Prodrome — The early signs or symptoms of an illness or health problem that appear before the major signs or symptoms start.

R

Râja Yoga — Higher energies.

Revenant — A spirit or animated corpse believed to have been revived from death to haunt the living.

Rupa — (Hindu) The Physical or Material body.

S

Sarcosôme — The Physical or Material body.

Shushupti — Hindu word where all thought, all sensation, all mental emotion ceases and the soul is freed from the Earthly body.

Spatulate — Having a broad, rounded end.

Spiritists — Those who believe that a spirit world exists alongside physical reality, which can be accessed by mediums.

Sthenometer — An instrument used to measure psychic strength.

T

Theophanies — An encounter with a deity that manifests in an observable and tangible form.

Theosophists — Adherents to an occult movement originating in the 19th century with roots that can be traced to ancient Gnosticism and Neoplatonism.

V

Vedantism — A significant philosophical and religious system rooted in the Vedas, the ancient texts of Hinduism.

Volitodynamia — Levitation.

Y

Yoga — In Hindu, the set of sciences that apply to the Self.

Z

Zoanthropy — A mental condition in which someone believes themselves to be an animal.

About the Translator

The author Cardelli holds a degree in Aeronautical Science. Combining his two decades of military experience and a lifetime of world travels as well as his passion for ancient history and comparative religion, he researches and decodes the truths and connections behind our ancient religions and mythologies to pierce the veil concealing the true nature of our reality.

He has documented nearly 600 conscious, out-of-body experiences over the course of his life.

He is the author of "*Maps of the Gods*", "*Nature of the Gods*", the English translation of "*Charles Lancelin's Out-of-body Method*", and two upcoming books: "*Nature of the Gods: The Lost Chapters*", and "*Dream Lord: A Lucid Dreamer's Education in Enlightenment*".

The author Cardelli currently resides with his wife and two sons in the state of Alabama.